Congregation & Community

Congregation & Community

NANCY TATOM AMMERMAN

with Arthur E. Farnsley II

and

Tammy Adams, Penny Edgell Becker,
Brenda Brasher, Thomas Clark,
Joan Cunningham, Nancy Eiesland,
Barbara Elwell, Michelle Hale, Diana Jones,
Virginia Laffey, Stacey Nicholas,
Marcia Robinson, Mary Beth Sievens,
Daphne Wiggins, Connie Zeigler

Rutgers University Press

NEW BRUNSWICK, NEW JERSEY

Library of Congress Cataloging-in-Publication Data

Ammerman, Nancy Tatom, 1950–
    Congregation and community / Nancy Tatom Ammerman with Arthur E.
Farnsley II and Tammy Adams . . . [et al.].
       p.   cm.
    Includes bibliographical references (p.   ) and index.
    ISBN 0-8135-2334-6 (cloth : alk. paper). — ISBN 0-8135-2335-4
(pbk. : alk. paper)
      1. Parishes—United States—Case studies.   2. Sociology,
Christian—United States.   3. United States—Church history—20th
century.   I. Farnsley, Arthur Emery.   II. Title.
BR526.A45   1997
250'.973—dc20   96-16173
                                                                CIP

British Cataloging-in-Publication information available

Manufactured in the United States of America

for Oakhurst

Contents

Contents

List of Tables

LIST OF TABLES

Acknowledgments

This has been a massive project that owes its existence to the labors of many people. It began with the curiosity and vision of James Wind, then at the Lilly Endowment, and it was Lilly that provided the generous funding that made our work possible. Jim's concern and interest have continued to guide the project through to completion, including a helpful reading of the manuscript in progress. Peter Berger saw the promise in asking questions about congregations in contemporary society and initiated this as a project of his Institute for the Study of Economic Culture (ISEC) at Boston University. The company of scholars in that place helped to provide an intellectual home away from home for this work. Peter's own role, of course, went far beyond providing an organizational home for the project. He challenged me in the beginning to go wherever my research instincts told me to go, to gather the best and most complete data I could, and then to say whatever those data allowed me to say about the state of religion in the midst of changing social circumstances. Along the way, he refused to allow any of us to get away with easy assumptions, constantly pushed us to look at what was before us with new eyes. As I have written this book, he has always insisted that I tell the stories *and* that I answer his insistent "So what?" For that I am grateful.

My most immediate partner in this work has been Arthur Farnsley. He did initial legwork in locating communities and recruiting researchers. He managed the day-to-day communication that kept things going, and he made sure that the volumes of data being generated (well over three thousand single-spaced pages) were organized in ways that made them accessible and analyzable. He read all the field notes and interviews, staying on top of substantive and personnel issues as they emerged in the research process. At every stage of the project, we planned the work together; and as I have written, he has read every chapter (often in several versions), offering the sort of insider critique no one else could. We come to these questions from very different places. As he put it "I emphasize the rational and individual, and you emphasize the community and personal connections—but we both recognize that neither side is the whole story and couldn't ever be." The result has been an extremely fruitful intellectual partnership.

The researchers who spent the better part of a year as part of this project were an exceptional team. They brought differing backgrounds and interests to this work, but almost without exception they allowed themselves to become immersed in the lives of these congregations in ways that enriched the vision the rest of us are able to have of those places. They not only did high-quality research, they also worked with each other, with us, and with their congregations in ways that speak highly of who they are. One of them, Tom Clark, has not survived to see this book to completion. His untimely death has grieved us all. He brought tremendous gifts of insight and caring to our work together and to the congregation he studied. That congregation, in turn, surrounded him with care in his last difficult months. We were privileged to have Tom among us.

Most of the research team took the opportunity we offered them to join in the writing task, and their names join Art's and mine on the title page. The accounts they wrote introduce each community and each congregation in the book. In addition, most of the researchers took time to read and critique my account of the churches they studied. Those who did research on a congregation but did not write material for the book include Robert Pierson and David Tripp, both of whom worked on the West Adams community.

The research team was assisted by faculty colleagues in each metropolitan area in which we worked. Professor Marilyn Halter, of Boston University, worked with the Allston-Brighton team. Professor David Bodenhamer, of Indiana University/Purdue University in Indianapolis, worked with our Carmel and Anderson teams. Professor Donald Miller, of the University of Southern California, worked with the West Adams and Long Beach teams. Each provided assistance in recruiting and supervising researchers, as well as their own insights on the research problems at hand.

Our circle of conversation during the project was enlarged to include participants in three key consultations. Bill McKinney and Stephen Warner joined the ISEC staff and Jim Wind in helping us to define the initial outlines of the project. Midway through the research, the research team was joined in Boston by David Roozen, James Lewis, and Robert Heifner, each of whom wrote very helpful reports and suggestions to us. At that meeting, our ethnographic training was provided by Stephen Warner. Finally, at the end of the data analysis, in July 1993 the team gathered again, this time in Atlanta; and we were joined by Emory colleagues Rebecca Chopp, Frank Lechner, and Tom Frank, plus Dan Olson from Indiana University in South Bend, Will Coleman from Columbia Theological Seminary, and David Martin from the London School of Economics. Also joining in the discussion were student colleagues James Nieman, Scott Thumma, Edward Gray, Carol Lytch, Susanna Jones, and Sue Crawford.

Vital support roles were played by a wide array of talented people. Karen DeNicola served ably as administrative assistant and bookkeeper at Emory. Laura Williams transcribed well over three hundred interviews with both accuracy and good humor. Carol Lytch did thorough and very helpful library background work. Edward Gray and Barbara Elwell joined Art and me in completing the coding of field notes and interviews. Barbara also produced the layout and graphics for the reports we provided to the congregations. Patricia Chang, then at Hartford Seminary, provided summary census reports for several of the communities. And Jackie Ammerman developed the software that we used to sort and analyze the data.

Most important in making this research possible, of course, were the congregations themselves. They graciously welcomed us, told us their stories, fed us, and offered genuine friendship that went far beyond obligation. I am delighted that most of them have agreed to the use of their actual identities in this book. They deserve to be known.

As the work of the project moved from research to writing, other groups of colleagues became sounding boards and wisdom givers. The Center for the Study of American Religion at Princeton became my home base for the 1993–1994 school year and provided the intellectual space in which to complete the majority of this book. Special thanks go to John Wilson and Robert Wuthnow for the invitation to Princeton and for their gracious hospitality during my stay there. The Center for Social and Religious Research at Hartford Seminary became, in 1995, my new academic home, and it has provided a similarly friendly environment in which to finish this work. Various pieces of my thinking were presented along the way to the Princeton Center's weekly seminar, to the American Religion "brown bag" at Emory, to the Congregational Studies Project Team, and to three separate gatherings of the Religious Institutions group at the Program on Non-Profit Organizations (PONPO) at Yale. Each of those conversations helped me to see my work more clearly. Special thanks go to Peter Dobkin Hall at PONPO, who challenged me to think harder about what difference congregations make in their communities.

The theoretical framework developed in chapter 1 was especially helped by conversations with and comments from the Princeton seminar, from Dvora Yanow, and from Paul DiMaggio. The implications that are drawn out in the beginning and ending chapters were given helpful critiques by Bill McKinney and Nancy Eiesland. Robert Wuthnow served as official reviewer in the process of moving this book toward publication, and his perceptive comments and suggestions helped to put the finishing touches on my work.

Because I am writing here about a number of religious traditions that are beyond my own experience or close knowledge, I asked several colleagues to read portions of this manuscript for the sorts of detail only a religious insider would notice. Charles Foster read the four United Methodist cases. Sally Purvis read the two United Church of Christ cases. Robert Franklin read the four cases involving African American churches. Mary Ann Zimmer read the three Catholic cases. Paul Light read the American Baptist cases. Laurel Kearns read the Quaker case. Edwin Hernandez read the Seventh-Day Adventist case. Fred Craddock read the Disciples of Christ case. Doug Hobson read the Church of God, Anderson, case. Richard Lee read the Unitarian case, and Roger Finke read the Lutheran case. Each of these people noted the nuances and terminology we had not gotten quite right and offered helpful encouragement and suggestions on how the cases were interpreted. Their willing assistance is gratefully acknowledged.

From the beginning of this project, I have enjoyed an ongoing conversation with Stephen Warner that has shaped and nourished both the project and me. He has given freely from his knowledge of congregations, his skills as a teacher of field methods, and his uncommon friendship. He has read the entire manuscript, offering the sorts of line-by-line suggestions that a keen outside observer could make. Just as Art could make sure that my analysis rang true to his intimate knowledge of the cases, Steve could note the places where I assumed too much. Beyond that, he has pushed me to think more clearly about dozens of issues. His own research concerns in these years and his thinking about American religion have dovetailed with mine in ways that sometimes made it hard to remember which ideas came from whose work. Warner's important work is footnoted throughout, but his midwifery affected many pages where no footnotes appear.

While these colleagues and institutions have provided the intellectual and research energy that made this project possible, its moral energy has been sustained, as well, in my own community of faith and in my family. Jackie and Abbey have laughed and cried and applauded as I have come home with countless tales of congregational life. And Oakhurst Baptist Church, in Decatur, was my spiritual home for the years this research was underway. The exceptional vision and grace of that place not only sustained me as a person but also showed me what congregational life at its best can mean for the persons and communities it touches.

Together, this vast array of colleagues and friends has provided wisdom and support for which I am deeply grateful. Ultimately I bear responsibility for what is in this book, but this research has been a remarkable collaborative effort that has been a delight to behold.

Congregation
&
Community

CHAPTER 1

Congregation and Community: Introductions

One of the most enduring features of the American landscape is the steeple, a landmark signaling the presence of a congregation. Whether small and simple or towering and ornate, whether soaring alongside skyscrapers or rising out of the rolling hills of the countryside or subtly blending into the sameness of a suburban housing development, the spaces set aside by Christian crosses, Jewish Stars of David, Muslim minarets, and other religious markers are the single most pervasive public gathering places in American society. From the moment Europeans landed on these shores, they began constructing meetinghouses—places for worship and for deliberation, for instruction in citizenship for this world and the next. Native Americans, of course, had their own sacred meeting places before the Europeans came. But by the time Alexis de Tocqueville arrived in 1831, voluntary organizations of all sorts—especially congregations—had become the center of American spiritual and democratic vitality.[1]

The nineteenth century saw an explosion of religious organizational energy that seemed to offer every new neighborhood, every new ethnic group, every new spiritual leader the opportunity to embody identity and commitment in a local assembly of the like minded.[2] By creating congregations—in cities and on the frontier—Americans embodied the cultural and religious values they cherished in ongoing institutions, structures that gave those values and traditions a place to thrive.[3] As communities grew and became more complex, social welfare and other functions were often moved from the congregation to associations of laborers and coethnics and lodge brothers.[4] Still, congregations did not disappear for lack of anything to do. As some of their functions were taken up by and shared with others, they continued to carve out a space for themselves in the lives of persons and neighborhoods.

American congregations have been characterized, almost from the beginning, by their voluntary nature and their consequent diversity.

1

With the early separation of church and state in the United States, citizens were freed to form congregations without hindrance from legal authorities. Nor would any one religious body get special privileges. The market would rule, as Roger Finke and Rodney Stark suggest.[5] One need not describe religion as a market commodity, however, to see that constitutional freedom created a climate for social and religious creativity.[6] The power of religion was not limited by denying congregations official access to political power but enhanced by their presence throughout the culture.[7] As people found that they had social and religious interests in common (and as they were motivated to see that fact by powerful populist leaders), they were free to create institutions that expressed and furthered those interests, that embodied their sense of who they were and what they saw as ultimately important.[8] There was no longer the pretense that all citizens must belong to one universal church tied to the interests of the state. Rather the sanction for religious diversity assumed that a diverse collection of institutions would build up the whole.[9] Indeed, Congregationalist preachers, such as Lyman Beecher and Leonard Bacon, coming to terms with disestablishment in the early nineteenth century, articulated a theology that would justify the voluntary system and would charge their hearers with the moral responsibility to form organizations that would benefit all of society. Out of the voluntary religious system came the impetus for other voluntary charitable activities.[10]

Since the beginning of the nineteenth century, the proportion of the U.S. population enrolled in local religious bodies has climbed steadily from less than 30 percent to well over 60 percent at latest count.[11] While there is a good deal of dispute about just how many Americans really attend religious services each week, for most of the last half century more than 40 percent have *said* they do.[12] With more than 300,000 congregations in existence, it would seem impossible to understand changes in U.S. society without taking these pervasive voluntary gatherings into account.

To say that U.S. citizens are free to create religious (and other) institutions that express their sense of identity and ultimate value is to imply immediately that change will be a fact of life. James Luther Adams has written that voluntary religious institutions "function as a creative principle by making way for free interaction and innovation in the spirit of community."[13] As social life evolves, as new populations arrive and shift, as communities grow and decline, our sense of belonging, of value, of vital interests shifts, as well. New visions of God's reign, new ways of worshipping, new congregational efforts at education or amelioration emerge alongside other new social arrangements. At the same time, old institutions fade away. With no governmental regulation or subsidy to keep outmoded religious institutions in place, *the social proc-*

esses of community formation govern the rise and fall of congregations, and the spiritual energies generated in congregations help to shape the social structures of communities. That interaction between congregation and community is the subject of this book. In the pages ahead we will glimpse the remarkable organizational energy generated in and by congregations. As some are dying, others are being born. In the midst of the most difficult of communities, congregations struggle to adapt. And in every community, congregations of every shape and color provide spaces of sociability, laboratories for civic participation, places of moral guidance and nurture, and points of contact with transcendent powers that can work transformative miracles small and large.

Formulating the Questions

Questions about the relationship between social change and congregational life were the starting point for this study. Change, of course, is a big subject. It is both ubiquitous and ongoing, conditions that make it difficult to study by looking at any given point in time. It is also multifaceted. Some changes are welcomed, others shunned. Some changes affect only small segments of life, while others seem to turn everything upside down. Likewise, changes that can be discerned in some larger cultural or societal unit may or may not be apparent in any given local community. The choice was to keep the focus local and to seek out places where changes were fundamental enough to have produced perceived dislocation. That is, we wanted to look at places where people knew that their immediate social order had changed. Aware that not all changes are perceived equally, we also wanted to examine a variety of kinds of dislocation in places that might be expected to give each of those changes different cultural and regional meanings.

In many ways, this study is a sequel—seventy years later—to pioneering work done by H. Paul Douglass. Based on data gathered in twenty-six parishes in 1925, his *Church in the Changing City* is a detailed analysis of sixteen cases.[14] These were congregations beset by challenges still present today that often kill city churches—the influx of immigrants, racial transition, or neighborhood deterioration. Most were downtown or near-downtown churches. All were mainline Protestant and in big cities. All were bigger than normal, with bigger staffs and more programming and more widely scattered constituencies than were typical in those days. In several ways his parishes were less representative than the ones we chose. But his emphasis on the importance of the context and his analyses of the resources available for adaptation will find echoes in the pages to follow.

The question of congregations and change returned with special urgency in the 1960s. In that tumultuous decade, community change

3

almost always meant changes in the racial composition of a neighborhood. Such changes presented churches and synagogues with fundamental challenges.[15] Would they stay? Could they survive if they did? How could they justify leaving? Religious values of fairness and inclusion ran square against the realities of racism and the natural particularity of congregations. In 1966, James Davis and Robert Wilson concluded of such churches, "Unless the church wins adherents from its community, its life is limited to that of the present members who make the effort to return to keep the institution alive. A white congregation in a Negro neighborhood simply cannot recruit a sufficient number of white members to keep the church going indefinitely."[16]

Indeed, the vast majority of congregations moved (or died), but not before a spate of books appeared, mostly urging them to accept the challenges of integration. Few issues in U.S. society have the power of race to touch chords of passion—on all sides. Theologians and preachers in those troubled times drew deeply on Jewish and Christian principles to proclaim God's favor for all persons and the obligation to treat one another as brothers and sisters, children of one God. Integrated congregations seemed to many an unavoidable obligation of the faith. Moving away or resisting change were seen as sinful compromises with human weakness.

My own interest in congregations and change began, in large measure, with this issue of racial transition. The congregation that nurtured me for the eleven years I lived in Atlanta was one of those rare congregations that stayed in a changing neighborhood and integrated. It is even the subject of one of those 1960s books.[17] I believe deeply that Christians must act like the family of God we claim to be, and that means learning to live with people who are different. But my sociological instincts also tell me that the issue is not so simple. In theological language, I am convinced that not every congregation is called to the same mission. In sociological language, I am convinced that there will inevitably be a wide range of responses to change, a range that will move toward a new religious ecology that serves a new community. My sentiments affected my initial passion for this study, and they have undoubtedly informed my study and writing in ways I have not even perceived. Yet, I have also sought to give a broad definition to institutional success, and I have genuinely come to admire many of the congregations that have chosen paths I would not have chosen.

Because earlier studies had attended almost exclusively to the issue of racial change—and because that particular type of change is so fraught with difficulty—we chose to concentrate on other transitions. Race is never far from the surface in these communities, but in none of them is white flight the immediate problem facing congregations.

Other studies that have examined the effect of context on congrega-

4

tions have often focused on the issue of church growth. In the midst of often heated arguments over why some congregations are growing while others die, many of the explanations initially focused on theological factors. Careful research in the 1970s, however, showed just how closely mainline Protestant church growth parallels changes in certain key demographic factors. Where there is a pool of white, middle-class, home-owning families-with-children on which to draw, mainline churches are likely to grow, no matter what their theological orientation. It helps if people are satisfied with the programming they offer, but the context alone explains a great deal.[18] As a result of studies like these, denominational offices have often engaged in careful strategies matching new church placement to the demographics of a community.

The congregations we wanted to study, however, were in no such prematched situation. Most would score low on the likelihood of growth, if context alone were the predictor. Most had formerly mirrored the population surrounding them, but today that is no longer the case. For others, both they and the context experienced economic dislocations. But our choice was to go beyond the simple question of growth or decline. While we would not ignore that issue, we wanted to look at a wider array of changes and responses. Success here is measured neither in number of members nor in theological or political correctness. If there is a measure of success, it is simply the congregation's survival as the institution it determines it should be.

Introducing the Communities

Beginning with a list of potential communities generated by the Boston planning group, Farnsley and I sought out a sample of places where rapid and significant changes had affected identifiable communities. We talked with sociologists and demographers, journalists and religious officials. We asked them what changes were happening in their regions and where those changes were most visibly felt. We asked them to consider basic structural changes like urban growth, basic economic changes like plant closings, and significant cultural changes like the presence of gay and lesbian populations or new immigrants. Out of those conversations, our list of communities and changes emerged (see table 1.1). This list is neither representative nor comprehensive. Still, these communities offer both regional contrast and a sampling of diverse changes. Their diversity gives us assurance that whatever patterns we observe are unlikely to be the result of the peculiarities of a particular type of change or of the cultural patterns found in one region more than another.

Some of our decisions about sites were made on frankly pragmatic grounds, especially the availability of researchers and supervisors with

Table 1.1. **Communities Studied**

Type of change	West	Southeast	Northeast	Midwest
Cultural	Los Angeles *(Long Beach)*: gay/lesbian influx	Atlanta *(Candler Park)*: gay/lesbian influx	Boston *(Allston-Brighton)*: immigration	Chicago *(Oak Park)*: integration
	Los Angeles *(West Adams)*: immigration			
Economic		Atlanta *(Southwest Atlanta)*: African American stratification		*Anderson,* Indiana: plant closings
Social/ structural		Atlanta *(Gwinnett County)*: suburban growth		Indianapolis *(Carmel)*: suburban growth

whom we could work. Our research team was assembled in the winter of 1992. For each community, a team of two researchers worked together to assemble materials on the community itself, while each individual took primary responsibility for one of the congregational case studies. They are the principal eyewitnesses to what was happening to these communities, and their words (in most cases) introduce each community and congregation in the chapters to follow. These brief italicized narrative descriptions are their summaries of what they saw and heard. Those who chose to, then, have become partners in both the research and in the writing of this book.

The first stage of our research was to document the changes that had taken place in the selected communities. In addition to compiling the hard numbers that could be provided by census data and Chamber of Commerce statistics, our researchers read newspaper clippings and community histories, talked to neighborhood old-timers and social service providers, even walked the streets and took pictures. Their assignment was to draw together a portrait of the community's experience of change.

One of the first challenges we faced was to establish the functional boundaries of each community. Beginning with the descriptions provided by our early informants, we asked the people we interviewed to tell us where they thought their community began and ended.[19] Taking that information, we went to census tract maps to determine the tracts that most closely corresponded to the area subjectively identified by our respondents and researchers. Those boundaries enabled us to put together information about the social, demographic, and economic changes that had affected each community over the last two decades.

LONG BEACH AND CANDLER PARK: COMMUNITIES WITH GAY AND LESBIAN ENCLAVES

Two communities, one on the West Coast and one in the deep South, were selected as locations where a gay and lesbian population has gained a visible foothold. Few issues have so divided U.S. society in recent years as has homosexuality. Denominations engage in bitter debates over whether to ordain lesbians and gay men. The federal government struggles over whether openly gay and lesbian people can serve in the military. And individual lesbian and gay persons continue to suffer under the condemnation and harassment of neighbors, co-workers, family, and strangers. They are not just neighbors; they are a political issue. Along with abortion, gay rights has become a central target of conservative political groups such as the Christian Coalition.

At the same time, the last decade has seen unprecedented growth in the legal and social acceptance of homosexual orientation and relationships. Gay Pride parades, municipal ordinances granting gay rights, and a growing gay-oriented retail trade are but the most visible of the changes. Parades, especially, have become major efforts at public redefinition of homosexuality.[20] In many large cities, gay communities have spawned everything from gay bowling leagues to gay twelve-step groups. Gay newspapers, of course, have been around for decades, as have gay bars. But with the advent of AIDS, gay communities seemed to shift their focus from the bars and bath houses to a broad range of voluntary activities and integrated recreations. And inevitably, the epidemic itself has created a need for a variety of community services and care-giving organizations that have absorbed much of the energy of gay men and their friends.[21]

While many writers have given attention to the *issue* of homosexuality or have described the culture and behavior of gay and lesbian people, few have looked at the communities in which they have begun to make their homes. In some cases entire neighborhoods are transformed, but in other instances integration of gay and straight is the rule. Frederick Lynch reports that in the suburbs, gay men are more interested in values of home ownership, career, and stable relationships than in identifying with an active and open gay culture. He reported that they "wanted to fit into the suburban environment, to be quietly accepted by and live and work among their heterosexual neighbors."[22] Candler Park is such a neighborhood in the suburbs of Atlanta,

Georgia, while Long Beach, California, combines that sort of integrationist orientation with a traditional urban gay enclave.

It might be easier to list what has not changed in urban Long Beach over the last twenty years than try to describe what has.[23] *For years, Long Beach was known as "Iowa by the Sea." It was a magnet for midwesterners looking for work, especially in California's defense industry. Every summer, the Iowa picnic drew hundreds who gathered by county to talk about old times. In the years between the turn of the century and World War II, these conservative families founded a full array of mainline Protestant churches in the city's downtown area. The Congregationalists and Presbyterians and Disciples and Episcopalians and Methodists were joined by two Catholic parishes in more and less stately central-city buildings. Most of the churches remain, and there are still lots of midwesterners in Long Beach, but both the demographic and the religious ecology have changed dramatically in the last two decades.*

It even looks different. The city's landscape is dotted with a startling number of new high rises, and an urban mall has replaced the old downtown shopping district. Along the oceanfront, dozens of office and condominium buildings were developed during the economic boom years of the Reagan era. Before that, the site where the World Trade Center and the other glittering marble and glass monuments now stand had decayed, as midwestern families fled the center city in the sixties. A downtown minister spoke eloquently of the bleak, desperate downtown that Long Beach had become in the 1970s, and of the changes that ensued. "Downtown Long Beach was just a battle zone. It was being ripped apart as the redevelopment agencies tried to change the makeup of Long Beach. All those ugly old stag bars were finally taken out. All the porno shops were taken out. The mall was built. There are some who say that the mall [is] a nightmare, but at least it was built . . . to try and stimulate the downtown and the shopping because the old stores were just closing left and right. It was terrible. It was a pit."

The years of downtown refurbishing and suburban growth have been paralleled by changes in the ethnic composition of Long Beach. We selected as our study area a rectangle that includes the downtown and close-in residential areas. In 1970, that section of Long Beach was 98 percent white; but by 1980, Asians, African Americans, and Hispanics had begun to move into the area in noticeable numbers (see table 1.2), a trend that continued throughout the 1980s. By 1990, 25 percent of the residents of our study area spoke some language other than English at home. Most of those (17 percent of the population) spoke Spanish, but the remaining 8 percent of the population were scattered among more than twenty other languages (3.3 percent speak one of six Asian languages, 3.6 percent, one of thirteen other European languages).[24]

Even the defense jobs that had drawn midwesterners to Long Beach have begun to disappear. In the 1990s, federal defense cutbacks have affected the navy (which has a huge base in Long Beach) and all the related industries in the area. Almost everyone we talked with knew people who had been laid off or were

**Table 1.2. Long Beach, California, 1970–1990:
Multiple Changes**

	1970	1980	1990
Population	47,432	50,481	57,023
No. of households	27,547	29,472	29,903
Age distribution			
<18	13.3%	15.2%	16.6%
18–64	54.3	60.1	69.4
65+	32.5	25.6	14.0
Households			
Married with kids	33.1%	22.8%	22.9%
Single with kids	8.4	9.2	12.1
Living alone	58.6	57.4	50.9
Unrelated adults	—	10.5	15.3
Housing			
1990 housing units built			
before	73.8%	85.9%	100.0%
1990 residents living at			
same address in	5.5%	15.6%	100.0%
Ethnicity			
White	98.0%	80.2%	62.5%
Black	0.3	2.9	9.4
Asian	—	2.9	5.2
Hispanic	—	12.3	22.0
Other	1.7	1.6	4.6

SOURCES: Bureau of the Census 1972, 1982, 1991.

*afraid they would be. The cutbacks put a general damper on the economy that
was felt by entrepreneurs, professionals, and businesses throughout the area.*

*Along with these economic and ethnic changes, less immediately visible
changes were happening in Long Beach. The population of this in-town area
was becoming somewhat more dense (probably reflecting the immigrant influx),
but more startling were changes in the demographics of age and household
composition. The proportion of older adults was cut in half in the twenty years
between 1970 and 1990, a change reflected in a decline in the proportion of the
population living alone. As older residents who were living alone died, they
were replaced by younger ones, not by other retirees. Those younger adults
were not, however, "married with children." Even with an increase in the
proportion of households headed by a single parent (from 8.4 to 12.1 percent
over the period), the total percentage of households with children declined from
42.5 percent in 1970 to 35 percent in 1990, and many of those were non-Anglo.
The biggest increase in household type was in households of "unrelated adults."
While that designation can fit roommates and significant others of any sort,*

9

there is good reason to believe that many of those households were lesbian and gay couples.

Long reputed to be home to a substantial population of lesbian and gay persons, Long Beach saw that community emerge into public view in the 1980s. Some observers estimate that about 15 percent of the entire city's population is either lesbian or gay. In 1981, the local newspaper ran a five-part series of articles concluding that the gay and lesbian population of the city was "beginning to change the fabric of Long Beach."[25] Our study area includes a new section of gay businesses along Broadway that have joined the gay bars long scattered throughout the town. In recent years, street harassment has declined enough to make gay and lesbian people comfortable in public as couples. Since 1977, they have had a central resource center, called simply The Center. There are also various voluntary associations that support gay and lesbian causes, as well as AIDS support groups. Although most of those we talked with said that the gay community lacked political and economic unity, it is nevertheless visible, and its members can come together to fight legislation deemed especially pernicious.

Probably the single event marking the emergence of that visibility was the city's first Gay Pride Parade, held in 1985. There were heated city council debates, as conservative Christians tried to stave off this event. In order to bring the parade off, gay and lesbian community leaders had to band together to win arguments with local officials and irate citizens—over insurance requirements and parade permits with the former, over the propriety of their "lifestyle" with the latter. The permit was granted and the parade held. Despite continued difficulties in obtaining permission and insurance, and despite the predictable presence of a group of conservative Christian protesters, the parade and its accompanying festival have continued each year. This monumental event signaled the public viability of the lesbian and gay community in Long Beach. Having successfully done battle in the public square, the lesbian/gay community found its public confidence bolstered and its political visibility dramatically increased.

Reflecting on how life has changed over the last decade, one gay community leader said, "I think a lot of it is, again, not being second class any longer. The young—not even young—the middle-aged gays that are with us now, most of them aren't living double lives. They don't feel oppressed, and pretty well their whole life they have been what they are. And that makes a big difference. It makes a difference in how you react to things and how you relate to people and how you take responsibility for things."

Especially since 1985, Long Beach has recognized its gay and lesbian population as part of an increasingly diverse population mix. In the midst of economic dislocations and immigrant arrivals, Long Beach is no longer the conservative "Iowa by the Sea" created at the middle of the century. That conservative midwestern population still exists, but largely in the suburbs. Downtown, Spanish speakers, economic wheeler-dealers, and homeless people are joined by gay couples who live, work, and play with decreasing fear of harrassment.

Across the country, Atlanta's gay and lesbian community is a smaller proportion of the city's total population and more scattered throughout the vast metropolitan region. However, even in this traditional southern city, there are neighborhoods clearly identifiable as enclaves, and Candler Park is one of them. It is also notable as an urban neighborhood that retains many public spaces in which people of different race, class, and sexual orientation meet. A mixture of people and a diversity of land use here defies the growing segmentation of urban areas.[26]

One really cannot speak of Candler Park as having undergone regentrification. Although homes are being fixed up, and new residents moving in, this was never a "gentrified" neighborhood in the first place. The people who built homes here in the late nineteenth century were ordinary folk, usually blue-collar. The Edgewood/Candler Park neighborhoods were a few trolley stops beyond the Inman Park area, Atlanta's first planned suburb, and many area residents worked in the nearby railroad yards or in an industrial area situated between them and downtown Atlanta. On the north was the Ponce de Leon corridor, with large houses separated by huge park spaces. And in the center of the community was the park from which the neighborhood took its name.

By the end of World War II, some of the area's residents were beginning to look for more spacious houses in newer, developing suburbs. By the 1960s, African Americans were moving into areas all around Candler Park, and a period of white flight increased the pace of home-owner exodus from the area. (Although most of the people we talked with mentioned this white flight, the census of 1970 found only 6.3 percent nonwhites in this immediate neighborhood; see table 1.3.) Little Five Points (Candler Park's major business district) became, by the 1970s, a hippie haven. Rents on apartments and houses had plummeted to a level where "alternative life-style" folk could afford to live in the neighborhood. At that point, only one-third of the neighborhood's households were owner occupied.

Since the 1970s, Candler Park has attracted an increasingly diverse group of residents. The neighborhood has become less white, but not dramatically so. The African American population rose in the 1970s to 14 percent and stayed steady in the 1980s. Tiny numbers of Asians, Hispanics, and others have arrived. But ethnic diversity is not what defines the neighborhood. Perhaps because of its hippie reputation and large health-food store, a more up-scale population of liberal, urban-oriented professionals, artisans, and community-minded lesbians and gay men began to purchase homes in the neighborhood and refurbish them. Throughout the 1970s and 1980s, the percentage of owner occupancy went up, as did the proportion of single-family housing. At the same time, the total population was declining. Houses that had been broken up into multiple rental units were being returned to their original state, and the neighborhood was becoming less densely populated.

11

Table 1.3. Candler Park (Atlanta), Georgia, 1970–1990: Multiple Changes

	1970	1980	1990
Population	11,911	7,947	7,800
No. of Households	4,489	4,288	3,880
Age distribution			
<18	28.5%	18.7%	14.5%
18–64	59.2	70.4	78.9
65+	12.3	10.9	6.6
Households			
Married with kids	54.3%	27.9%	27.0%
Single with kids	14.5	11.9	11.6
Living alone	30.5	35.3	39.9
Unrelated adults	—	24.7	21.4
Housing			
Owner-occupied	32.5%	41.2%	47.9%
Single-family units	42.7%	44.8%	55.5%
1990 residents living			
at same address in	4.9%	14.9%	100.0%
Ethnicity			
White	93.7%	84.0%	82.0%
Black	5.9	14.1	15.7
Other	0.4	1.8	2.3

SOURCES: Bureau of the Census 1972, 1982, 1991.

The population was also less dense because the types of households occupying those dwellings were changing. The presence of gays and lesbians showed up in the census figures by 1980. During the 1970s, the proportion of the population that fell into the "married with kids" category dropped sharply and the number of single-parent households declined; the total number of children and youth fell by more than half in the twenty years between 1970 and 1990. In addition, the number of older people was falling—to a tiny 6.6 percent by 1990. By 1980, one-third of the households were occupied by people living alone, and one-quarter by people living with "unrelated adults." While ownership of single-family dwellings was increasing, the families living in those dwellings were often not traditional at all.

Candler Park has now gained a reputation as a friendly, comfortable neighborhood for people of all sorts. The traditional families here do not seem to mind having lesbian singles and couples as neighbors. Gay and lesbian households often display rainbow flags or stickers on the houses, and an openly pro-gay candidate, Samantha Clare, ran for the state legislature in 1992. She lost, but the proliferation of yard signs promoting her candidacy—with pink triangles in each corner—were an indication of the strength of the lesbian and gay presence here. One woman recalled, "When we moved in here, we were like all alone in the gay and lesbian community here, but right across the street over there a couple more lesbians moved in. And we were like, 'Yes! We're not alone!' But now you just go down the street and count how many Samantha Clare signs you see. . . . I think we're really sort of taking over the 30307 zip code." In addition, Charis Books is an anchor of the Little Five Points business district and is a major source of feminist and lesbian books, as well as a sponsor for lesbian community events, book signings, and such. The Feminist Women's Chorus began its life rehearsing at First Existentialist, a Unitarian congrega-tion in the neighborhood. And Southern Voice *regularly publishes news of the gay and lesbian community. Economically, politically, and socially Candler Park has become home for a significant portion of Atlanta's lesbian and gay population.*

Whereas the Long Beach neighborhood we studied was an urban, downtown community, Candler Park is a collar suburb and more qui-etly residential. Both support identifiable gay and lesbian business es-tablishments, although they are more numerous in Long Beach than in Candler Park. Both have significant numbers of "unrelated adults" households, few older adults, and relatively few "married with chil-dren" units. Candler Park lacks the ethnic diversity of Long Beach, but both communities include large numbers of well-educated professionals. In the 1980s, Gay Pride Parades became important annual events in both. In the two places, new household patterns have brought cultural changes that have altered the basic identity of the neighborhoods themselves.

ALLSTON-BRIGHTON AND WEST ADAMS: COMMUNITIES WITH NEW IMMIGRANT POPULATIONS

Changes even more dramatic are wrought when the new population arrives from outside the United States and speaks languages other than English. Since the Immigration Act of 1965 lifted restrictive national quotas, the number and kinds of immigrants entering the country have changed dramatically. During the 1960s, 3.7 million immigrants ar-rived; during the 1980s, the number reached 9.97 million. In 1965, Ca-nadians and Europeans constituted 51 percent of the immigrant flow. In 1990, 80 percent came from Asia, the Caribbean, and Latin America. In part, this shift has meant that the minority share of the population has increased substantially—to almost 25 percent—and that African Americans constitute less than half that number. While the ratio of immigrants to total population is only half what it was at the turn of the century, increased absolute numbers and changes in the composition of the flow have raised the visibility of new immigrants. In many urban regions, such as Miami, Los Angeles, and San Antonio, concentrations of immigrants constitute significant segments of the population. Nor can today's immigrants be expected to melt into a single pot in the way earlier generations did. Their assimilation may be more segmented and less continuous. A growing number, for instance, do not stay permanently in the United States, moving back and forth across multiple international boundaries.[27]

The two immigrant communities we chose for study were dramatically different. Boston has been accepting immigrants (more and less eagerly) for well over a century. The old-timers now being displaced are themselves the children and grandchildren of earlier arrivals. West Adams, on the other hand, had barely weathered the racial transitions of the 1950s and 1960s, settling into its identity as an African American neighborhood, when Asian and Latin newcomers began arriving.[28] Both neighborhoods faced the challenge of immigration with somewhat depleted social and economic capital. In both places, the economic and demographic structure had already started to change before the immigrants arrived.

In 1874, when the adjacent communities of Allston and Brighton were annexed by the city of Boston, they were home to growing numbers of Irish and Italian immigrants. For nearly a century, the descendants of those immigrants dominated community life, building impressive churches and parochial schools in a community that was a combination of single-family homes, open spaces, commercial development, and growing private institutions.[29] Harvard University was just across the river to the north, with Boston College to the west, Boston University to the south, and St. Elizabeth's Hospital to the east. Until after World War II, none of those institutions was big enough to encroach on Allston and Brighton, but after the war, everything began to change.

Veterans Administration loans made it possible for thousands of veterans to buy homes in the suburbs, and Allston-Brighton's white middle-class population began to disperse. This decline in the home-owning population was accompanied by an increase in the community's college student population. The GI Bill and the student loan programs of the 1960s helped fuel the expansion of the three educational institutions on Allston-Brighton's borders. The homes sold by residents fleeing to the suburbs were converted to apartments and rented to the growing student population. Soon each house contained two or three or four apartments, and fewer homes were occupied by their owners. A longtime resident observed, "I saw families being brought up in that neighborhood, and it was family oriented. But now different families who have passed away, their children sold their homes, and I'd say 50 percent of them are owned by landlords who no longer live there, but rent. And this is changing the neighborhood. And we are close to colleges, and we find a lot of students in there." In 1965, the Massachusetts Turnpike was built, cutting off north Allston from the rest of the community, leaving it without effective mass transportation and dotted with warehouses and dead-end streets. In 1974, federal courts mandated busing in the Boston area, and the flight of white home owners accelerated further.

In the mid-1980s, many of the apartment buildings in the area were converted to condominiums. This slightly increased the rate of owner occupancy, but most of the conversions were bought by people who then rented out again, further aggravating the problem of absentee landlords. In the generation after World War II, then, Allston-Brighton had become an area dominated by rental property and transient populations. By 1990, only 20 percent of the community's properties were owner occupied, and 81 percent of the population had moved in since 1980.[30]

In addition, 20 percent of the population had entered the United States since 1980. A whole new wave of immigration was inundating Allston-Brighton (see table 1.4). Almost a third of the population (32.5 percent) reported speaking something other than English at home. The largest proportion of those (7 percent) were Spanish speakers; the remainder spoke Chinese, Russian, other Asian languages, French, and Portuguese.[31] Since about 1980, people from Hong Kong, fleeing the pending takeover by the People's Republic of China, have joined an existing Chinese community relocated to Allston-Brighton when the turnpike decimated Boston's Chinatown. In addition, Russian Jews have left the Soviet Union, replacing Allston-Brighton's earlier Jewish population, which had largely moved to the suburbs. People from all over Southeast Asia have fled the aftermath of the long war there, but Allston-Brighton's designation as a Cambodian cluster by the Refugee Relocation Act (and the focus of services at the Brighton Public Health Center) hastened the flow. Since the late 1970s, Haitians have fled the political and economic hardships of their island, and since the mid-1980s Brazilians have come seeking economic opportunity. There has even been a new wave of Irish. One older woman summed it up: "We have a lot of Vietnamese, and blacks, and everything moving in, all the minorities, you know."

Many in each of these groups are undocumented and live in cramped quarters, hoping to save money to send home or to get ahead here. They have also spawned a growing number of ethnic restaurants, groceries, and other businesses catering to this diverse new population. The streets of Allston-Brighton look and sound different today.

The long-term home owners who live in Allston-Brighton pride themselves on their acceptance and tolerance of the diverse racial and ethnic groups in the community. One community leader boasted that people are accepted whether they are "black, white, green, whatever. You know, if they're good people, they're good people; if they're bad people, they're bad people." There is remarkably little overt conflict. A late 1970s incident of violence against a young Asian man remains the sole case. Churches and civic organizations quickly rallied to repudiate ethnic antagonism.

The large number of civic groups in this community seem to focus the energies of its citizens on community improvement and fighting zoning battles

Table 1.4. Allston-Brighton, Massachusetts, 1970–1990: Shifting Ethnicities

	1970	1980	1990
Population	59,695	61,433	66,429
White	95.7%	84.4%	72.8%
Black	1.9	4.1	6.7
Asian	—	6.0	10.7
Hispanic	—	4.4	9.2
Other	2.4	1.1	0.7

SOURCES: Bureau of the Census 1972, 1982, 1991.

rather than on ethnic disputes. With four huge institutions constantly threatening to gobble up the last open spaces, further flooding the community with parking problems and more transient residents, various associations of Allston and Brighton residents stay busy. They especially oppose any development that might exacerbate the disturbances associated with a large student population. Dormitory construction and liquor licensing typify the issues over which Allston-Brighton residents, educational institutions, and businesses battle.

These civic associations are, however, overwhelmingly dominated by the long-term, home-owning, Anglo residents (now a tiny fraction of the population). Many of the immigrants are not yet legal and so do not even vote. Others have minimal facility with English. And the student population is too transient and otherwise occupied to pay much attention to civic affairs. (Students have, however, proven tolerant of their immigrant neighbors.) The dilemma of civic involvement is nicely illustrated by Allston-Brighton's annual Ethnic Festival and community parade. The parade includes the usual array of politicians, bands, and civic organizations—but few representatives of non-Anglo groups. The festival has a wide array of ethnic foods and entertainment, but most of the vendors and performers are businesses and professionals who live outside the community. The attenders, in turn, are mostly young Anglo families. The ethnic diversity of the community is represented by only a smattering of participants.

Direct contact among the various groups is perhaps most common in the schools and in some of the neighborhood's youth organizations. The West End Community House has been in existence since near the turn of the century, and its shifting clientele mirrors the community. The staff includes black, Hispanic, and Asian leaders, as well. The director said, "When you come into the club, then you see a real interaction amongst all races, creeds, and colors. And children judging each other by what they do, what they think, as opposed to the color of their skin, or their religion, or anything of that nature. And we've got, at this point in time, a real even balance. All of it happening by itself, as opposed to actively going out and recruiting more white children, or more Asian children, etc. So we've got a really incredible racial balance of children that come in here—play together, work together, chum together." Outside such youth organizations, however, there seems to be much less opportunity for various ethnic groups to meet. One community leader reported, "There isn't that much interaction. I don't know that I would describe it as harmonious. I think that in the schools, there's a lot of tension. Like in high schools, between kids." Among the parents, there may simply be a kind of live-and-let-live distance.

Realities of life in Allston-Brighton include a dwindling but still politically powerful Irish and Italian population holding on amidst economic and ethnic upheaval. The number of home-owning families is small, the number of transient students and immigrants large. The mix of immigrants here is, in fact, amazing, and the relative harmony of the community testifies to the openness of an older generation of leaders and civic organizations.

Across the country, in South Central Los Angeles, harmony is a bigger challenge. Any pretense of live-and-let-live tolerance was shattered by the Rodney King verdicts and the uprisings that followed in April 1992, just as our research was beginning. In many ways, West Adams is a poorer, more troubled neighborhood than Allston-Brighton. Much of the outrage of those days was directed at police brutality, economic deprivation, and the failures of the justice system. But the immediate targets were often the immigrant owners of neighborhood businesses. In the aftermath, issues of justice and issues of ethnicity were often intertwined.

From the turn of the century until World War II, the area now known as West Adams (for the east-west thoroughfare that runs through it) was home to some of Los Angeles's most distinguished citizens.[32] They built large stately homes on these hills south of downtown and surrounded them with beautiful grounds and wide boulevards. As the city began to grow rapidly in the 1930s and 1940s, this neighborhood stayed insulated from an increasingly diverse population, largely through the use of racially restrictive covenants. Deeds to neighborhood property forbade sale to persons of "Negroid or Mongoloid races."

In 1948, those covenants were declared unconstitutional, however, and the neighborhood began to change. Former home owners sold out, often to buyers who divided the large homes into apartments. A new freeway was built through the area, as well. By the time of the Watts riots in 1965, the area was already largely African American, but the riots hastened the remaining white flight. By 1970, the overwhelming majority (79.6 percent) of the neighborhood's residents were black (see table 1.5).[33] They owned black-oriented neighborhood businesses, and most of the churches in the area were predominantly black.

During this same period, a small number of Asians moved into the neighborhood. The Japanese who had first arrived on the edges of West Adams before World War II were taken away to internment camps during the war. One

Table 1.5. West Adams (Los Angeles), California, 1970–1990: Shifting Ethnicities

	1970	1980	1990
Population	28,281	28,747	44,651
White	11.8%	4.3%	3.2%
Black	79.6	64.3	48.0
Asian	—	4.8	3.8
Hispanic	—	25.6	43.3
Other	8.6	0.9	2.3

SOURCES: Bureau of the Census 1972, 1982, 1991.

African American woman remembered vividly the day that army trucks parked along every stretch of road in her neighborhood just to the east. She recalled with horror watching her Japanese neighbors entrusting treasured possessions to their non-Japanese friends before being carted away to an uncertain future. After the war, some of the Japanese returned, and they were eventually joined by Koreans and a scattering of other Asians. Their percentage has held steady at around 5 percent of the population, with only 2.5 percent reporting in 1990 that they speak some Asian language at home.

Koreans became visible in the community, however, far out of proportion to their numbers. Just north of the West Adams neighborhood, beginning in the late 1970s, "Koreatown" became a thriving commercial strip. Even within West Adams, Koreans were an increasing presence as small-business owners.

By the 1970s, there was also a growing Latino presence in the neighborhood, as Mexican Americans began to move west from the sections of East L.A. they already dominated. By 1980, a quarter of the population was classified by the Census Bureau as "Hispanic." During the 1980s, that proportion nearly doubled and changed to include significant numbers of Guatemalans, Salvadorans, and recent immigrants from elsewhere in Central and South America, along with people of more or less recent Mexican descent. By 1990, a quarter of West Adams's population had arrived in the United States since 1980. Latinos amounted to 43 percent of the population, and they were largely responsible for a major jump in the total number of persons residing in the area, from just under 29,000 in 1980 to well over 44,000 in 1990—and this with virtually no new housing stock. Only 11 percent of the structures in West Adams have been built since 1970. The population has become both more dense and more Hispanic. By 1990, people in nearly half of the households (46 percent) in West Adams spoke something other than English at home.

In the midst of all this change, the African American population held steady in numbers but grew increasingly restless. Older residents suddenly discovered that they did not understand their neighbors—neither their language nor their ways of life. After years of struggle to win civil rights and to make a place in the economy, they saw new groups threatening their gains. The Reagan years were especially inhospitable in South Central Los Angeles. Federal programs seemed to disappear, and many in the population began to feel a growing resentment at being apparently forgotten. The mix of Latin immigration, Asian economic success, and continued racism made West Adams anything but a cohesive neighborhood by the early 1990s. Rodney King was merely the spark that lit the fire.

The West Adams neighborhood was hit hard by the uprisings. Burned-out businesses abound, and the community is still struggling to regain a sense of its future. It is overcrowded and overflowing with people new to the United States. Beside them are African Americans who made their way into this area only within the last generation. The area's populations are trying to find a balance among themselves in the face of urban problems that range from poor schools and substantial housing to gang violence.

OAK PARK:
AN INTEGRATED LIBERAL ENCLAVE?

As Allston-Brighton and West Adams have been struggling to accept immigrants into their population, Oak Park, a suburb of Chicago, has gained national prominence as a place that has successfully integrated its housing and schools.[34] During the first waves of racial integration in the 1950s and 1960s, "community transition" often meant realtor-induced selling frenzies brought on by the arrival of a few African American families. Oak Park successfully organized to counter that pattern. Today, around the country, attitudes are less severe; whites are less likely to say they would move if a black family moved in. Still, the gains in neighborhood integration have been only modest. In many cities nearly 90 percent of the residents still live in neighborhoods that overrepresent their own race.[35] It is not yet clear whether a growing African American middle class will be able to (or want to) further reduce segregation by repeating the strategies established in Oak Park. Across the nation, suburbs that were white in 1980 were still white in 1990, and suburbs that were black remained black. Only the small number already open to blacks in 1980 showed substantial increases in black population during the next decade.[36]

Over the last generation, Oak Park has welcomed an increasing percentage of non-Anglo persons, but it has also suffered an economic restructuring that has introduced significant new strains. Its economic base has eroded, and the gap has widened between those who can afford to live in Oak Park and those who live next door in Chicago. The affluent liberals who engineered Oak Park's resistance to white flight are losing both economic and ideological capital in the 1990s. Affirmative action is no longer in vogue, and government regulation of all sorts is being phased out. The struggle to maintain liberal ideals in the midst of economic strain is very evident in Oak Park.

In 1970, Oak Park was 98.8 percent white, but just across Austin Boulevard to the east, Austin had already gone from an all-white community in 1960 to being one-third black in 1970. (By 1980, it would be three-quarters black.) The people of Oak Park saw the handwriting on the wall—or more accurately, the For Sale signs in the yards. They decided to fight the trend. Rather than try to resist integration—or run away—they undertook a program of planned integration that has since become a model for communities around the country. The community trained its realtors and strictly forbade the sorts of scare tactics that fueled white flight elsewhere. It even banned the posting of For Sale signs. A kind of unofficial quota system went into place to avoid concentrating all the new minority residents in one part of town. And the town provided an "equity assurance" program that guaranteed home values against steep declines. After a short period of uncertainty, in the early 1970s housing prices stabilized, and the community has remained prosperous ever since. The result is a community that is still three-quarters white, with 18 percent African Americans, 3.3 percent Asians, 3.6 percent Hispanic, and a handful of others (see table 1.6). The effort has been deemed so successful that the community has established the Oak Park Exchange, a network of communities in the nation seeking to maintain healthy diversity.

Some older residents did leave Oak Park as this transition got under way. They have been replaced by younger, well-educated professionals who want their children to grow up in a diverse environment. They also note that Oak Park has good schools and is a convenient commute either to downtown Chicago or to the western suburbs.

It is not, however, as affordable as it used to be. In 1970, the median price for a house in Oak Park was under $30,000. By 1980, it had more than doubled, to over $70,000; and by 1990, it had doubled again. Just over half of Oak Park's housing units are now owner occupied; nearly 20 percent are something other than a single-family dwelling. A recent sharp rise in property taxes has upped the cost of owning property in Oak Park. While half the households boast incomes above $40,000, the other half would have a difficult time making mortgage and tax payments on most of the property in Oak Park. Older people are afraid they cannot pay their taxes on a reduced income, and young families are increasingly unable to enter the market.

This is but one of the recent economic strains experienced in this community. Like many collar suburbs they have lost industry and retail operations to suburbs further west. In addition to a loss of jobs in the community, that has further strained the tax base. With little in the way of commercial property to tax, the village is forced to get all its revenues from home owners. Since Oak Park has historically been inviting in part because of its superior community services, the town is reluctant to cut back. The only alternative is, then, the large tax increase put into effect in 1992.

Table 1.6. Oak Park, Illinois, 1990: An Affluent and Diverse Community

Household income			
<$20,000			18.7%
$20,000–49,999			43.6
50,000–74,999			20.4
$75,000+			17.3
Average			$50,233
Housing			
Single-family units			40%
Median house price			$143,200
Education			
High school or less			22.4%
Some college			25.9
College degree or more			51.6
Occupations			
Professionals, managers & specialists			50.1%
Unemployment			2.7%
Ethnicity	1970	1980	1990
White	98.8%	82.6%	74.8%
Black	0.2	11.3	18.0
Asian	—	2.8	3.3
Hispanic	—	2.6	3.6
Other	1.0	0.6	0.4

SOURCE: Claritas, Inc., 1994.

Politics in Oak Park is rather low key. The progressive agenda of the last two decades seems to have been engineered by an informal network of residents who make sure that their candidates get elected to city council and school board seats. Despite a population of fifty thousand, they call themselves a village and cultivate a homey accessibility in town government.

Recently, the political assumptions of the last two decades have been under some challenge, however. While almost everyone points to harmonious race relations as one of the pluses to living in Oak Park, that, too, has been less sure in recent years. A new generation of African Americans is more insistent, and a new generation of Anglos is willing to listen. African Americans have become more vocal in demanding the right not only to live in the village but to have fair treatment within its local institutions. Particularly in the high school, accusations of unfair disciplinary practices directed to African American youth have caused controversy, and there have been one or two racially motivated assaults. In response, there has been formal organizing in the black community that has caught some white residents off guard. One African American leader reflected,

21

"When they [NAACP and an African American parents' group] first formed, it was like, 'Why do we need them?' you know. But we used to say to people, 'When you no longer need the River Forest Country Club, we won't need the NAACP.'"

More telling yet, the tensions in Oak Park focused especially on Austin Boulevard. Across that street, an all-black section of Chicago sits in stark contrast to Oak Park. As always, perceptions are important and instructive. A recent survey shows a concern about crime and personal safety that seems disproportionate to the rate of actual violent crime in the village. A local reporter said, "The reality is that I don't think that crime is any better or worse. I don't think a lot is different except for the presence of blacks in this community. And I don't mean in numbers, I mean in attitude and positions of leadership and prominence and such like."

In interviews, some white residents reveal that their crime concerns center on the fear of black young men from Chicago crossing over into Oak Park and causing trouble. Concerns about gang activities in the high school also contain this element of fear that the problems of the West Side will spill over the boulevard into Oak Park proper. A community long confident of its ability to absorb difference is now less sure of itself.

As part of a large metropolitan region, Oak Park has some resources for weathering its loss of industry and jobs, and it has a history of successfully tackling community problems. While both that legacy and its resource base are strained, Oak Park seems unlikely to fall apart. Its greatest challenge lies in dealing with the fear generated by its less-prosperous and integrated neighbors.

ANDERSON:
A COMMUNITY IN ECONOMIC DISTRESS

Unlike Oak Park, communities that stand on their own, not in a metropolitan region, can be economically devastated when a primary employer pulls up stakes. The closing of a steel mill or car factory has a ripple effect on a town's economy—a distressingly common occurrence in the last two decades. Of more than twelve thousand manufacturing plants open in 1969, 30 percent had closed by 1976. U.S. capital has been increasingly mobile, abandoning unprofitable operations in one place to invest in potentially high-profit locations elsewhere. This mobility most immediately affects the individuals—across the class structure—who lose their jobs. Studies of workers laid off due to plant closure indicate that they suffer longer periods of unemployment than do others more routinely laid off. Along with that unemployment go increased risks of physical and psychological ailments, with fewer and increasingly depleted family resources for coping with them. Whatever job they finally secure is likely to be a step down in money and prestige, and many workers may find themselves eventually giving up on their own employability. Because of investments in houses, friends, and family relationships, most remain in the community, if they can.[37] The result is a community where social service providers are strained to their limits and beyond.

At the same time that demands for social services rise, the community's resources are depleted. Losing a major employer means losing tax revenue and charitable contributions the company has made to the community. The overall loss of personal income in the community means a decline both in retail sales and in other aspects of the economy, along with a decline in individual income tax revenue. Those declines are muted in the first months by unemployment benefits, but benefits rarely last as long as the periods of lost wages many workers endure. Deficits in community resources are matched, in turn, by increases in requests for Aid to Families with Dependent Children (AFDC) payments and food stamps.[38] When Anderson, Indiana's General Motors–related factories began massive layoffs in the late 1970s, the town was no exception to these patterns of depletion and strain.

Anderson, a county seat forty miles northeast of Indianapolis, was a sleepy country town when natural gas was discovered there in the 1890s. That discovery began to attract manufacturing concerns and workers and to transform the community.[39] In the 1920s two of Anderson's manufacturing firms, Delco Remy and Inland Fisher Guide, allied with General Motors (GM), and the community quickly and gratefully became a company town. By 1970, almost twelve thousand persons in Anderson were employed in the manufacture of durable goods.[40] Jobs were plentiful, and the pay was good.

In the 1970s, however, the U.S. automotive industry went into a steep decline that quickly affected Anderson's GM plants. In 1978, GM's Delco Remy operated fifteen plants and employed 15,000 workers. In the next several years, those plants laid off or relocated 7,000 of those workers. Inland Fisher Guide added 1,100 more layoffs to that number, and Anderson's unemployment rate reached 24 percent in the 1980s. Delco Remy's local United Auto Workers union placed approximately 4,000 workers in GM facilities elsewhere, but thousands of others were forced to fend for themselves. Layoffs extended into months and then years, forcing younger workers to look for jobs outside Anderson and, often, to relocate. Older workers simply retired early and stayed in town. Retirees could exist comfortably on GM—sometimes referred to as "Generous Motors"—pensions. The result was an increasingly "grey" population. A local pastor talked about what had happened to young people in Anderson. "The word got around that if you're going to get anywhere in Delco, you'd better go to Purdue and get an engineering degree or something. So a lot of them were going to Purdue to get this training. And when they came back home, there was no job over there for them. So they had to move out. And they moved into other communities. For instance, we had a large youth group here just ten years ago . . . [but] only one young person out of this large group has returned to live in Anderson. And she actually works in Indianapolis, in counseling, and eventually she'll leave too. So that we've lost, in fact, the entire group." The results show up in the census figures. The number of school-aged children declined, while the number of senior citizens climbed (see table 1.7).

One local minister reminded his congregation that God is not spelled "GM," but the impact on the city was a plague of near-biblical proportions. From 1975 to 1990 unemployment soared, and the population of Anderson declined by almost fifteen thousand.

Today, Delco Remy is still the city's largest employer, with 7,100 employees, and Inland Fisher Guide is second with 4,400. But only the workers with over twenty years' seniority have retained their jobs at the Delco plants. Although Inland Fisher Guide has laid off fewer employees, both companies continue to allow natural attrition and early retirement plans to trim employee ranks. The post–World War II generation had counted on employment after high school at the GM plant where their parents had worked. But this group can no longer expect to see their own children working at these plants. One couple voiced thoughts we heard over and over.

He: Well, that was just a continuous state of affairs. It was one layoff after another.
She: There still isn't stability there. You can have twenty-five years at Delco and not know whether you're going to have a job tomorrow.

Recently, GM announced that Anderson's Inland Fisher Guide plant would be sold, as would some of the production lines at the Delco Remy factories. Each new upheaval sends ripples throughout the local economy. Smaller industrial establishments such as Prime Battery and Emge Meats also have closed in recent years, leaving the community with few alternate workplaces.

All of this change has strained the community's social services. One worker summed up her experience in trying to keep up with demand: "I just have been devastated with the amount of people." This flood of people has come to the doors of the township trustee, an official each Indiana township charges with caring for the indigent in the community. Anderson's trustee has been assisted by the Salvation Army, the St. Vincent de Paul Society (a Catholic charity), and an active community ministry at a local Episcopal church. There are a number of smaller agencies, as well, but when people hit bottom, there were not many places to go. One of the most knowledgeable people in this network talked about the additional hardship of handling this crisis in the midst of federal government cutbacks in social programs. A good deal of the human need generated by this economic crisis undoubtedly went unmet—or was met through the kindness of friends, neighbors, and fellow church members.

One thing that has not changed about Anderson is the blue-collar character of the community. One would search in vain for a trendy clothing boutique or a

Table 1.7. Anderson, Indiana, 1970–1990: Declining Fortunes

	1970	1980	1990
Population	70,787	64,695	59,459
Persons employed in manufacture of durable goods	11,936	7,775	6,252
Age distribution			
<18	36.0%	32.1%	24.1%
65+	9.4	12.6	16.1
Households/Housing			
Living alone	6.8%	10.1%	12.6%
1990 residents living at same address in	23.7%	42.9%	100%
1990 housing units built before	81.5%	94.0%	100%

SOURCES: Bureau of the Census 1972, 1982, 1991.

"fern bar." Instead, one would find strip malls and mini-golf, pizza restaurants and WalMarts. At the local cafe, if there is a nonsmoking section at all, it is tiny. And Anderson is segregated. There are even two separate ministers' associations for a church population that overlaps almost not at all. Nearly all the town's African Americans (a steady 14 percent of the population) are concentrated in three census tracts, and everyone seemed to know exactly where "the black community" was located. A few people also reported to us that the Klan was alive and well. In the heyday of Delco Remy, black workers often did well. In hard times, black workers have suffered.

The town's blue-collar character also shows in its housing stock. Almost two-thirds (64 percent) of the city's properties are owner occupied, and most are modest frame one- or two-story homes. The median price for one of those homes in 1990 was $38,500.[41] That amazingly depressed housing market is now, apparently, being turned to Anderson's advantage. The 1993 decision by the U.S. Census Bureau to count Anderson and Madison County as part of the Indianapolis Metropolitan Statistical Area recognizes the fact that 19 percent of the county's population now works in Indianapolis. One real estate agent reported that her listings were selling faster than ever before as young professionals who work in Indianapolis choose to live in Anderson, with its lower property taxes and small-town atmosphere.[42]

By the 1990s, Anderson seemed ready to recover. Town leaders resisted talking about the economic troubles of the 1980s and pointed us toward the signs of hope they saw. Still, the loss of jobs and people that Anderson experienced in the eighties left a lasting imprint on the people and institutions that remain.

SOUTHWEST ATLANTA:
CHANGING ECONOMIC REALITIES
FOR AFRICAN AMERICANS

Economy and race seem always entangled. In Oak Park, economic downturns have made a liberal agenda more problematic. In Anderson, economic hard times have fallen harder on African American residents than on everyone else. Over the last generation, African Americans throughout the country have experienced two divergent economic realities. On the one hand, especially since the 1960s, there has been a growing black middle class. While color has not disappeared as a determinant of access and prestige in U.S. society, avenues of education and occupational attainment have increasingly (if slowly) opened to African Americans. As a result, blacks have made striking gains in professional and managerial employment since 1960, especially if the gains are measured against the small number of those jobs held by African Americans before 1960.[43] Likewise, in absolute numbers, more African Americans are moving to predominantly white suburbs;[44] and in the cities, black political power is now an accomplished fact. In Atlanta, a historic concentration of black capital and black educational institutions has combined to produce a lively set of African American cultural institutions and an image as a black mecca.[45]

On the other hand, during the years in which the Huxtables (Bill Cosby's TV family) were creating a new image of black middle-class family life, worsening poverty afflicted the black underclass. Growing social isolation in black ghettos—rising rates of concentration there of poverty and joblessness—has increased the sense of hopelessness and bred greater social disorganization.[46] Those at the bottom are likely to be school dropouts, to participate in an underground economy, and to have unstable work and family lives. Their life chances are very poor, beset by crime and poor health. Their style of life is shaped by efforts to adapt to a white world that has excluded them and that they are not prepared to enter.[47] High levels of social distress are a reality for those increasingly left behind.

The realities of a visible black underclass and a visible black middle class have begun to present challenges to both groups. The potential for resentment is great. Expectations are high that middle-class African Americans will work hard for the betterment of those who have not yet made it.[48] Nowhere is the black middle class more visible than in the New South's capital city of Atlanta. And nowhere is a distressed lower class more present, even when the city pretends it is not there.

In the years after the Civil War, African Americans in Atlanta, with the help of northern white benefactors, founded Morehouse and Spelman Colleges on the near west side of the city. By the time the Atlanta University Center was cre-

ated in 1929–1930, drawing together all of the city's black colleges, the West Side was rivaling famed Auburn Street as the center of black commercial and cultural life in Atlanta. The universities provided many community services that might not otherwise have been available to black Atlantans. Until the 1950s, a strict color line kept African Americans from fully participating in the life of the rest of the city and kept them from moving south, out of the immediate West Side area. With the legal demise of segregation, however, population and economic pressures in such restricted areas pushed black families south and west, while Atlanta's white families moved north. At the same time, black contractors were taking advantage of the increasing number of black families who could afford to own a home.[49]

While the end of segregation meant increased choices for Atlanta's African Americans, it did not bring integration but greater racial distance. The story is distressingly familiar. Once blacks began to move in, whites moved out. That has certainly been the case in our study area, just south and west of the Atlanta University Center. A few university-related African Americans had begun to move into this all-white neighborhood in the 1950s. By 1960, the population was 18 percent nonwhite. In the 1960s, the pace increased. One longtime resident recalled the "block busting" that went on. "They started showing . . . houses in a predominantly white neighborhood, okay? And in some instances blacks would move into houses late at night, and whites would wake up the next morning to brothers in the neighborhood." He also remembered the white city government's frantic efforts to stop the flow. At one point a literal wall was built; at another, a literal bridge connecting white and black sections was delayed. But nothing worked. "First time in centuries that the white power structure couldn't control what was going on, because of the money coming in from the federal government. . . . Blacks could go up there and get a loan . . . blacks who were making money, who had good credit. . . . The whole thing just came topsy turvy." By 1970, the area closest to downtown was already two-thirds black; today it is virtually all black.

Despite the racial uniformity of this neighborhood, there is (as there has always been) a good deal of economic and social diversity among the residents (see table 1.8). In the areas closest to downtown, there are visible signs of urban distress—deteriorating properties, crack houses, and the like. Scattered throughout are stable working-class homes and apartments where people with modest incomes can raise a family. One of those residents lamented what he saw happening to his urban community: "There are some large houses in that area that at one time would usually be single-family houses. What has happened, because there are people moving out of that particular area, there's another class coming in. They're utilizing these houses as rooming houses and boardinghouses. . . . So, black folks are looking for new areas to move into. So that's why I see people moving into East Point and Decatur and even Stone Mountain."

Some, however, simply move slightly farther away from downtown in this same southwest Atlanta neighborhood. As one travels from Atlanta University

Table 1.8. Southwest Atlanta, Georgia, 1990: A Diverse Population

	Urban Section	Suburban Section
Household income		
< $20,000	49.1%	30.9%
$20,000–49,999	37.4	45.8
$50,000 +	13.7	23.4
Average	$25,770	$36,575
Education		
High school or less	64.4%	53.5%
Some college	20.7	25.3
College degree or more	14.8	21.2
Unemployment	7.5%	5.8%
Ethnicity		
Black residents, 1970	65.9%	41.7%
Black residents, 1990	97.7%	96.4%

SOURCE: Claritas, Inc., 1994.

Center west toward the "perimeter highway" that marks the symbolic boundary between city and suburb, this section of southwest Atlanta grows, in fact, more suburban. Whereas half (51 percent) of the households in the more urban portion live in single-family dwellings, three-quarters of those in the suburban section do. The lots get bigger, and there are more new houses under construction, with several complexes including offerings at and above $200,000. One recent resident noted, "This was the first time that we ever had the chance to buy a quality black home in a predominantly black neighborhood."

Black middle-class Atlantans can choose where to live, but many find the realities of racism still alive and well in predominantly white neighborhoods. Realtors may not conspire to keep them out, but they may still be scrutinized by passing police cars or mistaken for service employees by their neighbors. Many also have a sense that the larger black community needs them, and they do not want to walk away. The issues are complicated, but the result is black communities like this one that contain a mix of people from all economic and educational levels. People with enormous needs live within blocks of people with equally great resources. The degree to which one meets the other is unclear.

The economic dislocations of southwest Atlanta, then, go in two directions. Some people have made it into the suburban middle class, and others are struggling in urban poverty. The realities of racism bind them together, but the community itself has little cohesive power. The strains of class stratification are felt in the absence of causes and places that bring people together.

CARMEL, INDIANA, AND GWINNETT COUNTY, GEORGIA: COMMUNITIES TRANSFORMED BY SUBURBANIZATION

It is a long way from southwest Atlanta to Carmel, Indiana. While African Americans in Atlanta are adjusting to shifting economic and racial realities, the residents of Carmel are adjusting to rapid community growth and affluence. Those two factors, growth and affluence—typical of the suburban experience at least since World War II—have shaped Carmel's life in two distinct phases.[50] Those who have been there all their lives have seen a village transformed first into an outlying town, then into a full-fledged suburb of Indianapolis. Both transitions have left traces in the culture and institutions of Carmel. On one level, this has been a gemeinschaft-to-gesellschaft story. Yet it is not so simple. Each set of old-timers retains a great deal of power, and newcomers often come precisely because of the small-town appeal. Both here and in Gwinnett County, outside Atlanta, the story is not a simple one of old small-town patterns giving way to impersonal urban routines. Even before the city itself arrives at the door of such communities, the economy and culture of the city already shape the town. People begin working urban jobs and watching urban television long before they see the city as their home. Yet as those small towns grow, those who become their new residents often want to engage in a selective retrieval of rural culture. The result may be a peculiar mix of new and old, of "small town in mass society."[51]

These communities are not even described neatly by the term *suburb,* which usually refers to new blocks of housing on the outskirts of an urban area, occupied mostly by people who commute into the center of the city to work. In this picture, the city is like a wheel with a central hub and suburban spokes. Increasingly, however, the patterns of urban life are creating urban regions that look more like pepperoni pizza than like a wheel.[52] Centers of employment and commerce are dotted throughout the region, but especially along the edge. Rather than commuting in, people commute around. Nor is any one center likely to contain all the services desired by nearby residents. Shopping may be located in one center, recreation in another, cultural activities in another, and religious groups in another.[53] This decentralization is part of the challenge facing Carmel and Gwinnett County. They are taking their places alongside numerous other communities competing for the loyalty and involvement of people scattered all around the edge of a metropolitan region. These edge cities are the sites of complicated cultural negotiating in the midst of the enormous structural changes that have altered the economy, transportation, schooling, family life, and everything else for people in former small towns.

Quakers first settled the Carmel area in the 1830s. South of the county seat, their settlement was then a day's drive north of Indianapolis. Originally known as Bethlehem, Carmel was, throughout the nineteenth century, a small crossroads farming town. By 1900, still a small agricultural center, Carmel could boast a main street with a few businesses and professional offices, several mills, a newspaper, a small cluster of modest two-story wooden frame homes, and three churches. Population was still only 682 in 1930. Carmel, in fact, remained substantially the same until the beginning of World War II.

In the aftermath of the war, Carmel began to attract Indianapolis professionals who wanted to raise their children in a safe, small-town environment. Many of these newcomers commuted to Indianapolis and the surrounding area to work, but they still identified with Carmel as their home. They were willing to invest themselves in the community and planned to be there for the long haul. At first, local farmers and longtime residents were unhappy about this intrusion, but they soon realized that the demographic shift was unstoppable and that it would therefore be necessary to manage the growth of their community. Thus in 1958, with direction from new residents, Carmel began industrial and residential planning in anticipation of further population growth. One of those residents talked about attempting to protect Carmel from unwanted side effects of growth: "When the main avenues came out here, Keystone Avenue and others, that changed this into a truly suburban area. And then went all the problems, because being this close to Indianapolis we had to—or I did—go to the legislature and get the enactment of a bill that would protect Clay township and Carmel from the unloading of undesirable housing."

The 1960s saw an initial growth spurt, but the real boom occurred in the 1970s when Carmel surpassed both state and national growth rates. It went from a small town of 6,500 in 1970 to a small city of 18,000 ten years later (see table 1.9). Probably not coincidentally, this was also the period when Indianapolis was integrating its schools. Even in 1990, only 3 percent of Carmel's population was nonwhite, and half of those were Asian.

Today, Carmel is an incorporated suburban edge city with a population of over 25,000. The rapid growth of the 1970s leveled off somewhat in the 1980s, but by then Carmel had already lost much of its small-town flavor. Although it was still a safe, quiet place to live, the population growth translated to increased annexation, subdivisions, widened streets, strip malls and shopping areas, taxes, businesses, and city government. Growth also brought to the area more schools, golf courses, and churches. While Carmel is still primarily a residential community, it has recently added an increasing number of corporate headquarters and high-tech businesses along its major arteries.

The phrase "perpetual construction" aptly describes the whole city. New subdivisions seem to sprout like corn from the fields, and schools fill almost as soon as they can be built. All of this growth has strained the ability of the city to provide infrastructure and services. One person complained, "They were building so many new homes and creating all of these extra spigots in town, and

Table 1.9. Carmel, Indiana, 1990:
An Affluent and Growing Community

Household income
< $20,000	10.8%
$20,000–49,999	32.0
$50,000–74,999	26.5
$75,000 +	30.6
Average	$71,375

Education
High school or less	24.0%
Some college	27.2
College degree or more	48.8

Occupations
Professionals, managers & specialists	43.7%

Housing
Median house price = $131,800

Unemployment	1.8%

Ethnicity
Nonwhite residents	3.0%

Population and housing growth	1970	1980	1990
Number of persons	6,568	18,272	25,380
Number of single family units	1,539	4,618	6,912
1990 housing units built before	32.3%	66.4%	100%
1990 residents living at same address	8.6%	26.7%	100%

SOURCES: Claritas, Inc. 1994; Bureau of the Census, 1972, 1982, 1991.

doing nothing to provide more water and more services. We're still short of water. . . . If you pay your taxes and stand in the shower on Saturday night in August and hardly get enough water to rinse the soap off, that's out-of-control growth!"

Another said that developers seemed to be gobbling up all the land, with little planning for parks or open space. An older couple, longtime residents, noted how different life is now. "See, when our kids were in high school they could go two houses north up on this little hill and down to the neighbors and would play four-square right out in the road, because they could hear a car coming and would get out of the way."

Schools and youth activities have become, not surprisingly, centerpieces of the community's life. The high school prides itself on being state of the art. Soccer leagues abound. While dads and moms are on one of Carmel's numerous golf courses, kids can participate in any number of scouting or sporting or cultural activities. Carmel's churches take their place in the midst of this whirl of family and community activities. Part of what it means to live in Carmel is to be busy and to have a broad array of activities to choose from.

Being able to choose is a consequence of Carmel's affluence. The vast majority of those who live in Carmel are well-paid managers and professionals. As it grew, Carmel became known as the place to live for upwardly mobile professionals in the Indianapolis area, many of them destined to transfer out of the area after a few years. As a popular joke has it, "What are three words a Carmel housewife never hears? Attention K-Mart shoppers." She is more likely to shop in trendy department stores and boutiques. Even the grocery stores in Carmel can be depended on for a variety of gourmet foods not likely to be found in other parts of the city. One community leader noted that most people in Carmel probably do not know that there are occasionally people in need, even in Carmel. The city has little in the way of social services. More typical is the support group one of the local churches runs—for executives who have lost their jobs.

Carmel is no longer the small town of fifty years ago, or even the small town that became a postwar home to well-off Indianapolis professionals who wanted to live the small-town life. Today, it is a suburb, with all the mobility that implies. It is a community with tremendous resources, defining itself all over again.

Gwinnett County is neither as affluent nor as far along the path of suburbanization as Carmel. In Carmel, the old downtown has virtually disappeared, while the downtowns in several Gwinnett County towns are still very visible, even being refurbished. In the area of Gwinnett we studied, population did not begin to grow until after 1970, with the big spurt in the 1980s. Still, both communities continue to suffer the growing pains of infrastructures that cannot keep up with new construction, and both are full of people who have consciously chosen *not* to live in the city. People in both places shake their heads in amazement at the speed with which farm land can become a subdivision. The struggle to preserve a way of life is even more apparent today in Gwinnett than in Carmel.

During the 1980s, Gwinnett County had the dubious honor, several years running, of being among the fastest-growing counties in the nation. It really was phenomenal. In the section of the county we chose for study (a swath extending northeast from the county seat of Lawrenceville), almost seven thousand new single-family dwellings were built in the 1980s.[54] *In twenty years, the population more than doubled, from twenty-seven thousand to sixty-three thousand (see table 1.10). Only 16 percent of the current housing stock existed in 1970. Said one longtime resident, "Where there used to be pasture, now there are subdivisions; where you used to see cattle, now you see kids." And the county can barely keep up with the school needs of those children. At one school, a teacher recalled in amazement, "When we opened our building two years ago, we had one extra classroom we used as computer lab. The second year in the building that room became a classroom, plus we had two trailers. So*

Table 1.10. Gwinnett County, Georgia, 1970–1990: Population Growth

	1970	1980	1990
Population*	27,488	42,864	63,307
Housing			
Single-family units	7,640**	12,625	19,708
1990 housing units built before	16.2%	43.8%	100%
1990 residents living at same			
address in	7.6%	24.4%	100%

SOURCES: Claritas, Inc., 1994; Bureau of the Census 1972, 1982, 1991.
*Included is one section of the county, extending northeast from Lawrenceville.
**Estimate based on number of households. Detailed housing characteristics for census tracts were not available in Gwinnett in 1970.

that's approximately seventy-five additional students right there. This year in addition to those we have seven more trailers that will be set up."

Once the development began, county zoning and planning commissions seemed to compound the problems with tax policies that declared pasture and fallow land "vacant." Driving down two-lane state roads, one sees a For Sale sign on nearly every undeveloped piece of land. The pattern of growth in Gwinnett County, where only about 21 percent of the population lives in incorporated areas, has been remarkably decentralized and unregulated. While attractive schools and parks have been constructed in some places, many towns have failed to supply any major enhancement in streets, street lights, fire protection, policing, garbage, and sewer services. This deficiency has further encouraged the growth of high-density subdivisions beyond the town borders.

Many longtime residents feel as though their communities were simply overrun by growth and change. Sometimes they feel literally overrun trying to drive on their country roads, now dominated by fast city drivers. One woman voiced a common sentiment when she said, "We've grown too much, but there's nothing we can really do about it." Another resident speculated that the growth happened so fast and the change was so dramatic that there was no time for any resistance to take hold. If the growth had been slower or confined to certain areas, he speculated, "things might have turned out differently." Among those "things" is the old sense of community now lost. One man said ruefully, "Some people say, well, at least everybody don't know your business, but they don't look out for you either."

In part, all this development is the result of increased accessibility. Interstate 85 connects Gwinnett County to downtown Atlanta with as many as twelve lanes of concrete. Farther out, Georgia 316 adds a four-lane divided highway spur from I-85 south into the more distant sections of the county. People willing to drive up to an hour each way can own a less-expensive house in a quiet countrylike setting, while still working in the city. Yet Gwinnett residents are anxious that the county not be too accessible. Citing a fear of increased crime, Lawrenceville residents, along with the rest of Gwinnett County, consistently oppose the extension of MARTA, Atlanta's public rail system, into their area. Many residents and civic leaders would like to take advantage of the benefits that come with being a part of metropolitan Atlanta while avoiding the problems associated with large, urban areas.

Despite their absorption into the Atlanta metropolitan area, Lawrenceville and other communities are taking steps to maintain distinctive identities. Lawrenceville's downtown area—site of the courthouse square, historically the center of the community's life—has recently undergone a multimillion dollar facelift that leaders hope will "renew residents' sense of the past" and revitalize the economic center of the city. In numerous ways, Gwinnett communities are learning to use their past. Festivals and commemorations help to create a sense of nostalgia among new residents and old. Even the new subdivisions are often named "Plantation" this or that. In the midst of its growth, the area seems to be looking for ways to sustain and recreate its small-town identity.

Nine communities. The changes they face involve economic, structural, and cultural dislocations—for both good and ill—that have forced them to rethink who they are. Population shifts have changed the composition of each community's cultural base. What was once assumed to be true about what language is spoken, what sorts of families are present, what resources are available, how land is used—all has been rendered obsolete. Hundreds of human institutions are being transformed. Corner grocery stores are changing hands and stocking new foods. Social service agencies are increasing their staffs, and police forces are altering their patrol patterns. New roads are being built, and public transportation services are being revamped. Houses have been built and torn down or divided into apartments. Schools have come and gone, and the patterns of neighboring are being scrambled, as old friends move away and strangers arrive. Even governmental boundaries are eventually redrawn to reflect the new community that is emerging.

These are the communities about which this book will be concerned. This array of social, cultural, and economic change is the context in which the congregations we studied were attempting to survive and contribute to the well-being of their surroundings.

A Caveat

As segments of larger metropolitan areas, however, none of these communities are self-sufficient. The fate of each is tied to that larger region. (Anderson is the one exception. Although technically part of the Indianapolis census area, it still exists as a relatively self-contained community.) While many of the institutions in a given neighborhood may define themselves primarily in terms of that locale, others do not. Many businesses and cultural institutions, especially, seek to attract clientele from larger areas. The health and social services used by the neighborhood's population are unlikely to be located exclusively within its borders. And the individuals that call any given neighborhood home vary in their attachment to it. Sometimes the networks of affiliation are dense and tightly bounded by geography, but more often those local ties are combined with others, more loosely bounded and scattered, but no less real.[55] The neighborhood streets residents travel connect them to other communities as surely as they provide centers of local activity.

The two institutions most likely to remain connected to the immediate neighborhoods they serve are elementary schools and congregations. But even that has changed. In many places busing has strained the tie between school and community. And in most places, congregations are today less likely than before to be identified primarily by place. While every congregation is located in a specific place, not every congregation is defined primarily in terms of that location. The Roman Catholic Church still draws explicit parish boundaries, strongly encouraging people to attend the church to which they are assigned. Orthodox Jewish synagogues encourage proximity because of rules against travel on the Sabbath. But in most cases, people are perfectly free to live where they wish and attend the church of their choice. The choice of one's congregation is part of the freedom U.S. attenders have long cherished.

The possibility for choice has been greatly enhanced with the growth of cities. In an urban region, one can choose, for instance, among the "high church" Methodists and the "pro-life" Methodists and the "charismatic" Methodists and the Methodists with the woman preacher. Any given person's networks of affiliation—religious and otherwise— probably spread across institutions located in various quarters of a metropolitan area. Work may be in one place, populated by people from all over the region. Children's school and leisure activities often present transportation challenges to the most agile of car-pooling parents. And adult shopping and leisure may be equally distant from each other and from home. Rather than identifying with a particular neighborhood, urban middle-class residents may more readily identify with the cultural slice or life-style that binds the institutions with which they are affiliated. Those who teach in the local university, for instance, whose children are in the Montessori school, and who shop at the fresh-produce market may be especially likely to show up in the pews of the left-of-center Presbyterian church—which may or may not be in a neighborhood any of them inhabit.

The freedom to choose a place to worship is a powerful force pulling at the ties between congregation and local community. Still, powerful forces also anchor congregations in the particular place where they are located.[56] Small-town and rural congregations, of course, were always identified with a particular place—Big Piney Grove or Piedmont Ridge or Halfway—and they were populated with the people from that place. There were rarely multiple varieties of any denomination to choose from. If one were Methodist and lived in a small town, for instance, the choices, short of conversion, were limited. Even cities have been populated with congregations no less identified by location—Garden Hills or Fifth Avenue or West Side, for instance. Builders of suburban housing sometimes set aside a corner or two for new church buildings to serve the needs of the subdivision's residents. Even more than in urban areas, suburban communities—including their patterns of religious participation—seem to be defined by particularism and place.[57] People have often thought about religious participation much as they have thought about school attendance. The ideal was to have a friendly, attractive place to send one's children, preferably within an easy drive or short ride on public transit. Both congregations and schools are anchors for community. While people are not forced to attend close to home, powerful forces of culture and tradition still push them into neighborhood congregations.

Congregations, then, are related to their immediate contexts in a variety of ways. Some are strongly identified with the people who inhabit a given locale and are therefore tied into the dense network of affiliation that is the local community. They approximate the parish image. Others occupy a specialized niche, serving a culturally or theologically defined constituency.[58] Urban congregations probably always lie somewhere between the two poles of parish and niche; but identifying the poles is critical to understanding how congregations are responding to change in their communities. One of the responses to change we will see in the pages to follow is the transformation of neighborhood parishes into niche congregations.

Surveying Local Religious Ecologies

With such distinctions of context in mind, in the spring of 1992 our researchers turned their attention to these nine communities. After taking a measure of the changes they had confronted, we began to assess the state of the religious institutions they contained. Each research team sought to locate every congregation within the boundaries of the community and to visit a sampling of them for weekly worship. Such locating tasks are notoriously difficult. One can start with the *Yellow Pages* or with a published directory, but many congregations do not have telephones, and others are too new to show up in any published source. In addition, many new congregations meet in rented quarters that may not appear to be religious space except for the few hours the group occupies it each week. For all these reasons, we are confident that our count underestimates the number of congregations and that it disproportionately underestimates the number of new or small ones.

For similar reasons, we have much more complete data on some congregations than on others. Where a congregation is big enough to have a secretary who is in the office to answer the phone each day, it is relatively easy to find out when the congregation was founded, how many attend each week, what proportion are local and what proportion commute, and what sorts of activities they have. Where no such regular staff exists, it was often impossible to find out more than a name and location. From those two pieces of information we could make fairly safe judgments about the denominational or religious family to which the congregation belonged, and often we could make informed guesses about the dominant ethnicity of the congregants—but no more. In all, we found 449 congregations in our nine communities, and we gathered fairly complete information on the history and programing of about 300 of them. A summary of the religious ecology of the nine communities is contained in table 1.11.

One of the first things we discovered was that communities vary enormously in the density of the religious institutional population. With roughly equivalent populations of between fifty and sixty-five thousand persons, for instance, Allston-Brighton, Oak Park, and Anderson have 28, 57, and 121 congregations respectively. As a densely populated downtown area, Long Beach has the highest ratio of population to congregations, but Allston-Brighton (heavily concentrated into a couple of large Catholic parishes, but also heavily unchurched) is not far behind. Most of the southern and midwestern communities have a congregation for every five hundred to nine hundred residents. But fast-growing Gwinnett County has more population than church starters have yet caught up with. Attendance rates also vary, from a low of 5 percent in Allston-Brighton to a high of nearly 50 percent in Carmel. Both the density of congregations and the level of participation vary, then, especially by region.

Across communities, a significant proportion of the congregations is small. At least one-third (probably more among those we did not find) have average weekly attendance of under 100, and more than another third fall between 100 and 250, with most of the rest under 500. Almost

Table 1.11. Congregational Populations by Community

	Long Beach, California	Candler Park (Atlanta), Georgia	Allston-Brighton, Massachusetts	West Adams (Los Angeles), California
Population	57,000	7,800	66,400	44,700
No. of congregations	22	27	28	47
Ratio of congregations to population	1:2,591	1:289	1:2,371	1:951
Denominational family				
Mainline	64%	37%	21%	23%
Evangelical	14	33	43	21
Catholic	9	15	21	6
Black	—	4	4	36
Other	14	11	11	13
Size				
< 100	41%	50%	74%	29%*
100–499	47	50	17	38
500 +	12	—	9	33
Moved to present location since 1980	14%	25%	52%	28%*

*Because of large amounts of missing data, it should be assumed that the percentages of small and new congregations in these communities is seriously underestimated.

half of those small congregations are new and struggling to get established, having been founded since 1980.[59] The remainder have either settled into a stable niche as small congregations or are remnants of formerly thriving, now declining institutions. Most neighborhoods have only one or two really large congregations, and most of those are old and established (42 percent having been founded before 1946), Catholic (59 percent of Catholic parishes reported more than 500 in attendance), or both.

These communities also reflect an amazing amount of denominational diversity. Included are well over sixty denominational identities, from AME to Zen. Again, the amount and type of diversity vary across communities and regions. Not surprisingly, Gwinnett County, in suburban Atlanta, is full of evangelical Protestant churches, with almost no black churches, relatively few Catholics, and no new or sectarian religious choices, a pattern closely mirrored by Anderson. Anderson's evangelical character masks, however, the diversity *within* that evangelical presence. No less than twenty-two evangelical and Pentecostal

Table 1.11. *Continued*

Oak Park, Illinois	Anderson, Indiana	Southwest Atlanta, Georgia	Carmel, Indiana	Gwinnett County, Georgia
53,600	59,400	40,700	25,400	63,300
57	121	71	42	34
1:940	1:491	1:573	1:605	1:1,862
46%	22%	22%	45%	26%
28	53	17	38	59
12	2	—	7	9
5	18	56	2	6
9	5	4	7	—
38%	27%*	14%*	39%	18%
47	63	59	50	62
15	10	27	11	21
24%	22%*	26%*	47%	30%

denominations (and nondenominational groups) are represented among Anderson's sixty-four evangelical churches. Sectarian Christian (such as Jehovah's Witnesses or Mormons) and non-Christian alternatives (such as synagogues and Buddhist, Hindu, and Muslim groups) were most available on the West Coast, in Candler Park and in Allston-Brighton. Candler Park, for instance, was home in 1992 to a Reconstructionist Jewish congregation and a Krishna temple, in addition to a Quaker meeting, Maronite Christians, Anglo-Catholics, and an Antiochian Orthodox church.

The segregation of American Protestantism is still apparent in the uneven distribution of historically black denominations. Most of the communities have only one or two black churches. In predominantly black southwest Atlanta and West Adams, however, the mix of denominational types is dominated by churches from historically black traditions. Also present were a few predominantly white mainline and evangelical congregations, mostly populated by members who live outside the area, as well as a few congregations of mixed ethnic constituencies.

The one point of stability in the religious variety we found is a surprising uniformity across communities in the proportion of congregations that falls within the mainline Protestant category. The midwestern communities of Oak Park and Carmel, plus the midwestern outpost of Long Beach, were disproportionately mainline in their congregational offerings. Other communities weighed in, however, at a consistent 21–26 percent, despite significant variations in the numbers of other types of congregations they contained. Evangelical and Pentecostal churches are just as numerous as the mainline congregations overall, but not as evenly distributed.

Although these nine communities all contain a large number of congregations and a broad assortment to choose from, both the number and assortment vary quite widely by region and by several other factors. This accounting, of course, is a snapshot, taken at one point in time. It tells us only about the age, health, and size of the congregations found in these nine places at this one point in history. To find out more about the process of change, we will have to look more closely, gathering more nuanced information than could be gained in an initial inventory.

Selecting Focus Congregations

In each of the nine communities, we chose two focus congregations for more extensive study. In addition, five small, struggling congregations were chosen as "ministudies." Table 1.12 locates all twenty-three in terms of their denominational family and size. We tried to select a range of congregations that approximated the size and denominational range we had encountered in the communities as a whole. In that regard, we are aware of overselecting small mainline Protestant congregations and underselecting small evangelical Protestant groups. Otherwise, our range is fairly representative.

We were also attempting to select congregations that would represent the full range of apparent responses to change. Just what that range is and how these congregations are distributed will be the subject of much of the rest of this book. At this point it is sufficient to say that we wanted to include some congregations that did not appear likely to survive, some that were new, and some that were attempting to achieve various forms of adaptation. In addition, we discovered some congregations we came to call "rebirths." They had approached extinction before attempting adaptations that eventually transformed them into almost wholly new organizations. All of these types are included and distributed fairly evenly across the denominational families and regions. They are not, however, included in numbers proportional to their presence in the population. For instance, for only five of our twenty-three congregations is long-term survival in doubt, while our

Table 1.12. Study Congregations by Size and Denominational Family

Denominational Family	Average attendance		
	Less than 100	100–499	500+
Mainline Protestant	Brighton Evangelical Congregational *Brighton* Hinton Memorial United Methodist *Gwinnett County* Epworth United Methodist *Candler Park* Brighton Avenue Baptist* *Allston* Gray Friends Meeting* *Carmel* East Lynn Christian* *Anderson*	First Congregational *Long Beach* Good Shepherd Lutheran *Oak Park* First Baptist* *Anderson*	Carmel United Methodist *Carmel*
Evangelical Protestant	Carmel Wesleyan* *Carmel*	South Meridian Church of God *Anderson* City Baptist *Oak Park*	Northview (Assemblies of God) *Carmel* Grace Baptist *Anderson*
Catholic		St. Catherine's *Allston* St. Matthew's *Long Beach*	St. Lawrence *Gwinnett County*
Black Protestant	Incarnation Episcopal *Southwest Atlanta*	Berean Seventh-Day Adventist *West Adams*	Holman United Methodist *West Adams* Hope Baptist *Southwest Atlanta*
Other	First Existentialist *Candler Park*		

*These congregations were ministudies.

estimate is that nearly half of the total population of congregations belongs in that category. Our sample is a purposive one, then, although it attempts to be roughly representative in terms of size and denominational type. We will compare these twenty-three from time to time with what we know about the whole population of congregations in these communities; but for this study, it was more important to obtain adequate information on each of the possible response processes (oversampling and undersampling accordingly) than to work with a statistically representative sample of all congregations.

Each of the eighteen focus congregations received the attention of one of our researchers for the six months from July through December 1992. In addition, brief follow-up reports were done in late 1993. In 1992, they attended worship services and interviewed most of the staff members. They also attended congregational business meetings, board and committee meetings, Sunday school classes and fellowship groups, and whatever special events came along. Interviews were completed with ten to fifteen members besides the staff, including both old-timers and newcomers, both key lay leaders and ordinary members. For the ministudies, researchers visited the congregation for worship three or four times and interviewed the pastor plus one or two longtime members. We have 317 interviews on tape, including interviews with persons in the congregations and in the communities. Many of those involve multiple narrators—couples interviewed together and small groups, for instance. Beyond the interviews, of course, were the hundreds of conversations in hallways and over coffee, before worship and during committee meetings. Along with the researchers' observations, these conversations were carefully recorded in field notes that were then collected in our Atlanta office.

To get a firsthand picture of the places we were studying, I visited each of the focus congregations at least once, attending worship and some small group meetings, and interviewing a sampling of leaders and members. I had also visited each of the communities before we selected the congregations, and in a number of cases I made a third trip at some point during the project. While I do not have the intimate knowledge enjoyed by those who spent six intense months getting acquainted, my visits combined with the field notes and transcripts I read to give me a clear, firsthand sense of each place.

We were all guided in our task of observing by a set of questions worked out collectively by researchers and directors. The big question, of course, was how the congregation had changed, especially as a consequence of the changes in its context. But to give that big question a more concrete focus, we concentrated on learning how the members tell their story and what their primary theological tenets are. We looked for who belongs and how they are recruited. We mapped out the basics of the congregation's program and sense of mission. And we assessed how power is exercised and by whom. We also sized up the resources available to them—both material resources and the ideas that mobilize those resources. How they define their most pressing issues was also our interest, as well as what they think they can do about those problems. A complete list of our guiding questions, along with the instructions received by the researchers, is contained in Appendix A.

To supplement the wealth of data gathered by means of our observations and interviews, we also distributed a questionnaire in each congregation. These were handed out at the main worship service on two (and sometimes three) successive Sundays in late 1992, usually accompanied by an announcement by the pastor, the researcher, or both. In most instances people took them home to complete and brought them back to collection boxes at the church in the following weeks. In a couple of instances, pastors made time during the service for completing the survey, a process that at Incarnation Episcopal in Atlanta resulted in a near 100 percent response rate! At most other congregations we received completed surveys from about half the number of adults who normally attend worship, a total of 1,995 altogether. (We will note specific response rates as we look at each congregation throughout the book.) These surveys obviously overrepresent those most active in the congregation. Those who rarely attend probably never received a copy, and those less invested in the church's affairs may have felt less obligation to complete and return it. However, these aggregate numbers tell us more than our interviews could about the beliefs and practices, backgrounds and status of a broader cross-section of members, a cross-section that should adequately represent the regular attenders. A copy of the survey is contained in Appendix B.

Establishing a Framework for Analysis

Having mapped the religious ecology of these nine communities, and having gathered exhaustive data on twenty-three congregations whose experiences seemed to represent the range of possible responses to contextual change, what remained was to make sense of it all. The effort had been to allow the experience of the congregations to define our categories, rather than imposing a framework in advance.[60] This book is organized, then, around the types of strategies we observed.

Earlier writers have outlined the patterns they thought possible and likely in the face of environmental change. In a 1970s study of urban churches, Gaylord Noyce saw four options: (1) become a metro church (what we will call a "niche congregation"), (2) decline, (3) adapt, or (4) move.[61] H. Paul Douglass said that the large urban churches he studied could either move to a new location or attempt to appeal to a larger, metropolitan constituency (the niche congregation again). They could also attempt to hang on in their present location by appealing to "our kind of people," so long as there were enough of "our kind" to survive. A sort of compromise strategy, in his view, was drawing members from afar, while offering limited services to the immediate neighborhood.[62] Real adaptation, either intentional or cumulative, would involve changes in both the constituency and the program of the congregation. Finally, he noted, some urban churches may undertake such fundamental transformations as to cease resembling congregations at all.[63]

Rosabeth Kanter, Barry Stein, and Todd Jick, in their examination of changes in other types of organizations, sound a similar note. "As environmental movement presents pressures and opportunities for change, organizations can subtly change their identities by reformulating their relationships to their environments: changing the businesses in which they operate, the products they offer to the market, the investors who supply capital, and so forth. The most extreme version of identity change is when an organization becomes something entirely different (in its businesses, products, ownership, etc.) in order to allow a portion—the asset base, the products, some know-how, the employment base, even a tax carryover—to endure."[64] In such extreme circumstances, a building or a foundation may remain, but the round of activities and members that identified a congregation may be gone.

These organizational theorists and church researchers, along with our own observations, tell us that the outcomes of congregational encounters with change fall into four broad categories. First and most numerous are congregations thrown into decline. As we will see, many survive for relatively long periods with diminishing resources. Many who attempt various forms of adaptation are simply not successful in fitting their structures, resources, and expectations to newly available constituencies.

Second, many congregations reorient themselves to their locale. Some sell their buildings to new groups that will better serve the new community and move to a location to which they are better fitted. Others manage to establish an identity that transcends location. These are the niche congregations. Their program and constituency remain essentially stable, but they draw that constituency from throughout a metropolitan region.

Third, congregations adapt in one of three ways. Sometimes they manage to attract new constituencies without making appreciable changes in their own ways of doing things. They simply discover and decide to tap a new market. More often, however, those new constituencies require changes in the culture and programs of the congregation. Integrating new groups calls for doing new things and results in a congregation that looks noticeably different. Other times, the changes are mostly in the polity of the congregation. Changes in constituency and context require new structures of decision making that leave the congregation *looking* much the same, but significantly different in its internal dynamics. We examine all three kinds of adaptation.

Finally, we will look at two kinds of new beginnings. Some adaptations come only at the point of life-threatening crisis, and the result is a transformation so complete as to be a rebirth. These are not nearly so numerous as actual births, however. When contexts change, organizational entrepreneurs always move in to attempt whole new enterprises.

Births, deaths, adaptations, and reorientations to locale are, then, the broad categories in which congregational response to change occurs. In communities whose social infrastructure was being reconstructed, one of the most active institutional sectors, we discovered, was the changing religious ecology.

The social construction in which these citizens are engaged takes place within the possibilities and constraints of the institutional life of the congregations themselves. Understanding congregational response to change obviously requires more than understanding the external context; it also requires understanding the cultural work by which the congregations seek to shape that context. I have found helpful the perspective offered by Ann Swidler in a 1986 article, "Culture in Action."[65] She points out, following Clifford Geertz, that "settled" times are very different from "unsettled" times. Where culture is relatively settled, strategies of action are like well-worn paths. Everyone knows who belongs where and what to do next. There are readily recognizable scripts for the small episodes of everyday interaction in which we all participate— forms of greeting, bits of negotiation, exchanges of information, rituals of deference, and the like.[66] But in unsettled times, people have to invent new strategies of action, using the cultural tool kits of ideas and practices available to them (what Pierre Bourdieu has called "cultural capital").[67] Often ideological entrepreneurs are active in such times, promulgating new strategies and the rationales for them, answering the question not only of what to do, but also of why it should be done. All the congregations we are studying are living in unsettled times, faced with situations in which their old strategies of action no longer work in predictable ways. Survival may mean being able to invent new strategies of action with the cultural tools available to them.

Rosabeth Kanter and her associates point out that theorists have operated within three dominant understandings of how organizations change in response to their environments.[68] The population ecology theory might be called "survival of the fittest." These writers have been primarily concerned with the *population* of organizations, more than with how any given organization changes. They want to know why a given organizational type succeeds—under what conditions specialists are better able to survive than generalists, for instance. From this perspective, they often examine rates of foundings and rates of demise, as well as the effects of size and other resources. In fact, the competition for scarce resources is at the heart of this type of analysis. Selection processes eliminate the weakest competitors in any given population, while deposed competitors either leave (territorially) or differentiate (functionally).[69] If the resources dry up, organizations either move, die, or modify their activities so as to take advantage of different resources.

In contrast, the approach of the new institutionalist framework might be called "survival of the similar." Both frameworks note the "liabilities of newness," for instance. Organizations are much more likely to die in the first years of their existence than after they have gotten established. While population ecologists locate those liabilities in deficient resources, new institutionalists locate them in the lack of legitimation. New organizational forms do not easily mesh with the existing forms and patterns in a system. They may need supplies or skills that are hard to find or offer services not taken for granted as necessary.

Once established, however, there are powerful forces that create inertia in organizations. Population ecologists see that inertia coming from the efficient and predictable use of resources, while new institutionalists see it coming from established internal cultures coupled with legitimated patterns of interaction with other similarly constructed organizations. When everyone else has an affirmative action department, and there is a professional association of affirmative action officers, and all the government paperwork has to go somewhere, abolishing one's affirmative action department seems unthinkable.[70] New institutionalists, then, look for the cultural forces that legitimate existing and emerging forms of organization, while population ecologists are most concerned with resources.

A final framework for understanding organizational responses to change might be called "survival of the savvy." Some theorists have concentrated on studying how organizational leaders achieve adaptive change. The emphasis, almost inevitably, is on the mobilization of power within the organization, on effective use of influence and the building of coalitions—in short, on internal politics. While adaptation is certainly the goal of any leader who sees environmental forces threatening his or her organization, adaptation is, as we will see, more easily advocated than accomplished. John Freeman points out that it takes more than a charismatic entrepreneur to achieve change. Also involved are new technologies, unexploited markets, available capital, and not a little luck. One has to have tools, resources, and potential customers to achieve adaptation.[71] Similarly, Martha Feldman and James March note that organizational decision making is best seen as "an arena for exercising social values, for displaying authority, and for

exhibiting proper behavior and attitudes with respect to a central ideological construct of modern western civilization: the concept of intel-
ligent choice."[72] Legitimacy is established by having information, whether
or not that information can be shown to bear any relationship to the
decision made. Adaptation is not a simple process of gathering good
information and persuading others to change.

This summary of ways to understand organizational response to
change has some overlap with Gareth Morgan's identification of the
images that have dominated thinking in organizational studies more
broadly.[73] The earliest models were often mechanistic ones, looking at
organizations as highly structured and rationalized bureaucracies.
Those were followed by organismic images that pointed to the way in
which there is an "open system" between an environment that supplies resources (and stresses) and the organization seeking through
very human means to respond and adapt. There have also been images
of organizations as "brains," focusing on the information-processing
and decision-making capacities of organizations. Some have also used
psychological models to understand the irrationalities of organizational
life; but more common, especially recently, have been models analyz-
ing organizations as cultures. Standing in critique of all of these, however, are political models of organizational life that point out the
degree to which any organization is an amalgam of competing interests, tenuously held together.

Morgan's images are also rather like the "frames" offered by Lee
Bolman and Terrence Deal.[74] Their "structural" frame corresponds to
Morgan's mechanistic image and reminds us that organizations do
have structured hierarchies, patterns of communication, and the like.
Their "human resource" frame (like Morgan's psychological and organismic models) reminds us that much of organizational life is shaped
by the needs and desires of ordinary human actors—people who want
to be noticed and liked, as well as rewarded. That people also want to
have some control over what happens around them, and that there are
conflicting definitions of what to do and how to proceed, is at the heart
of Bolman and Deal's "political" frame (as it is for Morgan). And like
Morgan, they identify a "symbolic" frame in which the analyst focuses
on the culture of the organization.

Building out of all of this thinking about organizations, and about
congregations in particular, we will look at three broad dimensions of
congregational life: *resources, structures of authority,* and the congregation's *culture*.[75] That culture consists of physical artifacts, patterns of
activity, and the language and story that embellish those objects and
activities with meaning.[76] Changing environments mean changing
resources, and paying attention to a congregation's access to various kinds of resources is essential to understanding its response. But

neither organizations nor contexts are solely collections of resources. They are also sets of patterned and legitimated cultural responses. They are collections of symbols and rituals, as much as of materials and people. And all of that is given shape and energy by the lines of power and influence inside and outside the congregation.

RESOURCES

The first cultural tools we will examine in each case are the material and human resources with which the congregation has to work. We begin with the very mundane question of money. The vast majority of congregations support themselves from current contributions from their members. Paying their bills depends on how many members there are, how much money the members have, and how much of it they are willing to give to the church. It is generally true that people with more money give more dollars, but proportionately less of their income.[77] In addition, larger churches are able to command proportionately less from their members.[78] But both those facts are shaped by the particular culture, circumstances, and expectations of the congregation. Likewise, as communities change, constituencies may also change, along with the available resources those constituencies can or will bring into the congregation.

Beyond member contributions, congregations often have other material resources at their disposal. Most have a building, and that physical structure can be both a resource and a liability for the congregation. Most obviously, the building is a resource as a space in which the congregation and other groups can meet. But the congregation for which it was built may be very different from the one it now houses, with few spaces that meet the current congregation's needs. To the extent that the building is old and in need of repair, it may also be a significant drain on scarce resources. Old, drafty buildings may be exorbitantly expensive to heat. Leaky roofs may damage furniture and fixtures.[79] Inadequate lighting, unkempt grounds, and ineffective signs may harm the congregation's visible presence in the community. And congregations that have to deal with all these problems may have little money or energy left for dreaming up new programs and meeting new neighbors.

Sometimes, however, those mismatched buildings can be turned into an asset. Renting space to community organizations is, in fact, one of the most common ways churches raise a little extra money. In this way, buildings become a material asset that earns income for the congregation.

In addition, buildings may be a cultural asset, a status signal that helps to establish or maintain a congregation's place in the community.[80] In a congregation-friendly community, a key location along with ample space may attract new members and serve the needs of members already there. A congregation with lots of classroom space can imagine educational programs that another congregation might not, and a congregation without a gym is less likely to dream about an after-school recreation program. In short, buildings are resources both for the internal use of the congregation and for their potential as income and status producers.

In addition, congregations may have access to a variety of other income sources. Most commonly, they have an endowment that supplies them with regular payouts and with a cushion against which to borrow. Also fairly common are supplements supplied by a denomination. Given the dire financial straits in which most denominations find themselves, however, there is no guarantee that money will be available to help a congregation in trouble or a small congregation with big plans. Some congregations are also able to obtain funds from various secular sources, ranging from city government to charitable foundations. These outside agencies usually support specific programs, rather than general operating expenses.

In addition to these material resources, congregations also need human resources. The sheer size of the congregation makes a difference in what it is able to do.[81] And the bigger the congregation, the more likely it is to have an expanded professional staff, which in turn expands the range of activities and ministries the congregation can undertake. Congregations need personpower if they are to provide services to their members and to the community, and in most instances they depend for this energy on members' charitable impulses.[82] In some cases, the needed personpower is little more than warm bodies and willing spirits. But in other cases, the congregation needs skills— the ability to organize and plan, for instance.[83] Such planning skills often involve obtaining and reading background materials, contacting various officials, writing reports, and making presentations—skills often learned through higher education or in professional jobs.[84] Other times, the skills needed are relational—the ability to get along with diverse people, to raise money, to care for children, to make strangers welcome. These are skills not easily taught, but nevertheless necessary.

Most visibly, congregations need people with leadership skills, especially effective clergy.[85] They need someone who can envision what should be done and motivate others to participate in doing it. They need people who can help a group make a decision. They need people who can keep hundreds of details in order in the process of getting a large job done. They need people with whom members can identify, establishing an emotional connection that helps to bind them together as a congregation. They need people who make them feel both that things are under control and at the same time that everyone has a say. Such leadership can come from dynamic lay members, as well as from the congregation's paid staff.

Just as a congregation can supplement its own material resources with help from outside, so it can supplement its human resources through the networks in which it and its members are embedded. Co-workers, neighbors, and coparticipants in other community organizations are thereby indirectly connected to the congregation. They become potential recruits for the congregation's activities, potential contributors to the congregation's causes.[86] Their skills can often be put to use for special projects. Even people who may have no interest in joining this particular congregation may be willing to buy raffle tickets or help in a tutoring program. In addition to these individual connections, the organizations themselves are also potential resources. Business and community organizations in which members are active may join with the congregation in sponsoring events or supporting community programs. If connections are potential resources, then, the implication is that the better the connections between members and the larger community, the more resources they may be able to import into the congregation's ministry.

The congregation itself is also embedded in a network of organizations that are potential resources in its work. Denominations are the most obvious of these extracongregational connections, but there are others, as well. Many pastors belong to a local ministerial association, through which a variety of support is channeled. The pastors themselves get moral support from others engaged in similar work, but they may also use this forum for coordinating local services to indigent people, saving each local congregation from having to judge the merits of every case on its doorstep. In other cases, congregations may belong to coalitions that help them to pool resources in meeting the needs of the community.[87] Some of these coalitions may be explicitly religious, but others may include a variety of agencies and businesses and community organizations. In addition to these local alliances, congregations can extend their reach by participating with any of the hundreds of "parachurch" organizations, from Habitat for Humanity to the Christian Coalition.[88] These religious special purpose groups mobilize the energies of individuals and congregations around projects and specific goals. They may be evangelistic, humanitarian, educational, political, or any combination thereof. Again, the better the congregation's connections, the more extensive the pool of partners it has available for pursuing a variety of services to the community.

Money, time, skills, connections—all resources out of which a congregation can construct responses to the communities to which it is connected. However, all of those ingredients are only potential resources until they are mobilized by the commitment of the members to the group. Most critical seems to be the extent to which the congregation is able to offer its members a strong sense of identity and participation that is relatively distinct from anything available to them elsewhere. Groups that are more "sectarian" have a commitment advantage over groups that are more "churchlike." Maintaining a distinctive community requires commitment from everyone and rewards everyone with the benefits that come from participating in a solidary fellowship.[89] Rosabeth Kanter's study of nineteenth-century communes supports the notion that distinctiveness (and relative detachment from competing allegiances) is an organizational advantage. She also notes that commitment involves three dimensions: instrumental, affective, and evaluative. People are more committed to an organization when they have meaningful work to do, when they feel a sense of attachment to others in the group, and when they see the group as representing a moral good that allows them to transcend merely personal interest.[90] This transcendent moral authority is legitimated by the symbolic and cultural resources, the temporal and spiritual goods the congregation can claim to represent.[91] The ability of a congregation to mobilize its potential resources will depend on the extent to which its members find the good it offers sufficiently compelling to motivate their commitment.

Both human and material resources, then, are the building blocks out of which congregations construct their lives. They are the raw material without which there would be no congregation. They do not set absolute limits, but they do provide the backdrop and setting against which the congregation's story is told.

STRUCTURES OF AUTHORITY

Congregations vary greatly in the degree to which they are able to make decisions about how they will use the resources they have. A few of the congregations in our study, like a significant segment of the U.S. congregational population, are independent. They pay dues to no one and get no outside support. They design their own programs and decide for themselves what to believe and how to worship. They make their own personnel and financial decisions and pay for their own mistakes. Most congregations, however, are part of some larger organizational structure, usually a denomination to which they owe varying degrees of deference.[92] There is no single model for religious organization that prescribes how local bodies relate to regional and national units. Three broad distinctions are commonly made. Denominations with "congregational" polity allow local groups a good deal of autonomy, asking only voluntary cooperation with translocal efforts. Denominations with "presbyterian" polity still allow a good deal of local participation, but it is on a federalist model. Congregations send representatives to bodies that in turn have authority over those congregations. Denominations that are "hierarchical" in polity own the property, set the policy, and control the placement of personnel. But those neat labels are misleading. Even when there is ostensibly local autonomy, there may be strong reliance on denominational advice and support. And where official authority lies with a bishop, there may be a good deal of consultation between local congregations and church officials, with most members thinking of their religious membership primarily in local, rather than denominational, terms. Stephen Warner has suggested that a remarkable variety of religious groups—from American Catholics to Muslims newly arrived—have adopted a "de facto congregationalism."[93] It will, nevertheless, be helpful to ask whether the congregation can and does make its own decisions on three key issues: personnel, programming, and property and finances.[94] Official power structures—and how their power is exercised—create real constraints within which congregations must do their work, even though official structure itself is not the only determining factor.

The exercise of power is not just external, however. Every congregation has its own way of doing its local business, of making the decisions within its power to make. In every congregation there are governing bodies of some sort, although in some they are virtually inert, with the pastor effectively functioning as the sole decision maker. In most congregations a quarterly (or at least annual) meeting offers all the members who care to come an opportunity to hear reports and vote on major issues. And in the more participatory congregations, an extensive system of committees, intentional efforts at communication, and regular congregational meetings keep a broad range of members involved in the ongoing decisions that must be made. More important than the amount of control members exercise is their perception that decisions are being made in ways they see as appropriate and legitimate.[95] Each congregation, shaped in part by its denominational heritage, has its own way of defining how decisions should be made.

The most involved and influential person in most local congregations, of course, is the pastor or priest.[96] Beyond whatever sacramental power such persons may have over the souls of their parishioners, pastors also have a variety of more earthly ways of influencing what happens in the congregation. Most basically, pastors are the ones with the day-to-day knowledge of the congregation's operations. They are paid professionals and presumably know how to get things done. Pastors have pragmatic authority and are usually respected for their expertise. In addition, even in nonhierarchical traditions, that pastors are seen as having the divine legitimation of a "call" and ordination gives their words more than ordinary weight. Being the one who gets to stand before the congregation each week declaring God's intentions is an additional source of power for pastors. They are the primary persons charged with being interpreters for the congregation, making sense of what is happening in the world in light of the sacred texts and traditions of the faith.[97] Pastors with a clear sense of vision for the congregation's future can have an extraordinary impact through their religious authority. Because members grant them a certain legitimacy of office, pastors can sometimes lead congregations to do what the members' self-interests might predict was impossible.[98]

Pastors also have relational authority. They are often at the center of the relational web of the congregation. They serve as gatekeepers, recruiting new members and introducing them to the people who will become their friends, as well as rewarding loyal members with key jobs and visible worship roles. In times of distress and celebration, the pastor is often present as comforter and interpreter. Many in the congregation feel strong bonds and personal debts to the pastor.[99] A pastor who works effectively at building personal relationships, who is seen as expert and knowledgable, and who convincingly wears the mantle of religious authority can wield considerable influence in the congregation.[100]

But no organization functions solely within the bounds of its official decision-making structure. There are always informal networks of power, as well.[101] Some people wield great influence simply because of their longevity, not because of any office they hold. Others shape the agenda of the congregation because they are so well informed and communicate so effectively with others. Still others are heard because they are seen as especially skilled and others just because they are well liked. Official committee chairs may come and go, but most congregations can point to a core of dedicated members whose involvement and history make them key players whenever the congregation faces a major decision. They are the people everyone calls for advice and consent.

They are also the people who know all the everyday strategies that make the church functional.[102] They know where the fuse box is, how to coax the copy machine into working, which plumber can be trusted to come in a hurry, where the extra keys are, and how much the pastor's Christmas bonus is supposed to be. Theirs is a power that comes by way of experience and commitment to the group, exercised without notice in the hundreds of details of everyday life.

More overt efforts at influence are present, as well. People in congregations cannot exercise the usual array of rewards and punishments available to officials in economic or political enterprises. Because congregations are voluntary organizations, no one can threaten to fire or demote or dock the pay of a fellow member. Nevertheless, there are rewards and punishments in congregational life. Occasionally there are members who influence what happens because they are so unpleasant that no one wants to upset them. Occasionally members and leaders are even censured.[103] More often, however, the inducements are positive rather than negative. Members who give exemplary service are rewarded with recognition—rounds of applause, notes in the bulletin, even certificates or ceremonies of honor. Members may not garner pay increases from exceptional efforts on behalf of the organization, but they receive rewards nevertheless.

As congregations face a context that has changed, decisions will be made about how to respond. In part those decisions will be shaped by the everyday patterns of knowledge and influence inside the congregation; people who have the power to shape a congregation's life are always reluctant to see patterns change that will alter their power. Influence born of habit is strong indeed. In part, responses may be affected by decisions made outside a congregation in denominational hierarchies with their own larger agendas. In part, alternatives will be formulated in congregational committees, debated in business meetings, and put to official votes. But in at least equal part, they will be discussed over coffee, be wondered about in weeknight phone calls, be prayed about in women's groups, and emerge through the voices of trusted leaders. If we are to understand the story of a congregation's response to change, we will have to take this cast of actors into account.

CULTURE

To recognize that a congregation's ways of deciding are shaped by habits and informal patterns of friendship is to recognize that each congregation has a culture of its own—characteristic ways of acting, speaking, socializing new members, and the like. James Hopewell begins his book *Congregation* with the observation that "a group of people cannot regularly gather for what they feel to be religious purposes without developing a complex network of signals and symbols and conventions—in short, a subculture—that gains its own logic and then functions in a way peculiar to that group."[104] These everyday patterns of action and interaction are the mortar that holds the structure of resources and authority together. The small things of everyday life give shape and identity to a particular congregation, and those small things will prove the most resistant as the congregation faces new challenges and incorporates new constituencies.

Activities

The culture of the congregation is, first, a pattern of activity. It is what the congregation does.[105] It is gatherings of all kinds, as well as involvements of a more indirect sort (the congregation's presence, represented by their pastor, at an ecumenical event, for instance). The single most common congregational activity is a weekly worship event. The when and where of this event are heavily laden with the expectations of the larger culture and of theological tradition. After centuries of Christian dominance, a Sunday morning cultural niche exists in the weekly calendar, available for the religious observances of people who so choose.[106] Even groups for whom this day has no religious significance (e.g., Muslims or Buddhists) schedule their services on Sunday. As a result, people who do not meet on Sunday morning are conscious of operating on a countercultural calendar (something Jews have known for centuries, of course).

The worship event holds an importance far beyond how it is scheduled, of course. In this event congregations engage in their most dramatic rituals, their most intentional presentation of their sense of identity. Even "low-church" congregations, who pride themselves on informality, have their own version of the drama. There is a routine order of songs and prayers and sermons, even if it is not printed in a bulletin or prayer book. People know their places and what props are needed (Bibles, hymnals, and the like). They know who will do what and whether the service will move toward an emotional or a subdued conclusion.

In all sorts of congregations, the rhythms of the worship ritual are embedded in aesthetic sensibilities as much as in the minds of the worshippers. Standing, sitting, and kneeling embody one's relationship to the deity and to one's fellow worshippers and clergy leaders. Processing, receiving communion, being baptized (especially as an adult, or by immersion), and passing the peace encode religious truths in bodily experience.[107] Likewise, ritual music is first of all a sensual experience. In his stinging critique of current Catholic musical practices, Thomas Day notes that "congregational singing always begins as a sensuous experience, not an intellectual one; it flourishes wherever the congregation can feel the sensuous pleasure of musical vibrations."[108] Singing and chanting call for the worshipper to enact the faith she or he is recounting in song. Linda Clark writes that when "a community sings 'Were You There When They Crucified My Lord?' it journeys back to that hillside so vividly captured in the Christian imagination and relives the faith that image has carried throughout the ages."[109]

In a powerful sense, worship is an event that is meant to express the unifying vision of the congregation. All rituals help to create the community that enacts them. Even in highly rational modern societies, ritual forms of communication can create meaning-spaces that give shape to individual and group life.[110] However, rituals also create and celebrate differences. The very symbols they use set out the boundaries and the identifying categories for this gathering of worshippers, and their ritual practices highlight the internal differences that belie the picture of ritual unity.[111] Within the congregation differences in status and in levels of participation are apparent in the worship event (as well as elsewhere). Some congregational leaders are permitted access to sacred spaces and expected to utter sacred formulae that are forbidden to ordinary members.[112] Singers, readers, and announcement makers are likely to be otherwise influential members of the congregation. And throughout, divisions by gender are likely. Whether by habit or by fiat, men and women are likely to participate differently in worship (as in other congregational activities). As the congregation gathers for worship, differences abound, some of them generative of conflict.[113] One is even likely to be able to observe that some members are proficient, while others are inept, some enthusiastic, while others seem barely to mumble along.[114]

And in all of this, congregations are sending signals about who they are and what is important to them. The language they use and the kind of music they sing tell a story about the cultural, educational, and social-class backgrounds of the members no less than about the theology they espouse. Ethnicity and social class remain among the most visible categories in U.S. society, and they are no less so in the nation's worshipping communities.[115] People simply do not expect a congregation to be ethnically or economically diverse, and the practice of choosing a congregation (rather than being assigned to one) increases that homogeneity. Congregations that wish to be diverse have to be intentional in their openness, recognizing that usual patterns of action will likely lead to sameness.[116] In hundreds of tiny signals ingrained in everyday practices, congregations are shaped by the divisions of the larger cultural world in which those practices are also embedded. People who visit a new congregation readily sense whether "people like them" are present in this ritual event.[117]

They will also sense whether the symbols and events out of which this congregation constructs its worship evoke for them any sense of transcendence, of a presence connecting them to something beyond themselves—whether this is a place where they can meet God. We expect the time and space of the congregation's activities to be set apart from the ordinary.[118] A congregation's culture includes its habits of invoking God's presence—the degree to which it expects encounters with transcendence to happen regularly, through individual efforts or simply through the routine ritual actions sanctioned by the institution.[119] Whether it is a lay-led prayer asking for God's blessing or an especially reverent consecration of the elements of the Mass, worship services are intended as times when human presence meets divine, and that encounter can occasionally be transformative.[120] As Clifford Geertz has noted, religious symbols and rituals are both models *of* our social world (reflecting its values and categories) and models *for* that world, providing leverage and critique.[121]

While worship events are the most symbol laden of the congregation's activities, they are by no means the whole of the story. In most congregations, additional activities bring together all or part of the group. Most have religious education activities, for most Christian groups a Sunday school (Sabbath school for Seventh-Day groups) held before, during, or after worship. Classes, usually divided by age, offer children basic biblical knowledge and Christian principles. In congregations that also have adult classes, these are often support groups as well as forums for study and discussion.[122] In some congregations the educational opportunities go considerably beyond Sunday school to lecture series, missions education groups, special men's, women's, and children's groups, and weeknight Bible-study groups.

In addition to education, congregations also engage in activities explicitly designed to strengthen the bonds of members, what many congregations call "fellowship." Both in shared tasks, where a sense of kinship is the by-product, and in small groups intentionally formed for fellowship, the congregation's members forge bonds of mutual identification and obligation. The tighter the internal webs of affiliation, the more tangible the effects of the congregation on individual ideas and activities in the external secular world.[123] There are church suppers and holiday parties, outings and sports events, and especially coffee hours. Congregations are social collectivities no less than—indeed perhaps more than—places where ideological work is done.[124] They are gatherings of people who form a network of primary (face-to-face, familylike) relationships. Maintaining those bonds is a central "good" in the moral universe of congregational life.[125] The level of affective bonding is obviously correlated with the degree of cultural distinctiveness fostered by the congregation, but affective bonding of some sort is always present.

In addition to formal and informal building up of the congregation's collective bonds, there are also specifically task-oriented activities. There are meetings of committees and task forces, deacons or elders or church council, that plan the work of the church. Each of these bodies, with its own habits and routines, its own assumptions about *how* work is done, is as much a part of the congregation's authority structure as are the official patterns we have already noted. In addition to these decision-making bodies, there are activities aimed at serving people outside the church. Members come together to staff food pantries, visit people who need to be "saved," build a Habitat house, or go on an overseas mission trip.

Culture is, then, in part, patterns of activity through which the congregation communicates to itself and others what it is about. However, because congregations are voluntary organizations, the congregational culture is something members must choose to join and choose to support. No congregation has a guaranteed pool of members. More than at any time in U.S. history, the most recent generation has seen a vast increase in the degree to which religious affiliation has become a matter of individual choice (including the choice not to affiliate), a matter indeed of change across a lifetime.[126] The building of a congregation's culture begins, then, with the process of recruiting members. In this process a congregation declares its own perceived identity and is, in turn, changed (even if gradually) by those who choose to join.

Recruiting members is not, however, something many congregations do with any real intentionality. They rely on natural growth (births) and on their recognized position in the community to bring them a steady supply of new members. This assumes, of course, that the new people coming into the community recognize the image being projected and that it fits with their experiences of religious life and their perceptions of their own social identity. To the extent that the population in a given community changes, the natural pathways leading people into visible congregations in that community will change, as well.[127]

Just as visibility and position may not guarantee a continued supply of recruits, even births into the congregation cannot guarantee the long-term presence of those children. Both they and their families are likely to be gone before they reach adulthood. While a high fertility rate may increase the size of the nursery, it does not assure a thriving youth group. The service congregations render in providing religious education is one rendered to the religious community at large, rather than to any particular local unit. Most congregations think of "young families" as a sign of their vitality, and that is so—not because those families represent a guarantee for future survival, but because the impulse to provide one's children with religious education is one of the primary incentives for adult religious participation.[128] The congregation that establishes itself as an attractive provider of services to children can be assured that a segment of the community's population will be attracted to its door.

Passive recruitment, then, can bring members into congregations that are visible enough to be noticed and consonant enough with the values of a given population to be perceived as meeting its needs. But, as we have noted, changes in the population are likely to disrupt those passive patterns of recruiting. Populations with different cultural expectations about whether and what sort of religious participation is expected or populations without given incentives (such as children) for participation may mean that existing congregations can no longer depend on passive means of recruitment. If they are to survive (given the mortality of existing members), they are faced with the need for intentional recruiting.

Some congregations, of course, recruit members routinely, not merely for survival reasons, but for theological ones. Evangelicals believe that spreading the gospel is integral to their mandate. Members talk to their neighbors, co-workers, and friends about making a religious commitment and joining the church. Whether evangelical or not, such personal contacts are the most frequent bridge to congregational affiliation.[129]

Congregations can also engage in various sorts of public relations campaigns aimed at making themselves better known in the community. Many congregations put advertisements on a local newspaper's church page or in the *Yellow Pages*. They may try to convey in a few words or images the theological and programmatic emphases that make them distinctive. A quite different extension of the congregation's presence into the community comes from its efforts at ministry or service. Some congregations may offer food and shelter, while others offer space for public recitals. Some may be the place the town or neighborhood comes together in times of crisis, while others offer individualized psychological counseling or family crisis assistance.

Whatever the first contact, potential recruits must still be turned into practicing members of the congregation's culture. Congregations with especially distinctive cultures may have to work hard at training their new recruits.[130] But no matter how apparently minimal the need for congregational socialization, membership involves learning the appropriate behaviors and forming the relationships necessary to function within a congregation's culture.

Artifacts

Visit a new congregation these days, and you are likely to leave with artifacts—brochures about the congregation, printed orders of service, maybe even a visitor's badge. The congregation's culture is not just the activities in which it engages, but also the props for and residues of those activities. The congregation's culture involves both a structuring of time and a structuring (and filling) of space.

The building itself is both a material resource and a cultural artifact, communicating a great deal about the congregation's patterns of activity and value. Landscaping and parking, steeples and stained-glass windows, signs and banners—all establish the place of this congregation in this community, but they also reflect its assumptions about God, nature, humanity, itself, and others. Buildings, furniture, and grounds are visible, sensual clues to observers about the group that uses them.[131] The difference between a high fence and a wide driveway is not lost on a congregation's neighbors. The difference between a decaying children's wing and a high-tech nursery is not lost on potential new members. And the hallways and furnishings of the building itself shape the patterns of interaction contained in it. The size and condition of gathering spaces and their accessibility to people with various handicapping conditions determine what sorts of social interaction is possible, among what sorts of people.

Some of the congregation's space is marked off as "sacred space."[132] There are the obvious symbols contained in altars and banners, crosses and stained-glass windows, pulpits and organs. Those items tell stories about the faith tradition of the congregation. They honor the heroes and saints. Worship services use those spaces and call forth an extensive array of the congregation's cultural artifacts. They come complete with all the props, costumes, and scripts of a major theatrical production. People often wear "Sunday" (or Sabbath) clothes, and worship leaders may be garbed in elaborate symbolic attire.[133] There is special furniture, as well, whether fancy altar tables, containers for sacred objects, and elaborate chairs for worship leaders (visual signals that this is a special place and time) or simple folding chairs that signal the presence of God in ordinary things.

Like all cultures, congregations invent material objects that aid them in performing their routine tasks and express the values they hold most dear. Whether it is the set of accounting books and office equipment, the dozens of baby cribs in the nursery, or the extensive athletic equipment in the gym, physical objects tell us a good deal about the culture that uses them. The arrangement of buildings, furniture, landscaping, and ritual objects is critical to understanding the group's identity and its relationship to its community.

Language and Story

Cultures are both patterns of activity and patterns of objects, but they are also patterns of speech—what people do together and what they say. Because language is a basic orderer of reality, we can expect any group that spends time together to develop ways of talking about the experiences its members share.[134] They will develop distinctive words and phrases for the objects in their environment and for the events of their calendar. They will develop shorthand ways of alluding to ideas, people, and significant happenings in their history. Learning the group's jargon is part of becoming a member.[135] One learns that it is the "narthex" and not the "vestibule," a "carry in" not a "potluck." One will even learn to speak (and think) of oneself differently—as a communicant or a believer, for instance.

Since congregations are religious organizations, at least part of their unique language relates to sacred objects, actions, time, and space. Each religious tradition's language gives voice to the particular ways that tradition seeks to connect people with God. Rich and abundant language is available from both the professional theologians and the everyday practitioners. The mix of folk theological language with tech-

60

nical terms—as well as the degree to which theological language is present at all—is part of each congregation's unique culture.[136] Likewise, in some congregations, language and styles of speaking open up multiple possibilities for interpreting the relationship between God and humanity, while in other congregations, styles of speaking establish a given meaning as authoritative.[137] But the symbols and metaphors of even the most conservative congregations are often multivalent. Religious language can evoke in its hearers multiple images and interpretations.[138]

In addition to the words that name and order the congregation's time and space, there are stories that transmit the lore of the group.[139] These tales may be of its founding, but they are also likely to be about times of great success or about crises overcome, stories passed on from old members to new as a way of telling what this congregation is all about. Which stories get told at which time depends in large part on both the needs of the hour and the memories of those present. Sometimes the congregation's identity is captured not in a story so much as in an image or metaphor—an ark or a good citizen, for instance.[140] There are also, of course, in every congregation stories that go beyond the particular history of that one place—stories from a denomination, from the larger faith tradition, and from the Scripture. Jews and Christians alike hear the great sagas of Abraham and Sarah, Isaac and Rebecca, Jacob and Rachel, Moses, Joshua, King David, and the prophets. From Sunday school teachers and from the pulpit, these stories are told with enough frequency to make them familiar and with enough fanfare to reinforce their importance.[141] While questions asked in the official theologian's parlance may be interesting to contemplate, they may tell us little about how this congregation understands God's actions in the world. The theology of a congregation is best understood as its own telling of sacred stories.[142]

Because these sacred stories are so widely shared, they are also widely interpreted. Each group is likely to find in the stories elements that make sense of its own situation. As different groups come together and as life situations change, new meanings are likely to arise from the text. In turn, texts can infuse current situations with new meaning.[143] Congregations engaged in a process of change will find themselves listening to new stories and teaching new people old tales. But they will also find themselves listening to old stories with new ears.

This book tells the stories of twenty-three congregations, all within the Christian tradition, all situated in communities where various forms of social change are a fact of life. Each story is unique and complicated. It will quickly be apparent that the plots could easily have been written differently, that they may, indeed, eventually have a very different ending than now appears likely. Indeed, in the four years between our field research and the printing of this book, much has happened. We cannot tell stories with definitive endings here—no "happily ever afters." We must be content to understand the history and prospects of our congregations as they appeared in 1992 and 1993, with all the ambiguity that goes with tracing social patterns that can easily (or not so easily) be redrawn by the subjects of our artistry.

CHAPTER 2

Persistence in the Face of Change

As environments change, altering the supply of constituents, it would seem a simple matter for a congregation to assess the changes, decide on a course of action, and implement new programs and strategies in response. That rarely happens. Human organizations of all kinds are not as rational as they are sometimes assumed to be. At every stage of the process, the weight of habit and tradition maintain familiar patterns. Those familiar patterns often blind congregations to the change in the first place. Once they recognize change, their ability to imagine the future is blunted by the weight of the past. And even valiant, imaginative efforts to change are made more difficult by expectations and assumptions long in place. The most common response to change, in fact, is to proceed with business as usual.

Theorists who look at the "population ecology" of organizations note strong pressures toward structural inertia in all organizations.[1] Internally, change is inhibited by investment in plant, personnel, and equipment. We are reluctant to venture into territory that would make existing assets and skills obsolete. There are also constraints on available information. We simply do not ask the right questions. Internal politics (who loses in an adaptation) can also retard attempts at change, as can normative agreements about what we do and how. The organization's sense of identity and history often keeps it firmly within familiar patterns of activity.

Pressures toward inertia come from the larger culture as well. Legal and fiscal barriers may limit what an organization can do. And even where there are no official barriers, cultural norms defining the legitimate range of activity constrain the imaginations of organizational leaders. To attempt some kinds of adaptation would require reinterpreting the organization to its community and constituents, as well as reestablishing the networks of contact and supply that sustain it. For all these reasons, the most common response to change is inertia.

Carl Dudley's study of "transitional" churches confirms the prevalence of the urge toward continuity.[2] He notes that congregations often feel a strong sense of identity with the neighborhood, having experienced their greatest vitality when the neighborhood itself was growing. Their dreams and their memories are strongly tied to a particular place. Continuity is also premised on the congregation's sense of its history and mission in a given place. What they have accomplished would feel less significant if they were to leave it behind. They hope that they can somehow weather the changes around them unscathed.

Although we do not have enough information on all the congregations in each of these communities to be certain how many fit each pattern of response, it is safe to say that inertia is the most common pattern found in congregations—in changing communities or otherwise. We were able to gather data about the history and programming of just over 300 of the congregations in these nine communities. In about 175, we were able to sketch a rough estimation of what the recent trajectory of the congregation had been. Of those, nearly two-thirds (62 percent) reported no significant change in their congregation's programming. Over one-third (36 percent) reported no change in membership size, with an additional one-third reporting slight fluctuations either up (23 percent) or down (13 percent). For these congregations, things seem to be going along about as usual. They are doing what they have always done, and their membership is holding steady.

Many congregations are already relatively disconnected from the communities in which they are located. Again, nearly two-thirds (64 percent) reported little involvement in community programs or concerns, few if any programs that bring them into contact with people other than their own members. That distance may account for the fact that half (51 percent) reported that they perceive little or no change in the community. They are proceeding on an unaltered course in part because they do not see any need for change. And in part they do not see the changes because they are relatively isolated. So long as their own members continue to come, and so long as neither the congregation nor its members are in significant contact with the new realities of the neighborhood in which they are located, they have little reason to change their patterns of action.

Among the twenty-three churches we chose for study, ten were relatively unchanged in program and constituents and likely to remain so. They were not, however, all alike. They have different resources, face different challenges, and are in very different states of health. Three are in a community where an economic downturn has caused serious dislocations, and one is in an economically distressed African American community. Four are in communities experiencing a large influx of Asian and Hispanic immigrants, and two are in a community that has evolved from small town to suburb. But all ten share a basic continuity in membership and programming and a perception that change in their core identity is unnecessary, impossible, or both. Five of these congregations have chosen to maintain their current identities either by moving to a new location or by establishing a recognizable identity (a niche) that can draw constituents from throughout their region. We will look more closely at these five in the next chapter.

Here we will turn our attention to the five congregations holding onto existing patterns and staying in their current locations. All have experienced significant membership decline. Four—St. Catherine's and Brighton Avenue Baptist in Allston, Carmel Wesleyan and Gray Friends in Carmel—are struggling, clearly in decline, and unsure whether they will survive this latest challenge to their well-being. One—Berean Seventh-Day Adventist in Los Angeles—is attempting to alter its course of action, with uncertain success. All five are hanging on. Many in these congregations feel as if their community has left them. Such is certainly the case for the two Allston-Brighton churches. Their community is simply not the place it was in the 1940s and 1950s, when these churches were in their heyday. The Irish and Italian residents of those days are aging and gone, while Hispanic and Asian immigrants—and college students—have taken their place.

St. Catherine's Catholic Parish, Allston: Never Too Old?

At St. Catherine's in Allston, Massachusetts, the effects of change were visible both in the ten o'clock Masses I attended in the parish's lovely old sanctuary and in the raucous Sunday evening Salvadoran festival held in the school gymnasium next door.[3] At Sunday morning Mass, a scattering of people could not begin to fill the space, while on Sunday evening, the gym was packed to overflowing. On Sunday morning, the English words of the priests were often swallowed by a poor sound system. On Sunday evening, music and Spanish boomed from the loudspeakers. In between, the Salvadorans from all over the city who worship at St. Catherine's after the English speakers are gone carried their religious images through the streets of the neighborhood in a procession reminiscent of festivals for other saints in days gone by. The Irish and Italian members of the parish do not have processions anymore. What was once their thriving parish now struggles to survive. Gini Laffey of our research team tells the story.

St. Catherine's Parish was established in the late nineteenth century, as a mission of St. Columbkille's Church in Brighton, to make church more accessible to a growing number of Irish and Italian Catholic families living in their part of town. The church building, an attractive stone structure built in romanesque style, was completed in 1895 and named for St. Catherine. The walls are constructed of local Brighton stone and trimmed with buff-colored sandstone. Official church history describes the original parishioners as "coachmen, gardeners, maids and governesses," poor people who "gave largely of their slender earnings" and whose "performance of religious duties was often accomplished in defiance of intolerant employers."

The parish grew steadily over the next forty years. By 1907 the St. Vincent de Paul Society was founded to help the less fortunate of the parish. The Minstrel Show, a fund-raising extravaganza, was also started early in the century and has run annually to this day. By 1930 a rectory, an elementary school, and a convent had been built on adjacent land.

St. Catherine's was a focal point in the community well into the 1960s, a place of worship, the center of social activity, and a source of identity for area Catholics. A drill team and color guard were formed in 1949 and won national championships several times in the twenty-two years they competed. A drum and bugle corps, formed in 1959, played at the 1965 New York World's Fair. The church sponsored Boy Scout and Girl Scout Troops, as well as Cub Scouts and Brownies, with more than two hundred children participating by the midfifties. Thirty-one altar boys were available to serve Mass. During its heyday the church sponsored dances, festivals, and children's parties.

By the midseventies the number of children participating in Scout troops dropped to one hundred, the drill team and color guard had disbanded, and the altar boys numbered twenty-two. During the sixties and seventies school enrollment also fell, causing a cutback in the teaching staff. The Massachusetts Turnpike, built in 1965, cut across the northern section of Allston, making the church less accessible for part of the parish. By 1982 the convent had been closed and renovated into an eighty-unit subsidized housing project for the elderly. As the membership aged, a new, younger, generation did not take its place.

Since Catholic immigrants often prefer to worship in their native language, the Archdiocese of Boston has established foreign-language Masses at various points across the city, which draw these potential new members away from established English-language parishes. St. Catherine's has become the site for Boston's Salvadoran ministries. But the Catholic Salvadorans who worship at St. Catherine's on Sunday evenings are not connected in any way to the Anglo membership of the church, and most do not live nearby.

A typical Sunday morning Mass will find 125–150 people in attendance. The parking lot is seldom full, as many churchgoers live near enough to walk. A handful might come early to light a candle and sit in silent prayer, but most arrive five minutes before the service begins, or later. Some also leave directly after communion, before the Mass has ended. Consequently, seating is often heavily concentrated in the back and sides of the church. Because of low attendance worshippers can sit one or two to a pew and often do.

In the church's beautifully decorated interior, high vaulted ceilings are supported by four clustered and two single columns. The ceilings are painted light blue and deep pink with the details of the plaster molding and ceiling high-

lighted in gold. The stations of the cross, depicted in plaster bas-relief, line the side and rear walls at regular intervals. These scenes are also painted in light pastel colors with gold highlights. On sunny days the stained-glass windows along the walls and behind the sanctuary admit a good deal of light, adding to the bright and airy atmosphere. A rosette window of stained glass dominates the rear wall, and a large organ with gold pipes is visible behind and above the choir loft in the rear balcony. Behind the polished marble altar is a fifteen-foot marble screen inset with five panels of ornate gold grillwork. A large gold crucifix hangs on the center panel.

The congregation is predominantly white, although a few Asians and Afro-Hispanic or Haitian women and their children might also attend. More than half the congregation is over fifty years of age, and among that group two-thirds are female. Few young families or teens attend any Mass.

St. Catherine's follows a standard Catholic liturgy. Most congregants genuflect before entering a pew and kneel in prayer before sitting down to wait for the Mass to begin. The choir is made up of six to eight men and women, most of whom are over sixty. The music is often slow, and congregational participation is sparse. The choir and organ often compete with the coughing, whispering, and fidgeting of the congregation. Although singing is often lackluster, many congregants recite the Apostles' Creed with energy and enthusiasm. And the eucharistic prayer is the one time during the Mass when all parishioners are equally focused. During the consecration of the elements the congregation is still, quiet, and attentive. Virtually the entire congregation on any given Sunday will receive the Host; the wine is never offered to parishioners here. Most receive the Host in their hands, return to their seats, and kneel in prayer until communion is over. After communion the congregation becomes visibly restless, gathering their things as they prepare to leave. After Mass has ended most parishioners leave quickly, saying hello to friends and neighbors as they walk out the door. A few remain behind to light a candle and pray at one of the two shrines where a contribution of one dollar "lights" an electric prayer candle.

Members recognize the decline in the parish's membership but do not actively seek new members. Newcomers are not identified or welcomed in any routine way. In fact, there is no directory posted in front of the church, and potential worshippers must call at the rectory to learn the schedule of Masses.

The decline in membership has created a corresponding decline in resources. In recent years the church property needed several major repairs, which forced the parish to accept an archdiocesan loan to cover the expenses. Some members fear that this draws unwanted diocesan attention to their economic plight. A core of active members works hard at fund-raising efforts to cover the expenses of the church and school. However, in 1991, the pastor was forced to dismiss the two remaining nuns on staff due to budget constraints, to many members a tangible sign of the financial distress of the church.

The current pastor's main focus has been to revitalize the school. Many of the younger members who are active in the church work to support the school. A weekly Bingo game held in the school auditorium has helped to keep tuition relatively affordable. In recent years school enrollment has increased in the lower grades. K1 and K2 classes had waiting lists for the 1992-1993 school year. Many of the new students are the children of newly arrived immigrants who are not members of the church. While children are required to attend daily religion classes, many are not from Catholic families.

Within the parish, one of the most lively and committed groups is probably the Never Too Old Club, a group of thirty or so older women who have for years gathered on Tuesday mornings. They eat, trade stories, make crafts to sell at the Christmas bazaar, and occasionally go on outings together. Some of these women also attend Mass several times a week and take communion to others who are too infirm to come to the church. For these women, the care of the parish and its school is still an important concern. They also care for each other. One of the parish's nuns, and later the associate pastor, used to serve as a minister to this group. Now both those pastoral figures are gone, and the group meets only sporadically.

RESOURCES

Membership and participation at St. Catherine's have been declining for a generation. The Irish and Italian families that populated Allston from the late nineteenth century until the 1960s have slowly been replaced, first simply by renters, often transient students. They filled the gaps left by the generation that came of age in the 1970s and beyond, who chose not to stay in the old neighborhood but to move to the suburbs, to Florida, to wherever they could find work and space to raise their families. Many in this generation were first torn loose from the neighborhood by busing, transported across town and away from the schools that—along with the church—provided the community's identity.[4] Now they return to St. Catherine's only on rare special occasions. What they find in their old parish are mostly their aging parents. By the time the current wave of immigrants began to move into Allston, St. Catherine's had already lost much of its membership base.

As attendance dwindled, so did the programs, services, and eventually the staff of the parish. The convent was closed, and the school nearly died. The current pastor, who arrived in 1988, has worked hard to restore the school to health. But his energy can go only so far. Nearing retirement, he seems unable to engage the other needs of this struggling parish. The three part-time assistants who were there in 1992 were all gone by the end of 1993. Without enough money for new staff, the parish goes largely without leadership.

A small core of members struggles to provide the money necessary to run the parish and its school. Tuition provides part of the school's support, but the rest comes from the usual array of parish fund-raising events—the regular Thursday bingo game, the annual Christmas bazaar, and the famous Minstrel Show. Still, the school requires monetary and staff support from the parish that leaves few resources for the support of the parish itself. This is not a wealthy group. Almost no one (9 percent) who responded to our survey makes over $35,000, and many are elderly people on fixed incomes (see table 2.1).

With such a meager financial base, St. Catherine's building is perhaps both its greatest asset and its greatest liability. The interior, recently refurbished, is large and beautiful, a striking example of a pre–Vatican–II church. Shrines, candles, and stations of the cross encourage personal devotion. The sight of the priest celebrating the Mass in a sanctuary filled with marble and gold trim under a high-arched ceiling inspires awe. But in this church worshippers can barely *hear* the priest. Acoustics are not good, and the sound system works only sporadically. The huge organ that could provide thrilling solo performances is less well suited to accompanying a congregation in singing. And that congregation, scattered sparsely throughout the room, perhaps never quite senses what it must have been like to recite the Apostles' Creed or the Our Father with hundreds of other worshippers.

In addition, a hundred-year-old building poses serious maintenance and repair problems. Ancient wiring and heating systems, roofs that leak, furniture that is wearing out—all mean drains on the parish's limited resources. Heating the building is extraordinarily expensive, so the furnace is often not turned on until almost service time. The interior and exterior are kept clean, but there is no extra money for landscaping. In short, the people of the parish manage to keep their building looking very fine but have no financial cushion for preventive maintenance or crises.

When they have had to deal with disaster, they have fallen back on the resources of the diocese. The diocese, however, with a budget crisis of its own, is imposing austerity measures throughout the region. As its resources have gone down, demands for services have gone up, and it can no longer be counted on to have deep pockets. Indeed, asking the diocese for help is sometimes felt to be risky; needy parishes may be seen as the most easily expendable in the diocese's efforts to balance its books.

The other institutions that have traditionally formed St. Catherine's resource web are suffering similar strains, caused by the erosion of a constituent base. Each Sunday the back of St. Catherine's bulletin is advertising space, sold to support its publication. Businesses like the Shamrock Restaurant and the Blarney Pub, Anthony D'Angelo Insurance and Viteli's Exxon, buy small ads, and the parish urges its members to support these merchants. However, up to one-third of the space is sometimes empty. The businesses, clubs, and charitable institutions that once held together a "white ethnic" community (and could

Table 2.1. St. Catherine's Catholic Parish, Allston-Brighton

Ideas and priorities

Christian practices rated "essential"	Attendance at services
	Receiving the sacraments
Ministries rated "very important" or "essential"	Service to the needy

Resources

Average Saturday/Sunday attendance	300 (three masses)
Annual operating budget (1989–1990)	$232,983 (deficit $58,570)
Household incomes above $50,000	4%
College degrees or more	11%
Average age	65 years
Activities (beyond worship) participated in at least monthly	None

Relationship to the community

Live ten minutes or less from the church	91%
New to the community in the last five years	0
Ethnicity	98% European
Participate in civic & community activities more than once a month	16%

NOTE: Only 45 people completed our survey, amounting to only about 15% of average Saturday/Sunday attendance. This may be taken as only a tentative representation of all regular attenders.

be counted on to support church fund-raising efforts) are disappearing along with the white ethnics they served.

STRUCTURES OF AUTHORITY

St. Catherine's, of course, exists within the authority structure of the Roman Catholic Church. Decisions at any level are always subject to veto from above, just as needs at any level can be addressed by resources from throughout the Church. In practice, St. Catherine's Parish is dependent on the diocese for its staff and has little, if any, say in who is assigned to it. Within this parish, the pastor controls budget and programming decisions; there is effectively no parish council (common in many Catholic parishes) or other body to advise him. When people raise money and turn it over to the parish, it may be spent for any purpose the priest deems appropriate. And if the priest decides that the parish can no longer afford the nuns that have shepherded much of its ministry, it is the priest's decision alone to let them go. No mechanisms exist for the lay people in the parish (or religious workers in subordinate positions) to voice their needs or desires. The priest is in charge, and he answers to the diocese.

There are also few mechanisms for communicating with the parish's members. The Sunday bulletin contains various announcements, but there is no newsletter and no regular announcement time during the service. The woman who serves as secretary and bookkeeper for both the parish and the school is often a key link in the information flow. She is the single person who knows most about what is happening in the life of the parish.

CULTURE

For the traditional Catholics who populate St. Catherine's Parish, the Mass is the religious reality that defines both theology and practice. God is primarily known through the Mass; the gracious forgiveness, sacrifice, and divine presence of which the Mass speaks are the religious ideas most commonly voiced by St. Catherine's parishioners. When the bread and wine are consecrated and the bell is rung, the silence in the church bespeaks the awe most members feel at this moment.

Their awe is combined with a strong sense of mystery. They do not understand the finer points of doctrine, but they know what they experience in church. Most older members have never studied the Bible and depend on the priest to explain its lessons. God's word and God's ways are, for them, unfathomable mysteries to be accepted on faith. But to say that these are matters of mystery and faith is not to say that they are remote and irrelevant. It is to say that faith comes, for them, in the doing. The prayers of the Mass, the motions and gestures of it, the recitation of the Apostles' Creed or of the catechism they learned as children—these practices are deep in their bones, even if they cannot provide reasoned explanations for what they mean.

Beyond the mystery, of course, stands the community represented by the parish. In the old days, family, parish school, church, neighborhood, even businesses—all combined to create a pervasive milieu. People in the parish were surrounded by parish-related institutions and largely isolated from the larger, non-Catholic culture. That is no longer the situation for most American Catholics.[5] And St. Catherine's—along with the surrounding community—no longer has the institutional wherewithal to make it possible.

A remnant of that encompassing community can be seen in the Never Too Old (NTO) group, women who have shared a lifetime of involvement with the neighborhood, church, and school. One faithful member talked about the group to Gini and me. "We have a nice meeting. We're friends. And it also goes beyond the church. Like say you could come in new, and then in no time you'd be part of us. We'd offer you something to eat, and we talk about things that are going on around. It's very social for the women, and a lot of them don't do very much in this time of their life, and they need something. And they make crafts for our bazaar in December, and they work together on those things. We laugh a lot. And we do talk, don't we, Gini?" They do talk—about family and illness and travels. They ask each other's help with big problems and small. They put their skills to use in craftwork, caring for a larger circle of people in the parish, even as they care for each other.

There have been attempts to begin other small groups in the parish. A folk Mass lasted for awhile, but those who planned it did not get support from parish leadership to include fellowship or study times for those who came. Consequently the sense of community they tried to build during worship could not be sustained. A young priest tried to get a Bible study group started, but that did not work either. Even the NTO group has struggled with a lack of support from parish leadership, with each of their staff support persons successively let go.

The one place where internal cohesion, a sense of community, still holds the parish together is the round of fund-raising activities that support the school.[6] The people who run and attend the Thursday night Bingo game, and the Christmas bazaar, and all the other activities spend large amounts of time and energy (and money) working with each other in the service of the parish. The Minstrel Show (an annual vaudeville-style entertainment) draws together not only many parish youth and adults, but also many people from the community who are not otherwise part of the church. More than any other event, this extravaganza stakes St. Catherine's claim to a place in the community.

But the community in which the church is staking a claim is somewhat elusive. The new residents of Allston—students, Asians, Hispanics, people from the Caribbean—are not a part of St. Catherine's. And the people who are a part of St. Catherine's are a shrinking portion of Allston's population. The major point of contact between St. Catherine's and the new immigrants is the Salvadoran pastoral ministries office placed there by the diocese. The first Salvadoran Mass, held on a Sunday evening in November 1991, drew twenty-eight people. Within six months, however, the masses were averaging close to one-hundred each week. As the Salvadoran group has grown, it has added festivals and neighborhood processions to its activities. But not nearly all the participants are in fact from the neighborhood. As the single designated Salvadoran parish, the group draws from all over the metropolitan region. While this ministry gives St. Catherine's some point of contact with its immigrant neighbors, that contact is minimal.

The old neighborhood and the new intersect only rarely, then, perhaps most often in the schoolyard at St. Catherine's. About one-third of the students come from backgrounds other than European, thus reflecting the changes in the neighborhood. Some of their parents help with fund-raising activities, but neither children nor parents have been drawn into the life of the parish itself. They linger around the edges, never quite finding the activities of the parish inviting.

SUMMARY

St. Catherine's is doing what it knows to do. People gather on Saturday night and Sunday morning to celebrate a ritual that they value. Many of them work hard to keep open a parish school that serves—as it always has—the children of the neighborhood. But those children and their families are increasingly from a constituency not served by the church. *Neighborhood* and *parish* are no longer synonymous. Still, the strength of the school and the commitment of church members to it are perhaps the greatest institutional assets of the parish.

The church entered this period of change in a position of weakness. It had already suffered declining membership, which had meant declining finances and fewer programs. While its beautiful building remains a precious asset, it also drains parish resources and does not serve parishioners' needs well. The activities that remain suit the older members, who remember the days when the parish was the center of the community. Socializing, caring for each other, and raising money for the school are the activities that have historically held this parish together; and they still do.

The parish has experienced no strong leadership. Members do not come here with a ready set of leadership skills gained through education or occupational experience, and the parish offers few opportunities for developing those skills. Potential lay leaders have no forum in which to try out ideas or strategies and no one to lead them in doing so. Everyone feels at the mercy of an authority structure they find as mysterious as the theological world. No one knows what the diocese has in store for them. And members rarely know about or understand the administrative decisions made by the priest. Their greatest institutional liabilities are the absence of mechanisms for internal community building and decision making.

While those are not the primary liabilities of St. Catherine's neighboring congregation, Brighton Avenue Baptist, the two share a nostalgia for better days and bewilderment at the realities created by a needy immigrant population.

Brighton Avenue Baptist Church, Allston:
A Remnant of the Past

At the beginning of this chapter we noted that many congregations have few ties to their immediate neighborhood. Without such ties, these congregations may miss the early stages of change, only to discover too late that the demographic and institutional ecology has been altered beyond repair. What they may find eventually is that the well-worn paths that used to bring a supply of members to their doors have become isolated and overgrown. To varying degrees, that has been the case in all of these declining congregations. Each is struggling against an erosion of its natural demographic constituency that has been going on for at least a generation.

In each community we studied, some congregations had suffered sufficiently at the hands of demographic erosion to be in questionable states of viability. By the time the current changes were underway, they were already so depleted in human and material resources that their primary objective was to survive from one month to the next. About 15 percent of the congregations we surveyed reported that their membership was primarily elderly, that they had few, if any, younger adults or children, and that their attendance was less than a hundred (usually less than fifty) and shrinking. Many of these congregations are able to sustain no programming beyond Sunday services. Brighton Avenue Baptist in Allston, Massachusetts, is one of these, and Mary Beth Sievens and Virginia Laffey carried out our ministudy of the church.

The Brighton Avenue Baptist Church was founded in 1853. Until the past quarter century, the church was well attended and supported by many of the white middle-class residents of Allston-Brighton. The church filled both spiritual and social needs for those who came; spouses and lifetime friends were often met there. In the immediate post–World War II era church membership was at its highest, with more than five hundred on the rolls. The church was then free of debt and could comfortably fund missions when it chose to. However, a large portion of the budget was dedicated to maintaining the church property. Pride in their lovely brick building continues to be strong among today's surviving members.

In the 1950s the long decline in membership began, as newly married couples chose to move to the suburbs, and few returned to Brighton Avenue Baptist for church. By the 1960s and 1970s, that process was accelerated by "white flight," further eroding the traditional membership base of the church. From that time to the present, Allston-Brighton has become home to increasingly diverse racial and ethnic populations, while Brighton Avenue Baptist has remained white and middle class.

In the early 1960s a young pastor committed to civil rights filled the BABC pulpit for a short time. The congregation felt uncomfortable with his "radical" views on racial issues and asked him to step down, which he did. As member-ship continued to decline, congregants attempted to redress the problem by calling a pastor they felt would attract new members. They chose a young evangelical minister and charged him with filling the Sunday school and the pews. Unfortunately, they did not support him in his initiatives to increase membership (such as participation in a local Billy Graham Crusade). Frus-trated at the lack of support, he chose to leave.

In 1984 the current pastor, the Reverend Charlotte Davis, began her tenure at the BABC. She has worked steadily at focusing her aging congregation on the seriousness of its situation. Average attendance at a Sunday service is between twelve and fifteen.[7] Members are overwhelmingly elderly. While the church remains debt free, the dwindling congregation does not have the resources to maintain and repair their physical facility.

The church building itself is much larger than it seems from outside. The sanctuary contains small, hand-painted, glazed windows, decorated with bibli-cal figures and other traditional Christian symbols. The names of past members in whose memory the windows were donated are prominently featured. The wooden pews and floors are well worn. Divided by a center aisle, the pews form a semicircle facing the platform. On the platform, the pulpit and lectern are kept draped in the appropriate liturgical colors. A communion table and chairs for the pastor and Scripture reader are also present on the platform, with a velvet maroon curtain as the backdrop. The choir loft, which contains the or-gan, is located behind and above the platform. A balcony, no longer used, is located at the rear of the sanctuary.

Entering through the foyer on a Sunday morning, a visitor to the BABC would be struck by the silence and inactivity in the building. Before long, how-ever, the pastor's husband would likely welcome and escort a newcomer to a pew. Most of those present for a typical service are women who sit alone or in pairs, scattered throughout the large sanctuary. They greet one another on their way to their pews; however, there is little socializing before the service begins.

The pastor opens with a call to worship, conducting the service with energy and purpose. An organist and soloist—both women over sixty—lead the con-gregation in singing several traditional, stately hymns. Announcements tend to focus on the health and whereabouts of church members. A missing member is cause for great concern.

A lay member reads the Old and New Testament Scriptures assigned by the lectionary, but the sermons are not necessarily based on those texts. The pastor frequently emphasizes a personal relationship with God and stresses that this relationship should govern a Christian's actions and relations with others. She uses humor and stories from everyday life to illustrate her points. While she explores Christian themes, her sermons are not heavy with theology. The con-gregation is attentive, but they do not respond overtly, even to the humor.

After a final hymn and the benediction, everyone adjourns to the coffee hour, which often runs well over an hour as congregants are reluctant to leave.

Visitors are enthusiastically encouraged to attend; however, members are more interested in chatting with one another than with newcomers. For many, the coffee hour fills an important social need. It is one of the few opportunities they have to socialize during the course of the week. This small congregation provides for them an important source of friendship, memory, and inspiration.

The pastor has used her congregants' memory and their pride in the church building to convince them to begin reaching out to the community. The congregation rents space to a Brazilian congregation, a Haitian minister, and an alternative high school program. Members consider sharing this space a community mission. It is also vital to the church's financial survival. The congregation dreams of moving beyond these ministries to convert part of the building to a housing/day-care facility for the elderly.

Sharing the church building with the community allows BABC members to respond to the changes in their community without altering their own worship and fellowship. Offering the church building as a resource to the community has not changed the size or makeup of the congregation, and members seem resigned to its continuing decline. They are at a loss as to how this process may be reversed. They do not believe they can bridge the cultural differences between themselves and the new ethnic and racial groups in the community.

RESOURCES

The few who gather on Sunday morning at Brighton Avenue Baptist are the remnant of the white middle-class families who used to populate the community. For well over a century, Protestants have been a minority in this community; but over the last generation, people who were white and middle class also became a minority. The old constituency for this church disappeared from the neighborhood thirty years ago, long before the current wave of immigrants changed it again. By the time immigrants began to move in, this congregation was already depleted in members and resources. Those who remain are dedicated to the church and pitch in to do multiple jobs, but programming has shrunk to little more than Sunday services, a regular coffee hour, and an occasional picnic. The congregation has neither a demographic niche that can bring members in nor the programming resources to create a new niche.

With such a tiny congregation, money has also become a serious concern. In 1992, only twenty-two people pledged, and fewer than five of those were under sixty-five. Their pledges make up only about a quarter of the church's meager $50,000 budget. Half comes from investments and other income, while another quarter comes from rents. Keeping the building in minimal repair is a constant worry, and the pastor's salary is considerably below where it should be. There are simply not enough dollars to go around. Only the rental income enables the congregation to heat the building during the week and thereby use the church office. As part of a rental agreement, the Brazilian congregation that uses space in the building also does cleaning and some maintenance, something many of Brighton Avenue Baptist's members are no longer able to do.

Their building is, then, both a potential asset and a current drain on their resources. Its size and location give the congregation the potential for housing significant programming and ministry. Its age and long disuse, however, will require significant investment before that potential can be realized—investment the current congregation is unlikely to be able to make.

Nor are they likely to be able to qualify for money from their denomination, the American Baptist Churches. Like other mainline denominations, the ABC has suffered its own decline in members and dollars, but the real problem is that Brighton Avenue Baptist would have to submit a ten-year plan for development in order to be granted denominational assistance, something the church probably cannot do. Ironically, in earlier days, when Brighton Avenue Baptist's members were first moving to the suburbs, the denomination's money helped to fuel that shift. New suburban churches were supported; old urban ones were not. Now there is less money to help such churches rebuild.

The most important asset Brighton Avenue Baptist had in 1992, everyone seemed to agree, was their pastor. Rev. Charlotte Davis worked tirelessly and creatively to make connections and find resources. She was active in the local ministerial association and thereby connected the church to other religious activities in the area and to the community projects undertaken through the association. She secured a grant to fund an English-as-a-Second-Language program at the church for the area's growing Brazilian population. She tried to find money and volunteers to do necessary renovations to make the building suitable for weekday services to the elderly. She served as primary liaison with the groups that rented space in the building. It is her interpretive work, her help in making connections, that keeps these projects from being only business transactions. One long-term member described her as "a ball of fire. She works and she works hard. She's determined that she's gonna put the place on the map. She's succeeded in every way. . . . [N]ow when . . . they ask you what church, they know it. They know where we are and they say, 'Oh, that's where Charlotte Davis is.'"

In addition to all this work with outside groups, Reverend Davis was warm and caring in tending her own flock. She knew every name and what each member was concerned about. She was there when they were sick or grieving. And she prepared sermons and worship experiences that were highlights of the week for many of her elderly parishioners. Her extraordinary skill and energy seemed to keep the church going. Her departure in 1994 created a major deficit. An interim pastor was appointed, but the congregation's ability to call another full-time pastor was seriously in doubt.

STRUCTURES OF AUTHORITY

As part of the American Baptist Churches, Brighton Avenue Baptist is free to govern its own local affairs. Regional and national denominational organizations provide resources and connections, but each local church is on its own in matters of staff, property, and programming.

Locally, the primary decision-making body is known as the Standing Committee. It is a sort of combined trustee board and church council that considers major financial and property matters and important matters of church programming. There are also deacons, who tend to the spiritual well-being of the church, and a finance committee to formulate budgets. However, with so few in the congregation, most members wear more than one hat. At the least, all the committees are likely to meet on one night, share ideas, and work together on any matters that may need the attention of the entire congregation. If there are large expenditures to be made or major changes afoot, the congregation convenes as a whole to vote its collective will.

CULTURE

The most central practice in the life of Brighton Avenue Baptist is probably its weekly coffee hour. After worship each Sunday, the dozen or so elderly members who have made it to church that day gather in the coffee room. At round tables throughout the room, most members quickly find a congenial group with whom to share coffee and conversation. The pastor soon appears, having shed her preaching robe, and proceeds to check in with those who are there. Everyone lingers, savoring this time for conversation.

The members of this congregation have shared long years together, accumulating many memories along the way. In a nearby room, one of the women reflected on why the church is so important to her. "I always had the church, and I always had my friends in the church. I met my husband here, and most of my friends met their husbands here, so it really does have a special feeling. I was married right here [in the parlor]. I wasn't married in the sanctuary because I was married in 1942, and in wartime a lot of people—a lot of weddings were held here in this room. There are a lot of very good memories here." Every Sunday, in the rooms that hold those memories, this small band gathers to continue to sustain and care for each other. When asked what their faith means to them, they are less likely to offer theological pronouncements than to assert that God provides them the strength to carry on.

Much of that strength is garnered around these tables and over these coffee cups on Sunday.

Visitors are relatively rare in this congregation, but they are graciously welcomed. It is difficult, however, for the long-term members to get much beyond initial words of greeting. The gulf between them and newcomers is substantial, a gulf defined sometimes by age or ethnicity, often by family form, and always increased by the very lifetime of experience the current members already share with each other. There are no routines for bringing visitors into the fellowship or for teaching new members the beliefs and practices of the church. There simply have been no new members to teach.

The church's connections with its community have, however, increased during the tenure of Charlotte Davis, primarily in the form of rental agreements for use of space in the church building. An alternative school for troubled youth has been renting space in the church basement since 1986. The pastor tries to keep the church posted on what is happening to these students, and occasionally the church has a chance to help in some tangible way. Members have come to see this as an expression of ministry to the community. The relationship with the Brazilian congregation has sometimes been more problematic. Because this group uses the sanctuary, not the basement, it has directly entered the space that carries Brighton Avenue Baptist's memories and identity. A broken window raises the ire of longtime members. But when Brazilian and BABC members work side by side to clean and repair the space, a strong sense of common bond begins to grow. While neither the alternative school nor the Brazilian congregation has any impact on the worship life or membership of the congregation, their presence decreases the distance between the congregation and the neighborhood, establishing a tenuous place for BABC within the institutional ecology of the community.

The worshipping community of BABC, on the other hand, now appears to have a vanishing institutional niche, and the path of decline seems to its members inevitable. While fiercely loyal, they fear that the church cannot long survive. "It would hurt if we ever had to close the doors, which I hope we never have to do. But the community had changed so much through the years that everybody that . . . you know, I don't think there are very many original ones here. I'll keep coming for as long as I can," vowed one member. Another reflected on what has happened to the neighborhood over her lifetime. "Everybody moved out. And they didn't continue to come, like I did. And then the area changed . . . oh, there's a lot of oriental and other groups that don't—their religious affiliations are not—they're different. So they wouldn't be ones that would come to this church."

The conviction that the new residents of Allston-Brighton would not want to come to Brighton Avenue Baptist has been in place for quite some time now. The growing distance between the church and the neighborhood was set in motion when the differences in question were ones of race. The decision to reject the efforts of an earlier pastor who preached civil rights and wanted to reach out to the changing community seems to have had long-term repercussions. In the 1960s and early 1970s, the congregation wished neither to integrate nor to engage in evangelistic efforts.

Members chose instead to maintain their existing congregational identity. For more than twenty years—with slowly declining numbers—they have been able to continue as a remnant of the church they remember from the glory days of the 1950s. Even today, when they are asked to dream about what the church might be like in the future, that old vision returns. "I hope that this church grows, and that it will be filled again some day, as it once was. If we ever had another terrible depression, like we did before, that's when people turn to the church, I think. When things are going well, they don't feel like they need it. But I need it, and I think I always will. I do hope that it will fill up."

SUMMARY

The members of Brighton Avenue Baptist Church appear to have sufficient resources to sustain each other for the remainder of their days. But they lack the monetary resources and the personpower to make major changes in programming or outreach. Having chosen to maintain the identity that made them a thriving part of the community in the years after World War II, they have nurtured a caring community for those who remain, but with increasing distance of age, ethnicity, and experience between themselves and the community. They had strong leadership in Charlotte Davis, and exceptional commitment by the remaining members who want to keep the church open. But the decisions that shape their current situation, made long ago, seem irreversible.

These two Allston churches—Brighton Avenue Baptist and St. Catherine's Parish—responded to the changes wrought by immigration with a resolve to continue their existing strategies and programming for as long as a declining constituency could sustain them. The results by 1992 were serious deficits in resources. Such institutional liabilities are not solely the property of congregations challenged by dramatic changes like immigration, however. Other changes—changes that often look positive from the outside—also challenge the infrastructure of a community. Immigrants who do not speak English are a special challenge, but immigrants of other sorts can as easily disrupt old patterns. Just ask the people in Carmel.

Gray Friends Meeting, Carmel: Swimming Upstream

The patterns of community change and congregational decline present at St. Catherine's and Brighton Avenue Baptist are also apparent in a small, rural Quaker meeting on the edge of booming, suburban Carmel, Indiana. Here, too, the younger generation has largely left the community, while a new population has arrived. Here, too, congregations have lost a generation and failed to gain access to the new constituents that surround them. Our researcher Joan Cunningham picks up the story.

Gray Friends Meetinghouse sits across from its parsonage on the corner of 146th and Gray Road. At the juncture of three townships, this once rural area, called Gray, is now on the edge of expanding Carmel subdivisions. Although Gray lies outside the city limits, Carmel has historically claimed the church as one of its own. The unadorned white structure surrounded by trees looks quaint to many new area residents. An arch leading to the early Quaker cemetery behind the building reads "Garden of Memories." In the front, two doors—formerly the separate entrances for men and women—and several tall, narrow, stained glass windows add to the building's charm. A sign at the entrance, "Gray Friends Meeting," lists the pastor, Francis Kinsey, and the Sunday activities.

Inside, the walls of the sanctuary are a light green and the carpet a slightly darker shade. On a small bulletin board are posted old photographs of the congregation and church. The stained-glass windows and the lamps suspended from the ceiling provide the light. Most of those who attend meeting here are over fifty years old, but there are a few families with young children. While everyone dresses nicely, this is not a high-fashion sort of place. The sanctuary can seat nearly two-hundred, but while more of the pews are usually empty than full, the church doesn't seem vacant.

Among the first settlers in this area, Quakers established many of the early churches and schools and were active in the incorporation of the town, then Bethlehem, in 1833. An "Indulged meeting" was held around 1830 and a "Preparative meeting" on 31 July, 1852, and the church building was constructed around this time. Gray Friends became part of the Carmel Quarterly Meeting in 1868 and held their first monthly meeting on 4 August, 1874. Indicative of the Quaker emphasis on education, the first official committee was an education committee.

In 1879, a new church was erected to the east of the original building. The original structure became a post office, then a store, and later a residence. Eventually repurchased by the congregation, the land is now the location of the recently built parsonage, their first. The meeting became officially Gray Friends Meeting in 1887.

In 1912 the congregation had 159 members; by 1930 membership had increased to 210. In the 1920s the meeting had ten Sunday school classes and a twelve to fifteen member orchestra, which also played at other churches. In addition to Bible study and worship Sunday morning, a young people's meeting and a prayer meeting were held Sunday evening. This level of activity continued into the 1930s and 1940s and included musical programs and parties.

When Carmel began to grow after 1950, the meeting remained relatively isolated. By 1950, membership had decreased to 181, and a decade later was down to 166. During the 1970s as Carmel's population boomed, the meeting experienced some limited growth under the leadership of an evangelical pastor and saw a resurgence in Sunday school and youth activities as a new generation of children became active in the meeting. Soon, however, the pastor's evangelical style became a source of conflict, especially among longtime members who were uncomfortable with this form of worship. After voicing their dissatisfaction, many members, mainly from one family, left the meeting. Eventually the older, longtime members forced the minister and his followers to leave, after which most of the former members returned. Over this past decade, membership has declined gradually, as older members die and their grown children leave the area. Currently, more than half of the fifty active members are above the age of fifty.

Although the immediate area around the building has not changed much, Carmel has become a city of twenty-five-thousand. As suburbs creep north along Gray Road and more recently from neighboring communities to the west, the intersection at Gray Road and 146th Street sees more and more traffic. In the near future the church may be entirely surrounded by homes. For a congregation that historically considers itself rural, with members from farming backgrounds, the image of its building surrounded by expensive homes rather than by fertile fields is disconcerting.

For members, dramatic changes in Carmel reinforce a need for stability in the meeting. The usual Sunday service evokes just such a feeling of continuity. It begins with an organ prelude and announcements. Members share prayer requests, and the pastor includes them in her morning prayer. They sing familiar hymns, and there is a children's sermon. One recent sermon noted that these are tough times for Christians. The pastor began with a story from centuries ago in England. It seems a man reported a Quaker swimming in the river and was asked how he knew it was a Quaker. Because, he said, the swimmer was going upstream. The pastor observed, "Sometimes you have to swim upstream to get what you want." But, she concluded, "God gives us the gifts to use in building his kingdom and this may require swimming upstream. He calls us to do the difficult. . . . But we shouldn't be afraid because God keeps his promises." As always, the service ends with a few moments of silent reflection, after which the pastor asks if our "hearts and minds are at peace." A final hymn is followed by the benediction.

The members of the Gray Friends Meeting have deep roots in this community. Many family names that appear in the early meeting records are still on the current membership rolls. At least half the current members were born into the meeting, and many are related to each other. Only recently have younger, some of them newer, members assumed meaningful leadership roles. The congregation has also recently begun a new Sunday school class for the younger adults, providing a place where they feel free to ask questions about their faith. In the midst of a revered heritage and a strong desire for stability, there is some change.

RESOURCES

Like many traditional communities, indeed like the traditional ethnic community of Allston, the small-town farming community that Carmel once was has seen the exodus of its younger generation. Many who came of age in the 1960s and 1970s left the farms and small towns to find jobs in the cities. They left behind in rural Indiana an aging generation of parents and the few younger people who continue to work the land. Unlike the situation in Allston, in rural Carmel some younger adults remain as heirs to the community's traditions. They are now part of the church and bringing up their children within its fold. Indeed in 1993, five new babies were born to members of the meeting.

And unlike the people of Allston and St. Catherine's, the members of Gray Friends are relatively well off and quite well educated, with a reservoir of skill on which to draw. They seem able and willing to take on the tasks necessary to keep the church going. They also have a competent, energetic pastor who provides the sort of thoughtful sermons they value. Her husband, a lifelong Quaker and former pastor himself, provides valuable leadership as well, especially as teacher of the new young-adult Sunday school class.

Although their building and location do not place them in the heart of Carmel with the capacity for a vast array of modern programming, the facilities nevertheless have their own charm. As a typical country church, complete with cemetery, the building itself has the power to evoke the traditions embodied in this congregation. With no debt and no major repairs looming, Gray Friends—at the very least—is not encumbered by its building and is financially stable. When the meeting received a major bequest in 1993, members decided to invest most of it in capital improvements rather than establish a large endowment. Being financially self-sufficient seemed more important than having a financial cushion for the future.

STRUCTURES OF AUTHORITY

Quaker congregations are linked to Quarterly (regional) and Yearly (often state) Meetings, which provide advice and support, deliberating on policy issues that affect the whole. The Indiana Yearly Meeting, part of the Friends United Meetings, is among the most conservative Quaker groups in the United States. It is part of the "pastored" tradition, in contrast to the "unpastored" meetings found more commonly in the East. Once a meeting has gained recognition from the larger body, it is essentially self-governing, owns its own property, and calls its own pastor. It may, however, join with other meetings in policy statements and projects. Gray Friends Meeting chooses to cooperate with other Quakers in supporting various mission projects, for instance. The denomination plays both a supporting and a legitimating role, but its day-to-day presence is minimal.

Within the congregation, decision making is egalitarian and deliberative. While the pastor exercises considerable influence, she strongly encourages lay initiative. Any pastor who tried to exercise strong authority or leadership would likely be rejected by these folk. Everyone is expected to serve on committees, and committees are expected to take responsibility for doing what the people in the congregation think needs to be done. Most of that work has gotten done informally, of course. With a small group, well known to each other, little formal routine has been necessary. The 1993 bequest precipitated the first need for a more orderly decision-making and bookkeeping process.

Likewise, nothing is done in haste. In 1993, the meeting began discussions about making Reverend Kinsey a full-time pastor—discussions that would likely continue for a full year before a final decision was made. Reaching consensus, which is the Quaker way, is something Quakers are willing to take the time to do.

CULTURE

More than any other single idea, this congregation's Quaker heritage shapes its identity. When new people come, lessons about being Quaker are required before they can join the church. The members are proud of who they are and often explain why they do things by reference to the "Quaker way." Part of what they mean is that everyone is expected to be equally involved and to work toward consensus. They also expect a certain thoughtfulness and decorum in their worship. Worship, as all of life, is characterized by a simplicity that requires neither elaborate ritual nor elaborate clothing, none of the "conspicuous consumption" of suburban living. They know that their ways place them at odds with much of the larger culture. "Swimming upstream" is a powerful metaphor for them.

In the early days of central Indiana, Quakers were among the most numerous settlers. They built schools and churches and had an established place in the community. Today, the members of Gray Friends Meeting shake their heads in amusement at the ideas their neighbors have about Quakers. The new suburban residents of Carmel half expect Quakers to ride in horse-drawn buggies and dress in antiquated clothing (perhaps picturing the man on the Quaker Oats box). While the members of Gray Friends are traditional in many ways, these are not among them.

The traditions that permeate this congregation are those of land and family. More than perhaps any other congregation in Carmel, this one is still tied to the land. Its historic building sits in its original location on the edge of town. In its graveyard lie the ancestors of current members. The membership includes several people whose families have been in this congregation since they were deeded nearby land from George Rogers Clark. And many of the families are still working that land. The pervasiveness of 4-H activities in the conversations of these parishioners testifies to the continuity in their vocations as farmers. They worry about being pushed off their land by the encroaching housing developments and out of community life by people who are in too big a hurry to wait for a tractor to make its way down the road.

The traditions and family loyalties of this congregation sometimes stand in the way of incorporating new people into their membership. People do visit the services from time to time, and the meeting hosts an annual chili supper to which community residents are invited. But the members of Gray Friends take a cautious approach to these visitors— friendly, but never pushy. Only after someone has attended for several months is a member likely to inquire whether the newcomer might like to join the meeting. Some people have attended for years without formally joining.

Of late, only one or two families a year have become members, the first step in the process of becoming fully integrated into the church. To aid that process, the pastor works hard to get them onto the right committees and assigned to a long-term member as a sponsor. It will take awhile, however, for newer people to be part of the informal networks of communication on which the church relies. Gatherings that old-timers know about through long years of habit or because a friend or family member called, newcomers may never learn about. The members of Gray Friends Meeting are aware that recruiting and integrating new members is something they need to do, but as Quakers they shy away from aggressive evangelism. (That was one of the rules their evangelistic former pastor broke before he was finally pushed out.) Their methods of recruitment cannot violate their sense of what it means to follow the Quaker way.

SUMMARY

Gray Friends Meeting has a strong sense of its own traditions and identity and considerable resources on which to call. It is not hampered by debt and is able to pay its bills. While its building does not lend itself to the sorts of full-service suburban activities that many other Carmel churches offer, it does accommodate moderate growth that honors the traditions that are important here. If it were to emphasize its unique heritage and its picturesque location, it might be able to establish a long-lasting niche for itself in this suburb with small-town roots.[8] Most importantly, the congregation can build on the education and skills of its members, along with the flexibility and participation inherent in an egalitarian form of decision making. The largest liability for Gray Friends is the difficulty experienced by outsiders in becoming a part of this circle of tradition. And that difficulty overshadows the assets the congregation has, making continued decline very likely. While their resources and structures of authority provide the necessary base for adaptation, their culture leads them to choose continuity over change.

Carmel Wesleyan Church, Carmel: Camp Meetings for Suburbia?

Across town, another traditional rural church struggles with a similar set of circumstances. Carmel Wesleyan was another of the original three churches that served small-town Carmel. Today it too has been passed by in Carmel's transformation into suburbia. Researcher Michelle Hale describes this congregation.

Twelve Wesleyans began meeting in Carmel in 1897 and soon after merged with a nearby Westfield congregation. This merger included one family whose descendants have remained active supporters and members of the church to the present. The earliest members were converted at tent meetings or revivals held in nearby cornfields. The original church building was erected on its current site, along the old county highway leading north out of the small farming community. In 1932, it became a station church with a full-time pastor and financial obligations to the larger Wesleyan denomination.

The church's history through the mid-1950s is one of slow membership growth, gradual building and parsonage improvements, and yearly revivals. Membership almost doubled in the years immediately following the church's designation as a station, reaching an all-time membership high of sixty-four in 1944 and an all-time high Sunday school attendance of over a hundred in 1952. Members included many farmers and their families, as well as some teachers and clerical workers. Religion was an integral part of the members' lives, and they were very concerned with their "walk with the Lord."

By the mid-1950s, this small congregation was already beginning to shrink; membership had dropped to below fifty. Still, a history of the church prepared at the time noted, "Much new interest is being shown in the church and, situated in a rapidly growing community, we are anticipating and believing God for a much stronger Wesleyan Church soon in Carmel." Although Carmel still had only three churches, the Carmel Wesleyan Church experienced no substantial or long-lasting growth in the succeeding decades. In 1992, the membership numbered fifty-three, three less than in 1960. In the last three decades, church membership has dropped to an average of forty and fluctuated constantly.

In large measure, a continual turnover in pastors accounts for this lack of growth. Frequent changes in pastoral leadership led to subsequent fluctuation in membership and a lack of meaningful and sustained direction for the church. Still, the church has continually sought growth. With each new minister came a new plan for gaining members. Basically, all the plans called for a different combination of the same tactics: personal witnessing to the immediate neighborhood, reaching out to friends and family, and revivals. The church's programming has remained essentially unchanged for thirty years.

This strategy has been unsuccessful in reaching newer Carmel residents who have flooded the community since the 1970s, especially with more than forty churches now competing for members. Carmel Wesleyan has had an especially hard time trying to adapt to the community's new needs. In 1981, the congregation built a new sanctuary, but additional space did not transform its style of worship and programming into what newer residents were looking for. Under the burden of debt from this building and with shrinking membership, in 1985, Carmel Wesleyan became a "pioneer church" within the larger Wesleyan denomination. This change in status meant that the members traded control over running their church for financial assistance from the denomination.

Seven years later and still a pioneer church, Carmel Wesleyan received a new pastor who brought with him his former congregation, a dying Indianapolis Wesleyan parish. When Reverend Lightbourne came in the fall of 1992, the Carmel congregation added a few new members, in addition to the members he brought with him, and finances stabilized sufficiently for the church to revert to independent status. There were few initial problems merging the two congregations and accepting the Lightbournes, who are African American, but a year later, most of the African American members from Indianapolis had quit coming.

Throughout the church's history, a few families and their offspring have dominated the church membership and its decision making. These key families exercised added influence through generous bequests and offerings. They and other longstanding Carmel Wesleyan members have formed close bonds and remain committed to the church, having helped each other weather tough storms, both personal and church-related. There are obstacles to lasting renewal at Carmel Wesleyan, including a slowing of population growth in Carmel and the emergence of several other conservative Carmel churches that are better financed and have more to offer in terms of programming and facilities.

Today, a typical Sunday at the small, one-story, L-shaped church begins around 9:30 A.M. The front of the property is plain and unremarkable. The main entrance is at the rear, where members park in the tiny, newly paved parking lot that wraps around the building. In the foyer, they hang up their *coats and chat about the week's events. An attendance board on one wall shows that last week's Sunday school attendance was thirty and the service attendance was fifty.*

From the foyer one can see directly into the small sanctuary through the half-glassed wall. Two rows of ten pews face the platform. The walls are white, decorated by homemade felt banners hung between plain glass windows. Both Sunday school and morning worship include ample time for singing and prayer. Everything has a casual informality about it. The members are a diverse group: black and white, young and old, couples and families, farmers and professionals. They all know each other and carry on friendly conversations as they take their usual seats.

During the worship service, members call out prayer requests, asking the congregation to share their concern about an overworked husband, a hospitalized mother, a new missionary friend, a local evangelist about to start a new church, and a friend who has recently turned to Buddhism. This activity is not rushed, and members audibly sympathize with each other. Those who bring guests stand to introduce them, to which the congregation responds by singing "I Love You with the Love of the Lord" as everyone moves around the sanctuary to greet each other. After the sermon and the final chorus, people begin to leave. No one rushes, and some families may still be at the church thirty minutes after the service ends. They and others will return on Sunday evening and Wednesday night for services and Bible study, traditions that have defined this church throughout its life.

RESOURCES

Carmel Wesleyan has been small for virtually all of its life. While its membership has fluctuated, it has almost never seen more than one hundred persons in attendance on Sunday morning, and numbers have generally been half that since the 1950s. Like those of St. Catherine's, Brighton Avenue Baptist, and Gray Friends, this congregation has seen its young adults move out of the community, while the population of older adults slowly dwindles. Like the members of Gray Friends Meeting, many of Carmel Wesleyan's members work the land, and a few younger adults are carrying on that tradition.

Unlike the members of Gray Friends, the remainder of Carmel Wesleyan's long-term members have blue-collar jobs and average levels of education. Newer members are now bringing higher levels of education along with experience in the professions and management into the congregation. This mix of old and new members, the result of the recent merger, seems to have been accomplished with relative ease, but it is not yet clear to what extent the resources of the new members (in numbers, skills, and experience) will benefit the congregation. They generated a good deal of hope that the long journey to financial stability might finally be nearing an end.

Before the new members arrived, this tiny congregation had, in the early 1980s, taken a leap of faith. Declaring their old building unsuitable, they tore it down and built a new sanctuary. Partly the old building was in very poor condition, but partly the members hoped to better attract and serve the burgeoning population of Carmel. What they got in return was a modest, nicely appointed new building—and a huge load of debt. Although the members gave sacrificially to build the building and to retire portions of the debt, they have never been able to attract enough new members to fill the building, and paying the mortgage has strained their ability to do anything else. Finally, they were forced to fall back on outside resources. Since 1985, they have been partially subsidized by their denomination.

Their place in that denominational structure has brought them both resources and liabilities. The district has provided much-needed funds, but as a church that is not completely self-sufficient, Carmel Wesleyan has had little bargaining power in the competition for strong pastoral leadership. A small, rural, struggling congregation is often seen as a reasonable first or last step on the career ladder, rarely as the place a person of exceptional skill and experience ought to be placed. As a result, the tenure of Carmel Wesleyan's pastors has been quite short, over the last generation a maximum of four years and an average of two. With each new pastor, the church has formulated new goals and dreamed of growth and new programs; but before any of that could come to fruition, the next pastor, calling for newer goals, arrived on the scene. While no single leader seems to have been especially inept, the absence of continuity in leadership has been a problem for the congregation. Major decisions have been made more on the basis of available funds from particularly generous donor families than on the basis of a careful weighing of all the church's resources and priorities.

The recent paving of the church parking lot seems to mark a departure from earlier ways, an example of the congregation's careful planning and marshaling of resources. The pastor first took his idea to the local board of administration and to the congregation. But before they could go forward, the district (Wesleyan) board of administration had to approve the parking lot, as well. Once a financial commitment had been secured from the district, the pastor challenged the church members to raise the rest of the necessary money by pledging toward the paving of a specific square of the lot, and they soon had sufficient funds to proceed. The newly paved lot not only improves the appearance and maintenance of their grounds and building, it also stands as a symbol of their ability to put together the resources necessary to meet their own needs.

STRUCTURES OF AUTHORITY

Wesleyan congregations are part of a "connectional," hierarchical denomination. Bodies outside the local church have the authority to make decisions about that church, all the more so when the congregation is in the kind of receivership indicated by "pioneer church" standing. As a pioneer church, Carmel had less say about who its pastor would be and had to submit major expenditures to the district board of administration for approval. The decision to merge Carmel with Grace (the Indianapolis church), for instance, was made by the district, and the placement of Reverend Lightbourne in the Carmel pulpit was a district prerogative, as well.

Under normal circumstances, the local church board of administration has wide powers. Board members review the list of available pastors supplied by the district; they interview candidates; and they vote on who to recommend to the church. They formulate plans and approve expenditures, acting as the major decision-making body of the church. The congregation as a whole delegates much responsibility to this board, whose members would normally be elected by the congregation and seen as its legitimate representatives. For a pioneer church, however, the district, in consultation with the pastor, makes many of the routine decisions, including who will be on the local board.

In such a small congregation this hardly seems to matter, however. People who have been on the board for years are still there. And no official congregational conference is necessary to secure the advice and consent of a large portion of the congregation's members. A few phone calls and some after-church conversations work just as well.

Nevertheless, Carmel Wesleyan's members have felt relatively powerless in the face of a district office that has seemed to hold their fate in the balance. Although the congregation is quite involved in denominational mission efforts and fairly well connected to activities at Wesleyan denominational headquarters in Indianapolis, that involvement does not translate into leverage at the district level over the resources the congregation needs.

CULTURE

In August 1992, Carmel Wesleyan participated, as is their custom, in a camp meeting in nearby Frankfort at the Central Indiana Region Wesleyan Church campground. At this campground, simple cement-block buildings have replaced tents and sawdust, but the old-time camp meeting atmosphere remained—crowds gathering, friends reunited, gospel preached, and sin overcome. Nearly a thousand Wesleyans and their friends drove through the rural Indiana countryside to hear the music and preaching on that August night. Before they left, many had spent time on their knees at the front of the meetinghouse, seeking to get their lives right with the Lord. This is the world in which the members of Carmel Wesleyan are most at home.

The weekly and yearly rhythms of rural evangelicalism shape the life of this congregation. On Sundays, members gather, dressed in their finest, at 9:30 for Sunday school, followed by morning worship. They regather in the evening for traditional services of singing, praying, and exhorting the faithful. On Wednesday night, there is another gathering, this time for Bible study and prayer. During the rest of the week, members are urged to read their Bibles daily, to pray for each other, to visit the sick and those who are unsaved. And at least annually, the congregation gathers for a revival.

In the old days, such efforts at visitation in the community, evangelistic preaching, and regular revivals could be depended on to bring in a steady flow of converts and new members that would at least replace any who died or moved away. Those activities were part of the culture and intersected predictably the life stories of individuals within it. Many of the older members of Carmel Wesleyan remember fondly an earlier era in which their own children filled the Sunday school, and the traditional programming of the church seemed to match the needs of many in the community. For at least the last generation, this congregation has tried over and over to implement traditional evangelistic plans, seeking to reach the thousands of new residents streaming into the community—to no avail. Today, the members are discouraged at the failure of their efforts, mystified by the transience of their new Carmel neighbors. These newcomers are not rooted in the traditions that have nurtured the Carmel Wesleyan congregation; many seem not to be rooted in any tradition at all.

In contrast, the members of Carmel Wesleyan know what it means to be Wesleyan and are committed to both their faith and the community of saints in which they are nurtured. They have a strong, familylike loyalty to each other. One woman noted about the church's struggles, "I can't say we always really enjoyed it, but we just don't quit."

As this congregation gathers several times each week, prayer is one of its most important activities. A sizable portion of the Sunday morning service is set aside for prayer requests and prayer. People share all sorts of needs with their fellow church members. They ask for health and healing, but they also ask for patience with co-workers and spouses. They even confess their difficulties with each other and ask for forgiveness. There is a bond among these people that allows such candor and that elicits tangible aid in times of need. One couple recounted arriving in the Carmel area with few resources. The wife was pregnant, the husband jobless. They visited Carmel Wesleyan and were immediately invited to dinner by two different member families. Over the next few months, they were given a baby shower and a food shower—and they have been in the church ever since.

This family's experience demonstrates how this close-knit congregation can open the circle of its care to newcomers in need. Since the decision of the district to merge Carmel with Grace Wesleyan, that openness has been tested and found sufficient. More than a decade ago, Carmel Wesleyan accepted an Asian pastor. Now the church is home to Carmel's first African American pastor, and there have been few repercussions. One longtime member overtly demonstrated his objections to the new pastor and to the African American members who came from Grace. But the rest of the church, even the dissenting member's family, rallied to offer a warm welcome. Their already informal worship style lent itself to the more enthusiastic worship of some of the newcomers. Old-timers and newcomers alike could join in familiar gospel choruses, although old-timers seem nonplused when some of the newcomers lift their hands in praise and express verbal approval throughout the sermon.

The church is aware that they are something of a test case for the district, an effort to create an integrated congregation that will cross the lines between black city populations and white suburbs. The faith and the traditions these two disparate groups share initially seem to outweigh their cultural and social-class differences. Mixing working-class and rural white people with middle-class and professional black city-folk seemed at first to be working well, but the eventual loss of the black members belied that apparent success. The church must now reach out to groups that do not share the Wesleyan evangelical faith tradition. Carmel Wesleyan's future demographic niche is still being negotiated. It is clear that the congregation is ready to welcome a wide variety of newcomers; it is just not clear who those newcomers are likely to be.

SUMMARY

Carmel Wesleyan's situation presents a peculiar mixture of advantages and disadvantages. Their building provides them with the space in which to grow but saddles them with debt payments. They are genuinely welcoming, caring, and helpful. Their prayer and their worship provide a context into which concerns can be brought, petitions voiced, praise offered, and helping strategies spontaneously crafted. The irony is that those virtues are so seldom available beyond the circle of the congregation—not so much because members choose to be insulated and inward-looking, but because they so rarely get to welcome newcomers to their door.

And the ironies continue. They appeared to be on the road to successfully integrating two culturally different congregations, but neither of those cultures was likely to provide their future constituency. Neither is particularly attuned to the suburban ethos of today's Carmel. The city is neither blue-collar white nor African American, and Carmel Wesleyan does not appear well situated to attract either or both of those constituencies from a larger metropolitan region. This church is firmly rooted in evangelical traditions, but their efforts at evangelizing transient suburbanites seem to have fallen on deaf ears. Finally, they are part of a connectional system that has provided needed resouces, but at the price of a sense of congregational disempowerment. The growth since the merger and the resultant glimpse of financial stability are major sources of hope in this small congregation, but the path toward the future is by no means clear.

While Carmel is integrating mobile urban professionals into a midwestern small town, the challenges in Los Angeles are somewhat more volatile. Like Allston-Brighton, South Central L.A. has been host to recent waves of immigration. Those immigrants are arriving, however, in a very different sort of host community.

Berean Seventh-Day Adventist Church, West Adams: "Tent" Revivals for a New Neighborhood

They used to really pitch a tent. But more recently, Berean Seventh-Day Adventist Church's revivals have been indoors. In the fall of 1992, they invited a favorite evangelist and held their revival over a series of weekends that occupied much of the fall. The services were as emotionally intense as ever. This evangelist, who had been preaching revivals for fifty years or more, directed his message each night both at unsaved people who needed to repent and at backsliding church members who had failed to maintain Adventism's strict moral and personal standards. As always, the church advertised their revival widely throughout the neighborhood. Recognizing that their neighborhood now contains many Latinos, they printed flyers in both English and Spanish and offered a translator at the first services. The translator was never needed, but by the end of the revival, several Latino families had indeed decided to be baptized and join the church. Whether that trend will continue—and whether these new families will become an integral part of the congregation—is a story that lies ahead. The story that has gone before begins early in this century.

Berean Seventh-Day Adventist Church was founded in 1916 by a group of black Adventists led by Elder L. C. Sheafe. Disenchanted with the presence of prejudice in Adventism and in their local church, they formed an independent Adventist church, building a place of worship on Thirty-sixth Place, near

Normandie, in West Los Angeles. There they struggled along with a small membership for about twenty-five years. In 1940, with only three adult members remaining, a new pastor, Elder Peterson, arrived, and the church began to revitalize. It rejoined the Seventh-Day Adventist Conference and by 1948 had become a full-fledged recognized church.

The 1940s had brought migrants from all over the United States to California to work in the booming defense industries, a trend that continued into the 1950s. As the church grew, the members decided to sell their property on Thirty-sixth Place and plan toward building in a new location. For fifteen years, they rented space in a Methodist church at Forty-ninth and Western while they planned and saved and worked. In 1954, Elder Black came to pastor the church with the express goal of helping them to build. In 1958, the current site on West Adams was purchased. In 1960, the church broke ground, and for nearly four years, they worked to erect their sanctuary. They proudly report that only two people—a plumber and an electrician—were hired to help with the effort. On the last Sunday in November 1963, the church moved into its new space. One member recalls that as they were giving the building its final cleaning, they heard the news that President Kennedy had been shot.

Early the next year, they officially dedicated the building, and by June 1967 they were able to retire their debt and burn the mortgage. Soon thereafter, they began dreaming about adding a large youth center to serve the needs of both church and community. They broke ground for the multipurpose center in 1977 and opened it in 1979.

From the 1960s well into the 1980s, the church's membership continued to grow—from several hundred to nearly one thousand. During the 1960s and 1970s, the sanctuary was always full, and there was a full roster of activities for youth and adults. Berean helped to found several other black Adventist churches in the Los Angeles area during those decades, always sending a few of its own to seed the effort. Young ministers were often assigned to Berean as associates to learn under the strong senior ministers the church consistently enjoyed. And Berean's multipurpose building was often used for areawide gatherings of Adventists, as well as for Berean's own fellowship, youth, sports, and other activities.

As had always been the case, Berean's members came from across the metropolitan region; a 1986 survey reported that more than 60 percent of the members drove more than ten miles to church. By that time, a number of trends were becoming apparent. Many of the youth who swelled the church rolls in earlier decades had reached adulthood and had left the area, the church, or both. And the area immediately surrounding the church was increasingly populated by Latino and Asian immigrants.

While official membership has held steady, average Sabbath attendance has dropped to around 250, large numbers of elderly members can no longer attend, and many of the church's organizations are inactive. In the late 1980s, Elder Dawson, a young pastor, began to attract young adults back to Berean. How-

ever, when he moved to a nearby church in 1989, many of those new members went with him, leaving Berean again with a dearth of young and middle-aged adults—and without a pastor. By 1992, they were being led by a second interim minister—an able and well-liked man—but few had much hope that a permanent pastor would be assigned soon. The dire financial straits of the Southern California Conference of Seventh-Day Adventists, echoing the general recession in the California economy, had necessitated wide cutbacks. Since the conference places and pays pastors, Berean could do little to determine its own ministerial future. So long as the conference had a surplus of able retired ministers (who were already being paid anyway), it was unlikely to take on the burdens of a full pastoral salary. One of Berean's associates was even working without pay, after his position was cut entirely in the conference's attempts to balance its books.

Still, Berean is today a vibrant and friendly congregation. As members begin to gather each Saturday morning, they greet each other with "Happy Sabbath!" The group that attends the 8:45 praise service, followed by Sabbath school, is predominantly, but not exclusively, older; and everyone is dressed in their Sabbath best. Many of the women wear hats and gloves, but noticeably missing are jewelry and bright makeup. As Adventists, they keep their appearance modest and unadorned.

Berean's sanctuary and its balcony seat about five hundred; the balcony is usually occupied by the younger set. The contemporary architecture features a cantilevered roof, allowing indirect light to brighten the sanctuary. For the first-time visitor, perhaps the most striking feature in the room is the central stained-glass window in front, a colorful portrayal of Jesus and the little children—among them a Hawaiian girl, an Asian Indian girl, an African boy, a Chinese girl, and a European girl.

Adult Sabbath school classes all meet in the sanctuary, nine or ten groups of a dozen or so each seated in two or three pews, separated from the next class by a few pews or a center aisle. Each class is led by a lay teacher in study and discussion of a common lesson, based on a Scripture passage. They take an offering, check who is there, and note which class has won the various giving and attendance banners placed in the aisle each week. Toward the end of the hour, all the classes come back together for review and for other educational activities, often features on Adventist mission work.

Worship begins at eleven o'clock, and as Sabbath school ends, the crowd begins to get bigger, younger, and somewhat less conservatively dressed. Extended families fill their customary pews, and visitors are warmly greeted. The service begins with enthusiastic gospel singing (but very little in the way of hand clapping or other evidences of contemporary music styles). A period of announcements and welcome seems to include many in the congregation. Various visiting musical groups often add their voices to the congregation's worship, and Berean's own small youth and adult choirs contribute on occasion.

The sermons are extended exhortations on the necessity of accepting Jesus as

Lord and the need for disciplined Christian living. Members are reminded that Adventists have a special message for the world and that they must maintain strict standards of conduct. Every service ends with an invitation to greater commitment to Christ; and at least once a year, there are special evangelistic crusades where these messages can be preached with more frequency and intensity. The generations differ over how strict some of the standards ought to be, but all share a certain pride in the health guidelines they follow and the patterns of discipline necessary for Sabbath observance. They know that they have a "special message," and they remain eager evangelists about their way of life.

RESOURCES

In 1992, much about Berean felt tenuous, poised somewhere between security and insecurity, between strength and weakness. After years of growth in the fifties, sixties, and seventies, the last decade had seen the congregation in decline—fewer new members, smaller attendance, a major exodus when one pastor left, and an aging population of remaining members. Every Sabbath's bulletin contained a long list of people hospitalized, in rest homes, or otherwise no longer able to attend. Expenditures were exceeding receipts—at least by a little—almost every month. That they had been without a pastor for so long only seemed to confirm the precarious situation in which they found themselves. The cohort remaining at Berean has formidable resources still at its disposal; the congregation is nowhere near death. But the trends have been troublesome.

With two or three hundred active members, the congregation still has a secure membership base. (The other six hundred or so officially on the roll are both older members who can no longer come and members who have long since moved away. That their official membership never has declined would seem to indicate that members are rarely, if ever, removed from the roster.) While a large proportion (42 percent) of the active members is over fifty-five, a third is under thirty-five, and those younger members have made a deliberate commitment to being involved in this congregation. Their presence and commitment bode well for future membership strength.

Both older and younger members at Berean are exceptionally well educated (see table 2.2). More than two-thirds (70 percent) have at least some education beyond high school, and almost one-quarter have done graduate work beyond college. Forty percent are professionals or managers; several are doctors or other health professionals. Still, not everyone has a high-prestige occupation (or the income to match). An equal number (41 percent) hold or have retired from blue-collar or clerical jobs. That diversity is reflected in income levels. The poorest third reported household incomes of less than $20,000 per year. The next 40 percent falls between $20,000 and $50,000, with the top quarter (28

Table 2.2. Berean Seventh-Day Adventist Church, West Adams

Ideas and Priorities

Christian practices rated "essential"	Prayer
	Bible study
	Living Christian values
	Attendance at services
	Avoiding worldly vices
	Sharing faith with others
Ministries rated "very important" or "essential"	
	Helping members share faith
	Service to the needy
	Preparation for the next world
	An evangelism program
	Helping members resist this world

Resources

Average Sabbath attendance	250
Annual operating budget (1992)	$385,000
Household incomes above $50,000	28%
College degrees or more	41%
Average age	47 years
Activities (beyond worship) participated in at least monthly	Bible study

Relationship to the community

Live ten minutes or less from the church	33%
New to the community in the last five years	26%
Ethnicity	73% African American
	22% Caribbean
Participate in civic & community activities more than once a month	31%

NOTE: One hundred people responded to our survey, amounting to approximately 40 percent of average Sabbath attendance. This may be taken as a good representation of all regular attenders.

percent) reporting more than $50,000. Only 10 percent reported incomes above $80,000. While the reservoir of education and skill is great at Berean, income and occupational levels are quite diverse.

Across this wide range of incomes, tithing is the norm at Berean—both in theory and in practice. Only one-quarter of those who responded to our survey give less than $100 per month, while 41 percent give more than $200 per month. Even with reduced numbers of active givers, Berean is able to sustain a budget of around $250,000. Despite limited incomes, Berean's members are willing to give generously to the church. A few have even signed on as "investment leaders," giving more than 10 percent of their income and trusting God to reward them for their investment. There are also lots of special offerings—Sabbath school, revival, various denominational and mission causes—to which people contribute modest additional amounts. Berean, however, has no endowment and receives no rents. The church receives government and private assistance in running its food pantry but has no other programs supported by grants and gets no regular help from the denomination. Indeed their single largest expenditure is money *to* the denomination. In the second quarter of 1992, their regular contribution to the Southern California Conference amounted to 12 percent of their income. An additional 14.5 percent went to support the local SDA academy, and still another 5 percent to the revolving loan fund. Their current tight budget is not due to a lack of generosity among the members. Their reduced numbers and relatively low incomes, combined with high obligations to the denomination, inevitably mean fewer dollars available for the church. They have been holding their own (thanks in part to a comfortable bank balance), but little has been left after paying the bills.

Berean is fortunate to have a large, well-maintained, mortgage-free building that causes proportionately little drain on the budget. Utilities and maintenance take about 20 percent of their income, and they actually have nearly $100,000 set aside in a building fund. Present buildings include sufficient space for their needs (with room to grow), flexible enough for a variety of uses. They have, at various times, housed a day-care center and an after-school recreation program. There is room for a Haitian congregation to hold separate French-language services, and potlucks or other fellowship events can be handled with ease. The sanctuary will hold more people than currently attend.

They are also fortunate to have lay leaders and competent interim pastors who have kept the church on track during its long period between permanent pastors. A skilled and knowledgeable member served as clerk and office manager. Most of Berean's members (62 percent) are lifelong Adventists, and many have had years of experience running the organizations of the church. They were well prepared to carry on without a pastor. While they have suffered a certain inability to think about their long-term future during this time, they have not lacked for organizational continuity. The fall 1992 arrival of a new young associate minister with special responsibility for youth gave them an added boost. And when a new permanent pastor was finally assigned in 1993 the church was little the worse for its long interim. The most important thing lost was time for actively envisioning a response to their community.

STRUCTURES OF AUTHORITY

Seventh-Day Adventists are tightly organized into a worldwide structure that has a good deal of influence on the affairs of each local church. There are well over one hundred churches in the Southern California Conference; seven such conferences comprise the Pacific Union; and the nine or ten union conferences in North America make up the North American Division Conference. There are lots of conference events to attend—for youth, women, men, singles, and the like—and ample denominational materials for the various programs of the church. Strong denominational emphases on education and missions directly affect life at Berean. Besides the large subsidy Berean pays to the local academy, the church also encourages its children and youth to attend, which several have. There are colleges to support in the Pacific Union, but there is an especially strong connection to Oakwood College, the traditionally black Adventist college in Huntsville, Alabama. Several members attended there, and groups from the school regularly stop at Berean for concerts and other events. The emphasis on missions shows up in educational materials used in the Sabbath school, in special offerings, and in the number of Berean's members from countries outside the United States where Adventist missionaries are active.

The programs and organizations of the denomination, then, pervade local church life. But most significant is the denomination's control of the pastor placement process. In the case of the Southern California Conference, demands on the churches for support are high, but California's slumping economy made it hard for contributions to the conference to keep pace. That, in turn, made it difficult for the conference to place and pay a full complement of pastors.

Decisions about what sort of pastor is needed and whether any pastor is available are made at the conference level, where Berean is but one of a hundred churches, one of twenty black churches in the region. Indeed, in the entire Pacific Union, African Americans account for only 12 percent of the membership, while Latinos account for 17 percent. How the conference decides to balance and integrate the needs and opportunities among those populations will surely have a bearing on Berean's future.

Another factor in this pastor placement system is the possibility that members will be more loyal to a given pastor than to their congregation. With no real parish boundaries and most members of African American Seventh-Day Adventist churches traveling from all over the region to attend church anyway, no geographic constraints keep them from switching congregations. If a highly favored pastor is transferred to a nearby church (and the church he leaves has no equally good replacement), nothing prevents the sort of exodus Berean experienced. As part of a larger system, each congregation is subject to the forces affecting the whole, whether those forces are economic, ethnic, or the availability of attractive pastors.

While the people of Berean certainly carried on in competent fashion during their time without a pastor, it was clear that they felt unable to chart their own course for the future. There were no task forces studying mission needs or committees formulating new mission statements. They assumed that the conference would have some say about what kind of church they should become—at least by way of the sort of pastor they were sent. And they also assumed that their new pastor would be their guide. With chief responsibility for the spiritual well-being and administration of the congregation, the pastor will articulate whatever vision for the future emerges.

He is assisted by a board of elders that includes the other pastoral staff and several of the most respected men in the church, who are supposed to stand ready to be responsible for all the church's activities, even to preach, if necessary. In addition, deacons help to care for the congregation's members. The elders, heads of other church committees, and deacons make up the church board, which makes most of the key decisions about the business of the church. Because women chair a number of committees and hold other key organizational posts, the board has a substantial female contingent. In addition to this board, several committees and clubs (education, music, ushers, and the like) provide opportunities for Berean's members to be involved in both administrative and social activities. They stay informed about what is happening through Sabbath bulletins and announcements. About once a quarter a church business meeting convenes on a Saturday night, and the debate can often be lively, even about such a seemingly minor question as buying a microwave oven. The members of Berean seem to feel some ownership of their routine internal affairs.

There are, in fact, numerous opportunities for lay people to be involved in leadership roles at Berean. They direct the Sabbath school and the youth program, serve on committees, and teach. Still, the key roles of elder and deacon have stayed disproportionately in the hands of older, long-term members. Newer members have had to wait a long time before being accepted into the inner circle, and that is something that worries some of those who would like to see the congregation become more ethnically diverse. Concerned that even if Hispanics came they would not be included in decision making, one younger member mused, "If the older people can barely share it [power] with the younger folk, how will they share with the Spanish population?" The relative insularity of Berean's key lay leadership may work against the congregation's ability to change in any fundamental way.

CULTURE

Seventh-Day Adventists engage, by definition, in a distinctive way of life. They call themselves (using a biblical phrase) a "peculiar people." Getting up on Saturday morning to dress up and go to church places the Adventist on a distinctive calendar out of sync with most of the rest of the society. Even as they make their way through life the rest of the week, their dietary practices—no caffeine or alcohol and little if any meat—and modesty of dress often set them apart. Becoming an Adventist is not a decision made casually.

But for believers, it is a choice with eternal consequences. More than anything else, Berean is characterized by its evangelicalism. Having Jesus as Lord of life and anticipating the Second Coming of Christ are the central preoccupations here. That concern shapes Berean's worship, from the evangelical hymns they sing to the invitation that concludes each service. All the usual evangelical themes are here. People talk about God's answers to their prayers and about the threats posed by Satan in the world. They expect that people who have made a total commitment to Christ will have the power to live changed lives. Members are urged to be good witnesses, and people worry about the best ways to evangelize. The Bible is read and studied with care. The King James version is so ubiquitous that the pastor can invite members to read along in unison during the service. Even the various behavioral prohibitions here are but slightly stricter variations on the life-style that pervades evangelicalism at large.[9]

Still, the differences are important. Most especially, the members of Berean point to their emphasis on the whole person—mind, body, and soul. They want people to be well educated and physically healthy in this world, not just eternally secure in the next. Adventist dietary restrictions are backed by ample argumentation about maintaining a healthy way of life. Sometimes members defend their ways by turning to straight traditional authority (the Bible and church tradition), but just as often they turn to reason, bolstering their claims with scientific studies. They can also be heard making equally modern claims about individual preference ("It's something I've chosen") or practicality ("Your life will be better if you do"). All these styles of ethical evaluation are present in this congregation, in roughly equal mix, and they use all of them in explaining themselves to their neighbors and colleagues.[10]

Demonstrating and explaining a distinctive life-style is the primary way Berean's members evangelize. They think about health and personal discipline along with salvation. Their revival services, for instance, were preceded by health lectures each evening. When they plan their evangelizing in the neighborhood, they add cooking classes as a likely means of delivering the message. While as Adventists they are certainly concerned with the Second Coming, they talk at least as much about health in this world as in the next.

Berean also demonstrates its concern for this world by providing services to the community. Members used to run a day-care center but found that increasing government regulation made it impossible to continue. Now, their primary activity is a food pantry, open two mornings a week. Staffed by church volunteers, it serves more than four thousand families each year. In addition to church contributions, the pantry receives money from the Federal Emergency Management Agency and contributions from a food bank. Berean also opens its gym afternoons and evenings for neighborhood kids to use, and after the 1992 uprisings Berean's members were out on the street cleaning up alongside their neighbors; their existing food and clothing ministries became part of the area's vital relief efforts. Some members would now like to see the church undertake a tutoring program, but no concrete plans have been formulated.

A generation ago, when Berean's members talked about evangelizing in the neighborhood, they would have been talking about their own neighborhood. Most lived fairly near the church, and the same sorts of evangelism they now employ (demonstrating and explaining their Christian life-style) would have naturally resulted in the conversion and recruitment of nearby residents—their neighbors. That process can no longer be assumed. Most of Berean's members live fifteen minutes or more from the church; a quarter live more than twenty-five minutes away, and only 10 percent live in the immediate area. When they first moved into their building, in the 1960s, it was almost always open, and members were often there cleaning and fixing, as well as engaged in church activities. Today, the church building is carefully locked much of the time.

To mention the neighborhood is, of course, also to raise the issue of ethnicity. Berean's members express some bewilderment over their neighborhood. They do not understand who these newcomers are, do not know how to communicate with them. Berean is approaching the task using the tools at its disposal—doing what it knows to do. First, Berean is an evangelical congregation and has a tradition of targeting the immediate neighborhood in evangelism efforts, especially for revivals and vacation bible school. Despite difficulties, the church has continued this tradition, baptizing several Latino families at the end of the 1992 revival. Even though Berean's members come from all over the city, when they think about evangelism, they think about their church's neighborhood.

Second, the presence in the church of people who themselves or whose parents have come from Latin America and the Caribbean (as well as from Africa and the United States) is a resource for Berean. Berean's ethnic roots go back to Africa, but they do not always go there directly. The result is a congregation that is less distinctly African *American*. There is much less consensus at Berean over the meaning of ethnicity than in many black churches and little political commitment to the African American community. Berean's worship draws from African American traditions (in its use of time, especially), but the music the congregation sings is more evangelical than "black gospel." They inaugurated an African Sabbath in 1992, and many members wore clothing made of kinte cloth. But others did not, complaining that they just wanted to be Americans. Indeed, there is a strong message here that the gospel is no respecter of persons, that God does not see color or hear differences in language. "Those who have been born again see no differences, see no color, see only children of God." Although Berean is clearly an African American church, a number of factors keep it potentially open to a diverse ethnic constituency. That openness is indeed right before the congregation's eyes each Sunday. The stained-glass window behind the pulpit reminds them that Jesus welcomed the little children—"red and yellow, black and white."

The irony, however, is that the members of Berean rarely seem to notice that window and never comment on its significance. Its message of diversity in the Kingdom of God is a message not operative in their community. Their potential openness must contend with the natural insularity of a tight-knit congregation. People who live a distinctive life-style need each other and naturally form close bonds. Among Berean's members, 58 percent say that three or more of their closest friends are in the congregation. In addition, two-thirds of the members have been in the congregation for ten or more years, adding longevity to the natural intensity generated by the Adventist way of life. We have already noted the complaints of younger members that they cannot find their way into the inner circles of influence (which are matched by the complaints of older members who think younger ones do not take church life seriously enough). The strength of the bond among the congregation's long-term members is likely to remain a barrier to change. The primary mechanism Berean employs for integrating newcomers is its frequent fellowship events (potlucks, picnics, and the like). When newcomers are intentionally taken under someone's wing, such events are very effective at moving them into the life of the church. Without this intentionality, the events may serve more to reinforce existing bonds than to form new ones.

SUMMARY

Berean welcomed a new pastor in 1993; his guidance and vision would be crucial for the future of the church. Even with significant

membership loss over the last decade or so, Berean retains a sufficient base to make a strong organization possible. Similarly, finances
have become marginal, but the church's tradition of generous giving
bodes well for reestablishing a budget that will support expanded
programming.

Until now, Berean's place in the regional religious ecology has been
as a black Seventh-Day Adventist church, one of twenty in Los Angeles. Berean's location in an increasingly Hispanic neighborhood
throws that identity into question, for it is unclear whether the church
will continue to attract black members to this location. It is not politically committed to serving an African American constituency and appears to have no other distinctive mission that might draw members
from a wide, nonneighborhood area. Berean is in many ways already a
niche congregation, but with so many parallel congregations in its
niche, neither its distinctiveness nor its members' networks are sufficient to guarantee a flow of recruits from throughout the region.

Berean's theological tradition, however, pushes it in the direction of
evangelizing its immediate neighborhood, and its internal resources
would appear to prepare it for that task. With an educated, international membership, making room for a growing Latino contingent
seems possible. Berean's future seems to lie more with its immediate
community, changed as it is, than with becoming a niche congregation.
Whether it will be able to attract and hold new and different members
will depend both on the church's creative vision in seeking out these
neighbors and its ability to integrate them into the close-knit fellowship
of a church membership otherwise scattered throughout the region.
Long-established older leaders will have to give way to younger,
newer, and different folk. That process may take place through intentional recruitment and training and incorporation, but it may also be
the source of significant conflict.

Conclusion

The basic demographic facts facing these five congregations are remarkably similar, even though the root causes are different. Each of
the communities in which these churches are located has suffered a
dislocation that disrupted the generational flow. As youth came of age,
they left, and others moved in to take their place. In the case of Allston-
Brighton and West Adams, those others are culturally different, have
different economic and family patterns, and are not thought of as
"good prospects" for the church. In these cases, the newcomers generally occupy a lower rung on the socioeconomic ladder, while in the
case of Carmel, the opposite is true. Carmel's newcomers are seen as
very good prospects, but Gray Friends Meeting and Carmel Wesleyan

have found their upscale urban neighbors equally alien. In each case, the generational and demographic shift left a wide gulf between an older generation of church members and a new generation of neighbors who represented a significantly different culture. Whether the newcomers were immigrants or wealthy suburbanites, older middle-class white parishioners had trouble forging links between themselves and the newcomers, resulting in a slow pattern of decline in the strength of the congregation.

There are recurring patterns in how these congregations have confronted change, as well. In two cases—Brighton Avenue Baptist and Gray Friends—the congregation experienced an abortive effort at outreach into the new community. Both Brighton Avenue and Gray Friends had pastors who were too aggressively evangelical for the congregation's tastes and were pushed out.

These are also five congregations whose buildings play a crucial role in their destiny. St. Catherine's and Brighton Avenue Baptist, with beautiful but aging buildings to which many of the members are strongly attached, have to spend a disproportionate share of their resources on building maintenance. At Carmel Wesleyan, not an old building, but a new one—and the debt incurred—has posed serious difficulties. Among these congregations, only Gray Friends and Berean can comfortably carry out their ministries without undue concern about buildings and debt.

The question of leadership is much more complex. It is probably no accident that none of these congregations has pastors who would traditionally be seen as ranking high in the clergy market—two men nearing or past retirement (at St. Catherine's and Berean), two women (at Gray Friends and Brighton Avenue Baptist), and an African American in a traditionally Anglo denomination (Carmel Wesleyan). All have status strikes against them. Declining congregations cannot bargain for "the best" (defined in status terms, not in terms of actual skill) in the competition for clergy, whether in connectional systems or in systems where congregations call their own pastors. Decline sometimes becomes a self-fulfilling prophecy.

The exceptions, however, are the pastors who are low on the status ladder, but high on skill and energy. In the cases of the two Carmel churches, there is reason to believe that the pastors' strong leadership skills might bring renewal. In Allston, Charlotte Davis was unable to revive Brighton Avenue Baptist, but she attempted to lay a foundation for its eventual transformation when the current congregation is gone.

Inside each congregation stands a dedicated core of lay leaders whose commitment to the church is high. In Samuel Kincheloe's 1920s study of a dying Chicago church, he noted, "The principal reason for Monroe Park Church's continued existence in its critical community situation is the loyalty and determination of its small group of members."[11] The effort to keep a struggling church going is a monumental task. Some of these dedicated members bring the benefits of education and relatively high incomes (Gray Friends), while others bring high levels of generosity (Carmel Wesleyan and Berean). Only St. Catherine's and Brighton Avenue Baptist lack all of these advantages. In addition, the hierarchical structure of St. Catherine's has inhibited the development of its potential lay leadership.

What about the ideas and practices of these congregations? Have specific theological traditions helped them to weather the storm or, on the other hand, hindered their adaptation to new circumstances? The sacramentalism of St. Catherine's seems vital to sustaining those who remain; while the sacraments can bridge cultures, however, that does not seem to be happening. A vital system of small-group care and nurture is present in several of these congregations, but only at Carmel Wesleyan do we see evidence that the local system of caring can reach beyond itself to embrace newcomers. Certainly the record of evangelicalism is mixed, as well. Carmel Wesleyan has found traditional, rural, evangelical practices totally ineffective in reaching suburban Carmelites.

When communities face significant change, congregations that choose to maintain their existing identities may survive for a generation or more. Some may actively resist encounters with their new neighbors, but mostly these decisions for continuity are made by default. Eventually, however, most will face a crisis. As older members pass away and resources disappear, such congregations will be transformed. They will either move or die, and in either case they may be resurrected in a form their loyal former members might never recognize. The resources they leave behind will become part of the new religious ecology of the new community.

CHAPTER 3

Relocating: New Places, New Identities

W hen it becomes apparent that the neighborhood in which a church is located no longer matches the profile of that church, some congregations solve the problem by establishing a new place for themselves—either literally or practically. They either move to a new location or highlight their existing identity in a way that allows them to draw from beyond their immediate locale. In both cases, congregations are able to retain their basic programming while establishing new ways of maintaining a constituency base. Just as a store might move to a neighborhood more closely aligned with its shopper profile, one congregational adaptation strategy is to move to where the people are. Another is to establish a niche for oneself as the provider of a unique set of services that appeals to a scattered clientele willing to travel to obtain those services. In this chapter, we will look first at congregations that move, then at niche congregations.

LEAVING THE OLD NEIGHBORHOOD

The subject of congregations moving from one place to another brings to mind, for many observers, the 1960s exodus of white congregations from "neighborhoods in transition" (a code phrase for neighborhoods with increasing African American populations). As we noted in chapter 1, these moves were often the subject of agonizing debates within congregations whose liberal intentions often outstripped their ability to practice "unity amid diversity." Outsiders often condemned the exiting congregations as racist, and they were often right. The difficulties of interracial institution building were beyond what most congregations were willing and able to undertake. For many theologians the idea of abandoning one's location, giving up on incorporating a population from which one differs, is simply proof of the sinful ethnic and racial divisions that characterize American Protestantism.[1]

While theologians may certainly make their judgments, the purpose of this study is to take a sociological view. By understanding congregations as indeed reflective of the diverse particularities of the population, giving expression to the deepest experiences and values of those diverse peoples, we *expect* a shifting ecology of congregations, and one of the ways in which those shifts take place is through the relocation of existing congregations.

Because of the design of this study, congregations that had been in the community before 1992, but that had already moved elsewhere, were not included; we took as our focus the congregations that actually appeared in a given neighborhood in mid-1992. However, some of those congregations were considering moves, and three of them are included in our sample of twenty-three. All are in Anderson, Indiana. Here we have congregations that have concluded that ministry in the style to which they are accustomed is no longer possible in the location they have occupied. They recognize that they are different from the people who surround them, and they are looking for a place where those differences are smaller, where common interests and life-style will bring people naturally to the church's doorstep. As economic forces have restructured the town, its congregations are responding by reshuffling themselves to fit the new landscape.

East Lynn Christian Church, Anderson: The Struggle to Rebuild

Among the most needy is East Lynn Christian Church, a Disciples of Christ congregation not far from the center of Anderson. Like the congregations we surveyed in chapter 2, this congregation has experienced serious decline, only recently concluding that a move was in its best interest. Our researcher Stacey Nicholas recounts East Lynn's history.

If it were not for the concrete cross atop the southwest corner of the building, and the stained-glass windows, East Lynn Christian Church (Disciples of Christ) might easily be mistaken for an office building. Located on the south side of Anderson, the church is bordered on three sides by a residential neighborhood. To the south of the church building is Delco Remy World Headquarters, a division of General Motors. The congregation perceives that their residential neighborhood has declined in recent years. The members remark that it was at one time mostly single-family homes but now contains units rented by single parents and persons with transient life-styles.

And there can be little doubt that their other neighbor—Delco Remy—has also declined in recent years. East Lynn reflects the downward trend in Anderson's population and economy, with a steady decline in membership, as older members die and are not replaced by newer, younger ones. In 1957, East Lynn had 1,370 members, compared to 225 members in 1987. The church members are all white, mainly over fifty years of age, and primarily supported by General Motors pensions.

One recurring theme in the history of East Lynn, founded as a mission church, is movement. At least four times, the church has built a new building, moved the existing building, or built additions to the building. Each time, the move was successful, meaning that it resulted in more members or larger space with relatively little debt. The current plan to build a new church clearly fits into this overall theme, yet it differs in one substantial way. A growing congregation precipitated the previous moves. The congregation is now dwindling; this move is intended to initiate—not respond to—growth.

The Sunday morning service at East Lynn begins at 9:15, but by the top of the hour, most people are already getting out of their full-size GM cars and moving into the building. The congregation has very little parking of its own, but the members park in the Delco Remy lot across the street. Large enough to hold 350 people, the sanctuary, occupies the left side of the building. Assigned greeters welcome the seventy or so well-dressed members who typically attend the service. The five or six in their forties are the youngest people there.

On a typical Sunday, Dr. Sam Young, the pastor, enters the front of the sanctuary through a side door. Doctor Sam, as the members refer to him, is in his midfifties, dressed in a blue suit, looking somber and reserved. He begins with announcements about meetings to be held and donations needed for community ministry.

The actual service might begin with the organist playing Handel's "Aria in F." During the instrumental, two children come forward and light the two candles on the communion table. A lay leader calls the congregation to worship with a responsive reading, and Young asks the children (usually only a handful) to come forward for the children's sermon. As the children return to the warm security of their grandparents, the service moves on into the church's weekly observance of communion. This begins with a hymn, the nineteenth-century "Bread of the World in Mercy Broken," which the congregation sings somewhat languidly as the servers join the pastor around the communion table. These lay leaders, the church's elders and deacons, say the communion prayers and distribute the elements to the members.

There are two readings from the Bible each week, for which many members follow along, sometimes joining in a unison reading from the pew Bibles provided. Before the sermon, there is also special music, usually a vocal solo.

Dr. Young preaches from carefully prepared notes. He emphasizes that all of Christianity is based on the assumption that God created all things and that humanity was made in his image. As his creation, we have dignity and worth. Being made in the image of God means that we have the ability to grow spiritually and physically with honesty, integrity, and truthfulness. Jesus believed *that people could change, grow, and realize the potential that was placed in them at conception. Jesus knows something good about us, something we have yet to discover because we are still becoming.*

The service closes with an invitation, usually a traditional evangelical hymn, sung from the Hymns for the Family of God *hymnal. Dr. Young asks anyone who wants to choose Jesus as their savior to step forward. After the song, Young gives a short benediction, and he and his wife join the assigned greeters in the lobby to speak with people as they leave the service.*

During the fifteen-minute interlude between the service and Sunday school, which follows, there is a bustle as some members go to the parlor to have coffee and juice and others collect grandchildren and children from the nursery. Some may gather around the blueprints of the new church, anticipating how good it will be to have a new building that better meets their needs.

RESOURCES

East Lynn's records indicate an average worship attendance of about one hundred, but we never counted that many. During the summer, attendance was barely half that number, and the vast majority of those present were over sixty-five. Like the declining churches we saw in chapter 2, East Lynn Christian has seen a generation of its young adults leave the community. As Anderson's once thriving Delco Remy and Inland Fisher Guide plants downsized during the 1980s, those who could retired, while younger workers by the thousands either transferred or were laid off. Today, East Lynn starkly reflects those dislocations. Its young families are mostly gone, while its older members are living off the pensions they earned in their years in GM-related plants. While neither money nor membership have reached the crisis proportions present at Brighton Avenue Baptist in Boston, the absence of a block of younger adults and the steady decline in membership numbers are worrisome.

So far, money has not become a critical problem. East Lynn has been quite successful in raising funds for its proposed building project. In 1990, the congregation purchased a five-acre site for $118,000. They took a three-year, $50,000 mortgage on the land, but repaid it in full within six and a half months. By early 1993, they had well over $200,000 in their building fund. They hope to have $300,000 to use as a down payment toward the $800,000 cost of a new church building. While this is not a congregation with deep-pocket contributors, members' willingness to give generously from modest incomes is impressive. Despite their attachment to a building that holds long-time sentimental value, these older adults seem committed to moving.

Still, a $500,000 mortgage would require monthly payments of nearly $5,000; current giving averages just over $6,000 per month. They rent out some of the space they are no longer using, which has helped enlarge the building fund. The income from the sale of the current building will make a dent in the cost of relocating, but it cannot be sold until they move out, and once they move, the rental income will be gone. It would appear that relocating may only be possible with a significant influx of new members, which ironically is not a likelihood so long as the congregation remains in its current location, persevering in the patterns and programs to which it is accustomed. This may be a classic catch-22. When members were first advised by a denominational consultant to move—in 1981—they chose to stay. Now, their resources have dwindled to the point that moving is barely possible.

East Lynn's primary resources seem to be its committed and loyal members. They attend regularly, volunteer to teach and do other church duties, and give sacrificially, both to make this move a reality and to sustain the church's programming. They bring to these tasks the skills, connections, and resources of a solid middle-class constituency. But ironically, it is precisely that constituency that is disappearing in Anderson, and those skills that may no longer be sufficient.

STRUCTURES OF AUTHORITY

As a Disciples of Christ congregation, East Lynn has many of the resources of the denomination at its disposal, with very few strings attached. The congregation can get advice on locating a pastor, consultation in planning their move, and help with strategic planning without the obligation to comply with any of it. In fact, the denomination's early advice about the need for adaptation, relocation, or both was set aside for ten years.

Major decision making, then, devolves to the local congregation, and within the church several committees and a general board chart the congregation's course. In theory, the pastor works under the direction of these groups, but in practice, his influence is much more pervasive. The members are ready to be involved, but they look to the pastor for guidance.

But just as the congregation can refuse the advice of its denomination, so it can resist the pastor's leadership. When Dr. Sam Young came to East Lynn in 1989, he knew he faced a challenge. He was aware of the denomination's study of the church and the recommendation that East Lynn move to a new location, and he thought the church had made that decision. He was impressed with the people he met and eagerly set out to rebuild the church. The process has been slower than he expected, however. At the time he arrived, the church had not really made the decision to move. He has since become aware that teaching this congregation to be genuinely open to newcomers and new activities is a formidable challenge.

111

CULTURE

Like the members of Brighton Avenue Baptist, the members of East Lynn feel a strong affection for their building and for each other. They have many memories in this place and have put many of their resources into keeping it beautiful. The thickly carpeted and immaculately furnished parlor is witness to that care. What they experience in their building each week are the traditional worship, Bible study, and fellowship that have sustained them over the years. They gather into Sunday school classes that have traditions going back decades. They sing traditional hymns and celebrate the Lord's Supper each week. They have adopted the high-church practices of using the lectionary and having acolytes, but they have retained the low-church informality of a nonrobed minister. Young presents well-prepared sermons, and they enjoy well-rehearsed musical numbers. It is all part of a routine that reflects their high expectations and their strong sense of community. The tone of worship and the content of the sermons at East Lynn reflect a positive message about the goodness of life and its potential fulfillment in Christ.

This is a congregation with a traditional sense of obligation to support denominational and other efforts at good works. The women's mission group, the Christian Women's Fellowship, studies about and supports Disciples denominational mission efforts, and reports on denominational fund-raising appear in the Sunday bulletin. The church has an active food pantry and rents office space to a local welfare program. Members recently decided to put an information table in a place where people coming for that program could learn about the church.

Their other major effort at making themselves known is their annual fish fry. In 1992, they fed more than seven hundred people in a tent pitched on their new property. They put out a table full of brochures about the church and posted a drawing of the proposed new building. Most of the attendees, however, seemed to be either current church members or area residents who simply stopped in for the meal.

The members who remain at East Lynn are connected to the organizations and extended families that make up the middle-class world of Anderson. Nearly everyone has some extended family in the community, and except for two people, all those who filled out our survey have lived in Anderson for thirty-five years or more. Several are also active in the Masons; indeed some of the highest ranking people in that organization have been part of the East Lynn congregation. The constituency of this church has been the working- and middle-class families who brought up their children in Anderson in the 1950s and 1960s. It is a tightly knit network with uncertain room for newcomers.[2]

No routines exist for orienting and welcoming new members at East

Lynn, since new members have been quite rare. When visitors do come to the church for services, they are warmly welcomed by official greeters and pulpit announcements. There are, however, considerable barriers between the visitor and full acceptance into the traditional routines of the congregation. As at Brighton Avenue Baptist, the rich store of memory and experience shared by the current members stands between them and persons who do not share that experience. Age and generational ties also create distance between current members and younger families who might visit. As welcome as they might be, children and newcomers inevitably disrupt the decorum to which East Lynn members are accustomed.

The dearth of new members is not just a result of the absence of a younger generation—the children of older members who have not joined as they came of age. It is also the result of the growing gulf between the congregation and its neighborhood. Over the years, East Lynn has seen the neighborhood surrounding the church change from working-class family home owners to absentee landlord rental property. Along with that change has come a perception among church members that the people in the neighborhood were not good prospects for their church. A 1991 church report lamented that the percentage of single parents and unemployed families living in the surrounding neighborhood had increased dramatically. Those in the neighborhood who do attend church, the report continued, are usually affiliated with the Holiness type of church whose worship service is informal, dress code casual, theology fundamentalist, atmosphere of worship emotional, and preaching characterized by defining social and theological issues in terms of absolutes.

None of these are characteristics East Lynn members would list to describe themselves. By 1989, the divide between the church and the neighborhood was pronounced enough to provoke Disciples associate regional minister Dr. C. Edward Weisheimer to write in his "Listening Report": "There are deep and compelling reasons out of our faith, to direct you to see the neighborhood as your mission area. To fulfill this kind of mission, I believe, would call for substantial change. I am not sure that as a *congregation* you can make such changes. Some *individuals* may do this. I do not believe that you, as a congregation, can do this. I am deeply saddened to say I do not believe that you can successfully evangelize the neighborhood." In choosing to move, East Lynn has given tacit assent to that assessment. Its members have chosen to maintain the programming and constituency that has identified them from the beginning. Their hope is that a move to a new location can precipitate the reestablishment of links with a younger, 1990s version of the middle-class families who have sustained the church until now.

SUMMARY

Having lost both its sense of connection to its neighborhood and its younger generation of adults, East Lynn Christian has faced a crisis in membership. The members that remain are remarkably committed to the church and generous in support of the congregation's planned moved. Their generosity cannot, however, outweigh their sheer lack of numbers, and assimilation of new people remains a significant problem. The traditional Disciples of Christ programming that has sustained them through all these years suits the current members perfectly. Building bridges between old and new will involve more than just moving into a new building, and the necessary resources for significant changes in worship, leadership, programming, and fellowship are probably beyond this congregation's reach.

First Baptist Church, Anderson: Moving from the Center

Not far from East Lynn, Anderson's First Baptist Church is struggling with similar dilemmas. Connie Zeigler of our research team describes its history and current situation.

First Baptist Church sits on the corner of Fourteenth and Lincoln streets in Anderson, Indiana, a few blocks from downtown in what was once a middle- to upper-middle-class neighborhood. The homes nearby date from the early twentieth century with some added during the 1940s. Some are in good condition, but most are deteriorating. Most of First Baptist's neighbors are now African American.

Like many Anderson churches, First Baptist was founded in 1890, around the time natural gas was discovered near the city. Within two years the congregation grew to 186, purchased a lot on the near west side of town—across the street from its present location—and erected a small frame church building under the leadership of Rev. U. M. McGuire. In 1923, under Rev. Edgar Laurens Hamilton, the congregation erected an educational unit and auditorium on the site where the present building is located. The following October they proudly hosted the Indiana Baptist Convention.

In 1937, the congregation hired L. Elizabeth Wright as assistant pastor to build the church school and youth programs. At the time of the church's fiftieth anniversary, in 1940, Rev. Elbert J. Smith announced the end of the church's indebtedness on their building; membership was 1,212.

After World War II, Anderson expanded east and south away from downtown and First Baptist Church. Some longtime west-side residents moved to the new suburbs and sold or rented their older homes to people who could not afford new houses. By the 1960s, First Baptist Church began to recognize these trends. In 1962, a study by the American Baptist Churches showed the new settlement patterns and recommended that the church, then pastored by Rev. Mel Phillips, consider moving to the city's east side. Reluctant to leave their debt-free building, the members decided instead to add an education wing to the existing facilities. The new building did not, however, bring new members. First Baptist Church had begun the stasis that would bring it to a crisis in the 1990s.

When Rev. Edward Dorsey came to the church in 1977, First Baptist's future on the corner of Fourteenth and Lincoln streets still seemed secure. Membership had declined from the 1940s but was still near eight hundred. Although most members continued to view Anderson's near west side as an appropriate location for their home church, they acknowledged the population's move away from the city center by establishing mission churches, first on the southern, then the northern edge of the city.

As the 1980s began, General Motors layoffs soured Anderson's economic future, although they were not the immediate problem at First Baptist that they were at other Anderson churches. The church had many retired GM workers as members, but most of its middle-aged or younger congregants were professionals. Still, as the city's economy plummeted, the members of the church's youth group—which had been one of the strongest in the state—no longer saw futures for themselves in Anderson. They left the city to attend college, but they found no market for their skills in Anderson once they completed their degrees. These young people joined the fourteen thousand residents who moved from Anderson in the 1980s. Their departure left First Baptist Church without a new generation of members. The neighboring young African American families whose homes surrounds the church were not attracted to it, nor did First Baptist encourage them to attend.

Today, the First Baptist Church of Anderson still meets in their red brick templelike building on the near west side. Limestone columns frame the three stained-glass windows on the facade. Across Fourteenth Street is Anderson High School, whose parking lot, west of the church, does double duty as the church's lot on Sunday. Inside, the sanctuary seems cavernous; fewer than two hundred people attend on an average Sunday, but there are pews enough for several hundred more. The room is painted a pale gray-green; the woodwork is white, with white floor-to-ceiling pilasters along the side walls. Tall, stained-glass windows depicting grape vines and flowers separate the pilasters. There is elaborate white millwork throughout the sanctuary, and above the baptistry (center front, behind the choir loft) is a stained-glass window that portrays a modified celtic cross. A balcony spans the width of the room at the back. On a typical Sunday, most of the congregation is elderly; a few younger couples and some teens sit in the balcony. Everyone is of European descent.

Before the 10:30 worship service begins, a layperson gives the announcements. They might include a church family dinner, the sale of church cookbooks, the availability of the bylaws for the American Baptist Churches, USA, and rehearsal schedules for the Temple Choir. The service begins as Rev. Dorsey, wearing a black robe with a white stole, enters the sanctuary and steps to the pulpit. The congregation joins in a unison reading from Psalms, found in the hymnal, and a pastoral prayer that concludes with the congregation reciting the Lord's Prayer. A stately hymn of praise is sung, and a small group of children enters to sit on the steps in front of the communion table. Reverend Dorsey talks to the youngsters for a few minutes about Jesus, and they lead in a verse of "Jesus Loves Me" before filing back out of the sanctuary behind their teacher.

Dorsey steps back to the pulpit at this point to begin a time of prayer. He mentions members who are ill or who have died, and the congregation responds by singing "I Need Thee Every Hour." There is a time of quiet prayer, concluded by the pastor. After the offering is taken, the congregation sings the Doxology as two ushers carry one offering plate each to the communion table.

At one service in August 1992, the sermon was titled "Liar, Lunatic, or Lord," a paraphrase of a C. S. Lewis quote; the text was John 20:24, about doubting Thomas. Dorsey reminded his listeners that if they have not made a decision for Christ, they have said that his claims of salvation are false. Asking "Has he touched your life?" the pastor led the congregation in singing the invitation hymn, "Jesus, I Come." As they sang, two women walked forward to meet Dorsey in front of the communion table. After the music stopped, he explained that he would be baptizing these women before he retired at the end of August. He asked the congregation to raise their hands if they were happy these new members were joining the church. After the benediction, most of the members formed a line, conversing with each other as they moved forward to greet the two women at the front of the sanctuary.

Today the median age among First Baptist Church's three hundred members is sixty-three. More than 50 percent of the congregation have been members for more than twenty-five years. Finally in 1991, faced with an aging membership and increasing crime in the church neighborhood and unable to attract new members, the congregation voted to move to Anderson's northwest side. Here they hope to draw young professionals from the nearby subdivisions and condominiums, people who have survived to establish a place in Anderson's reconstructing economy.

Many church members remain hesitant to leave their large facility for what will be a much smaller one. They also worry about their ability to finance a building project. The church did not hire an architect until December 1992, more than a year after the building committee's proposal was approved. In addition to deciding if and when to move, the congregation has been searching for a new pastor since Dorsey retired. Members hoped they would find someone who could build the church membership as well as the new church physical plant. First Baptist Church realizes it will die if it remains where it is.

RESOURCES

The most obvious difference between First Baptist and East Lynn is that First Baptist has more members, more of whom are under sixty-five. Its base of persons and dollars for making a move is considerably stronger. The churches face the same set of demographic and geographic constraints—a relatively absent younger generation that has left to find jobs elsewhere, an aging older generation, and a neighborhood that no longer contains the white, middle-class families it once did. The processes of decline look similar; at First Baptist, the decline is simply less advanced.

First Baptist still has a relatively strong base of resources within its own membership. While this is not a wealthy church, its members are fairly comfortable. More than a quarter of those who completed our survey reported household incomes of above $50,000, and the incomes of another quarter fall between $35,000 and $50,000. Their giving to the church is relatively generous; almost half give more than $150 per month. They should, therefore, have little difficulty raising money for a building. To aid them in that project, the American Baptist Churches Extension Corporation (a denominational agency) has arranged a million-dollar loan that will require only interest payments for the first year.

The congregation has adopted a rather conservative strategy for their building project, perhaps reflecting the caution with which they approach this move. Their strategy will be to build in segments, adding parts of the new building as fund-raising moves along. This will also allow them to move, selling the current building, before having to invest in the entire physical facility they hope eventually to have.

Their current building has always been, for First Baptist's members, a symbol of their central place in the community. Even today, despite increasing levels of crime in the neighborhood, most members would like to be able to stay. And with good reason. The building is old, but it is large and designed to accommodate a wide range of programming. The beautiful sanctuary is one of the most inviting worship spaces of any of the churches we studied. Besides location, the only significant advantage they see in the new building over the old is that the new building will be more easily accessible to older people, eliminating the stair climbing necessary in the current facility.

More than the money it can potentially have in the bank or invested in property, First Baptist also, of course, has assets in its members and leadership. This is a relatively well-educated congregation. More than a third of its members have at least a college degree; many are (or were) teachers and principals. Some of Anderson's more prominent citizens are in the congregation, and members of First Baptist have long been active in civic affairs. The members of this church have the knowledge, the experience, and the connections to allow them to envision and enact a future for themselves.

To lose their pastor at this critical juncture poses both advantages and disadvantages. The disadvantages are the most obvious. At a time when they need their energy for planning and fund-raising, they are diverted into searching for a new pastor. At a time when they need a clear vision for the future, they are without a designated leader. However, First Baptist did not wait for a new pastor to continue fund-raising for the move but hired a California consulting firm and raised $300,000 in pledges during 1993, after Dorsey left. Indeed, such times between pastors can generate just the new energy and vision a congregation needs. After a long tenure with a pastor, they can reassess their strengths and envision their future. The process itself creates pressures toward such introspection, as candidates ask the church to describe itself and its future, and the church determines what sort of image it wants to project.

The existing ministerial support staff and the younger lay leaders who are shouldering the administrative burdens at First Baptist are significant signs of the church's potential future strength. The church's minister of education brings a good deal of energy to his job. His work, combined with his wife's leadership of children's choirs, provides a solid core of programming for families that bodes well for the church's ability to rebuild. The new pastor called by the church in late 1993, Dr. Arlo Reichter, came committed to that rebuilding process, as well.

STRUCTURES OF AUTHORITY

First Baptist, like Brighton Avenue Baptist, is affiliated with the American Baptist Churches. That means that the church has a good deal of freedom to make its own choices about property, staff, and programming. However, unlike Brighton Avenue Baptist, this congregation has forged close ties with its regional denominational headquarters and has often turned to them for consultation. The denomination's placement service has supplied the congregation with profiles of available pastoral candidates; a recently retired area minister stepped in as interim pastor, after Reverend Dorsey retired. Reverend Dorsey had cultivated friendships with various denominational officials over the years, and the church has been a consistently strong supporter of denominational causes. In turn, First Baptist's members called on the resources in Valley Forge (national denominational headquarters) as they assessed their needs and resources for making a move. They received assistance from the American Baptist Extension Corporation in compiling a survey of their community and of the congregation's program needs, and that agency arranged for the loan that will help them meet their building goals.

Locally, the church depends on a long list of committees and boards for its routine decision making and direction. The congregation gathers twice a year for general business meetings, but between those times, the boards and committees do the work. In addition, there are Sunday school classes to be taught and choirs to be filled and led, youth groups to be directed, and women's missionary work to be done. The number of roles to be filled stretches the capacities of a mostly elderly congregation. The pastor works alongside this structure exercising influence and leadership, but having no official control over it. Also operating in tandem with this official structure is the unofficial structure of lay leadership in the congregation—a core of older members who combine longevity and respect into a formidable base of influence. They routinely circulate among the key elected positions. Only in the very recent past have younger members begun to make their way into these key roles, a process that seems to be happening with little conflict and that bodes well for evolving a new leadership cohort.

CULTURE

Throughout much of its history, First Baptist, Anderson, has been a prominent church—both in the community and in its denomination. In the community, where its size and location placed it at the heart of things, it was known for its music programs and for hosting community events. Within the denomination, the church admirably filled the role of "County Seat First Church." It hosted area Baptist events, developed a youth group that was the envy of the state, and made generous gifts to denominational causes. Some of its past ministers have been renowned preachers, known throughout both the city and the denomination. For a variety of reasons, the people of First Baptist have thought of theirs as an important church, occupying a central place in their community, and being "a powerful influence for Christ." When a consultant first suggested that they move, nearly thirty years ago, they could not imagine giving up their location. Even today, the decision to move has been hard.

That sense of place in the community has also shaped their ideas about their building, their worship, and their programming. In the 1989 "Program Committee Report," the word *quality* is used over and over again. The people at First Baptist want to do things right. The report emphasizes that they want their teachers to be well trained and to have the "finest curricula and resources." They want to maintain the worshipful atmosphere of their Sunday morning services, making sure that they are "organized, dignified and on time."

That sense of decorum may be one of the reasons that the church had such difficulty with the outreach activities begun by their former associate pastor. He put together a lively Wednesday evening program for children and youth that began to draw as many as a hundred participants, many of them otherwise unchurched and many of them African American children from the neighborhood. The 1989 report says, diplomatically, "The Wednesday evening bus ministry is a source of pride to some while all agree that it still needs some fine-tuning." The friendly midweek fellowship dinner traditionally enjoyed by one hundred or so longtime members had become a bustling, somewhat chaotic event. While they liked having youth drawn to the church, they were unwilling to put up with the disruption. The young minister who developed the program eventually left, and Wednesday night returned to normal.

Normal, for First Baptist, includes a fairly predictable round of activities. There is Sunday school at 9:15, before the 10:30 morning worship service. When the 1989 program survey was conducted, the committee returned a recommendation that the order of these two activities be reversed. However, their arguments were not nearly so persuasive as the force of tradition. In addition to education, Sunday school classes provide an enduring source of support and fellowship for church members—and Sunday school always comes before worship. These groups also plan outings or dinners together. There is, in fact, concern that the young adult class has disbanded because virtually all its members are involved in teaching and other responsibilities that prevent them from gathering for this traditional time of mutual support. People are aware that these overcommitted adults need the study and fellowship Sunday school would provide.

On Sunday evening, there are BYF (Baptist Youth Fellowship) meetings, and on Wednesday evening—besides dinner—there are children's choirs, adult Bible study and prayer time, adult choir, more youth meetings, and the like. Numerous women's missions "circles" meet once a month, during the day (which, of course, assumes that those who attend are not working outside the home). They study and support denominational mission efforts and help to keep the church informed about them. They also engage in small, local works of charity, as well as provide yet another arena in which friendships are sustained. The church also holds annual camp outs and banquets and picnics, as well as routine gatherings with the local Baptist association and state convention. It is a way of being church that has been in place for many years, at least since today's older members were raising their children.

The ideas that shape this routine are drawn from the evangelical tradition, but not rigidly so. It is important here to know Jesus Christ as one's personal savior; the church has a traditional altar call each Sunday to invite people to publicly proclaim their faith and practices adult baptism, by immersion, for those converts. But the church also dedicates its infants, asking parents and congregation to make promises about participating in the spiritual nurture of the child. Members emphasize the importance of scripture but do not interpret it literally. The pastor's sermons cite traditional evangelical writers like C. S. Lewis, but they may also draw from more liberal sources like Paul Tillich. Those we surveyed listed outreach to the unchurched and personal faith-sharing as their top two ministry priorities, but the church has no regular organized effort for either. The evangelism of this church seems more a rhetoric and a reflex—a way of talking about what they ought to do—than a defining discourse or practice.

First Baptist's efforts at outreach, as we noted, have had mixed results. When a large number of neighborhood children were successfully brought into church programming, the disruption proved too much of a strain. These children were the visible reminders of the differences between the members of First Baptist and the neighborhood that surrounds them. As with nearby East Lynn, once the surrounding homes were no longer occupied by middle-class white families, church members sensed an increasing gulf between themselves and the community. That gulf is widened by neighborhood crime and vandalism. First Baptist's members now see their church's near-downtown location as not only alien but hostile.

When, in the 1989 report, the congregation dreamed about possible outreach and mission efforts, they included better advertising and more staff involvement in civic affairs, as well as continuing their strong support for denominational mission efforts overseas. They mentioned the possibility of cooperation with nearby churches, but there were no specific proposals for ministries that would directly involve the neighborhood.

The alternative, of course, is their move to a safer location more hospitable to the traditional ways of a church like First Baptist. They will no longer be located near the heart of the city, but they will not have ceded their influence. By locating among the new houses and condominiums on the north side, the church will again be among the sorts of people likely to be attracted to the moderate evangelicalism and quality traditional programming that First Baptist is still able to do. While the preponderance of older adults creates for this congregation the same hurdles in recruiting and assimilating new members present at East Lynn or Brighton Avenue Baptist or either of the Carmel churches, First Baptist has the resources of money and personpower to make this move possible, beginning the process of transformation necessary if the congregation is to survive and grow.

SUMMARY

Although First Baptist has lost large numbers of members and has a disproportionately aging membership, neither its numbers or its flow of money is yet at a critical point. With a well-educated and generous membership, there are still time and resources enough for establishing a new future in a new location. As the core of younger leaders gains more influence—and as a new pastor comes on the scene—some of the church's traditional and predictable programming will probably begin to change. What is not likely to change is the church's sense of itself as an important influence in the city of Anderson and beyond.

South Meridian Church of God, Anderson: Prayer and Praise through Thick and Thin

Like East Lynn, South Meridian Church of God lies on the outskirts of Anderson, Indiana's central city area. Like First Baptist, South Meridian thinks of itself as a leading church in town. And unlike either, this is a congregation that represents the single most important religious tradition in the community. It has brought a variety of strengths to this moment in its history and has, in fact, weathered the downturn in Anderson's economy with apparently minimal disruption. People barely recognize that there has been a problem, and the church seems as healthy as ever. The decision to move is being made from strength, not weakness. Research team member Stacey Nicholas tells the story.

In 1905, South Meridian Church of God began as an in-home prayer meeting. The Church of God movement was still young, an outgrowth of nineteenth-century revivals and Holiness movements, but not Pentecostal, like its younger namesake, the Church of God of Cleveland, Tennessee. Nine years later, in 1914, the congregation constructed its first small wood-frame church building at 2427 Meridian Street, across the street from the congregation's current location. By 1941, the congregation had burned its first mortgage and was ready for the changes that would follow World War II. The church experienced a period of rapid growth in the years after the war, purchasing nearby properties and its first parsonage. A Sunday school building and gym were completed in 1954, just as the baby boom began to swell Sunday school enrollments. The sanctuary building was completed six years later. Families in the small, neat homes nearby walked to South Meridian, and when thousands of Church of God families arrived from all over the world for the annual "camp meeting" in Anderson each summer, many would choose to attend South Meridian as one of the two or three leading Church of God congregations in town.

As its name suggests, South Meridian Church of God is located on the south side of Anderson. The sand-colored brick building erected in 1960 is almost hidden by the tall shrubs along its walls. Parking lots surround it on three sides, and to the south are a few two-story, wood-frame homes. Four doors lead into the building, and a quick way to recognize visitors is to notice who uses the door that fronts Meridian Street. The building comprises three disjointed sections. The center segment includes classrooms and the Chan Memorial Gym— begun in 1948 as a community center—with a fellowship hall and kitchen in the basement. At one time, this section was an independent, freestanding building. North of this area, connected by various steps and stairways, the sanctu-

ary and more classrooms have been added. To the south, classrooms, church offices, and the library were added in the late 1970s to form the third segment. The building is not accessible to handicapped people, and the many levels of stairs are sometimes difficult for elderly members to negotiate.

Within a three-block radius of South Meridian Church of God lie two other churches—both also slated to move soon—and a sprawling urban hospital. Collectively, the four institutions absorbed most of the property in this one-time residential neighborhood. Only six families from the immediate neighborhood attend the church, and church members surmise that the area has changed from an upper-middle-class, all-white neighborhood to a lower-middle-class, racially mixed one. Some members of South Meridian report that the neighborhood is "bothered by crime," but the fear of crime is not as pervasive here as at First Baptist downtown.

The cross-generational membership of the church is all white. Many people hold manufacturing jobs, either at one of the Delco Remy/Inland Fisher Guide plants or at Warner Press (the Church of God's publishing house, located in Anderson). Some members are employed as teachers and nurses and about one-third of the congregation is retired. The women, if they work outside the home, tend to occupy gender-traditional jobs, such as nurses or day-care supervisors.

Sunday morning services begin at South Meridian at 10:45, following the 9:30 Sunday school. The building is filled with the continuous hum of activity as children reunite with their parents and as parents with toddlers and infants usher them toward the nursery. The sanctuary is decorated in a green, blue, and gold motif. The carpeting and the seating pads for the wooden pews are a spring green. The large, abstract, stained-glass window in the front of the room encompasses all three colors. The raised platform in front holds the choir, pulpit, and altar table. Behind the altar table is a fifteen-foot, dark brown wooden cross; beneath it, hidden by a five-foot wall, lies the baptismal pool.

The murmur in the sanctuary matches that in the hall, and the volume increases as more of the 450-member congregation fill the seats. Called to worship, they stand to sing twice through the refrain from "Blessed Assurance": "This is my story; this is my song, praising my Savior all the day long." Music plays an integral part in the worship service. The traditional, nineteenth-century songs are usually upbeat and praiseful. During an average service, the congregation sings four songs, there are three piano solos, a soloist or a group sings, and the choir sings a special number.

Every service also includes a time of anointing with oil. Members who wish to be prayed for walk to the altar rail, in front of the pulpit, and kneel. As the organist plays a sober piece, Pastor Gary Ausbun meets and prays with each of them, touching them with a drop of oil. Praying for each other is very much a part of this congregation's life. Nearly every meeting includes a prayer time, and there are multiple support groups—among them, cancer support, parenting, TLC small groups, and weight loss—in addition to Sunday school classes. Here people share concerns about health problems, accidents and disasters, finances and jobs, marriages and families. They expect concern and support on these issues from their church community, feeling that others in the church have been through such problems, as well. People take the requests they hear seriously, writing them down to remember later.

The sermons remind members to live as faithful Christians, to be more faithful in their prayer life, more faithful in church attendance, more faithful in giving, more faithful in witnessing. At the end, people are again invited to come forward to the altar rail if they wish to accept Jesus as their savior or make a renewed commitment to their faith.

When asked, most people at South Meridian Church of God say that GM's downsizing barely affected the church; membership and finances remained constant. But a cursory survey of annual reports from this period suggests that this opinion is not entirely correct. As with most organizations in Anderson, the low point of South Meridian's history parallels the economic downturn of the 1970s and 1980s. The years 1974–1975 brought financial difficulty because some church members lost their jobs, and the country was in the clutches of the gas and energy crises. During the five years between 1979 and 1984, 160 people left the church or died, and only 90 new persons joined the church. The pastor then, Emmitt Whalen, commented on the economic problems facing Anderson in the 1981–1982 annual report: "In light of the circumstances in Anderson this past year, it is likely that the Lord has blessed us in a much greater measure than we may be aware of. Our city made the national news by having the highest unemployment in the nation. Many businesses have failed, many people have moved away and the number of bankruptcies having [sic] increased. It is miraculous that the South Meridian Church of God is still prospering."

Financial constraints also affected the church's programs. In 1981–1982, the church council periodically approved special funds to restock the Helping Hand Cupboard, which provided food for families in need. Hindered by the city's economic problems and the need to repair the building's heating unit, the board of finance was forced to cut the budgets of many programs.

Still, even without special fund-raising efforts in 1982, there was a significant increase in giving. During this time, the church established a Social Needs Committee, allotted it five thousand dollars for the last six months of the fiscal year, and charged it with helping the needy people of Anderson. At the end of the year, the committee report listed its accomplishments: "Food was put on tables where there was none, heat was turned on in homes where people were cold, and clothing was put on the backs of little children."

Today, South Meridian's mission is "to worship God, walk in the faith, and witness to the world through the love of Jesus Christ and in the power of the Spirit." One of the current issues facing the church is how to carry out this mission. The congregation retired its new building debt in 1992 *and faced what to do next—build a new building or remodel the current one. The Building Improvement Committee and the Ministries Council examined the programs needed in the future and the space that will be needed for those programs. By late 1993, the church had decided that moving to a new location made more sense than spending nearly one million dollars to remodel the current property. Members recognized in the process that they really are not a neighborhood church and would be better served by being in a visible, accessible location on the edge of the city. They will seek to sell their buildings, perhaps to the nearby hospital or to a Christian school; and they will take about five years to make the full transition to the new facilities. They hope to raise nearly half a million dollars toward the project and finance the remaining $2.5 to $3.5 million. With a strong and generous membership, no one is worried about whether this move is possible.*

RESOURCES

South Meridian entered Anderson's economic downturn in a position of strength. In the early seventies, the church was the leader in and beneficiary of a major revival that swept the community. Spreading from Asbury College in Kentucky, the religious fervor was intense. One man recalled, "We had a monumental revival when I was a child. . . . I was in elementary school, but I still remember it very well. It went on for, like, fifty days. Every night. And I remember when it started, because it began on a Sunday morning, and the service just never ended. Then it sort of spread and started affecting the whole city. . . . We had services at our church every evening for around fifty days. But every Sunday they had Unity Services for all the churches in the city, at Anderson High School."

The church, which had grown throughout the 1950s and 1960s, got an added boost from this revival. While there would be membership losses during the worst of the layoffs, the congregation could sustain those losses without threat to their survival.

The congregation was also sustained by its emphasis on generous giving and a strong tradition of tithing. Although not nearly everyone gives 10 percent of their household income, enough do to make this one of the most generous congregations we studied, able to maintain a professional staff of three ministers and a broad-based program of activities, despite the fact that there are very few wealthy people here, and many whose household incomes are less than luxurious. Almost half—47 percent—have household incomes under $35,000. But with a manageable debt (now paid off) and relatively new buildings, the congregation has weathered the community's economic woes with only minor (and temporary) cutbacks.

South Meridian was also blessed during this period with capable, stable leadership. The church certainly lost members to Anderson's recession, but not the younger generational cohort that East Lynn and First Baptist lost. Fewer of South Meridian's youth seem to have left for college, and fewer young adults left town in search of better opportunity. Times were hard for those who stayed, but their staying kept membership numbers relatively strong. In turn, as a strong church, South Meridian could attract and hold experienced pastors. The current pastor has been in place since 1987, and the previous pastor had served for ten years. In the inevitable pecking order of any denomination's career system, this would be seen as a good job. It would not carry the highest prestige—that belongs to Anderson's Park Place Church—but it is close to headquarters and clearly among the leading churches in the Church of God's "mecca." With high visibility, a comfortable salary, a medium-sized membership, and two associates, South Meridian is a plum appointment. Once on the scene, a pastor would find few material incentives for leaving.

As a Church of God congregation in the center of Church of God territory, South Meridian could also reach easily beyond its own resources into the network of people and institutions that are the stuff of denominational life—guest preachers and conference leaders, ample colleagues for the church's ministers to consult, various models at hand for how to "do church." The denomination itself is so strong in Anderson that Church of God ministers have their own ministerial association and are not part of any larger community association. That, of course, can be a problem. It leaves South Meridian relatively isolated from the ecumenical and social service institutions of the city. Still, the congregation managed to combine forces with others beyond the denomination to support a Crisis Pregnancy Center and a downtown rescue mission. While the resources of the Church of God network were usually more than sufficient, South Meridian could forge connections beyond the denomination when necessary.

Having paid off their building debt, the congregation also had a serviceable facility that created little drain on their budget. During the worst years of the economic crises, the congregation struggled to make their payments and to make do in that building. But by the early 1990s, they were starting to feel the pull of dreams about newer, more up-to-date facilities. Their numerous additions over the years had created a maze of corridors and steps that were hopelessly inaccessible to handicapped persons. The decor was distinctly 1960s, and parking was scattered over several small lots. The building was paid for and mostly met their needs, but they had ceased to feel proud of it or of the neighborhood in which it was located. Because they had ample resources of money and people, they were able to make the decision to move.

Theirs was not a decision born of desperation, but of aspirations long delayed and now possible to fulfill.

STRUCTURES OF AUTHORITY

As part of the Church of God movement (the term members prefer to *denomination*), South Meridian has a polity that is "congregational."[3] That is, members have control over their own personnel, buildings, and programs. They can call on the resources of the denomination, but the denomination does not dictate what they do. When they are without a pastor, for instance, a committee of church members is formed to search for a replacement. They may consult with denominational headquarters, but they are not constrained to follow that advice. They are free to seek the person whose skills and faith best match what they think they need.

Inside the church, business is conducted through a system of democratically elected committees on which staff have no official vote (although they certainly have influence). People in the church seem accustomed to planning and strategizing and organizing and have the skills to make things happen. This is a relatively well educated group, with 40 percent of the active members claiming a college diploma or more. Support groups and ministries are usually begun because a person or group of persons sees a need and has the vision and energy to organize to meet that need. Big decisions are brought to called church conferences (and there is an annual church business meeting), but the day-to-day business of the church can move fairly flexibly through committees and the church council. When a new need arises, the structures of decision making make response possible.

CULTURE

As an evangelical church in the Holiness tradition, South Meridian places its primary emphasis on individual piety. Prayer, Bible reading, witnessing, and attending worship are high priorities (see table 3.1). A Sunday school teacher reminded her class, "Arm yourself daily by doing morning devotions. Remember that the Lord does not see success the same as the world does. If we are to fulfill the job that he has planned for us, then we must find the success that he has planned for us. . . . Every morning, there is something special in there [the Bible], just waiting for us."

The congregation, in turn, places a high priority on preparing people for a world to come. Members view this world as a vale of tears to be endured, a time of temptation to be resisted. In a fall 1992 letter to his members, Pastor Gary Ausbun reflected on the deaths of two members and how much they would be missed. He said, "This is what our faith and our church is all about. This is what makes us different from other

Table 3.1. South Meridian Church of God, Anderson

Ideas and Priorities	
Christian practices rated "essential"	Living Christian values
	Prayer
	Bible reading
	Attendance at services
Ministries rated "very important" or	
"essential"	Service to the needy
	Preparation for the next world
	Helping members resist this world
	An evangelism program
	Encouragement of individual witnessing
Resources	
Average Sunday attendance	400
Annual operating budget (1992)	$347,000
Household incomes above $50,000	26%
College degrees or more	40%
Average age	48 years
Activities (beyond worship) participated	
in at least monthly	Bible study
	Fellowship
Relationship to the community	
Live ten minutes or less from the church	53%
New to the community in the last	
five years	11%
Ethnicity	100% European
Participate in civic & community	
activities more than once a month	38%

NOTE: Two hundred fourteen people responded to our survey, amounting to 53 percent of average Sunday attendance. This may be taken as a very accurate representation of all regular attenders.

social organizations. We are in the business of preparing persons for another life."

But this emphasis on the next world does not mean that South Meridian members are indifferent to this world. They are insistent that the daily living of one's Christian values is the most important mark of a Christian. And they are insistent that the most important priority for their church is serving people in need. To that end, the church has long supported a plethora of support groups and charitable ministries. These groups provide a prayerful environment in which to deal with cancer, being overweight, parenting problem teenagers, and the like. Meanwhile, Sunday school classes, fellowship groups, athletic teams, and women's mission circles provide a routine forum in which the needs of members are shared. A young woman in the church recounted one such time in her life. The most important group for her, she said, was "our Sunday school class—in their prayers, in their caring. I just felt that I was able to share real easily. . . . I've sometimes felt that I went through all that infertility treatment for a reason. . . . It's the hardest thing I can remember going through in my life. I had people ask me, 'Why aren't you mad at God?' because I wanted a child *so* badly. But I knew that it really wasn't God's fault that I wasn't able to conceive, and I thought that he would know when the best time is. And now looking back, I truly believe he knows." A man in the church recalled that when his family first arrived in Anderson, they had a very rough time economically. It was hard for him to share such things with others, but, he said, "I'm a prayer partner with one of the associate pastors here, and we get together every Wednesday morning, and we get together and talk about our families and problems and what we're thankful for, and have a time of sharing together." That time of sharing—whether with a prayer partner or in a Sunday school class—means both moral support and, often, concrete assistance. These church members simply know that it is their Christian duty to take care of each other.

That structure of caring can extend fairly quickly to new members, although the church has not been very intentional in making that happen. Visitors are usually greeted by ushers and often by people sitting near them. If they sign a visitor's card, they will get a letter from the pastor; but what happens after that depends on the mutual initiatives of the visitors and people who happen to connect with them. All of this, of course, takes place naturally when the visitor has come with a friend, neighbor, or family member—as is usually the case. When members bring their friends, as they are strongly encouraged to do, the making of connections is eased. Because so very few members live in the immediate neighborhood, those natural connections rarely extend into the streets surrounding the church. The congregation, as a result, increasingly finds no human connections to the particular place they come to worship.

Because there is no formal membership in the church (no official distinction between members and nonmembers), there is also no membership orientation process. Once a person has made it clear that they intend to be a regular participant, they receive a packet of information describing the church's activities and ministries, urging them to become even more involved. As soon as they learn enough to choose to become involved in any of the church's small groups, they also enter the congregation's circle of care.

That circle of care extends in some ways to people beyond the membership. This is a church that has a strong tradition of missions involvement. Mostly that means support for overseas missionaries, but the same compassion that leads them to care about the souls of people in Hong Kong or Hungary also makes them concerned about the souls and bodies of people closer to home. When greater economic need arose in the community, this tradition led to establishing a Social Needs Committee and restocking the Helping Hands Cupboard more often than usual. What they already knew to do helped to sustain dislocated members of the congregation, as well as people in the community.

Within the congregation, there is a culture of mutual support. In countless small groups, a climate of openness and sharing means that needs do not go unnoticed. Their confidence in the power of the Holy Spirit means that they expect things to change, expect healing and tangible comfort, expect to weather economic ills. Their convictions about what it means to live a Christian life make them likely to become partners in that healing and comfort.

SUMMARY

South Meridian faced Anderson's economic downturn from a position of strength. Their material and leadership resources were up to the challenge. Their structures of authority allowed them to make adjustments as necessary. And their central ideas and practices were well suited to the demands of the times. They did what they knew to do, and those forces of structural inertia kept their place in the community secure. People came to worship, sang and prayed, and—most of all—cared for each other. With their extensive system of small groups and the addition of a Social Needs Committee, the strains of economic hard times were absorbed so effortlessly that most people in the congregation do not think the downturn ever affected them. When the dust cleared, they were ready to move to a location more suited to their strong and growing sense of place in the community.

ESTABLISHING A NICHE

All three of these Anderson churches have, until recently, thought of themselves as belonging to a particular place. While not official parishes defined by a denomination, they nevertheless identified themselves with a section of their town. Similar parish-style congregations may be in a small town serving a particular segment of the local population, or in a suburb, surrounded by the sea of tract houses in which their members live, or in an urban ethnic enclave of traditional Catholics or Orthordox Jews. Changes in their immediate neighborhood and an increasingly scattered congregation may lead them to find a new place.

In contrast, niche congregations do not serve a specific locale. They reach beyond an immediate neighborhood to create an identity relatively independent of context. While many forces still bind congregation and community to each other, making parish-style congregations a recognizable part of the religious landscape, there are also strong forces creating a larger urban religious ecology with many choices not tied to residential neighborhood. The implications of a mobile, cosmopolitan culture, where congregational choice is the norm, make such specialized religious sorting more and more likely. Condemnations of "church shopping" abound, but there is good reason to believe that an increased range of religious alternatives may actually enhance overall religious participation rates by raising the likelihood that matches between individual commitments and institutional programs will be possible for a greater range of a diverse population.[4] The community that is operative for any given congregation, then, may not fall neatly within geographic boundaries, being defined instead by the social niche it has established.

Although the future is still uncertain for both Holman United Methodist and Incarnation Episcopal, both appear headed for such a niche identity. Both are still struggling with how to respond to their changed neighborhoods, but their existing, distinctive identities prepare them well for establishing themselves independent of their immediate contexts. For Incarnation, the context is an economically diverse, but largely distressed, Atlanta neighborhood. For Holman, the context is the West Adams neighborhood, a part of South Central Los Angeles that is increasingly full of Latino and Asian immigrants.

Holman United Methodist Church, West Adams: African American Community Leader

If the congregations in the West Adams neighborhood of Los Angeles had not noticed that their community was changing, the events of April 1992 certainly provided a wake-up call. As burning and rage filled the streets around them in the aftermath of the Rodney King verdict, whatever sense of comfort and stability they may have earlier enjoyed quite literally went up in smoke. In the days following, Holman mobilized its feeding ministry to provide immediate assistance to thousands. But in the weeks and months that followed, they and other congregations that had traditionally served the African American residents of this community were faced with new dilemmas. In many ways, Holman United Methodist is typical of both the neighborhood's history and its current dilemmas. Telling this congregation's story will make the issues more clear.

Near the end of World War II a tiny group of black Methodists gathered in a backyard to talk about the need for a church on the west side of Los Angeles. As in cities all over the country, African Americans were arriving by the thousands, drawn by California's rapidly expanding wartime economy. In February 1945, the group met for the first time for worship, and over the next two years moved from rented location to rented location. Finally in 1947, they purchased a former synagogue building, officially took the name Holman United Methodist (after the district superintendent at that time), and received L. L. White as their pastor.

The years that followed are recalled by longtime members as a time of struggle. Theirs was the first black congregation to purchase property in the West Adams area. The racially exclusive covenants that were in place had not yet been ruled unconstitutional, and white residents made sure obstacles stood in the way of the purchase. But the congregation saw the old Pepperdine estate on West Adams, which the church purchased in 1951, as a gift from God. The church added a sanctuary on the back of the mansion and soon filled it with the young black professionals who were flocking into the city. In 1958, a new sanctuary was built next to the mansion, and in 1967, a second new building for classrooms and offices. By the 1960s, Holman was the place where anyone who was anyone in the black community wanted to be seen. One man who grew up in the church recalled, "It was very big. It was packed, standing room only every service. . . . We were the church. . . . We had the doctors and attorneys. . . . It was packed, and on special days like Christmas and Mother's Day, if you didn't come early you couldn't get in." Other black churches had slowly moved into this area of South Central Los Angeles, but Holman was the biggest and most prestigious.

In 1974, Pastor White resigned after twenty-seven years of service to become a district superintendent and later to begin a new congregation. Some of his longtime supporters left to join that church, but the majority of the congregation stayed to welcome James M. Lawson as the new pastor. Most people agree that the church has taken on a more activist role in the community since Reverend Lawson came. Given his history, that was to be expected. A trusted and visible associate of Martin Luther King, Jr., Lawson had been in the inner circle of the civil rights movement. Even today, he continues to be a respected teacher of nonviolence, called on when national issues are at stake.

Reverend Lawson preaches twice each Sunday in Holman's striking sanctuary. The entire seating area (with room for at least five hundred worshippers) is surrounded by sliding-glass doors, the walls above studded with brightly colored glass in the shape of crosses, circles, triangles, and the like. The effect is one of openness and light. While a sense of awe pervades the place, it is never a true "sanctuary," a place to withdraw from the world, since the world is never really shut out. Behind the altar, a scrim of glass beads creates a backdrop. They can be rotated to create different color effects as the seasons of the liturgical year pass. A banner and a simple cross complete the decoration.

Uniformed ushers, both men and women, are posted down each aisle of the church, greeting and seating people as they arrive in their Sunday finest (including several lovely fur coats and a number of stylish hats). About 350 persons attend the 8:30 service, with another 200 or so at eleven o'clock. The later service tends to draw people who have been coming the longest, while the earlier one is more youthful and enthusiastic. The service follows United Methodist tradition, and everything moves like clockwork, both in the service that is broadcast on the radio and in the one that is not. There are numerous responsive readings and unison prayers, mostly printed in the bulletin. The ambiance of the service is dignified; rarely is there any clapping during or after musical numbers, and almost no one says Amen. The large choir sings from a split loft—men on one side, women on the other. It has a justified reputation as an outstanding ensemble, especially noted for the dramatic, technically demanding arrangements of Negro spirituals it presents in an annual concert attended by people from all over the city. The choir is occasionally joined by other instrumentalists—a brass player, a guest violinist, a bass and drums duo, and the like. Several people told us how important the worship service is for them—its inspirational music and its moments of quiet reflection.

Each service includes an extended announcement period in which concerns like deaths and illnesses of members are noted, community activities and issues emphasized, visits of political and religious dignitaries announced, and people urged to become involved and vote. Other activities mentioned might include a vigil to be held on the site of a random shooting or an upcoming African heritage event. In addition, the church's financial needs are noted.

The sermons remind Holman's parishioners that the Kingdom of God is both now and not yet. Christ has come and the Spirit is present with us, but we hope for the time when God will finally reign in peace and justice. The Christian's task is to pull the world toward the light of God's kingdom, becoming like Christ in the world in order to transform it. "This is not about struggling through this life in hope of a better life beyond," preaches Associate Sandy Olewine. "It is about this world. It is about going into the broken places with faith." Pastor Lawson often emphasizes the necessary relationship between spirituality and doing God's work in the world. Without prayer and Bible study, the sacrifices demanded in the pursuit of justice are not possible.

As the services end, people disperse rather quickly, making their way to expensive cars in the newly constructed church parking lots. They will return to homes scattered all over the Los Angeles area; relatively few live nearby. A small number (less than a hundred children and fewer adults) attend the church school classes held between the two services. During the week, several small groups of adults will gather for various social activities or Bible studies or to plan the church's involvement in the community.

Pursuing justice in Los Angeles often involves the people of Holman in politics. They hosted a debate between two city supervisor candidates as well as a forum on the Christopher Commission Report (which called for reforms in the Los Angeles Police Department following the 1992 uprisings). In 1994, on the eve of South African elections, they hosted an event for one of Nelson Mandela's closest aides, continuing a connection to South Africa long present in the *congregation. Pursuing justice also involves them with the physical needs of their neighbors. They have had a feeding ministry for many years, and after the uprisings they distributed food to more than five thousand people.*

The events of April 1992 caused them to rethink their church's role in the community. Many long-complacent members were impressed with the need to volunteer their energies toward making a difference in the neighborhood and beyond, and a revitalized political action group was formed within the congregation. Both they and the Council on Ministries have been pushing the church to define more clearly just what its mission is to be. In addition, a Visioning Task Force has generated a good deal of energy as it set out goals for the church's ministry, especially its use of its new multipurpose building.

The Christopher Commission forum was one of the first events to be held in the congregation's newest building. In the fall of 1992, the church moved into a 24,000-square-foot multipurpose building on the site of the Pepperdine mansion it originally occupied. Getting permission to build was a challenge. Preservationists (mostly white) did not want the old building destroyed and fought the church to save it. But church members turned out in force at the hearings and persuaded city officials to let them build. Now they are immensely proud of what they have constructed—offices, chapel, class and meeting rooms, state-of-the-art choir room, library, parlor, and especially the fully equipped kitchen and large fellowship hall. That hall is increasingly the site for African American community events, including the 1994 ecumenical breakfast during Martin Luther King Week, a citywide gathering of (primarily) the black and Jewish communities.

Holman has always thought of itself as a center for black community activities and concern. The new building is making that even more the case. As the church settles into a new pattern of activities made possible by this new space, members are also reassessing what it means for their church to be a community center. Just which community or communities will they serve in the years ahead?

RESOURCES

With twenty-seven hundred members and a parking lot full of Mercedes cars every Sunday, Holman seems the picture of a comfortably endowed congregation. They have both numbers and affluence on their side. Still, appearances do not tell the whole story. There is, in fact, no endowment—only the routine cash contributions of members. Over one-third of our respondents did report household incomes of over $50,000, but an equal number reported incomes under $35,000 (see table 3.2). The fur coats and expensive cars here do not necessarily indicate a uniform affluence. While many in the congregation are indeed very well off, others, mostly older members, are not. Most of the younger members (under forty) have comfortable, growing salaries, and nearly half of those in their forties and fifties have achieved in-

Table 3.2. Holman United Methodist Church, West Adams

Ideas and priorities	
Christian practices rated "essential"	Living Christian values
	Prayer
	Attendance at services
Ministries rated "very important" or "essential"	Service to the needy
	Cooperation with other groups for community improvement
	Encouraging good citizenship
	Sponsoring social action groups
	Outreach to unchurched people
Resources	
Average Sunday attendance	600
Annual operating budget (1993)	$695,000
Household incomes above $50,000	37%
College degrees or more	64%
Average age	53 years
Activities (beyond worship) participated in at least monthly	None
Relationship to the community	
Live ten minutes or less from the church	30%
New to the community in the last five years	5%
Ethnicity	90% African American
	5% Caribbean
Participate in civic & community activities more than once a month	55%

NOTE: Two hundred six people responded to our survey, amounting to approximately 34 percent of average Sunday attendance. This may be taken as a good representation of all regular attenders.

comes over $65,000. In contrast, median family income in the West Adams neighborhood is $19,767.

Many people at Holman, then, have ample monetary resources, but not nearly all of them give substantial amounts to the church. Indeed, with weekly attendance at between six and seven hundred, nearly three-quarters of the members are absent on any given Sunday. There is good reason to believe that our two hundred survey respondents represent most of the church's faithful givers. The amounts they report giving—an average of $150 per month—account for half the church's actual operating budget of just under $700,000. That leaves the other twenty-five hundred members to make up the other half. In 1993, Holman took in an additional $350,000 in building-fund receipts and $130,000 in other income (mostly brought in by the choir). Still, the church ran a deficit of $54,000, made up by borrowing against special funds and not paying $92,000 in apportionments to the United Methodist Church. During the fall, the church's leaders had wondered whether they would be able to pay the bills. Given the stark outlook then, the final manageable deficit came as a relief.

The new multipurpose building has cost the church $4.5 million, straining its resources in all sorts of ways. The extended period of fund-raising wore on some people's patience (as did some of the white fund-raising consultants sent in by the United Methodist district). Planning and overseeing construction stretched an already reduced staff to capacity and beyond. Normal church functions were sometimes neglected, and construction work dislodged the feeding ministry. There were predictable cost overruns and errors in construction. Throughout the long process, then, there were costs in money, time, goodwill, and other projects foregone. Now that the building is finished, members who have persevered are enjoying the rewards of having facilities for things they would like to do. Having tied up so much of their time, money, and energy in the building, they also now have those resources to reinvest.

One of the first things that struck me in talking with the people at Holman was the extent to which their sense of mission and their dreams for the future were tied to this building. Discussions about what the church ought to be doing with itself quickly became discussions about what it ought to be doing with the new building. After long feeling constrained by lack of adequate facilities, many of the congregation's leaders have found that the richness of this facility has unleashed their imaginations.

Those leaders and their imaginations are among Holman's greatest resources. The skills and knowledge present in the congregation are very impressive. Over half the respondents to our survey are in professional or managerial occupations, and nearly half (44 percent) have at least some education beyond college. The congregation's most active members are young adults in their thirties, along with an experienced cadre of members in their fifties. When these people gather in the Council on Ministries or in a planning retreat, they bring professional skills and experience in problem solving.

They also bring a vast network of contacts in the political and business world. They know people in city hall and in the legislature and in dozens of city and state agencies. They are well connected and active in their professions and able to call on the resources of colleagues and employers for projects Holman plans. When I attended a meeting of the political action committee (HOPE, for Holman Organization for Political Empowerment), members were planning an event in honor of

Patrick Lekota, African National Congress (ANC) executive committee member and close associate of Nelson Mandela. There would be music and food and a general celebration of Holman's African heritage and connections. Lekota wanted to come to Holman to express his gratitude for the support of churches and pastors whose civil rights activities have been both example and direct support for South Africa. Jim Lawson, it seems, is well known within the ANC. As the group planned, nearly every detail involved contacts with other churches, schools, businesses, and especially other civil rights organizations. Each person around the table (fewer than a dozen of them, at that) mentioned people who ought to be involved and people they would be willing to call for help. It was a remarkable example of the potential power of a few people willing and able to mobilize the resources in their large networks of involvement in the community.

No one, of course, has a larger network than Lawson himself. His longtime involvement in national and local civil rights causes has put him in touch with countless organizations and leaders whose presence and message are often brought to Holman. Having Jesse Jackson or Desmond Tutu in Holman's pulpit is almost routine. Hosting citywide events or taking the lead on a community project follows naturally out of the position Lawson occupies in the civil rights community. He brings to the church visibility and vision, constant encouragement to dream about how the world might be better and what can be done to make it so. Of course, his position carries costs for Holman, as well. When he is involved in city and national causes, he is not present in the pulpit, as an administrator, or for the routine pastoral care of his parish. Holman's members seem to think he has achieved an acceptable balance between his outside work and his pastoral duties, but they also recognize that they miss his leadership when he is not there.

Holman's two associate ministers and choir director are also highly valued. One active layperson noted that Sandy Olewine is a real asset. She has high energy, is very able to communicate with the youth, and is a capable administrator. Not long out of seminary, Reverend Olewine, a white woman, had been active on race issues in her first pastoral assignment and in 1989 was tapped for Holman as a result. The choir director is the staff person with the longest tenure and gets considerable respect as head of the congregation's well-recognized ensemble. The second associate is Rev. Okechukwu Ogbonnaya, a native of South Africa and recent graduate of Claremont School of Theology. He is the second African associate minister the church has had, a fact that has helped strengthen members' sense of connection to that continent and to their heritage. This African connection, along with Lawson's civil rights involvement, clearly establishes this congregation's identity as a place where the traditions and concerns of African Americans are foremost.

STRUCTURES OF AUTHORITY

As part of the United Methodist connectional system, Holman comes under the authority of the bishop of the Los Angeles Conference and a district superintendent. Reverend Lawson serves Holman at their discretion, and it is a board of the conference that sets the amount due the denomination in apportionments. It is the conference that ultimately owns the buildings Holman occupies, as well. On paper, Holman is quite thoroughly dependent on this outside denominational authority.

In practice, the denominational connection is much more lightly worn. The conference shows little inclination to move one of Holman's pastors if neither the pastor nor the church wants that move to happen. Nor has the conference yet begun to agitate over Holman's non-payment of apportionments. Indeed, Holman is still able to get special conference grants for innovative programs the conference wants to see happen. Various Holman members serve on denominational committees, and they report that the congregation has the well-earned goodwill of others in the conference.

That goodwill does not translate into carte blanche, however. For several years, Holman has asked for an Asian or Hispanic associate minister as a way of beginning to build bridges to the changing neighborhood. That request has not yet been honored. Whether because the conference itself does not have the necessary resources or because officials have decided to use those resources otherwise, this situation illustrates the degree to which Holman's own sense of mission can be limited by the actions of the larger structures of which it is a part.

Inside Holman, decisions are made in a labyrinth of committees and task forces. When faced with a problem or challenge, the church's usual response is to form a committee, have a planning meeting, and produce a report. The maze of committees is sometimes bewildering even to people who are active in it. One man complained that he felt like there were too many hoops, that one could never get anything done because it had to go through too many committees. Those committees, however, not the congregation itself, make decisions. Once a year, reports on all the church's activities and decisions are made to the district superintendent in an all-church Charge Conference. The annual conference ratifies important budgetary and personnel decisions, in addition to hearing reports. It is the primary point where the official work of the congregation and the structure of the larger Church intersect.

For the most part, Holman's roster of committees follows the prescriptions in the United Methodist *Book of Discipline:* church and society, religion and race, education, evangelism, and the like. In addition, special task forces occasionally spring up. HOPE is one of those. When people see a need and an opportunity, they are free to organize to respond. There are also an official lay leader, a staff-parish relations committee, and various officers to tend to the administration of the church. They, along with representatives of the usual church organizations—church school, United Methodist Women (UMW), and the like—serve on an administrative council of more than thirty members. It was recently decided that a subset of those members should form a Council on Ministries to deal especially with questions of mission. However, at the meeting of the Council on Ministries I attended, the members were not altogether clear which council's meeting they were attending. The functions and membership of each had not yet been fully clarified.

When one reaches past the official structure to look for how things get done, the role of the pastor becomes more apparent. He (along with the associates) is certainly involved in guiding the official councils and committees, but he also plays a critical role in mobilizing resources for the projects he wants to see done. While he describes himself as a very democratically oriented leader, active lay people note that he also likes to be involved and that important church business needs his support. Those same active lay people worry that too many of the church's members are uninformed and uninvolved. Although the congregation produces a weekly newsletter, some fear that its format and appearance do not attract the attention of many. As the front page of the national "United Methodist Reporter," it comes attached to four pages of national church news and one page of news from the western jurisdiction of the Church. Much of what is happening in committees, task forces, and other small groups is not reflected there, and major church issues are primarily addressed from the point of view of the staff. As one member of the Council on Ministries noted, the congregation needs a way to "blow its own horn." There are so many things happening—both inside the congregation and in its work in the community—that few members really know about or come to take for granted.

Holman's way of doing business does not easily invite broad participation, but it can provide the spaces for individual and small-group initiatives. The process of gaining support for such efforts is likely to involve the influence of the pastor and a series of committee meetings for approval. Sometimes new energy and initiative are simply channeled into existing structures, but there is also room for new ones to be invented. Sometimes the support of the denomination is also sought, and occasionally the denomination's lack of support is critical. As the members sometimes joke, they really are very Methodist—lots of committees and lots of meetings, plans, and reports.

CULTURE

But Holman is also very African American. Members think of themselves as leaders, activists, and spokespeople for African Americans in Los Angeles, as a rallying point for the community. Increasingly, they also think about the actual African content to their heritage, and they have begun to maintain ties to African culture and politics. They think of themselves as preservers and exponents of the African American religious heritage, as well. In all of this, they see themselves as stewards—people to whom much has been given and of whom much will be required.

Their commitment to spirituals, for instance, tells us a good deal about their sense of identity. In an earlier day, singing spirituals roused some controversy among Holman's members; some worried that spirituals were undignified and would be used to stereotype them as ignorant and backward. But others argued that spirituals are central to what it has meant to be African American, that the songs embody a religious heritage of which they can be justly proud. Holman's accomplished choir performs this music in a manner to please the most demanding and sophisticated of musical connoisseurs. The emphasis on spirituals, then, embodies the congregation's concerns with preserving the African American religious heritage and with doing so in a way befitting a respected community leader.

Issues facing African Americans in Los Angeles are foremost among the concerns that shape Holman's sense of mission. Whether it is a question of police misconduct or random street violence or continuing discrimination and economic disadvantage, Holman's members are individually and collectively aware. They hear it from the pulpit, and they read it in the books and periodicals they receive at home and at work. They use Holman as a base for organizing responses and for connecting with other community organizations. They raise money for scholarships, participate in vigils at the sites of killings, and host forums in which politicians and government officials are quizzed and held accountable. In addition, the new building makes possible the hosting of large community events—the Martin Luther King Week ecumenical breakfast or the visit of Patrick Lekota, for instance.

When they talk about these issues and concerns, they do so in the context of God's work in the world. They are convinced that the power of love is greater than the power of hate, that God is in the process of transforming the world. Even when evil powers seem to prevail, there is strength to endure. A typical prayer contained these lines: "Let not the evils of these times and this society break our spirit. May our journey transform these days into Your day. Amen."

In all of this, they are combining "civic" and "activist" mission orientations.[5] As a civic church, Holman calls on its members to be good citizens, to work for the betterment of the community, to celebrate and uphold the community in which they live. As an activist church, it is attempting to change the world, to alter the basic structures of life, especially for African Americans. The members, in fact, want their church to do lots of things. Those who completed our survey rated as "very important" or "essential" a long list of ministries, including cooperating with other groups for the betterment of the community, sponsoring social action groups in the congregation, serving the needy, reaching out to the unchurched, and encouraging good citizenship. Their ideal church is a very active and involved place.

That activist orientation sometimes raises issues that go beyond the African American community. At one Council on Ministries meeting, a member of the council gave an impassioned speech about the need to reach out beyond "our kids." She asked why the church was not tutoring Spanish-speaking kids, why so many programs for church kids do not include kids from the neighborhood, why kids that come for something like the UMW's Christmas party for children of prisoners are not back for other activities, why people from the church are not providing transportation to people like that who could not come otherwise, why everyone in the church is not learning Spanish. She worried that the church was losing its vitality, was too satisfied with itself. She was clearly not alone in her sentiments; fellow members of the council urged her on with "Amen" and "That's right." No one seemed to have a concrete plan, but many of the council members seemed to see her call as a legitimate challenge.

Those sentiments, however, must struggle against the weight of accumulated church tradition and existing patterns of doing mission. Holman's activism occurs in three organizational modes. First, the church is represented by its pastor. James Lawson, as a visible leader on civil rights issues, often speaks out publicly and lends his influence to efforts to organize protest and reform. Second, the congregation builds and joins coalitions that include other religious and political groups, the Southern Christian Leadership Conference, for example. Individuals from the church are recruited to provide organizational and front-line energies for a variety of efforts. And third, multiple small groups in the church undertake projects. Sometimes these are one-time or occasional efforts incidental to the usual purposes of the group. For instance, the United Methodist Women's groups or various social groupings may take on an annual effort to raise money for scholarships or work with an AIDS hospice. Other times, the group itself exists to carry out efforts at outreach and change.

All of these efforts exist in a relatively decentralized system that depends largely on individual and group initiative, not on an overall congregational strategy. After the uprisings, for instance, a number of people were shocked into a new level of concern. That concern got mobilized into HOPE. Their projects have focused largely on developing awareness of Holman's African identity and roots, not on specific responses to the diversity and tension in South Central.

What the members know very well how to do, then, is to organize political and charitable and civic efforts addressed to the needs of African Americans. Existing networks and resources and ideas—existing strategies of action—make these responses sensible and routine. Because this congregation is, in fact, a recognized leader in such actions, it can draw a constituency from all over the metropolitan region. Almost always, people first come to Holman because someone they know (not always a Holman member) recommended the place. This pattern of recruitment means that new constituencies are unlikely to be brought in. So long as the church recruits primarily along existing lines of relationship, the current constituency will replicate itself. As a result, they are, in effect, a niche congregation, rather than a neighborhood one. Their mission statement echoes what is tacitly acknowledged by the congregation: Their first priority is to be an African American congregation.

Holman members actually find their immediate neighbors rather mysterious. Almost everyone I talked with said that they did not know much about who was now in the neighborhood, that they were pretty sure that their neighbors were different from themselves and had different needs, but that they were not quite sure what those needs might be. Many members, like the woman who spoke at the Council on Ministries meeting, feel called to include the needs of the neighborhood in Holman's ministry; but such a move would require some very intentional development of new patterns of action, learning of new skills—literally new languages—and acquiring of new networks. It seems to me unlikely that Holman will encourage such an investment. Its current identity, constituency, and patterns of ministry are sufficient to sustain its place serving those who wish to be advocates for the African American community and stewards of its cultural traditions.

To speak of such activism and cultural preservation might sound to some ears like an agenda as easily pursued in a secular organization as in a congregation. A secular approach however, would not adequately encompass the way Holman's members understand and live their commitments. Sociologists are used to asking people about how religion influences their everyday lives, but when I asked people at Holman that question, they seemed puzzled, unable to answer. I soon discovered that their puzzlement was not an indicator of a faith that was irrelevant to their lives outside church. It rather had to do with the seamlessness of faith, as they experienced it. They could not talk about how faith informed their work; work and faith were inseparable. One young woman said, "So I found myself in a situation where the thing that I loved to do most, which is public policy, could also take shape in my daily religious life. And I found that to be very powerful." Another added, "I find a lot of compatibility, always have over the years, between my professional choice and my church life . . . it really does all revolve around issues of social justice." Pastor Lawson often preaches about the necessary relationship between faith and social action, between piety and working for social justice. At least some of his parishioners live that connection. They have selected jobs that let them work toward a better world. Some of them go in early to spend time in prayer before work begins. Some bring co-workers to events at church. But most of all, both their work and their church involvement are expressions of who they are. Their individual vocational lives are very much an extension of the mission of Holman United Methodist Church.

Not nearly everyone who belongs to Holman, however, is so thoroughly integrated into the life and mission of the congregation. On any given Sunday, around two thousand members of the church are not there. Some come sporadically, some only rarely. Some are fairly new and have not yet found a place for themselves. Many of those I talked with described their involvement in the church as coming very gradually. For a fairly long period, they visited the church, keeping it at arm's length. In some instances they had been hurt in other churches and were not yet ready to make a full commitment to a new congregation. In other instances, they had been highly committed somewhere else and wanted a rest. In still other instances, they were coming from another tradition and wanted time to decide whether this was a place they could find comfortable.

Those I talked with had all subsequently made the move into active participation, but obviously not everyone has followed that path. Nor do the structures of the congregation particularly encourage it. People who present themselves for membership are welcomed in on the spot, at the end of a worship service. The congregation turns to the back of the hymnal to read the vows of membership, and that's that. There is a new-members class, but it is not required and elicits only minimal participation. Our researchers, in fact, never found a class in session; on the day I attended, I had to ask several people before I found anyone who knew where it was meeting. Two new members attended along with me.

Even those who come fairly regularly may be uninvolved in any activity beyond worship. Those who responded to our survey are probably among Holman's most active members, but fewer than half ever participate in any social action ministry; almost half never participate in any Bible study; and over half participate in fellowship activities no more than a few times a year. There are "double ring" clubs for couples, a couple of Sunday school groups, and the UMW circles, but they involve barely 10 percent of the church's population. Holman has, then, neither any intentional program of recruitment nor any systematic effort to integrate its new members. Maintaining arm's length is easy to do, and many of the congregation's members obviously take this option.

SUMMARY

The question of how to respond to a neighborhood that is no longer home to most church members is still an open one at Holman. Voices within the congregation call for a more intentional strategy of ministry to immigrants and others in the immediate community. Still, the weight of evidence seems to indicate that Holman will continue to do what it knows to do: be an African American congregation speaking to and for that more dispersed community. Because it has metropolitan visibility already, it can pull in members from all over the region and need not depend on the immediate neighborhood for constituents. It will be a niche congregation.

While Holman is a remarkably active church, it accomplishes its ministries through the efforts of only a handful of its members. The great majority is relatively absent, gives little money, and holds the congregation at arm's length, a situation that results in far fewer available resources for the congregation than might be imagined, based on the size and affluence of its membership. The new building has strained Holman's resources to the limit. It has also unleashed the imaginations of many members, who are envisioning how the building can further establish Holman's place in the community and provide space for expanded ministries. Making those dreams a reality, however, would seem to depend on finding ways to increase the personpower available to the congregation. Only as the church is able to increase expected levels of commitment—and provide the structures to foster and sustain that commitment—can it expect to increase substantially its involvement in the community.

Across the country, in Atlanta, another African American neighborhood has gone through its share of changes in recent years, the result not of immigrants of different cultural heritages but of economic fluctuations. What was once a uniformly blue-collar neighborhood has become both poorer and richer than it used to be, creating space for greater diversity in the kinds of congregations located there.

Episcopal Church of the Incarnation, Southwest Atlanta: In Search of a "Signature Ministry"

If you have a mental image of Episcopal Church Women, the ECW members at Episcopal Church of the Incarnation in southwest Atlanta are likely to violate it. In the first place, most are African American. But in the second place, this is a church that prides itself on not being "stuffy" Episcopalian; and surely the ECW's trip to Dollywood, Dolly Parton's Great Smokies theme park, would prove the congregation right in that assessment. To be fair, the ECW also plans more traditional trips—to the theater for instance—and raises money for charitable causes. Like many other things about Church of the Incarnation, the church women's organization manages to hold a number of seemingly contradictory forces together. Its African American members have to explain to their friends why they go to an Episcopal church, and its white members have to explain why they go to a predominantly black one. There are evangelicals and charismatics in the congregation, along with old-fashioned liberals. But they are all held together by their commitment to this congregation and to the liturgy that is performed here each week. Their story is told by our research team member Daphne Wiggins.

The area surrounding the Church of the Incarnation was, before the mid-1960s, predominantly white. A few blacks lived on nearby streets, but the apartment complex right next door to Incarnation was all white (with no children allowed). Today, the area is 95 percent black, and the economic picture surrounding Incarnation is distinctly mixed; within a mile of the church one finds both abject poverty and comfortable affluence.

As the population changed, so did the churches. A large new independent church, Hillside International Truth Center, was built across the street from Incarnation. Many other churches changed hands as white congregations moved out, and black congregations moved in, many from the West End area. Others, like Incarnation, stayed but were transformed.

The Church of the Incarnation is located on Cascade Road in the heart of southwest Atlanta. Approaching the church from the east, one passes through a small commercial strip. Just beyond an apartment complex, a long driveway appears. Across the street, a vacant lot is overgrown with brush and trees. The church, sitting about a hundred feet back from the street, is not immediately visible. The drive leads past the building to a modest parking lot at the rear. (There are lockable gates on this driveway, and a steel fence all around the property.) From there one can see the Sunday school rooms that face the parking area and a play yard with slides, jungle gyms, and the like. Beside the main church building are two small temporary classroom buildings. For several years, until 1993, the Progressive Academy ran an Afrocentric elementary school in this space.

The one-story brick church building makes a square around an inner courtyard. Entering from the rear, as most members do, one passes through the parish hall, goes past the nursery, the vestry room, and the pastor's office, and finally arrives at the narthex. Here, and throughout the church, the walls are covered with pictures from different cultures, depicting Jesus as they see him.

The church has occupied this building since 1958, but only since about 1973 has it had a predominantly black congregation. It was established as a mission church in 1882 and in 1896 built its first building, on Lee Street, becoming the third Episcopal parish in the Atlanta area. The church grew steadily over the next half century under the leadership of just four priests. The congregation was noted for its ministry to servicemen from nearby Fort McPherson, especially during World War II.

Following the war, a boom in births and church attendance and the expansion of the suburbs resulted in further growth for this middle-class, white congregation. They decided to follow suburban growth west (leaving behind an increasingly black residential area in West End) and relocate to their present property on Cascade Road. However, the congregation had hardly moved in before the racial transition began here as well, along with white flight. By 1981, the diocese recorded 121 parish members, down from 618 in 1961. From accounts of members, many of the remaining few were not even in active attendance. Membership was undoubtedly not helped during this period by the two successive priests who left under a cloud of suspicion. In addition, Church of the Resurrection was opened in nearby College Park, and many white Incarnation members who remained in the neighborhood transferred there.

The appointment of Father Kim Dreisbach in 1973 marked a new phase in the parish's life. A proven social activist, Dreisbach was ready to lead the church to full integration. That intention perhaps showed most in his efforts to help Incarnation develop new traditions and symbols reflecting its members' diverse cultures. Many of the traditions practiced today, as well as much of the art on the walls, can be traced to Father Dreisbach's initiative.

Many current black members remember first coming to the church under Father Dreisbach. Some transferred from St. Paul's, the city's historically black Episcopal parish, because they preferred a smaller, more intimate parish. Members recollect the transition from predominantly white to predominantly black as nonproblematic. Black members say they were surprised at the openness and warmness of the white parishoners; they assumed that the white members who stayed were committed to the church regardless of the race of its occupants.

Father Dreisbach was followed by two more white priests, and by the time the second of them was chosen, many members were beginning to resent this pattern. The parish was, by the 1980s, overwhelmingly black, although a sizable number of long-term white members remained. Finally, in 1990, Father Rick Britton, the parish's first black priest, arrived. Since then, attendance, mem-

bership, and giving have increased. *Sunday attendance often exceeds 130. And black members are more thoroughly involved in all aspects of church life, now finally assuming key leadership roles. They are sometimes reminded by the remaining 10 percent who are white that "this is not a black church." But black and white are united in their love of the liturgy. These parishoners are loyally Episcopalian—they don't want a Baptist or Pentecostal service. Even those influenced by the charismatic movement continue to love the ritual, the prayers, the feeling of community that distinguish this congregation from others.*

As people enter the sanctuary each Sunday, they face a striking cross over the altar, with new stained-glass windows along the right wall and the old stained glass from their Lee Street church along the left. Most of those arriving genuflect in the aisle, facing the cross, before they enter a pew and pull out the kneeler for their silent prayer before the service begins. Soon the organ strikes up a brief prelude before the choir processes in. Father Britton, from the back of the church, announces the processional hymn, and the congregation rises and starts singing. "I Love Thy Kingdom" or "Rejoice Ye Pure in Heart" are among the favorites, but occasionally the hymn is something like "We're Marching to Zion."

The opening part of the service proceeds in standard Episcopal fashion. The sermon usually lasts between fifteen and twenty minutes, weaving all the day's texts into messages that emphasize moral decision making and Christian duty. After a period of confession, the congregation stands to exchange the peace. At this point, the mood shifts from solemnity to gaiety. People move around, hug, chat, shake hands, and welcome newcomers. After about three minutes one of the acolytes rings the bells to draw the congregation together again, and Father Britton, from the floor level, welcomes visitors and gives the announcements. The communion service that follows is from the Book of Common Prayer, *but several newer songs from the special music booklet are inserted along the way. As the service concludes, Father Britton, again at the rear of the church, pronounces the benediction.*

Immediately people pour out into the aisles. Many then head for the parish hall for coffee hour, but no one eats until Father Britton comes in and blesses the refreshments. Sometimes a table is set up for tending to various items of church business or mission opportunities (getting pledge envelopes or a directory; signing up for Habitat for Humanity or for a finance workshop; purchasing calendars, Girl Scout cookies, or imports from an African congregation; solicitations for Episcopal Church Women functions, and so on). This activity does not, however, disrupt the chit chat, as people ask about each other's families, work, fraternity events, and the like. Church is usually over at noon, but the coffee hour does not disperse until around 12:30. Members exit into a neighborhood that increasingly challenges them to ask just what they should be doing as a church, but they leave having been strengthened and inspired by the worship and fellowship of Incarnation.

147

RESOURCES

A relatively small congregation, Incarnation has struggled during the last twenty years to reestablish itself in the wake of a community transition from white to black. In the booming fifties, it was a white suburban congregation bursting at the seams; but by 1980 almost all those white members were gone, and the church was a shadow of its former self. Today a regular attendance of around one hundred, half of them under fifty, is a real sign of hope. Almost half those now in the congregation have come in the last ten years (and not nearly all those were new to Atlanta). At least some people are again seeking out this black Episcopal church in the heart of Southwest Atlanta.

Those coming are upper-middle-class professionals with high levels of education. Half the people who responded to our survey reported household incomes above $50,000; almost one-quarter said their incomes were over $80,000 (see table 3.3). Fewer than one in five lack a college degree, and over half (58 percent) have some graduate work beyond college. An equal number (58 percent) are in professional or managerial occupations. While small in numbers, Incarnation's members have ample resources at their disposal, both the money and the skills to make things happen.

Incarnation's building offers advantages and disadvantages for the church. Probably its greatest disadvantage is its low visibility. Even if a person is intentionally looking for it, the hidden driveway and set-back location make it hard to spot. Once spotted, who occupies it or how one should enter is unclear. People in the neighborhood are not likely to wander in while "church shopping." Indeed, because the church is not tied to a traditional African American denomination, many neighborhood residents may assume they are not welcome. Still, the Cascade Road neighborhood is improving, with new grocery stores and banks going up, and new housing just three or four miles west continues to draw African American professionals into the church's vicinity. With minor improvements in visibility, Incarnation's location could become more of an asset.

The building Incarnation occupies, while not large, is adequate for members' needs. They have no debt or major repairs facing them. Building expenses require about one-quarter of their budget. After a 1993 remodeling, the fellowship hall is suitable for dinners and other events for both the church and the larger community. And the artwork and stained glass collected over the last twenty years create an atmosphere inside the building in which God's presence in diverse cultures is celebrated. The classroom buildings behind the church provide space either for rental or other uses, should the church so choose. Until the spring of 1993, those buildings had in fact brought in rental income

Table 3.3. Episcopal Church of the Incarnation, Southwest Atlanta

Ideas and priorities	
Christian practices rated "essential"	Living Christian values
Ministries rated "very important" or "essential"	Service to the needy
Resources	
Average Sunday attendance	100
Annual operating budget (1992)	$175,000
Household incomes above $50,000	50%
College degrees or more	81%
Average age	51 years
Activities (beyond worship) participated in at least monthly	None
Relationship to the community	
Live ten minutes or less from the church	31%
New to the community in the last five years	22%
Ethnicity	77% African American 15% European
Participate in civic & community activities more than once a month	47%

NOTE: Ninety-four people responded to our survey, amounting to approximately 94 percent of average Sunday attendance. This may be taken as an extremely accurate picture of regular attenders.

roughly equal to the cost of maintaining the church's physical plant for the year. In sum, Incarnation's building is a usable resource both for the church's ministry and as a generator of income, but it does not create a visible and welcoming presence in the neighborhood.

Incarnation is not, in fact, a neighborhood church. Less than one-third of its members live within a ten-minute drive of the church, and one-quarter live more than twenty minutes away. That geographic dispersion is part of the difficulty this church has in making demands on the time and resources of its members. They are busy professionals living at some distance from the church and not eager to come for meetings or activities except on Sunday morning.

The church is also rather marginal to their personal budgets. Barely more than one-third (37 percent) give more than one hundred dollars per month to the church. Almost as many (27 percent) give less than fifty dollars per month. In recent years, the church has made stewardship a priority. Members have attended conferences on how to plan for and encourage giving. There has been a major effort to encourage tithing, but this notion has seemed rather foreign (or at least uncongenial) to many. In addition, the church has attempted to draw members into discussions about the importance of its ministries, hoping to elicit commitment in that way. Such efforts have had disappointing results. Those who are already giving generously seem willing to give more, but others continue to contribute at a minimal level. The result is a budget that can barely maintain the staff, building, and contributions to the diocese, with little left over for other efforts.

The staff is small but effective, with a full-time rector and a part-time administrative assistant to run the office, along with a paid sexton and a paid organist. The administrative assistant is effective at organizing volunteers—mostly retired women—to help in the office during the week. They produce the newsletters, for instance. The rector, who arrived in 1990, has become a highly valued asset. As the congregation's first African American rector, he has been a symbol of the maturing of their new identity. He has worked hard to recruit new members, get old ones more involved, and improve the church's standing with the diocese. For years, the church had been unable to convince the diocese to invest in it by sending a strong black pastor. Father Britton's arrival has had positive effects both on the life of the church and on its self-image.

Incarnation's human, physical, and material resources are, then, sufficient, with the potential to be greater. At the moment, the church seems content to mobilize its resources for a stable, minimal program that will support a place for regular worship and occasional special events, along with a basic pastoral staff.

STRUCTURES OF AUTHORITY

As a part of the Episcopal Diocese of Atlanta, Incarnation's ministry is lodged in a larger church structure. The advice and resources of that body are available to them, and they, in turn, are subject to the wisdom and discretion of the diocese. A number of members have participated in diocesan events and committees, and the rector is serving as a national consultant on stewardship. The church is now contributing 10 percent of its budget to the diocese and is therefore eligible for low-interest loans, should they be needed. In general, the denomination's hierarchy seems to be a benevolent but rather remote presence. The church's life is certainly shaped by the fact that it is Episcopal—its worship and programs clearly follow Church forms—but denominational officials are relatively invisible in everyday decision making at Incarnation.

The effects of being in a hierarchical denomination were probably most evident in the congregation's long wait for a pastor who would match their needs. In the 1970s, they had the very effective leadership of Father Dreisbach, who helped them survive their racial transition, indeed to promote themselves as an integrated congregation. From 1985, when he left, until 1990, the congregation floundered somewhat under unsatisfactory leadership. As a small mostly black congregation in an all-black community, they were probably not high on the list of easy parishes to staff. Had the diocese not placed Father Britton in the parish—had there been neither the will nor the resources to make this match possible—Incarnation might not have survived many more years.

Internally, the church is administered by the usual array of committees and boards. At an annual meeting of the congregation, to which forty to fifty people come, all the church organizations make reports, and major decisions can be made. Between annual meetings, a vestry does most of the actual work of governing. Its minutes are posted so that all the members can be informed about the business of the church. Father Britton has worked hard to get more people involved and trained for leadership positions in the church. He has also led them to revise their bylaws for the first time in thirty years. The educational and professional experience of the members gives them plenty of background for full participation in church life, but because they are such busy people, they are likely to let their church work slip. Committee tasks that could be done in a few weeks stretch out over months as members miss meetings and meetings are canceled. In general, members of Incarnation spend relatively little time on governance. The church runs fairly smoothly with little attention to governing detail.

People gain influence at Incarnation through a variety of means— through longevity or service to the congregation, as major contributors, or because they have the skills and expertise the church needs. Because longevity has been honored, only under Father Britton's leadership has the older, white leadership begun to move over to include younger, black members in significant numbers. That shift, along with the other changes he has introduced, has not come without resistance, but no one seems to have gotten unhappy enough to make a real fuss.

The church's approach to governance is well illustrated by its 1992–1993 effort to assess its mission and choose a future course of action. Early in the process, the church did a survey to determine what the members saw as the most urgent needs to which they should respond. During this same early period, the church also rewrote its mission statement. In the fall of 1992, the pastor spearheaded the establishment of a task force, which met sporadically for the next year, charged with recommending a "signature ministry" for the church. During this time, the task force did additional surveying and gathered members into "cottage groups" to discuss the church's priorities. None of this, however, seemed to lead to a clear vision of the church's role.

Finally, in the fall of 1993, a church member persuaded his company to donate the computer equipment it was replacing. Combined with a general feeling that the church should focus on black youth, a consensus began to emerge that the computers ought to be used in some sort of youth educational program. This decision-making process had involved busy lay people who attempted to apply the sorts of information-gathering and consensus-building techniques they know well from their work lives, but with little time to make those techniques work effectively. In the end, pastoral guidance provided the critical push that brought the task to completion. The results of this task force's work remain, however, unclear. Whether the church will wholeheartedly adopt this new program to reshape its identity will depend on more than whether it receives a majority vote.

CULTURE

Finding a signature ministry has proved a difficult task for the Church of the Incarnation in part because its own sense of identity and culture are still being formed. It is no longer the suburban white congregation it was a generation ago, nor the congregation that struggled for a decade to become successfully integrated. There are now enough young families to think of this as a family church again (although nearly half of the adults who completed our survey are either single or widowed). But these new families do not form a cohesive neighborhood parish like the suburban one of old. They are, instead, scattered over the city and busy with dozens of activities away from the church.

Busy is perhaps the best word to describe the lives of Incarnation's members. Most are in professional occupations that demand a great deal of them. Many spend their days serving people in need. And many spend time away from work participating in clubs and charities that also involve mental, emotional, financial, and moral investment. Almost half (47 percent) participate in some civic or professional group at least once a month, and a quarter have some leadership role. When one member was asked what sorts of groups people at Incarnation belonged to, she offered a long list. "100 Black Men, The Alphas of course, all the sororities—the AKAs, the Deltas, many in the church are in those two—and The Guardsmen, that's another exclusive club. . . . Jack and Jill, the Ladies of Distinction. Of course you have specialty organizations, like the women attorneys groups. . . . There are several who are members of those. Or the Urban League, or what is the other one? NAACP, several very active members there." In all of this, they are much like the members of Holman, African American adults who have an economically secure place *and* a sense of obligation to be involved in activities that benefit their community.

Unlike Holman, however, Incarnation has no history as a leader in

152

African American community affairs, and neither church is part of a denomination recognized as rooted in the African American tradition. In fact, although Incarnation is now more than 80 percent black, its white members (and many nonwhite ones, as well) adamantly insist that this is not a "black church." When Incarnation members participate in African American community affairs, they do so as individuals, not as representatives of their church. While their community activities may be connected in some way to their personal sense of service and vocation, the connections between church and community activism are much less explicit than at Holman.

The result, as at Holman, is a church of busy people in which proportionately few members participate in any church activities beyond worship. The busyness even carries over to the youth in the acolyte program. One of the things Father Britton has to stress most is simply taking responsibility for being present on a regular basis. There are few other church activities for these youth or children. Among adults, a small core of mostly older women plans projects and outings for the Episcopal Church Women's group. Some of the same women form a small Altar Guild to care for the sanctuary and help out in the office when needed. A group of fewer than ten, mixed in age, gathers for a weeknight Bible study at irregular six-week intervals. Another group, with some overlap with the first, gathers for prayer and Bible study on Sunday mornings before worship. In all, only about 15 to 20 percent of the church's members participate in these activities with any regularity. About half regularly attend the after-worship coffee hour, but few join in any other form of fellowship activity. Only about 20 percent have more than two close friends among their churchmates. A core of two dozen or so members, then, is active in various church affairs, while the remainder confine their involvement to Sunday worship.

A similarly small number are involved in the one outreach ministry in which the church has been engaged in recent years. On one Wednesday each month, members provide a meal for the residents of Cascade House, a shelter for homeless women and children. In past years, the church has taken on a variety of efforts to "aid the less fortunate" (as one older woman put it), but as the church has struggled for its own survival, most of these fell by the wayside. For some members this lack of connection with the community's needy—some virtually at their doorstep—is a source of concern.

Member: We don't do anything for that apartment building right next door to us. One time they were throwing trash out the window and over into the yard, and I said if we'd go over and say "Good morning" sometime, we wouldn't have a trash pile in the

yard. [She laughs.] But we don't do any outreach in the community. I'm talking about around the church.

Daphne Wiggins [reading, after some conversation about the church's
official mission statement]: "We acknowledge a global vision of
mission, aiding those living in other countries of the world."

Member: Now we go *way* into the world. And we can't get the apartments right next door.

Daphne Wiggins: So you're saying more than you're doing?

Member: You know we are.

More than one person voiced such concerns, but at the same time that
they wished for a more active congregational ministry in the community, they also worried about who would staff it. Several acknowledged
that, while they would like to see the church more involved, they were
not sure if they would commit the time to participating.

One of the places where the community and church involvements of
Incarnation's members have begun to come together is in their annual
Women's Day activities. Drawing on their members' extensive connections in the community, in 1993 Incarnation invited as a speaker a local
judge whose concerns about the problems facing black youth match
those of many of the church's members. The program, planned and led
entirely by the church's women, included a guest celebrant, a guest
pianist, a guest soloist, and a special choir of about twenty women.
There was also a commemorative book, which was one of the ways the
women raised money for their special offering of the day. One of the
leaders recalled, "This was the first year that we tried to do something.
And I don't really know how much we raised yet, because I leave that
with the treasurer; but we sold about four thousand dollars' worth of
ads and everything, which means that once we pay our bills, we ought
to have fourteen or fifteen hundred dollars left [to contribute to the
church]." In this special event, the energies of more than the usual
number of the church's women were mobilized. Their connections in
the community paid off handsomely, and the church was called together around some of the issues on which individuals spend a good
deal of their moral energy.

The one thing that regularly calls the people of Incarnation together
is, in fact, worship. For almost everyone we talked with, the liturgy
itself, especially the Eucharist, is the essential element in their spiritual
lives. They speak of the service as a time that is holy, a place set aside
for meeting God. Some talked about it as a time of "refueling," others
as a time when they are reassured of God's love and care for them.
Several of the young adults we talked with spoke of returning to
church after a long time away. One man talked about the differences
between Father Britton and the dogmatic preachers he had known.

Father Britton's approach was a whole lot different one that seemed to know that here is a pilgrim who is searching . . . and over a period of time people grow. And it seems to take that confidence. I know that's how I accepted it. Sometimes I'm thrilled with the notion that ten years from now my spiritual life will be a lot different than it is now . . . , [but I will still be] daily praying to the Lord, daily reading the Bible. If you had told me five years ago that I would be doing that, I would have just looked at you sideways and said, "Yeah, that's for weak folks; that's for folks that can't figure out what life's about. I know what life's about."

Another young woman said simply, "I'm glad I'm back."

The people of Incarnation come each week, then, from many different places. They bring to their weekly ritual strikingly different theological perspectives. The congregation includes not only charismatics and noncharismatics, but people for whom the labels "conservative" and "liberal" are apt. One group is pragmatic and this-worldly. For them, God is the spirit within, one's inner strength, one's joy, one's confusion, one's anger, one's conscience. Said one woman, "I believe in myself." For others, that is exactly what one should not do. Trusting self over God is a sure way to get into trouble. This more evangelical group is very willing to talk about God's intervention in their everyday lives, about praying every day, and about the peace God gives them. But both these conservatives and their more liberal colleagues find something to unite them in their weekly worship experience.

Two-thirds of Incarnation's members grew up in other traditions— mostly traditional black Baptist and Methodist denominations—but they now find the solemnity of the Episcopal ritual much to their liking. They also enjoy the smallness and relative informality of Incarnation. It feels more like a family and is not as utterly high church as some other places they might go. The use of an African American Episcopal hymnal, *Lift Every Voice,* has also allowed the congregation to claim a musical heritage that might not be present in the typical Episcopal church. It is for many good reasons that one member described the church's style as "middle Anglican." It falls between the high pomp of a large cathedral and the casual spontaneity of many traditional black churches or the emotional intensity of the charismatic gatherings some of them attend.

Just how much of their African and African American heritage to claim is another of the ways in which Incarnation offers a middle road. The use of *Lift Every Voice* is new, and Father Britton reported that he now notices people singing its familiar hymns by heart. Every service includes musical selections both from that hymnal and from the older "standard" Episcopal hymnal. Father Dreisbach began the process of introducing visual symbols and art from many cultures, and the halls and sanctuary now house a rich mixture of images from Africa, Europe, and beyond. In 1992, one member reported to an after-worship gathering about her trip to South Africa. That country's oppression and violence were often mentioned in sermons and prayers, as well. Although an awareness of connections to the continent of Africa seemed to be growing, it did not begin to match the sustained attention given those connections at Holman, for instance.

This middle road makes sense for persons in a particular niche. What Incarnation members seem to share are their high levels of education and comfortable incomes, their involvement in African American community affairs, and their sense of spiritual searching that is satisfied by the relative solemnity of the Episcopal style of worship. What the older white members add to that mix is a commitment to this particular congregation and its history, including a history of successful integration. With an increasingly diverse black population, the black religious scene is increasingly diverse, as well. Incarnation represents that specialization—a church that appeals to one segment of the population and not to others.

Incarnation is not likely to remain an integrated congregation, however. The remaining white members no longer live in the neighborhood, and neither do any other white people. The possibility that white Episcopalians from other parts of the city will choose to travel to a predominantly black church in a marginal neighborhood is remote. The white members who remain have a history with this congregation that cannot be replicated for a new generation of members.

Although white people are not joining the church, black people are. In recent years, the congregation has demonstrated an ability to attract new members entirely by word of mouth, with no intentional recruitment effort either in the neighborhood or beyond. Because Incarnation's members are so involved in the community, however, with so many friends outside the church, the lines along which this sort of natural recruitment can happen are many. The church can certainly not rely on visibility—either physical visibility in the neighborhood or symbolic visibility in the community. Its corporate presence is slight. But the presence of its members in civic and professional affairs brings the church into contact with others likely to fit the niche Incarnation occupies—busy people seeking a congregational involvement that allows them opportunities for worship and reflection, but not necessarily another place in which to invest large amounts of money or energy. Their moral investments will probably lie elsewhere.

While Incarnation's members have extensive contacts with fellow professionals and others active in the community, they do not have similar contacts with the church's less well-off neighbors. The members do not live in the neighborhood, and they are unlikely to run into neighborhood people at their clubs or civic organizations. Nor has the church itself created any significant points of contact with this population. Incarnation simply has no natural lines of recruitment into the disadvantaged black population of Atlanta, and Incarnation's members have every reason to believe that such folk would not feel at home in their church anyway.

SUMMARY

Incarnation seems well on its way to establishing itself as a niche congregation, serving a particular kind of person, drawn from all over the Atlanta metropolitan region, and relatively disconnected from the immediate neighborhood in which it is located. Its struggle over a signature ministry is unlikely to represent a fundamental change in orientation for the congregation. While some members would like to see the congregation more involved in outreach, more connected to the neighborhood, that sentiment is not widespread; and it is tempered by the realization that the congregation probably could not mobilize sufficient time and money from its members to mount a substantial service ministry in the community anyway.

With strong pastoral leadership and slow, steady membership growth, the future of the congregation looks bright, however. Incarnation is likely to remain a place where only a small proportion of members invest significantly in the activities of the congregation itself. The remainder will commit enough of their time and money to maintain a basic level of staff and programming. The church is likely to continue to attract busy African American professionals for whom weekly worship in the Episcopal style meets a deep spiritual longing and who will serve the community more through their individual career and volunteer activity than through the vehicle of this congregation.

Conclusion

The ability to become a niche congregation depends, it appears, on two things. First, the existing constituency must have wide network connections not tied to the church and neighborhood. Second, the congregation must be able to establish and project an identity that clearly distinguishes it from other potentially competing congregations. Both Holman and Incarnation are becoming, it appears, niche congregations. Each has sufficient strength and distinctiveness to draw together a particular population, a particular spiritual community. That community, in turn, need have little relationship with the immediate geographic parish in which the church is located. Both congregations have developed internal task forces to chart their futures, including the question of how they should relate to their neighborhoods. As well-educated professionals, that is what their members know how to do. In neither case is the work of the task force likely to change the course of the church's history, but the fact of the task force symbolizes who they are and how they do business.[6] It says to potential observers that they are deliberate planners, smart people able to gather information. That identity, along with many other aspects of their congregation's life, further establishes their place in their niche.

For Holman, that niche is affluent African Americans who are politically active in behalf of African American causes. For Incarnation it is affluent African Americans who appreciate the warmth of a relatively small church and the inspiration of the Episcopal liturgy. Both the constituencies and the interests that draw them together are present in sufficient numbers in the general population to make it possible for these congregations to recruit among the wide networks their busy members already occupy. And neither the constituency nor its interests are likely to be widely present in the immediate neighborhood.

Holman, like the parish congregation of South Meridian, comes to its current strategy from a position of strength, having never gone through any significant decline or disruption. Both congregations have maintained places prominent in their communities through all the difficulties those communities have endured. Both have had the resources—especially connections and denominational prominence—to weather the storms. Both had buildings that were no particular drain on their resources, and aspirations for new facilities that would better represent them. Holman has built its new building in its current location. South Meridian will build in a new suburban location. But both are continuing well-established identities that transcend the buildings and locations they own.

Both also had a broad constituency base and programming that has met the needs of that constituency. As a Church of God church in a Church of God town, South Meridian could expect to be recognized as part of the culture, a culture that was not fundamentally changed by the economic decline the community suffered. While Anderson, Indiana's economic woes might erode the base for other religious groups, the Church of God never lost its constituency. Similarly, as a leading African American church in a region with strong African American community leadership, Holman can expect to retain its place in that culture. South Meridian offered its members the piety and tangible support they expected; Holman offered its members the advocacy and social service they expected. Both maintained a good match with a viable constituency.

Incarnation and the other two Anderson churches come to their current strategies after periods of decline. For East Lynn Christian, that decline is sufficient to make its survival doubtful. For First Baptist, Anderson, formidable challenges remain, while Incarnation seems to have moved past its period of crisis. For these congregations the historic ties to neighborhood were much stronger than for either of the more prominent churches, South Meridian and Holman. Their earlier constituency *was* a neighborhood constituency and no longer is. In addition, the members of both First Baptist and East Lynn had ties to their buildings that delayed a decision to move until at or past the critical point where the congregation could raise the necessary funds to make a move possible. Like the congregations we looked at in chapter 2, they experienced a radical disjuncture between their ties to place, which were largely gone, and their ties to the physical structure located in that place, which seemed to grow stronger with age.

Also like the churches in decline, East Lynn and First Baptist have actively resisted the efforts of outsiders to get them to change. Both had the resources of a willing denomination available to them and rejected the strings attached to the aid. Neither the Disciples of Christ nor the American Baptists could force them to do otherwise. Holman United Methodist and Incarnation Episcopal, on the other hand, are in denominations that could—theoretically—impose decisions from the outside. Because of its size and prominence, however, Holman manages to chart its own course. It, too, rejects the advice of unwanted denominational (fund-raising) consultants. Incarnation, by contrast, has had neither interference nor help from its denomination. It suffered for years without the pastoral leadership that could build on its growing strength. While denominations cannot impose change, they can sometimes withhold crucial support.

Ideologically, these five congregations differ greatly. Holman and Incarnation represent a combination of evangelicalism and social activism that is not unusual among African American churches. In Anderson, First Baptist and East Lynn Christian practice a sort of civic evangelicalism, while South Meridian's version of evangelical holiness emphasizes prayer, healing, mutual support, and Bible study, along with evangelism. Each of these sets of ideas combines an emphasis on Bible reading and prayer with the sort of this-worldly citizenship that makes a given community work. They all pray, but they also work at doing the things that make people's lives better. These beliefs and practices, however, tell us little about who they will pray for or whose lives will fall within their circle of care. Caring for the souls they see as intrusted to their care has led each of these very different congregations to preserve their identity and practice.

For these five congregations, the constituents brought to their neighborhood by economic and cultural upheavals seem not likely to become potential members. By either highlighting the uniqueness of their existing identity or moving to a new location, the congregations have persisted in their current structures and programming and established new relationships with old constituents. In most instances, that strategy is likely to be successful.

CHAPTER 4

Adaptation: Integrating Gay and Straight

$\mathbf{I}$f the congregations we have examined so far have maintained their historic sense of identity and purpose, the nine to which we turn in the next three chapters, have decisively turned toward new and unfamiliar ways, while remaining recognizably themselves. When we asked their members to imagine what the congregation would be like ten years from now, they described a significantly different picture from who they used to be. They are not whole new creations (we will turn to those churches in chapter 6), but they are amalgamations of old practices and new, of enduring rituals and new programs.

Changed environments have confronted these congregations with new potential constituents and new challenges in retaining their old ones, with needs for internal restructuring and new mission outreach. They have responded by altering their programs and activities to accommodate their changed circumstances. Their faith and the world they live in have touched each other. They have called on their imaginations as well as their own history and tradition, their own skills as well as the resources of outsiders, to construct new patterns of action. Among the congregations we studied, these nine have responded to the change in their communities by instituting new policies, activities, and programs, adapting their offerings to the needs of the altered environment. Their paths have not been without struggle, and they have often encountered conflict and failure. But what has emerged for these congregations is a new sense of who they are and what they are about, an acknowledgment that they have changed and that the future does not look like the past.

This chapter and the next will examine six congregations that *look* different today than they did ten years ago, whose new constituents differ significantly from their old members. The third group (in chapter 6) are congregations that do not look so different on the outside;

changes in constituency are not especially visible, but changes in internal structures have made it possible for these congregations to serve in altered social and economic circumstances.

The congregations in this chapter have absorbed a particular new population group—gay men and lesbians. As we surveyed Long Beach, California, and Candler Park in Atlanta—the two communities in our study where such folk are visibly present—we discovered that most congregations were ignoring the issue, some more deliberately than others. Surprisingly few were openly and verbally hostile to homosexuality, but fewer still were openly welcoming. The dominant strategy was what we came to call the "elephant in the living room" response.[1] In family therapy this metaphor is used to describe the problems everyone knows are present but refuses to talk about, instead working uncomfortably around their massive presence. Many people we talked with in these communities acknowledged that there were probably gay people in their congregations. Some were sure of it. But, as in the military, the policy was "Don't ask, don't tell." The issue itself is simply too volatile for most congregations to confront. So long as they relate to their gay members as if sexuality were out of the picture, they think the conflict can be avoided.

Despite the issue's volatility, three of the congregations we studied have opened their doors to people otherwise outcast and often quite convinced that churches are their worst enemies. St. Matthew's, in Long Beach, has undertaken the task of integration in a quiet and uneventful way. First Existentialist, in Candler Park, outside Atlanta, has become predominantly lesbian without even trying. First Congregational, also in Long Beach, after engaging in a deliberate process of choosing to become "open and affirming," has taken integration one step further—to advocacy. Members not only welcome lesbian and gay persons into their midst, they have taken up the cause. Working out of their long activist heritage and downtown visibility, First Congregational has become not only open and affirming, but adamantly, publicly so. Each church's story is different, but as we will see, they share many things in common.

St. Matthew's Catholic Parish, Long Beach: Gay and Straight Breaking Bread Together

Research team member Tom Clark had alerted me to the usual seating habits of the guys from Comunidad who attend the seven o'clock Sunday morning Mass at St. Matthew's Catholic Church in Long Beach; sure enough, the row to my left began filling up with single men, along with men in couples. They were clearly at home here, happy to see one another. Indeed, when it came time to serve communion, a couple of the men from this row slipped out to take their places as eucharistic ministers, and everyone in the row filed forward to receive the elements along with their straight neighbors. The service is a quiet one, befitting the hour, and relatively brief. When it ended, all of the parishioners made their way to the patio to chat and to contribute to various parish-related activities. Before long, a group had gathered for the second "communion" of the morning—brunch at the Park Pantry. This group of gay men is such a fixture at the restaurant that their table is always waiting. They were kind enough to take me along and to regale me with stories about vacations and pets and houses. This communion, unlike the earlier one, is anything but quiet. It was clear to me that this group, brought together in worship at a Roman Catholic parish, draws enormous joy and strength from each other's friendship. Just how that combination—gay and Catholic—came to be is the story Tom Clark will tell.

St. Matthew's Catholic Church sits on the southeast corner of Temple Avenue and Seventh Street in Long Beach, less than two miles from the city's downtown. The immediate neighborhood is predominantly residential, except for the small businesses that line Seventh Street. St. Matthew's, neither old enough nor large enough to be imposing or even striking, was built in 1933, after the original 1920 structure was destroyed in an earthquake. Although the exterior hints at the Spanish influence common in southern California, the most notable thing about this church is not its architecture. Rather, the careful observer who passes St. Matthew's will see that the front door of the church remains wide open from morning until evening, in apparent defiance of the usual urban concerns about safety.

To step through that door is to notice the dark mahogany altarpiece, with its intricately carved crucifix and lilies. The wooden ceiling is supported by thick cross-beams from which are suspended wrought-iron light fixtures. The darkness of the wood is complemented by cream-colored adobe walls, and brightened by the large, multicolored stained-glass windows depicting scenes from the Gospels. Across the front of the church ranges an assembly of angels and saints: six angels are painted at the top of the sanctuary walls, while statues of saints stand nearby. The presence of so many images from traditional Catholic piety, together with the generally traditional appearance of the church, elicits feelings of familiarity and "at-homeness" for many lifelong Catholics, whatever their theological leanings. More than once parishioners remarked to me, "It reminds me of the church I grew up in."

That at-home feeling is consciously fostered in the worship life of the church. There is an effort to build a feeling of community from the moment congregants arrive. One of the priests stands outside greeting people, while lay ministers do the same at the church doors. Though there is a quiet, almost hushed atmosphere inside people often greet one another and exchange a few words as they arrive.

Before the liturgy begins, the song leader rehearses any new music with the congregation and generally receives a satisfying response. During the opening song, the ministers—the presiding priest, the server, and the lector—process down the main aisle to the sanctuary. The server and the lector are adult members of the parish; both women and men fill these roles. The readings for Mass are those prescribed by the lectionary. The homily, generally about two to three minutes, takes its direction from the Scripture readings. The message is usually one that affirms the congregation, assures them of God's unfailing love, and encourages and challenges them to put their faith commitment into action in their daily lives. After the homily, the liturgy proceeds to the eucharistic prayer and the distribution of communion, during which the priest is assisted by lay eucharistic ministers—women and men of various ethnic backgrounds—who come forward into the sanctuary from their places in the congregation.

When parishioners describe how St. Matthew's arrived at this place in its history, they generally talk only about the last twenty years or so, when the parish has undergone its most significant changes, especially the growth of the Hispanic population. In 1973, the parish added its first Spanish Mass to the schedule of six English Masses. Twenty years later, there are three Spanish Masses on the weekend, at which attendance ranges from 150 to 500 or more. The number of English Masses, by contrast, has decreased to three, at which the number of congregants rarely exceeds 175.

Many longtime members remark poignantly that today's Hispanic community is what the Anglo community once was at St. Matthew's. They recall a time when St. Matthew's was predominantly made up of young Anglo families for whom the parish was situated close to the center of their lives. Parish-sponsored dances, potluck dinners, and bazaars provided frequent opportunities for members to come together as one community. The elementary school and religious education programs helped parents raise their children in the faith. And, over the entire parish enterprise, from 1932 until 1972, loomed the figure of the much beloved pastor, Msgr. James Lynch, an "old-time Irish priest." It is the shadow of this encompassing parish experience that some longtime members detect in the present life of the Hispanic community—and that they miss in their own.

In part these changes result from the eastward shift of the Anglo family population in Long Beach. In its place have come Hispanic, African American, and Asian American families and single Anglo adults, many of whom are lesbian or gay. Still remaining are many retired and elderly persons. This study's focus on the lesbian and gay population could just as easily have been a focus on ethnic change; both have been part of the transitions in this section of Long Beach.

It would, in fact, be inaccurate to depict the direction of change at St. Matthew's as one in which the Hispanic community has taken over where the English-speaking community left off. For a portion of the English-speaking community, St. Matthew's continues to serve as both a dynamic worshipping community and an important source of social connectedness. A pervasive goal at St. Matthew's is the creation of an ever greater sense of community that recognizes the social diversity that now marks the English-speaking membership of the parish. Members often say, "St. Matthew's is not your traditional family parish." They note an increase in the number of single-parent families and in the number of persons living alone (including the widowed, the divorced, and those who have never married). Likewise, the lesbian and gay membership, both single and partnered, has grown at St. Matthew's. All of these trends have been more apparent since the closing of the parish school in 1981.

In one sense, it is not surprising that gay and lesbian membership should have increased over the past several years. Significant numbers of gays and lesbians have lived in Long Beach since World War II, but in the 1970s, their presence emerged into the civic consciousness. Indeed, Belmont Heights, the neighborhood in which St. Matthew's is located, has become one of the centers of gay and lesbian life in Long Beach. A cluster of gay restaurants, bars, and shops—something of a gay business district—lies within the parish boundaries, only six blocks south of the church.

In early 1986, Cardinal Mahoney invited parishes throughout the archdiocese to establish formal programs that would respond to the needs of their lesbian and gay members (including, but not limited to, needs arising from the AIDS crisis). In response to this invitation, St. Matthew's sponsored a parish Mass of healing for persons with AIDS. People present were invited to sign up if they were interested in a parish ministry for lesbian and gay Catholics. Between ninety and one hundred people signed the list, and Comunidad was soon started.

In its early days, the group's activity consisted primarily of a monthly meeting to hear a guest speaker, including some discussion and time for socializing. But by 1990, the group was ready to take fuller responsibility for its own mission and existence. A new mission statement committed the group "to actively reach out, welcome, and support Lesbian and Gay Catholics and non-Catholics in their pursuit to develop, integrate, and nurture their own spiritual and social well being within the spirit of the Catholic Church." The group now helps members attend to their own faith formation, organizes projects of service to the broader parish and civic community, and sponsors social and recreational activities, such as potluck dinners and theater outings.

Since the reorganization of Comunidad and the creation of its mission statement, membership in the group has grown steadily. Attendance at the monthly meetings averages about thirty people, though it sometimes grows to as many as fifty. Many new people are brought to Comunidad by friends who belong to the group, while others are referred by the archdiocesan Office of Pastoral Ministry to the Lesbian and Gay Community. Most members of Comunidad are men; the number of women has grown only slowly, from four or five to about *twice that many by early 1994. It's simply easier for men to return to the Church. Even when a parish welcomes lesbians, women often find the Church's stands on abortion, ordination, or both difficult to swallow.*

Not all members of Comunidad are members of the parish, though a majority are. Likewise, not all gay and lesbian parishioners are active in Comunidad, often because membership in the group entails, at least within the limited confines of the parish, a public expression of one's sexual orientation. Others simply feel no need to belong to a separate group. Indeed, the members of Comunidad are quite clear in their insistence that they are not a separate or parallel parish, a "gay church," as it were. One reason they are drawn to St. Matthew's is that the group exists within a parish and is part of a larger faith community. Comunidad members are quick to point out that they are integrated into all areas of parish life as lectors, altar servers, eucharistic ministers, choir members, song leaders, and members of other parish committees, especially the Peace and Justice Committee.

For many nongay parishioners, the presence of gay and lesbian members at St. Matthew's is not an issue. In fact, they point out that Comunidad members are among the more active parishioners and express gratitude for their work for the parish. This attitude is modeled by the priests and the deacon of the parish, who consistently display openness, acceptance, and concern for all the members, gay and straight.

Still, confusion, discomfort, and objection have arisen in response to St. Matthew's acceptance of gay and lesbian persons. However, these reactions have been few and isolated. St. Matthew's continues to serve, in the words of one young parishioner, as "a home for many different people." Keeping the church door open has not always been easy or comfortable for the parishioners of St. Matthew's, and some have left through that door, precisely because it is open. Yet the door stays open and will likely remain so for the foreseeable future. For, as St. Matthew's pastor, Father Meisel, has observed, in all the years they've kept the door open, the church has never been harmed.

RESOURCES

As with many of the other churches we have observed, St. Matthew's has experienced a significant population shift that has resulted in a loss of members—at least among its Anglo population. We might easily have focused, in fact, on the parish's active response to its new immigrant neighbors. A growing Hispanic population has been welcomed at St. Matthew's, where there are now half as many English Masses as a generation ago, and attendance at none of them comes close to filling the church.[2] As with the other churches, long-term members vividly remember the thriving, family-oriented parish of the 1950s. And as we have seen again and again, population trends have moved those families to other locations, replacing them with other demographic groups. By 1981, the loss of its natural constituency had become acutely apparent at St. Matthew's. The enrollment in the eight grades of the parish school had fallen to 117. There were no longer enough nearby Catholic families raising children to justify keeping the school open.

That decision has had lasting effects on the character and resources of St. Matthew's. The parish lost an institution that had helped it attract young families; and when the archdiocese decided to demolish the school buildings, it also lost classroom and meeting space. It gained, however, freedom to tailor its programming to adults and to spend its energy on things other than school fund-raising.

As a result, significant numbers of adults in "nontraditional" families have now begun to make St. Matthew's their home. Only a quarter of those who responded to our survey of the English-speaking congregation said they are currently married, and only 13 percent have children in their households. Total parish membership numbers are at least holding steady, and many of these new members have offered the church real energy and commitment. As word of Comunidad has spread, a growing number of gay (and some lesbian) Catholics—often long alienated from the Church—have returned with real enthusiasm to active parish life. As the demographics of the parish's neighborhood have changed, then, St. Matthew's identity has changed accordingly (table 4.1).

Unfortunately, years of keeping a shrinking school open created a serious financial drain on the parish from which it has never really recovered. They have since sold two houses. The pastor rarely makes special appeals for the parish's needs, and few realize that more money is needed. While there are few really well-off people in the parish, it is solidly middle class. Almost half those who responded to our survey have household incomes over $35,000, yet fewer than 40 percent give more than fifty dollars per month to the church; and fewer than 20 percent give more than a hundred dollars. Given that response to the survey over-represents people who are more active and committed to the parish, actual averages are probably lower. The potential for more abundant financial resources is clearly present.

Presumably the parish could call on the archdiocese should it need extra support. Instead, the archdiocese calls on each parish to meet an assessed goal in an annual special appeal. People at St. Matthew's worry that meeting those goals will deprive the parish itself of needed funds—that parishioners will give to the archdiocese rather than giving their regular gifts to the parish. Still, no parish wants to be in debt to the hierarchy, if it can be avoided, so St. Matthew's is likely to look for resources within its own control before asking the larger Church for help.

The parish has also been unable of late to demand sufficient pastoral staff. During 1992, the pastor was assisted by one Spanish-speaking

Table 4.1. St. Matthew's Catholic Parish, Long Beach

Ideas and priorities

Christian practices rated "essential"	Living Christian values
Ministries rated "very important" or "essential"	Service to the needy

Resources

Average Saturday/Sunday attendance (English Masses)	450
Annual operating budget (1992)	N/a
Household incomes above $50,000	28%
College degrees or more	60%
Average age	54 years
Activities (beyond worship) participated in at least monthly	None

Relationship to the community

Live ten minutes or less from the church	79%
New to the community in the last five years	26%
Ethnicity	88% European
	6% Hispanic
Participate in civic & community activities more than once a month	40%

NOTE: Only eighty-nine people responded to our survey, amounting to approximately 20 percent of average Saturday/Sunday attendance at English masses. This should be taken as only a tentative representation of all regular attenders.

associate, two part-time priests, and a deacon. In 1993, the deacon left to gain additional schooling, and both part-time priests became seriously ill, which forced the pastor to rely on visiting priests for many of the liturgies.

In addition to this pastoral staff, a sister oversees religious education, and there is a part-time music director and a part-time liturgy director. These staff efforts have produced a thriving catechism program (especially among the Hispanic children) and worship services of consistently high quality, now embellished by a growing choir.

The pastor himself has set the tone for a strong and healthy parish, both by his insistence on openness and inclusion and by his hands-off style of management. His stance of no-questions-asked acceptance diffuses criticism of the presence of gays and lesbians in the parish. And his willingness to let parish groups run their own affairs has made space for a good deal of creativity and responsibility. Indeed, the current vitality of Comunidad would not be possible but for his initial willingness to answer the archdiocesan appeal for response to gays and lesbians.

This archdiocesan ministry has, in fact, been the major resource St. Matthew's has claimed from its denominational hierarchy, with the archdiocesan Office of Pastoral Ministry to the Lesbian and Gay Community providing programmatic, theological, and pastoral resources to Comunidad. It refers people to the group and provides official Church sanction for the ministry.

While St. Matthew's has fewer Anglo members than in its heyday and barely enough financial resources to get by, it has good pastoral leadership and a membership base that is shifting along with the demographics of the community by including both increasing numbers of Spanish-speaking parishioners and people in "nontraditional" families.

STRUCTURES OF AUTHORITY

As a parish within the Roman Catholic system, St. Matthew's is heir to two differing traditions of authority. The first and most prevalent is the tradition of obedience to the teaching authority of the Church. As represented and interpreted by priests and bishops, up to the pope, the Church's teachings are to be accepted by the faithful. The other tradition, more pronounced since Vatican II, emphasizes the "primacy of conscience." In other words, each faithful Catholic must weigh the teachings of Scripture and the Church and follow the dictates of his or her own Spirit-informed conscience.[3] The tension between these two views of authority is nowhere more apparent than in the relationship between Comunidad and the parish and Church of which it is a part.

When, for instance, Pope John Paul II declared in 1992 that it was the duty of faithful Catholics to oppose all gay rights legislation, the traditional view of authority called for simple obedience. Those who depend on primacy of conscience, however, sought the deeper spiritual principles that might help them interpret such a teaching. Members of Comunidad, along with the archdiocesan pastoral office director, struggled over their disappointment with this declaration. However, they concluded that at heart it had not altered the Church's basic love and acceptance of all persons who seek to live a Christian life under its care.

While a good many people at St. Matthew's are comfortable with traditional authority and traditional teaching, the weight of the Church's hierarchy generally falls rather lightly on this parish. The archdiocese has been a resource in supporting the ministry of Comunidad, even if it has also been a burden in its unilateral requests for funds or its decision to demolish the school buildings. People at St. Matthew's deeply respect the tradition and authority of which they are a part, but they also claim a good deal of freedom to pursue their ministry under the primacy of their own consciences.

Indeed, the weight of their own pastor's authority falls lightly on this parish, as well. Father Meisel's style of administration can best be described as laissez faire. Once a committee or task force has gotten started, he is content to see it run on its own. He often provides initial encouragement and leadership, then delegates authority to others who have a special interest in seeing something happen. In fact, things at St. Matthew's often seem to happen because a few people have the interest and energy to pursue them. In the case of Comunidad or the Peace and Justice group, this freedom has meant a good deal of responsible creativity on the part of the lay people thus empowered. With an Anglo membership that is very well educated (60 percent of our survey respondents have a college degree or more), such freedom and encouragement seem to be a successful leadership strategy.

The pastor's avoidance of administrative entanglements also means, however, that no parish council exists, and thus no forum for discussion of issues that concern the parish as a whole. Nor do the parishioners have access to financial information and decision making. While a few worry about the lack of opportunity for democratic participation, most in the parish are quite satisfied. So long as they can get involved in ministries and committees, using their creative energies unhindered in those ways, they seem content to see their pastor take care of the larger concerns of the parish. As a result, the pastor alone deals with the occasional disgruntled parishioner angry over the presence of gays and lesbians in the parish. The issue is framed, in those instances, as a pastoral issue between priest and parishioner, and he tries to make them "teachable moments." Were there a parish council, the frame might well be partisan debate in a struggle over policy. Both the loose structure of the parish and the freedom with which parishioners interpret their relationship to Church teachings have facilitated the ministry St. Matthew's is able to extend to gay and lesbian persons.

CULTURE

Comunidad is listed on the front page of each Sunday's bulletin at St. Matthew's as a "Lesbian and Gay Outreach." Many Anglo members of the parish, if they notice it at all, probably assume that the group is just another outside or diocesan group that uses their building. From its Spanish name, they might think it is an activity of the Hispanic parishioners. They may notice the large number of single people or clusters of same-sex persons at Mass, but they do not acknowledge consciously the presence of gay and lesbian persons in their midst. Others, however, notice and adopt a live-and-let-live attitude; they simply do not ask questions. A few notice and complain. The pronouncements of Rome are held in very high regard by some in the parish, and those who do not conform to official Church teaching are seen as less than adequate Catholics. Still others are convinced that whatever God has made must be good. They may not understand why some people are homosexual, but they are convinced that if God made them that way, they should be treated with the respect every part of creation is due.

The parish itself, however, does not raise these issues. Issues related to homosexuality are not on the public agenda at St. Matthew's. What happens in Comunidad, like what happens in the Peace and Justice Committee or the Religious Education Committee, is relatively self-contained. Each group goes about its task, meeting the needs of its members, making few demands on the larger whole.

It has become the conviction of most of those closest to Comunidad, however, that its outreach affects the larger parish. Even though Catholic parishes do not typically recruit members, a parish's reputation as a hospitable environment for a particular kind of person or worship style or ministry is likely to draw Catholics of like mind. In this case, the parish has extended a welcome to a population that might otherwise stay away from church entirely. Many gay and lesbian members talk about the sense of alienation they felt in their years away from the Church, feeling lost and alone, unsure of God's love. But they were drawn back to church and then reassured that God did indeed love them. "I needed a friend so much that it led me to Christ," said one. Another said, "This seems to be where I belong. . . . I am committed to the Catholic faith, to the Catholic church. This is where I experience my spirituality, and I don't believe that it's something I'll have to lose again."

Those who return to the Church come with a strong commitment to being fully engaged in parish life. As Tom Clark points out, the members of Comunidad do not want to be a separate "gay church." Says one member, "We are part of the body of Christ, we are not the gay body of Christ. It doesn't matter what happens on this earth, I know that I'm a part of Christ. And I'm grateful." He and the other members of Comunidad want to be involved alongside their straight neighbors in worship and service—and they are. When the group spent time at the beginning of 1994 talking about goals for the new year, many voiced a desire to be even more fully integrated into parish life.

In turn, many in the parish have recognized that gay and lesbian members have something to contribute, that much of the energy for the parish's worship and service comes from these new members. Says one priest, "They're not *better* because they're gay, and the straights aren't better because they're straight. They're just children of God. They just are. We need them, God needs them, they need us." While Comunidad members are anxious to continue to reach out into the gay community to bring others back into the Church's fold, they are just as anxious to be a visible and accepted presence in that Church. Their mission is as much internal as external.

As the priest's statement indicates, much of the acceptance of these new parishioners has been grounded in a gospel message that emphasizes God's inclusive love. As is the case at Brighton Evangelical Congregational Church (see chapter 5) and elsewhere, St. Matthew's parishioners hear a good deal from their pulpit about God's unconditional acceptance of all who have faith—regardless of social distinctions. They hear about the need for a unity that does not require uniformity, about the richness that comes with diversity.

Theirs is also a "sacramental" faith. In part that means that the Eucharist is taken very seriously as the source of the Christian's strength for living in the world. But more profoundly, it means that St. Matthew's parishioners expect God's love to be embodied. They expect to see God in the faces of others and in the natural world around them. This, in turn, affirms for them the goodness of that natural, embodied order. It challenges them to make a difference in this world. For those who responded to our survey, more important than any other Christian virtue is the need to "practice Christian values in work, home, and school." And more significant than anything else their church can do is "providing aid and services to people in need." The Bible itself is, in their view, stories and teachings that "provide a powerful motivation as we work toward God's reign in the world." Theirs is a this-worldly, practical faith, tied nevertheless to rituals, symbols, and traditions that have much deeper meaning.

The opportunity to make a difference in the world is often a part of parish life at St. Matthew's. People from the parish participate in the local CROP walk (raising money to fight hunger), and they have been involved in the Heifer Project, an overseas development effort. A small group marched together in the L.A. AIDS walk. At Christmas, Comunidad coordinated a parishwide effort to collect food for baskets and went caroling in nursing homes. The Justice Bakery sells bread at the church after Masses. There was also a table one Sunday selling crafts made by Latin American refugees, with proceeds to benefit them. When Comunidad members talked with each other about their New Year's resolutions, many concerned getting more involved in service projects like this.

A good deal of political awareness and activity are apparent in the parish as well. A voter registration table was set up at the church during the fall of 1992. The Peace and Justice Committee circulated information about a proposition on welfare reform. The Respect Life Committee routinely keeps pro-life issues in the parish's consciousness and urged parishioners to oppose the California "death with dignity" proposition.

Not surprisingly, AIDS-related issues are also of concern at St. Matthews. A number of parishioners participate in the care of persons with AIDS, and several volunteer at a local hospice. St. Matthew's clergy are among the few in the city who will visit those with the syndrome.

The Peace and Justice Committee sponsors many of these activities. They have established links with a variety of outside groups—Long Beach Area Peace Network, the archdiocesan Peace and Justice Commission, Catholic Peace Coalition, Seamless Garment Network, South Coast Ecumenical Council, and various hunger organizations—to channel information and concern into the parish, and funds and support out of it. Members recognize that not everyone in the parish shares their concerns, but they are anxious to get as many people as possible involved. About half of those who responded to our survey said that they participate in social ministry activities at least a few times a year.

The committee's most successful activity by far is their series of Monday night Soup Suppers during Advent and Lent. These evenings are significant not only for the money they raise, but also for the sense of community they foster in the parish. Here more than perhaps anywhere else, Anglo parishioners come together in an informal setting to share more of their lives than is possible on Sunday. There are no Bible study groups or Sunday school groups to provide a similar venue. Adult Christian education is usually a video attended by a few older members who slip in and slip out without discussion. Although the various committees and task forces provide fellowship opportunities for the small groups they involve, the Soup Suppers are where all the Anglo members of the parish come together. And here one can see the extent to which many social boundaries really do not matter; young and old, gay and straight, married and single—all enjoy these meals together.

SUMMARY

Despite having lost much of its traditional constituency, St. Matthew's seems to be succeeding in reaching two of the new population groups that have moved into its neighborhood—Hispanics and gay and lesbian persons. Our study focused on the relationship between the old Anglo constituents and only the latter of these new groups. At present, parish resources appear sufficient for the task, but eventually the parish will need either budget cutbacks or a significant new emphasis on giving. The relatively well-off, well-educated congregation has both monetary and personnel resources as yet untapped. A fairly loose administrative and authority structure seems to be serving parishioners well, allowing them to create ministries without waiting for hierarchical approval or a clear doctrinal rationale. What their theology says to them most clearly is that God cares for everyone, and Christians should be about putting flesh to that concern. Both Comunidad and the other outreach ministries of the church are their attempt to live the values they hear preached.

First Congregational Church, Long Beach: Open and Affirming Advocates

The first Sunday I spent in the Los Angeles area looking for research sites, I found myself in downtown Long Beach at church time. There on a prominent corner was the imposing building of First Congregational Church. There were homeless people on the doorstep, as there are throughout downtown Long Beach, but services were clearly about to get under way. Inside, a healthy number of parishioners—young and old—had gathered, and sprinkled among the traditional heterosexual couples were sizable numbers of single persons and same-sex pairs. Worship that day seemed pretty typical for a mainline Protestant congregation (an associate pastor, a man quite up in years, was preaching). I made a mental note, however, that this might be an interesting place to explore. Our research team member Brenda Brasher describes what we learned when we spent a good deal more time at First Congregational later that year.

During the years in which downtown Long Beach was in decline, First Congregational's attendance shrank and shrank. One member told of the changes since he arrived. "When I came in 1971, we were running two church services every Sunday—a 9:30 and an 11:00 A.M—which was typical of a lot of churches at that time. . . . It was a very fast drop from '71 to '74. It got to be so low, . . . it was decided, let's cut our losses and put everybody into one service at ten o'clock. . . . In about 1974, there was an actual motion to sell the church property. Demolish the building. Sell the property and relocate First Congregational Church to the suburbs." Clergy advocates counseled against this move, pointing out that the building was still a valuable resource. In the midst of this uncertain time in the life of downtown Long Beach, First Congregational decided not to move. In order to protect its property, it applied for and received historic landmark status for the building, built in 1914, meaning that the city could not touch it.

But the congregation still had to regain its footing and rediscover its role in this downtown location. During all the years of change in the city, the church's programs, outreach, and membership cultivation efforts didn't change a great deal. It remained a traditional "family" church where prominent members of the community attended. Although there were gay members, no one openly acknowledged that fact.

In 1987, the congregation called Rev. Dr. Mary Ellen Kilsby, a dynamic, activist pastor. Under her leadership, the church's role at the heart of downtown Long Beach has been firmly reestablished as a result of active neighborhood interaction and outreach, along with significant internal change.

Probably the most significant internal change has been the decision to become an "open and affirming" congregation. This is the United Church of Christ's formal designation for congregations who not only are open to lesbians and gays, but affirm them by supporting them for leadership positions and taking their concerns seriously as a congregational issue. This decision was preceded by a series of small Getting to Know You groups whose membership was half straight, half lesbian/gay and who got together to talk about their similarities and differences. By the time the decision was actually made, very few of the older members were upset, and many new people found that they really had a spiritual home.

Indeed, the congregation has flourished. Worship attendance hovers between two and three times what it was before Kilsby came. The church has employed a part-time staff person for children's music and an associate pastor who devotes about half-time to urban housing concerns. Members have even written and published a church history. The congregation has reconnected with its urban, downtown identity.

Because this is an urban church, the typical churchgoer is likely to be accosted outside the building by a homeless person asking for spare coins. Inside the nearly century-old elegant Romanesque building, groups of five and six parishioners scattered throughout the narthex and sanctuary are happily chatting away. "Here you are in the house of the Lord and saying that! [laughter]" "Did you cook a turkey?" "How's our friend Vala?" The ushers talk among themselves: "We've changed communion. Did you know that?" Getting each Sunday's ritual perfectly orchestrated at FCC can be a last-minute process.

During the prelude, children enter from church school and sit on the front pews, to the right. Babies and small toddlers remain in the nursery. The prelude, like nearly all music at FCC, is a professional-level classical performance, surprising and delighting the first-time visitor. Once it's over, people continue to enter. By the time the sermon begins, 250 will be present in this quietly ornate sanctuary.

The call to worship is given from the back of the sanctuary by Reverend Kilsby. Her lilting voice and excellent diction command attention. Her words articulate an inclusive, loving spirit of the Divine that calls all to worship and service. The congregation sings new and sometimes complicated hymns, beginning with a processional. Announcements are brief and mostly deal with events of that day.

The choir usually offers an anthem, although there are also often solos. About thirty-five people sing in the choir, many from some of the oldest families of the church, but interwoven with many newcomers. Their execution of classic sacred music is flawless, and the congregation is often moved.

Scripture reading and pastoral prayer are usually led by Associate Pastor Kit Wilke, who asks the congregation to pray with him in different ways each week. During this time, congregation members voice their concerns for Somalia, the Bosnians, and the homeless and the need to deal with hatred. This is followed by prayers for those within the community who are ill or in distress.

True to the church's heritage in the Reformed tradition, the sermon is the focal point of worship at FCC. Attention is riveted on the preacher as she steps up to the podium and begins to paint vivid word pictures, making real and present a vision of what the Christian life can be. Twenty minutes later she sits down, but the time passed seems but a moment. It is a moment (kairos) in which these worshippers are gathered together into a community. They have shared this experience, glimpsed the vision, and by so doing have affirmed the connections among them. Not many are able to explain what makes Reverend Kilsby's preaching so remarkable, so important to them, but all agree that it is.

The offertory that follows moves quickly, with members discreetly placing their envelopes in the plates. A recessional hymn ends worship; and from the back of the sanctuary, Reverend Kilsby pronounces the benediction. As the organist begins his postlude, most of the congregation sit back down to enjoy this last bit of magnificent music. At the end, they break into applause, and the organist, whose back has been to the congregation for all of worship, sticks out a slim hand from behind the organ screen and waves acknowledgment. Only then does the congregation begin to move back onto the streets of downtown Long Beach.

What First Congregational does on Sunday and what it does throughout the week have both changed over the last few years. An active lay member spoke at length about the difference Kilsby's presence has made.

It's the 1990s. . . . We've been at the site for a hundred years, and we're just starting to interact with the neighborhood. We want to grow. . . . Yet I think it's finally dawning on people that growth means change. . . . And Mary Ellen has brought that. She brought new vitality and new life and new growth, but tied into all that is this change. . . . I think the congregation is coming to terms with it. It doesn't mean that we're becoming a gay church. It means that we are—as our tradition calls for—being active people in society, and this [the presence of gay and lesbian persons] is a societal issue right now.

RESOURCES

Being actively involved in addressing societal issues is a primary concern for the people at First Congregational. That concern helps to shape what resources they need and how they define and use what they have. Their building, for example. When the downtown was in decline, and members were fleeing to suburban churches, FCC chose to stay. That decision was tested again when new earthquake building codes forced a $2.5 million "retrofit" of the sanctuary building and the demolition of the educational wing. They were able to undertake this massive project in part because a previous pastor had raised considerable endowment funds, but also because the members took on the task of raising money (and carrying a debt) in order to stay downtown.

The result is a building visible for blocks around that stands as a symbol of the church's presence in the midst of the community. It provides meeting space for community groups and worship space for Jewish high holy days, concert space for community and regional events, even space for a major senatorial campaign debate. Reverend Kilsby recalled sitting in the balcony one day, "listening to a steel drum band concert from the university, in the sanctuary. Next door to us was a neighborhood meeting with the police about gangs; downstairs the Hispanic church was meeting in the chapel for their Wednesday night prayer service; down below that was Adult Children of Alcoholics in one room and the Gay Men's Chorus in another." A busy space all week, even more importantly it is the space in which this congregation worships each Sunday. The richly carved wood, the dramatic organ pipes, and the soft light of the stained-glass windows create the backdrop for the music, prayers, and sermons that punctuate the lives of FCC's members and draw them together into a community.

Those members are, of course, another of the resources on which FCC draws. Since Reverend Kilsby arrived, the number of members has been growing, now standing at about five-hundred, up over a hundred. The average age is fifty-five (see table 4.2), and adult members are spread fairly evenly across the age spectrum. Many of the younger members are lesbian or gay; about 15 percent of those who completed our questionnaire reported a same-sex partner and nearly 40 percent reported being single. But there are also a good number of young straight families, enough to begin to swell the nursery and the church school and to precipitate a new children's choir.

Those who call FCC home are a well-educated group; more than half have completed work *beyond* a college degree, and only 3 percent have not gone beyond high school. Two-thirds work in professional and management occupations. That education and experience shows up in members' ability to plan ahead, to manage complex events, and to design new programs. There are also a good number of well-paid persons in the congregation; 21 percent have incomes over $80,000. Still, half have incomes in the $20,000 to $50,000 range, and 8 percent make even less. Fewer of Long Beach's most prominent business people attend the church than was the case a couple of decades ago, but the congregation is not lacking in human capital.

Table 4.2. First Congregational Church, Long Beach

Ideas and priorities	
Christian practices rated "essential"	Living Christian values
Ministries rated "very important" or "essential"	Service to the needy
	Social action groups in the church
Resources	
Average Sunday attendance	300
Annual operating budget (1992)	$490,000
Household incomes above $50,000	41%
College degrees or more	75%
Average age	55 years
Activities (beyond worship) participated in at least monthly	Fellowship
Relationship to the community	
Live ten minutes or less from the church	33%
New to the community in the last five years	20%
Ethnicity	95% European
Participate in civic & community activities more than once a month	50%

NOTE: Ninety-nine people responded to our survey, amounting to approximately 33 percent of average Sunday attendance. This may be taken as a fair representation of all regular attenders.

Those who attend have a fairly high level of commitment to the congregation. Members contribute, on average, between one hundred and two hundred dollars per month, supporting a regular annual budget of just under half a million dollars. A large proportion of the membership makes an annual pledge, and most of that group contribute at least as much as they pledge.

They are also willing to give a good deal of themselves to the tasks of the church and in service to the community. The high number of single people in the congregation has meant a high level of energy for investment. More than a third (38.8 percent) report being involved in the church's social ministries at least once a month. And half are involved in civic, political, or other community events and organizations more than once a month.

The high level of individual community involvement here is consonant with the church's own multiple connections with the Long Beach region's social service and political systems. First Congregational rarely undertakes a project alone. Sometimes they are in the lead, sometimes simply one among many. Their partners include the regional ecumenical association, the housing coalition, Christian Outreach Appeal (a local provider of services to people in need), and various AIDS organizations, with funding from local businesses, civic groups, even federal and state sources. In addition, FCC's arts programs connects them with local arts organizations and with Cal State, Long Beach. Although the denomination provides little material support, the regional United Church of Christ is able to help connect the church with various suburban churches that want to be involved in FCC's urban ministries. This habit of working in coalitions multiplies the congregation's resources of time, money, personpower, and visibility.

And visibility must certainly be counted among First Congregational's most valuable resources. When a meeting is held in the community and Mary Ellen Kilsby stands to speak, most of those present already know who she is and what the church does. When the annual Gay Pride Parade is held, she and her husband are invited to ride in it, representing the church. Local reporters often call her for comment on issues facing the city. The church also has gained something of a regional and national reputation. As the largest United Church of Christ congregation in the region pastored by a woman, it is watched carefully. When the *Wall Street Journal* was doing a story on the struggle over inclusive language in churches, religion writer Gustav Niebuhr visited FCC and began his story with an account of its worship services. If working in coalitions multiplies FCC's efforts, so does its visibility. Having determined to be a physical presence in Long Beach's downtown, the church has also become locally and nationally visible for its determination to make a difference in the world. Both the physical presence and the influence are resources of which FCC is increasingly aware.

STRUCTURES OF AUTHORITY

Among the most interesting aspects of First Congregational's work is the way it structures its relationships to all these outside organizations. Most often, staff and members participate in a loose coalition to accomplish some specific task. However, from time to time FCC takes on bigger, long-term projects for the good of the community, projects that need a more enduring structure. For instance, FCC began the local Farmer's Market, which was at first run through the structures of the church and eventually became an independent organization with a board of its own. Similarly, the church has been providing after-school services (tutoring, recreation, and the like) for a number of years. Now that the program is large enough to require a broader base of support, it, too, will probably become an independent ministry. The church will retain a significant interest in these efforts: FCC property will still be used, and members may be involved as contributors, volunteers, and board members. But having birthed these efforts, FCC has sent them out into the world.

The other major point of broader connection for FCC is its membership in the United Church of Christ (UCC). It remains, however, an autonomous congregation, able to make its own hiring, programming, and budgeting decisions. The pastor and several members are fairly active in the local UCC association, but that body has no direct authority over the congregation. It and the regional conference can, however, provide resources. In the pastor selection process, conferences nearly always play a key role in matching congregations and clergy. Churches in trouble can go to other UCC churches and to the conference for advice and support, and the denomination can help with connections that benefit everyone involved. First Congregational's denominational connections have helped in these ways, but perhaps the largest benefit FCC has gleaned from its membership in the UCC is the larger denomination's forthright stance supporting gay and lesbian persons. The UCC is among the few places a noncelibate lesbian or gay person can be ordained to the ministry, although the decision is still in the hands of each local church. More to the point for First Congregational, the UCC has produced materials that support churches that choose to become open and affirming. The phrase *open and affirming* itself provides a recognized label for the actions FCC (and other congregations) wish to take. FCC designed its own way of educating the congregation and making this decision, but public support by the denomination made its work easier.

The process of becoming open and affirming is, in fact, a good window on First Congregational's internal authority structures. In a Congregational church, decisions are made in democratic fashion by the members. But at FCC, long before there is a vote, decisions are being shaped by key leaders and by broad-based democratic discussion.

Even before the congregation called Mary Ellen Kilsby to be its pastor, several key lay leaders had discerned that becoming open and affirming was a direction they felt the church should take. They recognized the presence of large numbers of lesbian and gay people in the community and knew that many were already quietly making their way into the congregation. Citing Congregationalism's history as a forum where key issues are confronted and debated rather than ignored, they felt compelled to face the presence of this new (or newly visible) constituency. As the search committee did its work, this issue was subtly included among points to consider. That Kilsby had already led a church through the open and affirming process certainly counted in her favor.

Soon after Kilsby arrived, she began to meet with these lay leaders (some but not all of whom had official positions in the church) and others to dream about how the process might take shape. Reverend Kilsby describes her style of leadership as like a "mother hen." She both shelters and encourages. She is everywhere, constantly exerting the sheer power of her presence. She more often leads by her own contagious enthusiasm than by wielding any overt authority. When an idea is being "hatched," she knows how to bring together the energy and resources of the congregation to make it happen.

It was in her informal talks with lay leaders that the Getting to Know You groups were conceived. These would be small discussion groups in which gay and straight people would have a chance to learn at a personal level what was really at stake in being open and affirming. They would hear each other's stories, grieve and rejoice together, answer each other's questions. In addition, there would be educational forums, with in-house and guest experts. These two strategies allowed members of FCC opportunity to voice their opinions, but they also disseminated the two ingredients most critical to members like these— the kind of hard, critical, expert evidence that can appeal to the minds of such a highly educated group and the kinds of personal, emotional experiences that bind people together even when they disagree.

This was a process conducive to building something close to consensus, and as a result it also felt rather oppressive to the few who did disagree. A very few dropped out of the church along the way, but even most dissidents emerged from the final vote convinced they had been heard and were still respected.

CULTURE

To be heard, disagreed with, and still respected exemplifies much of what belonging to First Congregational means. This is a place that combines a near-sacred view of the individual with an intense commitment and loyalty to a group that often feels like home and family. A paradox, it lies at the heart of this congregation's life, held together by grace—perhaps the central concept in this congregation's theology. For members of First Congregational, salvation is experienced as an encounter with a love and acceptance so amazing that it transforms life. That is perhaps nowhere so evident as in the stories of gay and lesbian persons who find here a home, a reconnection with church traditions they thought lost, a place that acknowledges their spiritual longings *and* accepts them for who they are. As well, parents of gay and lesbian children find here a place where they can talk about their children's lives (and deaths) without censorship.

Accepting people for who they are means that First Congregational allows a good bit of room for doubt and exploration. The United Church of Christ is a noncreedal denomination. Although most members hold basic beliefs in common, these are subject to a wide range of articulation. When youth are confirmed at FCC, each one writes his or her own vows, and the congregation responds by welcoming them to a journey of faith. No one has to believe what everyone else believes, but they are able to accept and celebrate the beliefs people *do* hold with conviction. Members have a keen sense that what they learn and experience at church has implications for how they live their lives, implications that may force them to stand up against a perceived injustice or protest a situation that harms another. An influential lay leader put it this way: "I think that what this church holds sacred is the individual and how the individual relates to God, to Christ, how we live our lives relative to those around us, what value we place on human life." Speaking of being "open and affirming," she continued, "I don't think those things have changed, but they've expanded. The definition of what that encompassing love is about has changed."

First Congregational creates spaces for members to experience love and acceptance in a variety of ways. There are several "social groups" that meet regularly, drawing together couples in the empty-nest stage, young families with children, or just people who enjoy each other's company. Kindred Spirits, the group aimed especially at gays and lesbians (FCC's version of Comunidad), includes many people who have not yet made FCC their church home. But other groups contain both gay and straight people, often mixed in roughly equal numbers. In this, as in committees, worship, and everything else they do, the church asserts that sexual orientation is only one aspect of a person's identity, not the whole of it. These social groups, as well as the weekly coffee hour, the warm greeting visitors are likely to get from those on their pew, and the church's many other social activities are opportunities for members to share all the things they care about, from the most frivolous to the most serious.

The other place where God's love is encountered by First Congregational's members is worship. The beautiful music performed by choir, organ, and soloists reminds them of God's presence in the world. The sight of their fellow parishioners sitting in the semicircle of pews and the prayer requests shared during the service link members to each other and to God. But above all, the sermons they hear each week create moments of awareness—Brenda Brasher in her description used the theological word *kairos*—times when people see anew what God is up to in the world.

The way First Congregational worships is also a reflection of more profane realities. That this is a well-educated congregation that appreciates the musical and literary qualities of a worship service has made the integration of gay and straight people easier. The new constituency shares many of the cultural attributes of the old. All love the beauty of their historic old building and revel in the excellence of the music and in the way a well-crafted sermon stimulates their thinking. Many share common political causes, as well. The culture and expectations they bring in from the outside, shaped by their social class positions, have helped to establish common ground within the congregation.

Reverend Kilsby's sermons are often the bridge between the love experienced inside the congregation and the need to love and take responsibility for the world in which they find themselves. She reminds members that the gospel is good news to the poor and unwelcome news for the rich. In a November 1993 column in the newsletter, she recounted seeing an ad in which a large department store chain claimed to "stand ready to help" those affected by recent fires. Curious, she picked up the phone to find out what sort of help they meant. When she discovered they only meant that they would extend payment schedules for people who had been burned out, she sighed. Exposing and denouncing the hypocrisy of such commercial techniques, she went on to say that the church, in contrast, stood ready to offer concrete assistance and spiritual support.

These are not just people who make each other feel good, then, nor are they a group solely intent on finding their own individual spirituality. This is a place that attempts to combine worship and social action, love and justice. In fact, members talked to us about their conviction that in order to live a moral life, they needed both the sense of support they got from belonging to a community like First Congregational and the sense of transcendent power and direction they got from their experience of God, especially in worship.

The result is a congregation deeply engaged in work that addresses needs in its community. It is still involved with the Farmers Market and with the after-school program. A fledgling Spanish church uses FCC's building. Associate Pastor Kit Wilke spends a portion of his time working on issues of homelessness. The church sponsors a group for families of people who are incarcerated and hosts another group for Adult Children of Alcoholics. Other support groups crop up from time to time, including groups related to AIDS concerns. And myriad coalitions constantly involve the church in other ministry to the community, as do the vocations and volunteer activities of the members themselves. The church often disseminates information about ministry groups (from Habitat for Humanity to "third-world" self-help projects), expecting that individual members will become involved on their own.

Although the church has become more active and visible since Reverend Kilsby came, these qualities are not completely new developments. The church participated in earlier civil rights struggles and has always seen itself as the inheritor of the Congregationalist tradition of providing a public forum at the center of the city. First Congregational's response to the presence of gays and lesbians with *both* openness and public advocacy is therefore not surprising. Some in the congregation wish the church could quietly accept everyone, regardless of sexual orientation, but others believe that this issue is one they have to stand up for. Not to be public might perpetuate, they fear, the injustices faced by gays and lesbians. Neighboring St. Matthew's strategy of quiet integration of this new constituency would not work at FCC, where the role of the church in public life is central, and whatever issues face church and community will be publicly faced in the congregation and in its outreach.

Being public about its openness does have effects, however. FCC often serves as a lightning rod for conservative criticism, but that has little real effect. More critical is the way its new policy affects patterns of recruitment. Since the church has become open and affirming, increasing numbers of gay and lesbian persons have found their way into FCC. They have provided a real burst of energy for the congregation, but both they and the rest of the congregation worry that straight people will quit joining. Everybody in the church is clear that they do not want FCC to be a "gay church." Other places meet that need, and this congregation values diversity and integration. They want to be a church that brings gays and straights together, which cannot happen if only gay people join. Perhaps for this reason, there was extraordinary rejoicing over a rash of infant baptisms in late 1993 and extraordinary pride in the new children's choir. The parents who are committed to FCC have made a conscious choice to raise their children in this sort of open and tolerant environment. The coming years will tell whether the number of such straight parents and older traditional adults will balance out the number of gays and lesbians flocking to the worship, fellowship, and community involvement of this open and affirming congregation.

SUMMARY

For First Congregational, responding to external change is part and parcel of their identity. As a church committed to its downtown location and with a history of civic involvement and political activism, they found that gay and lesbian concerns were not different in kind from earlier issues they had faced. With the growth of recent years the congregation has found itself with ample resources of money, facilities, visibility, leadership, and personpower to tackle both the internal changes implied by integrating a new constituency and the external involvements implied by taking on a new set of concerns. Their own internal decision-making processes served them well, and their denomination provided needed support and encouragement.

The integration of gays and lesbians has probably been eased by the similar social-class and education levels of gay and straight members. Those joining First Congregational share the same occupational and educational backgrounds, enjoy the same sorts of music, have like political commitments. Members' theology and history told them they should become open and affirming, but their place in the social system helped build the necessary bridges. They have not, for instance, built similar bridges to the various immigrant communities in Long Beach, where the social differences would be much greater.

Across the country, in Atlanta, First Existentialist has built social bridges of its own. Not a visible downtown presence but a maverick on the margins, it has managed to draw together a variety of people who share that sense of marginality. First Existentialist has little sense of history but rather a sense of making its own history as it goes along. This is an experimental congregation full of seekers who nevertheless value this way station along the road.

First Existentialist Congregation, Candler Park: An Alternative Community

First Existentialist, in the Candler Park section of Atlanta, is not your run-of-the-mill church. In fact, most of its members call it a congregation rather than a church. The Bible and traditional Christianity are mostly irrelevant. Many who gather here have found traditional churches hostile, unwelcoming, and personally unfulfilling. The fact that some of their neighbors derisively call their congregation "First Lesbyterian" is not lost on them. Still, this small group gathers each Sunday morning at eleven o'clock to sing, have announcements, take an offering, and listen to a sermon, all traditional churchly activities. Theirs is a curious mix of tradition and antitradition, a haven created by people who often feel they have no other home. Research team member Diana Jones has listened in on this unusual congregation's life, and she describes its history.

In the 1970s, a small group of individuals interested in learning more about existentialism began to meet weekly in the home of Lanier Clance, a trained minister and practicing therapist. His family partners—Pauline, a university professor and therapist, and Nancy, also a college professor—were also instrumental in these early days of the congregation's life. As the group grew they began to hold meetings at the local YMCA. In 1979 the group had grown large enough to warrant purchasing their own building, and with the help of the Unitarian Universalist Association they did just that. Now, almost two decades later, the congregation is still going strong.

First Existentialist's sanctuary overlooks the golf course and park that lie in the heart of the Candler Park community. As people gather on Sunday morning, some sit on the steps outside, while others pace near the coffee pot in the

185

kitchen, waiting for the little red light to come on. People arrive at a leisurely pace and move about casually even after the service begins. The sanctuary could hold 250 persons, but it is usually set up with 120 or so folding chairs on its newly resurfaced wood floor. About two-thirds of those seats will be full before the morning is over.

At least three-quarters of those who come will be female, most between the ages of thirty and fifty, a large majority white. Those attending dress quite casually in shorts, t-shirts, jeans, cotton pants, or dresses. At least 60 percent of the congregation is lesbian/gay or bisexual, with lesbians making up the largest segment. This characteristic of the congregation is fairly new, beginning in about the mideighties when the congregation's attendance peaked at approximately 120 persons at each service. Until then the congregation comprised mostly, though not exclusively, heterosexuals.

The space itself is plain, with the chairs facing a large stage on which stands a lectern. A large piano sits in front of the stage. But the space is filled with a changing display of artwork that gives it meaning. The stage may have various pieces of sculpture, while the side walls of the sanctuary are adorned with paintings and photographs. The figures on the stage and paintings on the walls feature mostly female and goddess forms.

The service begins with singing from the Unitarian Universalist hymnal, which contains many folksongs, union songs, and classic spirituals with some radically altered lyrics. Two of the congregation's favorites are "This Little Light of Mine" and "All the Colors." Tambourines and other rhythm instruments are passed out to those who wish to accompany the lively singing and gospel-style piano. As congregants continue to arrive, they greet one another with hugs, getting coffee or tea before they sit down. People, straight and gay, sit with their arms around one another, holding hands or leaning shoulder to shoulder. Some expressing this physical intimacy are friends, while others are lovers or spouses who have been together for many years.

Lanier Clance, the congregation's founder and minister, is likely to be dressed in a shimmering silver shirt, silver slacks, a black velveteen jacket, and black suede shoes with silver sequins. His hair and full beard are a mix of silver, gray, and white, and his ear is newly pierced. Standing on the stage, he asks if there are any community announcements. Someone may stand to announce the need for volunteers to work with the Project Open Hand program serving meals to people with AIDS. Others announce a meeting time for the newly formed finance committee, recent research investigating the relationship between mammograms and breast cancer, the amount of money raised at a recent art show sponsored by the congregation, and an upcoming concert of the Atlanta Feminist Women's Chorus.

Lanier then asks if there are any birthdays or anniversaries, a regular feature of the Sunday service designed, in part, to fill the void many experience by being either emotionally estranged or geographically distanced from their families of origin. One Sunday, for instance, the congregation sang "Happy Birthday" to one woman and then celebrated with two other women marking their third anniversary as a couple. One of the women joked, "That's a hundred in lesbian years."

A period of meditation follows, in which Lanier invites the congregation to "sit quietly with our brothers and sisters" or to light a candle located on small tables at either side of the sanctuary. Announcements from the congregants follow. People often talk about illnesses or deaths of those close to them, struggles dealing with childhood abuse, experiences of "coming out" to family or colleagues, personal health concerns, or loss of jobs. Many also talk about positive developments in relationships, progress in therapy, and work achievements. Musicians or artists in the congregation announce upcoming shows, performances, or tape or album releases. Others in attendance comment on issues in the media they find particularly interesting (such as Maya Angelou's poem at President Clinton's inauguration) or disturbing (such as the Republicans' interpretation of "family values").

The congregation sings another song while baskets are passed and the offering is taken. The offertory is often a reading by Lanier from authors such as bell hooks, Maya Angelou, Jean-Paul Sartre, or Martin Luther King, Jr.

The sermon is a kind of stream-of-consciousness exposition on personal and political issues. On one Sunday morning, Lanier began by talking about the danger and destructiveness of secrets within a community, addressing a recent crisis the congregation had faced. The twelve-person board had been petitioned by a long-term member of the congregation to use the building to hold Cub Scout meetings. Because the Boy Scouts of America has an explicit anti-gay/lesbian policy the request resulted in a heated discussion among several board members. Some argued that supporting a Cub Scout group was, fundamentally, about supporting and nurturing children. Others argued that it legitimized an organization whose policies are discriminatory. Although the board finally voted not to allow the Scout group to meet in the building, tempers had flared and feelings had been hurt. Many of the gays and lesbians on the board felt that some of the straight board members failed to recognize and honor the pain and discrimination they have experienced in their lifetimes. One or two of the straight board members felt that they were experiencing "reverse discrimination." After explaining this turn of events to the congregation, Lanier talked about how people often think that diversity is beautiful, but, in reality, it often leads to conflict. He encouraged everyone to continue working to find creative ways of respecting one another's differences. Knowing that many communities and organizations in the country are unwilling to face the pain of working through intense conflicts, "We've got to work it out here," he said. "If we can't do it here, it won't happen in other areas."

Lanier views the Existentialist Congregation as a group whose very existence is risky, for it rejects many mainstream U.S. traditions, while actively supporting and promoting alternative belief systems and types of relationships. This stance, he claims, often elicits passion, rage, fear, and terror in the larger *community. And yet, Lanier says, he is proud of First E and its strong support of the lesbian community. He feels privileged to be in a position where he can be exposed to and be a part of a politically lesbian feminist culture. The congregation is a place where all its members can go to rally the energy to continue being political.*

Part of being in community at First E is finding a place where people can acknowledge their terrors and let them out, he says. But it is also being able to reach out to others and to celebrate life. Though Lanier and most in the congregation understand that the South in general is unsafe for most gays/lesbians and bisexuals, the congregation is described as a place where one can feel both safe and whole. Associate Minister Marsha Mitchener said of coming there, "I didn't have to pretend like I was somebody different on Sunday when I went to church. I could just be who I was."

The service ends each week with the singing of another hymn. A few people leave immediately, but most—gay, straight, and otherwise defined—linger for up to an hour visiting with one another, continuing the sharing of lives that is at the heart of First Existentialist.

RESOURCES

With a relatively small, not especially rich congregation, First Existentialist (or First E, as many refer to it) lacks a firm financial base. Money is a perennial problem. More than half the members (58 percent) have household incomes under $35,000, and almost three-quarters (73 percent) give less than fifty dollars per month to the congregation. At the end of 1992, the congregation had taken in almost $6000 less than it spent for the year and had very little cushion with which to make up that shortfall. Its budget of just over $70,000 comes mostly from pledges ($50,000), with the remainder coming from rental of the building, miscellaneous offerings, and numerous fund-raising projects (see table 4.3).

A good deal of energy, in fact, goes into finding ways to raise money. Since most of the members are also active in other community organizations, they bring to the congregation their experience with the projects that keep other precarious voluntary associations alive. Fund-raising has become one of the primary social activities of the congregation. Dances and dinners, art shows and clothing sales provide opportunities for members to work together and play together in behalf of a cause they support. They recognize, of course, that the more practical way to raise money for the congregation is to secure routine pledges from the members. But like everything else about this congregation, giving is a highly personal decision, and each person's needs are respected. Still, they are reminded often that they need to contribute so that they can "keep our experience financially viable," as one

Table 4.3. First Existentialist Congregation, Candler Park

Ideas and priorities	
Practices rated "essential" to a good life	Seeking to bring beauty into the world
Ministries rated "very important" or "essential"	Individual participation in social & political issues Social action groups in the congregation
Resources	
Average Sunday attendance	75
Annual operating budget (1992)	$71,000
Household incomes above $50,000	30%
College degrees or more	83%
Average age	38 years
Activities (beyond worship) participated in at least monthly	None
Relationship to the community	
Live ten minutes or less from the church	55%
New to the community in the last five years	29%
Ethnicity	88% European
Participate in civic & community activities more than once a month	44%

NOTE: Seventy-one people responded to our survey, amounting to approximately 95 percent of average Sunday attendance. This can be taken as an extremely accurate cross-section of regular attenders.

newsletter plea put it. The finance committee asks for pledges each year and the pastor often reminds members that they cannot keep the doors open without sufficient funds. But regular financial commitments are hard to come by, and sometimes they have to cut back on projects they would like to do because the money is not available.

Fortunately, however, this is a congregation with an infrastructure that requires minimal financial support. Their pastor, who works as a therapist, is not paid a full-time salary by the congregation. When they can afford it, they have additional part-time ministerial staff, often more for the sake of training them than for urgent programming needs. In short, the congregation's size and limited program allow it to get by with minimal staff support. The building, adequate for members' needs, accounts for about one-quarter of their expenses, but they are able to take care of most routine work with volunteer labor. In addition, over 10 percent of their income comes from building rental. Making their space available to outside groups has the double advantage of bringing in income and making the congregation visible in the larger community of arts, political, and gay and lesbian organizations. The Atlanta Feminist Women's Chorus has been perhaps their most visible tenant.

That larger community of organizations, comprising Atlanta's arts and radical political sector, is a network of which First E and its members are very much a part. Nearly a third of the members (30 percent) report holding some leadership position in a civic, political, or other community group, and nearly half (44 percent) participate in such a group more than once a month. Those attachments show up in the Sunday morning announcement period. Members tend to be widely informed about causes to support and happenings in the community. They think of First E as a place where they can share their concerns and get sympathetic support for the political and humanitarian work they do. Almost any concern or need can find a potential channel for action in one of the community connections represented within this congregation's membership.

That vast network of connections is part of the richness of the human resources First E enjoys. Within its ranks are artists of various sorts and a wide range of professionals and service providers, along with a contingent of students. Nearly half (44 percent) have some education beyond college, while only 10 percent of those not currently in school have less than a college degree.

This skill combines with a good deal of political passion at First E. Members are well connected in the community because they care a great deal about people who are marginalized and suffering. That concern, however, has another side when it comes to maintaining First E as a congregation. Because they are so active, they come to the congregation relatively needy and often burned out. Rather than undertaking projects of its own, First E is therefore often a place that heals and energizes its members for the work in which they are already involved. It is difficult to generate collective energy for new causes when so much is already being done. While the congregation can boast a wealth of skill, experience, and connections, it mobilizes those resources for its own purposes less often than it might if its members were not already so engaged.

This dilemma also affects the congregation's efforts to recruit leaders. Various committees (guilds) go understaffed, and it is sometimes hard to find twelve people to serve on the main governing board. Since the pastor is not a full-time employee, he too may sometimes prove unavailable when the congregation needs to work through a crisis. Between the intense commitments these members often make and their own existentialist quest for self-fulfillment, this congregation's high level of ability to say no sometimes leaves it without the internal leadership it needs.

The relative unavailability of the pastor for administrative and pastoral duties does not mean that his leadership has been less than crucial in building the congregation. As with any experimental religious group, the devotion of followers is often mobilized by their loyalty to a visionary leader. Everyone recognizes that First Existentialist has grown from the dream of Lanier Clance, and recently his health problems have reminded the group of how much they depend on him. His sermons offer the reflective opportunity members seek each week, his commitments challenge and energize the group, his openness sets the tone, and his own connections often translate into recruits for the congregation. Despite being a man pastoring a congregation populated by lesbians, he successfully proclaims First E to be "woman space," a safe place where feminist values are the guiding norm.

STRUCTURES OF AUTHORITY

First Existentialist has at least a nominal affiliation with the Unitarian Universalists (UU). Some members consider themselves Unitarian and attended another Unitarian church in town before coming to First E. A few participate in regional UU events and keep the congregation informed through the newsletter. Congregants use the Unitarian hymnal, and the Unitarians helped them buy their building. But the affiliation is otherwise little noticed. Lanier does not participate in denominational affairs, and the denomination has no direct authority over the congregation. When First E chose to ordain Marsha Mitchener, the service was designed and conducted by the congregation itself. First E is even willing to put itself at odds with the denomination on occasion. The congregation sets its own agenda and only calls on its denominational affiliation when those resources of connection and legitimation prove useful.

Internally, First E's guilds address the various functions of the congregation—building and grounds, social action, membership, publicity, finances, and the like. Although they sometimes operate without a full complement of members, they manage to do the work that has to be done. The congregation is kept informed by a well-produced newsletter that contains articles about congregational issues, information about who to call for what, news about members and upcoming events, and so on. Actual decision making is entrusted to a twelve-person board, which has overall responsibility for planning, administering, and dealing with crises. Here critical issues are debated, for example, the Cub Scout question. The request for use of the building went to the board for approval, where it ran into trouble because of the Boy Scouts of America position on homosexuality. Gay and lesbian members felt the sting of BSA discrimination acutely. Straight members wanted to support community children. Neither could quite understand why the other was so upset. It was a critical test of the congregation's ability to hold together its diverse elements. In the end, the board voted not to rent space to the Scout troop, but its decision could gain full legitimacy only through an extensive effort at personalized negotiation and fence mending. Lanier's sermon on the subject simply acknowledged the difficulty people were already working through.

The conditional nature of the board's authority was reinforced in another crisis situation a year later. For many months, Sam (not his real name) had been attending services at First E. Homeless and mentally unstable, he had gained a reputation as somewhat disruptive. His behavior at potluck dinners was so unpleasant that the congregation had essentially quit having them. Still, his presence was tolerated, even welcomed, until he physically pushed one of the women. After that incident, the board deliberated long and hard about how to respond and decided that he should be barred from the building. Others in the congregation, however, were unhappy with this act of exclusion and rose during the personal announcement period to invite others to brainstorm about alternative ways of handling Sam. Even before this crisis, one laywoman had said, "If we are an open congregation and we believe in the goodness of all people, then our mentally ill people and our homeless people need to be welcomed." The radical individualism of these seekers includes a strong sense of protection for people otherwise not protected in society. But it also limits the authority of the board. The associate minister reflected, "What I've come to believe is that people temporarily give you authority to perform a certain function, and that that is a gift they give you to do that. But at the same time, I claim to have no answers that are true for anyone else but myself. I'm willing to share those, but not to mandate that this is how it is." Situations that affect the group's sense of identity are ultimately decided in the forum of personal and congregational discussion. As existentialists, it could hardly be otherwise.

CULTURE

When members of First Existentialist tell their friends about the congregation, they are likely to emphasize first of all its openness and warmth and safety. When Lanier describes it as a haven, he is reflecting both the hostility of a world that does not welcome unconventional folk and the caring experienced by people who come to First E. "I believe this is a sanctuary," Lanier says. "I need a place where I can come back and feel whole." A member says, "The people here are supportive and good, and they're people who will listen to you and who have gone through a hell of a lot themselves. But they're willing to talk about it, and look at it, and listen to what's happening with you."

The personal-announcement time each Sunday is the collective representation of this commitment to listening, and it can sometimes be emotionally intense. On a single Sunday, a woman in her forties talked about recently coming out to her mother; it was difficult, but finally positive, she said. Another woman talked about the suicide of her disabled son. A man shared that his doctors think he should begin treatment with antidepressants. A woman in her fifties talked about a recent reconciliation with her former lover's daughter. A young woman asked for the congregation's support as she comes out to her parents. And still another woman celebrated that she would be able to spend holiday time with a daughter she had lost custody of years earlier, as a result of being a lesbian.

Sharing such personal concerns is part of the unique mix of individual and communal that characterizes this congregation. On the one hand members are existentialists—ultimately concerned with finding what path is right for each individual, being in touch with their own minds, bodies, and spirits. On the other hand, they have found that their quest for self-realization has led them into this community. Say the members, "Part of being alive is looking after one another;" and "If I am what I am, I am most able to connect and have community." They recognize and celebrate the paradox of a community dedicated to helping individuals be all they can be. It happens, they say, both in the announcement times and in the informal conversations before and after services. It also happens in the times of meditation and in the sermon. "I guess having other people around and having that time set aside for examining whether I'm doing right in my life and in my relationships [really helps]. Am I caring about more than just me and my family? Can I reach out to a broader range of people? It really reminds me of my very human connection, and my obligation to give as well as to get things." Said another member, "I like people working together to do things to help one another. It feels like a good place."

Working together to help one another extends to supporting each other in a wide range of social and political activism. The activities of this very involved group include delivering meals to persons with AIDS; support for a battered women's shelter; various congressional letter-writing campaigns; mobilizing on issues of discrimination, war, sexual abuse, and violence; hunger walks and support for aid to Somalia—and the list goes on. Rarely does the congregation act *as a congregation.* Instead, the members are encouraged to share their own involvements and concerns and ask for help from others who are interested. This approach avoids the long debates that might accompany

any effort to commit the congregation as a whole to anything. It also solves the problem of having to make decisions about allocating the congregation's scarce resources of time and money.

This way of handling social and political involvement illustrates again the curious balance First E maintains between individual and community. People are invited to act collectively, but only as they individually so choose. This highly individual form of action poses problems for First E as an organization. It cannot take for granted the support of its members in time, energy, and money. Supporting institutions for their own sake is not high on the priority list of most people here—it is something of a miracle that this congregation exists at all, a tribute to the power of what people experience at First E. Still, there is a recurring pattern of joining and regular participation—including perhaps taking on congregational leadership roles—followed by dropping out. The high energy of the congregation occasionally produces burnout. Sometimes people have simply reaped the benefit the congregation has to offer them and moved on. Occasionally they move to more conventional religiosity; more often they cease any religious participation at all. Sometimes they return in a year or two, again seeking the sense of community and empowerment the congregation offers.

The kind of emotional vulnerability and intense political activism that membership in this congregation involves (as well as the particular issues it addresses) is very good news to many who make their way through First E's doors. But it is not for everybody. The congregation recognizes, in fact, that it suffers from a kind of double bind in recruitment. Many people in the community who share the radical political and life-style commitments of First E's members are not at all interested in things spiritual, while most of the spiritually minded in this southern city are at least uncomfortable with, if not hostile to, the concerns and constituency of a place like First E.

The sort of spirituality found at First E would not be congenial for much of this Bible Belt city. In fact, Lanier and many of his listeners joyously reject most traditional Christian beliefs and practices. The Bible is, for them, too often used to stifle individual spiritual quests, rather than to aid them. Christian ideas about sin and guilt are seen as major impediments to self-realization. The notion that one might need a savior represents, for First E members, an unhealthy dependence on forces outside oneself. In short, traditional evangelical Christianity is something to be escaped and gotten over. Part of the "healing" First E members experience in the congregation is a reconnection with a spiritual life that carries none of the old baggage of sin and condemnation and otherworldliness. What they find instead is a this-worldly engagement, combined with a spirituality that borrows liberally from a variety of religious traditions.[4] In this they are not unlike other Unitarians.[5]

194

Solstices are celebrated, crystals hang in the windows, chants and ceremonies are borrowed from Wicca, and meditation techniques are borrowed from Zen. No one is ever expected to participate in anything
they do not personally find meaningful, but space is created in each
service for practices that help each person to touch their spiritual center, as one member put it, "that little place inside that is greater than
what I am as an individual and that touches me into that power that is
out there that is beyond just me."

First E clearly occupies a specialized niche. While many members
live in and identify with the Candler Park community, others come
from throughout the Atlanta area. In 1995, they were voted "most welcoming congregation" by Atlanta's *Southern Voice*, an alternative newspaper. Whether that niche will be predominantly lesbian or contain a
strong mixture of straight members, as well, is still being negotiated.
First E began as a predominantly straight congregation that was open
to gays and lesbians—much like First Congregational in Long Beach.
The straight people who remain at First E share the radical politics and
the sense of marginality felt by their lesbian and gay compatriots. Because there are so few places for gay and lesbian persons to worship,
they inevitably flock to those that are available. Most straight people,
on the other hand, not only have more choices but are less likely to
want to worship alongside lesbians and gays. Maintaining a balance
will be difficult for any congregation that is visibly open. Over the
years, the mix at First E has shifted so that only 10 percent of the congregation is in conventional marriages, while another 10 percent live
with roommates and 25 percent are in long-term same-sex partnerships. The remainder are single, the vast majority of those gay or lesbian. Many people in the congregation wish it could be a genuinely
mixed group, longing for the integration and acceptance that would
model. But others are glad for a space in which their issues are granted
privileged status. Here those otherwise without a voice can speak
freely.[6] With so few such safe spaces, this one seems especially important. This struggle perhaps explains the intensity with which the congregation debated the Cub Scout issue. For one set of people the Scouts
represented a hostile invasion of their safe space, while for others it
represented a world where "conventional" families with children could
accept the hospitality of gays and lesbians.

SUMMARY

Having created a radically unconventional congregation in one of Atlanta's few countercultural neighborhoods, the people at First Existentialist were naturally open to the lesbian and gay people who began to
attend almost from the beginning. By also opening their building to the
Atlanta Feminist Women's Chorus, as well as to other lesbian activities

and various arts endeavors, the congregation soon became a magnet for lesbian and gay people who wanted the sort of spirituality and communal support offered there. The congregation constantly struggles to maintain adequate institutional commitment among its highly individual members. They are not exceptionally well-heeled, and they do not give generous amounts to the congregation. However, they *are* exceptionally well connected and skilled, and the congregation serves as a focal point for their wide-ranging community involvements. They find in First E a haven, a place to share concerns with sympathetic others, a place that challenges them both to grow personally and to care about others. Out of this combination of radical political commitments and intense personal sharing has come a congregation whose openness made adaptation to the presence of lesbian and gay persons a natural outgrowth of their existing identity.

Conclusion

These three congregations found themselves in communities where lesbian and gay persons were a recognizable presence. Rather than ignore that presence, they have chosen to open their doors. In each case, that has meant the establishment of new programs: FCC's Kindred Spirits, St. Matthew's Comunidad, and playing host to the Feminist Women's Chorus at First E. It has also meant changes in the persons and symbols included in worship. The involvement of gay men as eucharistic ministers at St. Matthew's symbolizes their inclusion, just as does the music and art of First Existentialist. First Congregational and First Existentialist brought to this task a tradition of activism and of serving nonconventional communities. St. Matthew's, however, is less reformist, more simply a community parish seeking to serve the populations it finds within its parish borders.

All three congregations are also struggling with the task of remaining integrated, not losing their original straight population. Some of the traditional parishioners at St. Matthew's are tempted by the more accommodating schedule of Masses at a nearby parish. First E recognizes that it is a very adult place, with little room for families with children. And FCC rejoices when it can baptize a bevy of infants and start a new children's choir. With varying degrees of success, these three congregations are avoiding conversion into places defined solely by sexual orientation.

The process by which they arrived at their current state of integration differs in each case. At First E, it just happened. At FCC, the process was deliberate and involved the whole congregation in debate and conscious decision. At St. Matthew's, the denomination made the first suggestion and provided initial resources. In all three cases, denominations either provided active support or stayed out of the way. And in all three cases, visionary pastors provided necessary guidance for the process.

The most striking characteristic these three congregations have in common, however, is their extraordinarily high level of education. As a group, they score higher than any other group of congregations in the study. While the incomes and occupations in all three tend toward the comfortable and professional, there is some variation on those factors. First E's congregation is much more economically and occupationally marginal than FCC's, for instance. However, for all three the norm is a college degree and the presence of large numbers with postgraduate education. Both the gay and straight populations share the experience of higher education, perhaps having learned in the process some of the skills necessary for guiding an organization through the transformation necessary for integrating diverse groups, along with the norms of inclusion that they have put into practice in their congregations.

CHAPTER 5

Adaptation: Integrating across Cultures

While the issue of homosexuality is perhaps the most divisive issue facing much of U.S. religion, the three congregations we met in the last chapter discovered a strong sense of common background and common mission with the gay and lesbian people they welcomed. Old and new members, though of different sexual orientation, shared political commitments, educational achievements, aesthetic values, and the like. They were urban in orientation and almost all white. The three congregations we will look at in this chapter have discovered formidable challenges in attempting to integrate cultural groups of different races, languages, and heritages. They can make few assumptions about shared educational backgrounds, common political agendas, or agreed-upon aesthetic styles. The people who find their way into the pews of these churches are in many ways worlds apart, and creating a working congregation from such diverse elements goes against many of the norms of U.S. congregational life, where sharing a cultural identity is much more common. Finding grounds for commonality among apparently different peoples has been the task these congregations faced.

Brighton Evangelical Congregational Church and City Baptist Church have undertaken the inclusion of diverse ethnic groups, a process they find entails changes in long-held patterns of action. Hinton Memorial United Methodist is attempting to integrate traditional small-town southerners with mobile suburbanites. In three very different communities, facing very different cultural challenges, all three congregations have embraced the notion that there is beauty in diversity, that they can find common ground in a religious community. We will turn first to Brighton Evangelical Congregational Church, which takes us back to Allston-Brighton and its growing immigrant population. In the same community where St. Catherine's Catholic Church and Brighton Ave-

198

nue Baptist are struggling to survive, BECC has begun to change in some fundamental ways.

Brighton Evangelical Congregational Church, Brighton: From Morning Coats to Community Food Pantry

On the day I met Eunice Taylor, she was working in the church food pantry, which was not an unusual place to find her. An imposing African American woman now approaching retirement age, she has a passion for people in need that makes her impatient with church activities that have no clear purpose. That was how she felt one night several years ago when she was working at a church bingo game. At the end of the evening, with tired feet and an equally tired spirit, she thought to herself, "There has to be something better than this for this church to do with itself." From those tired feet—and Eunice's imagination and passion—a new vision has begun to emerge for Brighton Evangelical Congregational Church in Brighton, Massachusetts.

BECC is one of the most fragile congregations we studied. With barely fifty active members and liabilities at least as formidable as its assets, it nevertheless seems to be on a path toward a new future. Mary Beth Sievens of our research team tells BECC's story.

The Brighton Evangelical Congregational Church was established in 1827, a product of the Second Great Awakening, and is the oldest religious congregation that continues to meet in Allston-Brighton. The church is located in Brighton Center, in the third building the congregation has occupied, a lovely federalist-style brick structure with a white steeple, erected in 1927 after a fire destroyed the building the church had used since the middle of the nineteenth century.

The congregation was at its strongest, both financially and in terms of membership, from the 1930s to the 1950s. During this period, members numbered in the hundreds, many of them were among Allston-Brighton's most affluent residents. The community was predominantly Irish and Italian, home-owning, and solidly middle class. The Catholic presence had been dominant for half a century, but Protestants were still numerous. As Allston-Brighton lost many of its middle-class residents to the suburbs, the membership of BECC also began to decline. By the mid-1980s, active membership had dropped to the low fifties.

Today, ethnic enterprises abound in Allston-Brighton, and on the streets one is likely to hear a medley of languages, including Portuguese, French, Vietnamese, and Korean. Likewise, the once homogeneous white middle-class congregation of BECC is now a multiracial and multiethnic mix. This transformation has occurred with little overt conflict, but the congregation is still grappling with the multiple consequences of the community's recent demographic shifts.

For instance, the precipitous decline in BECC's membership has affected the church's leadership and finances. Until the late 1980s, the congregation had always been served by a full-time minister. In June 1990, the congregation installed its first part-time minister. Rev. John Eller, who holds a full-time job in the banking industry, is expected to devote another thirty hours a week to his congregation (although he actually devotes considerably more). This change in pastoral leadership has necessitated other administrative changes. Reverend Eller launched a complete revamping of the church by-laws and revived a committee system to handle much of the administrative business of the church. The new style of leadership has created some tension between older members who are used to being in charge and new members who frequently have new ideas and new ways of doing things.

BECC has experienced some growth in membership under the current pastor, mostly adding new members who are ethnically and economically different from its traditional constituency. A congregation that was once almost exclusively middle-class Anglo-American has opened its doors to African Americans, Asians, Asian Indians, and Caribbean islanders. Many new congregants are also of a lower socioeconomic status than are older members. Some rely on public assistance, and some have had difficulty finding employment during the recession of the early 1990s.

These new members are full participants in the congregation's life. They belong to all of the church's auxiliary groups; serve on committees, often in leadership positions; teach Sunday school; and take their turns in those roles (such as scripture reader) that the laity fill during worship service. Class differences present more difficulty to the congregation than ethnic ones. Older members fret about the way some new members dress for worship service and worry that some new congregants might be attracted to the church more for financial assistance than for spiritual reasons.

Most members, new and old, identify church finances as one of the most important problems facing BECC. While they foresee no imminent financial crisis, money is tight. In spite of increasing membership and a high percentage of pledgers in the congregation, donations have declined in recent years, as some of the new members have been less able to contribute.

Despite financial constraints, BECC maintains several high-profile community ministries. A thrift shop offers inexpensive clothing, housewares, and other items for sale. A weekly soup kitchen feeds close to one hundred people every Wednesday night, and a food pantry provides food baskets to needy community residents. The teen group offers community youth activities ranging from arts-and-crafts workshops to trips to amusement parks to after-school tutoring. BECC is able to carry out these ministries because of the extensive institutional partnerships it has developed. Local supermarkets and restaurants donate food for the soup kitchen and food pantry. College service organizations *provide much of the staffing for these food ministries, as well as tutoring services for the teen group. The mayor's Office of Youth Services provided a grant to fund many other teen group activities. Church members also actively support these ministries by volunteering and donating food and clothing.*

All of BECC's community ministries have been created in the past ten to twelve years, in response to the needs of the new population groups entering Allston-Brighton. Both old and new members take pride in them; they are glad to obey Christ's injunction to feed the hungry and clothe the naked. Long-term members describe the BECC of forty to fifty years ago as a less friendly place, not very open to newcomers. They pride themselves now on the prevailing atmosphere of friendliness and openness. My experience as a "newcomer" confirmed their perception. Never did I feel unwelcome: Congregants accepted me warmly as a person, not a researcher, although all were aware of my reason for attending services and asking so many questions. Other newcomers receive the same enthusiastic welcome.

The sanctuary of the church, plain but elegant, invites visitors to pay attention to the people who gather there. There is no stained glass, only simple multipaned windows. The wooden pews are padded, and the entire floor is carpeted. The open platform contains a center pulpit and, to the side, a lectern in the shape of an eagle. Both are draped in the appropriate liturgical colors. Behind the platform is a raised choir loft, now occupied only by an organist. The only other prominent decoration, a framed piece of stained glass that depicts the face of Jesus, recovered from the ruins of the second building, hangs below the organ pipes on the front wall.

At a typical worship service average attendance ranges from forty to fifty, although the sanctuary would comfortably hold four or five times that many. About one-third of those present are nonwhite, with a strong contingent of elderly ladies, many of whom sit together. However, most congregants are in their forties and fifties, with a few younger adults and a handful of teenagers. Few people sit alone; most are with family members or friends.

On the surface, the service appears staid. It begins with a responsive call to worship printed in the bulletin. A paid soloist leads the congregation in singing three fairly traditional, stately hymns at regular intervals throughout the service. The congregation recites the Lord's Prayer and sings the Gloria Patri and Doxology at set times during each service. Scripture readings follow the United Church of Christ lectionary. The service formally ends with a threefold amen sung by the congregation.

Important breaks in this formality, however, permit a glimpse into the openness of the congregation. Passing the peace is no mere ritual here but a true greeting time, characterized as much by hugs as by the prescribed handshake. When making the announcements, the pastor always comes down from the platform onto the floor of the sanctuary; people frequently speak out to amend what the pastor has said or to remind him of announcements he has not mentioned. After announcements, when the pastor asks for prayer requests, which are freely shared, he calls each congregant who makes a request by name and frequently knows the names of family members or friends mentioned in requests. In his prayer, the pastor then mentions each request, goes on to point out larger community needs, and ends by requesting God's assistance in such global problems as the civil war in Yugoslavia and the famine in Somalia.

The sermon, the center of the worship service, is based on one or more of the Scripture passages read earlier in the service and tends to stress actions Christians can take to demonstrate God's love to the world. The pastor particularly emphasizes the role of Christians in accepting and loving the outcasts of society, those who are too different, too poor, and too dirty to be at home in mainstream, middle-class America. The implications for this congregation are obvious, for much of Allston-Brighton does not fit the white, middle-class norm of years gone by. The message reinforces the congregation's sense of mission in this new community.

For the most part, the congregants appear to heed their pastor's sermons. The coffee hour held after each service is often a lively time of fellowship among all congregants. African American and Asian women hug and chat with elderly white women. A dozen or so young children of all races emerge from the nursery and proceed to wreak havoc playing games in and amongst the adults. After about forty-five minutes, congregants begin to trickle away. Older members frequently walk or drive their cars to the family homes they own. Many new members do not own cars and rely on the church van and a volunteer to take them home to their apartments, some of which are in the two housing projects in Allston-Brighton. BECC serves as a common meeting ground for people who return to very different homes and lives.

RESOURCES

BECC can claim neither an abundance of members nor members with deep pockets. As the church entered the 1980s, its situation was not unlike that of other Protestant churches in Allston-Brighton. Indeed the story might have been Brighton Avenue Baptist's—a white middle-class constituency that disappeared, leaving an aging remnant occupying a lovely building that reminded them of better days. Pictures on the walls, and in the older members' minds, recalled a day when church dinners were china and silver affairs, and deacons wore morning coats when they served communion. While BECC could claim both longevity and a certain historical place of privilege, the community no longer recognized anything special about the congregational church at the center of town. Their numbers, through the 1980s, dwindled toward extinction. Today, official membership has not rebounded significantly, for new members are balanced by deaths and continued pruning of long-inactive members from the rolls, but the number of active members is inching slowly upward. Average Sunday attendance approaches fifty, and the Sunday school is growing.

The new members cannot match the financial resources of the older members who are dying and moving away. Average household income among those who completed our survey was $24,000 (see table 5.1). Still they show a remarkable willingness to commit what they can to the church. In 1993, out of a possible sixty-five "pledging units," forty made a pledge, and thirty-eight kept their pledge. The amount of money generated directly by member gifts in 1992, however, was less than $30,000, not even enough to pay their part-time minister.

The remainder of the church's $111,000 income comes from endowment funds, miscellaneous fund-raising, and fees paid by people who rent parking and office space from the church. Income from an endowment fund of well over $300,000 covers a variety of church expenses. In addition, the church has borrowed from itself on occasion in recent years, always paying itself back in good order. Because its former constituents left a financial legacy to the church, the BECC of recent memory has had a cushion to assist in its transformation.

Various fund-raising activities (a fair, a flea market, and the like) add small amounts to the church's coffers, but the more substantial income comes from rent. A Haitian congregation and an AA group use the main church building and pay rent. Next door, the church's former parsonage has been converted into office space. The church uses part of the building for itself and rents out the rest. Again, the assets of a former era (a building) have been converted to assets useful to the church today. Rents plus parking fees amount to almost as much as the church's own combined offerings. Total income, then, comes in roughly equal thirds from offerings, endowment, and rent. While not generous, it is sufficient to keep the church going.

The most remarkable set of resources this church has assembled is its partnerships with various community and governmental agencies. As Mary Beth Sievens points out in her description, much of the legwork for the feeding and youth programs comes from Boston College (BC) volunteers, while the mayor's office and local merchants supply funding and food, respectively, for other programs.

That network has developed, in large part, through the efforts of Eunice Taylor, well-known among city officials as someone who can make things happen. While her passion and organizational skills have made her a key figure in the church's life, hers is an influence that readily gives away power. Remembering the early days of the thrift shop, she said, "At the end of the second month I had worked myself out of a job. The older ladies who knew more about old clothing had taken over. It was their shop. And they did the scheduling, and the bookkeeping, and everything. I was delighted."

Those older ladies are still a force to reckon with in the church. Fiercely devoted to the congregation they have supported for so long, they have time and resources to staff much of the church's outreach, as

Table 5.1. Brighton Evangelical Congregational Church, Allston-Brighton

Ideas and priorities	
Christian practices rated "essential"	Living Christian values
Ministries rated "very important" or "essential"	Service to the needy
Resources	
Average Sunday attendance	50
Annual operating budget (1992)	$111,000
Household incomes above $50,000	16%
College degrees or more	44%
Average age	52 years
Activities (beyond worship) participated in at least monthly	Fellowship
	Building maintenance
	Bible study
Relationship to the community	
Live ten minutes or less from the church	67%
New to the community in the last five years	19%
Ethnicity	71% European
	7% African American
	7% Asian
Participate in civic & community activities more than once a month	64%

NOTE: Sixteen people responded to our survey, amounting to approximately 32 percent of average Sunday attendance. This may be taken as a fair representation of all regular attenders.

well as its internal structures. That the congregation is not today rich in skilled, well-connected members is a concern for the future. But those it has seem exceptionally willing to give their time and energy to caring for each other and for the community. The personpower of the congregation, though stretched thin, is enough.

The church's pastoral leadership has also been a key resource in recent times. Having a part-time minister has meant that laity have had to become more involved and responsible. Meanwhile, the pastor has provided both spiritual and managerial leadership as BECC has struggled to survive and reach out beyond itself. His community connections and commitment to urban ministry have enhanced the church's role as an organizing hub for responses to the community's needs.

STRUCTURES OF AUTHORITY

Brighton Evangelical Congregational Church, as part of the United Church of Christ (UCC), has a good deal of congregational autonomy.

Members can choose their own pastor, although the local denominational office assists with resumés. They govern their own finances, although the local denomination sometimes provides assistance. And they can design their own programs, although local and national denominational resources are there to call on, if they choose. In recent years, BECC has used the resources of the local UCC Association in finding a new pastor and, occasionally, for short-term loans. But most of the church's programming reflects members' choices rather than denominational directives. In fact, two key programmatic resources—the hymnal and Sunday school materials—come from other sources. The hymnal is published by the evangelical publishing house Zondervan, and the Sunday school materials come from the Southern Baptist Convention.

Still, BECC has been more tied to its denomination under John Eller than it had been for some time previously. Each Sunday's bulletin identifies it as "A Congregation of the United Church of Christ" right under BECC's name. Various denominational offerings and meetings are announced from the pulpit, and members are encouraged to attend association and conference events. Sometimes they come back quite enthusiastic about what the denomination is doing, but there is never any sense of obligation to follow what higher-ups want the congregation to do.

Internally as well, the congregation has undergone a transformation under Eller. A largely dormant committee system has been revived, the bylaws rewritten, the budget a more carefully planned, and attention paid to managing the church's endowment. In general, a system that operated rather haphazardly from one crisis to the next has been given some order. One member said of the pastor that "he doesn't encourage a 'lone ranger' way of going about doing the business of the church. He thinks it should be done in committees, and the decisions of the committees should be honored and adhered to and followed."

The structure that has evolved includes three committees—finance, prudential (building and grounds), and religious education—along with a diaconate and a church council. The first two committees tend to the material well-being of the church; the religious education committee and the diaconate tend to the care and spiritual nurture of the members. Major decisions are taken to congregational meetings, as needed; and once a year all the committees and ministries of the church report to the annual congregational meeting. The pastor retains a good deal of influence in all this, sitting on all the committees and helping to set their agendas. As the balance between the new system and the old is still being worked out, it is often the pastor who makes sure that things happen. Still, the extent to which the congregation is in charge of its own life is probably best reflected in the announcement period each

Sunday. The pastor's rarely is the sole voice. Others contribute information in a way that clearly communicates their sense of ownership.

Achieving some degree of explicit order has, of course, meant colliding at times with the implicit order that governed the church before. Through years of difficulty, various of the older members had exercised a good deal of unofficial authority. And, for a time, some of the newer members had tried to exert their individual influence. Having official committees and official job descriptions has forced the people in the congregation to take responsibility for their own designated tasks—but only for those tasks. They have made the transition Max Weber described as a move from "traditional" to "rational-legal" authority.[1] What had been a matter of (often contested) personal influence or longevity or patrimony is becoming a matter of rules and offices and systematic planning. With an increasingly diverse membership, no implicit norms could hope to provide effective governance. And with precarious finances, careful planning is essential. A few key members still shoulder heavy responsibility in this system, but they are generally people who have the time and commitment the church needs.

CULTURE

In the rhythm of BECC's life, Sunday morning and Wednesday evening are the defining moments. On Sunday morning, much of what the congregation does to sustain its own life is visible. On Wednesday night, as members and student volunteers serve supper to the community, the church's sense of mission comes to the fore.

Sunday morning begins with breakfast, served to those who wish either the physical or social nourishment it provides. Both this meal and the van service that brings some parishioners to church are evidence of the congregation's care for its less well-off constituents. In the Sunday school hour that follows, the economic and educational diversity of the congregation is even more apparent. Some members are dressed well and deal with written materials with ease. Others dress more modestly and shy away from reading. While a few who remember the old days may grumble in private about these less-refined ways, the overt message is welcoming and inclusive. The adult Sunday school teacher attempts to find ways for all his pupils to participate.

In such a small congregation, no one can stay a stranger long. Those who choose to join BECC go through a formal orientation class and an initiation ritual ("The Reception of New Members") in which they and the congregation make pledges to each other. Those pledges take on flesh in the prayer time each Sunday. Here members share stories from their work and neighborhood and family, asking for prayer and support. In this sharing, and in Reverend Eller's pastoral prayer, one has the distinct impression of a congregation in which the caring is very real and extends across surprising boundaries. Says one member, "Most times all anybody really wants is an ear, somebody to listen to them and give them a hug or whatever they need. And we've been doing that."

As Mary Beth Sievens points out, social-class differences have actually been harder for the congregation to deal with than their growing ethnic diversity. Cultural differences are both visible and celebrated on Sunday mornings at BECC. The pastor has used breads from various cultures, for instance, in the celebration of communion. He points out that Jesus took the common, everyday elements of his culture in instituting this special meal, and the church can do likewise. On most Sundays, at least one-third of the congregation is non-Anglo, with a kind of easy mingling at coffee hour and cooperation in church business that signals real inclusion. When neighborhood ruffians insult nonwhite people coming and going from the church, Anglo members leap to their defense. People at BECC have come to *think* of themselves as multicultural and to think that is a good thing.

This emerging self-image seems to be a product of both their everyday experiences as a congregation and the messages they hear from their pastor. What he says about the gospel combines with what they experience in Sunday school and coffee hour and the food pantry or thrift shop. In many ways, his messages are classic social gospel. He emphasizes the love of God, God's care for marginal and outcast people, the call of God to live out the Gospel in this world rather than waiting for the next. In one sermon, Eller proclaimed that "God don't make no junk." Everyone in the church is special, he said, each one has received an invitation from God to God's table. The image of sitting together at God's table is a prevalent one, perhaps fitting for a congregation that feeds its own community's marginal and outcast each Wednesday night.

This social gospel theology exists at BECC alongside a strong strain of evangelicalism. Many members insist that everything they do must be biblical and evangelistic—hence the choice of Southern Baptist Sunday school materials (replacing equally evangelical David C. Cook materials) and a Zondervan hymnal. Hence the Wednesday night Bible study and the prayer partners meeting after worship on Sunday. For most of the older members, such activities fit a piety that has been part of their church experience since learning to sing "Jesus Loves Me" in their preschool days. A few other members have adopted this piety as part of a self-conscious evangelicalism. Both these self-conscious evangelicals and the evangelicals-by-habit are willing to live with Reverend Eller's theology—so long as he remains firmly grounded in Scripture. For his part, Eller seems to recognize the strengths of evangelicalism. If he disagrees with his more conservative parishioners on matters of doctrine (the virgin birth, "substitutionary atonement," or other controversial ideas), he does not involve himself in fruitless debate over them. Rather, he concentrates on basics—God's love and our need to love and serve each other. And he relies on the church's evangelicals for their biblical knowledge, their willingness to pray, and their eagerness to give witness to their faith.

The congregation's sense of service is felt by at least two hundred people every week. Those in need of life's basic necessities often find their way to BECC's door, but none of the church's activity is undertaken as a direct means of recruitment. In fact, BECC makes no routine effort to seek new members. Although some members may engage in individual evangelizing, the church usually waits for newcomers to take the initiative. There is no expectation that people served by the church will become a part of the congregation and no hard sell when they come. The congregation simply welcomes whoever enters its doors, making of this church an increasingly heterogeneous mix.

SUMMARY

Brighton Evangelical Congregational Church is a paradoxical mix of social gospel and evangelicalism, of long-term middle-class pillars of the community and a rag-tag assortment of newcomers, of precarious finances and creative resourcefulness. It still teeters dangerously close to extinction. The effort to find supplementary money will have to continue, at least until membership has grown significantly. And there are no guarantees that this theological and ethnic mix can continue to hold together. Still, the sharing that happens among congregants both in the worship service and in coffee hour bodes well. Their developing self-image as a place where God has brought a surprising mix of people together is likely to shape their future. Likewise, their ways of reaching out into the community—both in finding resources and in serving people in need—are likely to shape their future. What remains is the development of a conscious strategy for recruiting new members. The congregation cannot continue indefinitely to serve the community without additional personpower.

City Baptist Church, Oak Park: Singing New Songs

Among many striking features about City Baptist in Oak Park, Illinois, the music and the hugs impressed me most. Combining white evangelical favorite hymns with traditional black favorites has created an engaging musical experience for both groups. Congregants sing with almost as much enthusiasm as they bring to their greetings of one another after the service. While researcher Penny Edgell Becker and I stood waiting for the pastor to be free to talk with us, he slowly made his way back down the aisle, and everyone got a hug—old and young, black and white, men and women. It was contagious. Later, downstairs, we too were greeted by parishioners on their way out, welcomed as warmly as the pastor was welcoming others upstairs, right down to the hug.

If Brighton Evangelical Congregational has been struggling to integrate people whose social class and national origins are unfamiliar, City Baptist has been struggling—rather successfully, it would seem—with the sort of integration that usually defines the word in the United States: racial integration. With troubled Austin right next door to comfortable, middle-class Oak Park, this independent (nondenominational) Baptist church chose not to ignore or run from their neighbors. Penny Edgell Becker describes how they have confronted their neighborhood.

Until the 1980s City Baptist was an Oak Park congregation, drawing most of its members from that suburb. One older member confides that it was a little stuffy, and certainly the large building and the church's endowment signaled prosperity. Today, in contrast, City Baptist is an Oak Park/Austin congregation, with members, community ties, and outreach programs in two communities quite different in demographics and life experience.

Sunday morning begins with Sunday school at City Baptist, with both age-based and interest-based classes offered for all members. The hallways fill as the Sunday school classes break up, with a lot of talking and laughter, especially among the teens and young adults. Children play in the foyer. The seniors emerge from their Sunday school class in a group and go up to the sanctuary. The service starts promptly at 10:30, but latecomers arrive for the next twenty minutes, many going up to the balcony. Some are dressed casually, but most of the women wear dresses and makeup, and most of the men wear jackets or sweaters and ties, if not suits. About 60 percent are white, 40 percent black.

The worship service lasts at least an hour and a half, and its format is flexible. The order of worship includes a prelude, a congregational hymn, the invocation, a chorus sung by the congregation, a choir special, another congregational hymn, communion, praise choruses, the offering, announcements, more special music, another hymn, the sermon, an invitational hymn, the benediction, and a postlude. Announcements may be interjected at various points in the service, and it is not unusual for an adult baptism or a baby dedication to be included, as well. The choir sometimes sings spirituals along with other types of music. Special music can be instrumental or a contemporary Christian ballad. The congregation sings both hymns and praise choruses; for the former the music leader stands at the podium and directs the standing congregation, and for the latter everyone is seated and the man playing the keyboard offers prayers or inspirational words between songs. Congregation members also participate in sharing joys and concerns; a period for testimony is included on some Sundays, with a roving mike to make access easier.

The choir members are mostly African American, and the pastor, assistant

*pastor, organist, and chorus leader are white men. The benediction is some-
times given by a black man, a minister who is a member of the congregation,
and the Scripture readings are done by men and women, black and white. Often
an exegesis of a specific passage, the sermon may be one of a series lasting from
two to several weeks. Sometimes it will follow a specific theme throughout the
Bible, but the emphasis is always on applications to contemporary life in Oak
Park and Austin. One sermon on parenting (from 1 Thess. 2) stressed the
importance of role models for children and mentioned the problems both of absent fathers and of families too busy with work and accumulating wealth to
spend time with their children.*

*At the end of the service, the church clears slowly. Once a month, a well-
attended potluck dinner allows this period of fellowship to continue well into
the afternoon.*

*Putting down roots in both Oak Park and Austin is the result of a conscious
strategy of church growth. The congregation's leaders concluded in the
mid-1980s that to grow and survive they needed to be local, to have ties to their
immediate neighborhood; for City Baptist, the neighborhood spans both communities. This strategy is also the result of the pastor's and elders' interpretation of the New Testament mandates concerning the church—"In Christ there
is neither Jew nor Greek." To target mostly white Oak Park and not African
American Austin in recruiting new members would have been racist and was
specifically rejected by this conservative Baptist congregation.*

*But why did City need to go out and try to bring in new people? The racial
changes in the community had some effect on City as they had on other churches
in the community. Membership and attendance reached their peak in the 1950s
and early 1960s and then began to decline. Some of City's members left the area
when blacks and other ethnic groups moved in. But despite these losses, City
was still a large congregation in 1981, with more than four hundred members,
almost all white. Then, a series of events began that led to a devastating conflict
within the congregation.*

*Among the several versions of what happened to City, all agree that in the
early 1980s, the pastor and his brother-in-law began preaching more and more
on personal holiness, demanding higher and higher standards of strict living,
and condemning those who did not agree, thereby driving many members
away. In 1984, after a year of struggle, the church dismissed the pastor, and he
and his followers left. A few people today will say that the tension over what to
do about integration led to the conflict, but others point out that the same pastor
who was finally dismissed had favored trying to attract African American
members.*

*This conflict left only eighty people at City Baptist. The church had lost a
generation of leaders, people in their late thirties to middle fifties with families.
But during the long hiatus that followed, City determined to try to attract
members from the whole neighborhood, not only white Oak Parkers. Pastor Bill*

Smith was finally selected and called partly because he had training and an interest in multicultural ministry.

Pastor Smith came to City in 1987 and left at the end of 1992, five years that were a period not only of numerical growth and increasing financial stability, but also of explaining and developing the biblical rationale behind a multicultural ministry. The biggest challenge has been meshing the cultural styles of the various congregational subgroups, who have disagreed about worship and music style, and about the timing and duration of church events.

These tensions have been managed by open and communicative decision making and by appealing to a vision of community based on the New Testament. City's emphasis on healing and reconciling human divisions in Christ's ministry has been a powerful incentive. One reason so much music is performed in the service is that the congregation has a strong musical heritage; another is that the mix of musical styles lets everyone listen to everyone else's music and so develop a tolerance and acceptance of difference. Even a multicultural ministry is not seen as an end in itself, but as following the biblical mandate to preach the gospel. When City Baptist's pastor and members marched with members of churches from Austin after the Los Angeles riots, or when they tutor Austin children or contribute to other types of community ministry, they are doing so as a compassionate outreach and as a witness for Christ.

City Baptist members do not tell of a congregational resurrection. They talk about a leadership sobered by conflict, with a strategy to grow and a reason to believe their continued presence was a good thing for them and for the neighborhood. They believe they are simply about the task that is set before them by their place and circumstances. The miracle is not their adaptation as a congregation; the miracle is Christ, and the work they have done is simply that which is required. When Smith announced that he was leaving to pastor a church in another part of the country, people were saddened, but they were confident that their ministry and their identity were firmly grounded and would not change.

RESOURCES

Although City Baptist entered the 1980s in good financial health, with an abundance of members, it soon underwent a crisis that threatened its very existence. Many of the strongest and most faithful members left before a remnant united to depose a difficult pastor. While this crisis does not appear to have been directly connected to questions about how the church would relate to its neighborhood, it nevertheless presented the church with an imperative for change. With much of its dependable base gone, this was the time to be serious about the outreach goals church members had already talked about. They had no choice but to engage in intentional outreach, and their theological convictions refused to allow them to seek only white Oak Park recruits. They began to spread the word, and over the next decade, the church steadily grew, adding both white and African American members, to establish today's solid base of membership.

Those members represent a range of backgrounds, training, and material resources. Sixty percent have joined this church in the last five years. Over half the membership grew up in a tradition other than Baptist. Almost half of those come from other evangelical groups, but the rest come from mainline Protestant and Catholic backgrounds. Three-quarters are forty-five or under, with 16 percent sixty-five or older, leaving a scant 9 percent in the forty-six through sixty-four range. Though the church clearly lacks a cohort of settled, middle-aged adults, it has a strong contingent of young adults raising families who, having chosen this church and this tradition as their own, bring to it a good deal of energy.

Partly because it is such a young congregation, it is also relatively well educated. Only 16 percent of its members have not been educated past high school, while 24 percent have training beyond college (see table 5.2). Occupationally, the congregation is divided in nearly equal thirds among professional/managerial people, other white-collar workers, and blue-collar workers. While roughly half have household incomes between $20,000 and $50,000, more fall under that range (34 percent) than fall above it (17 percent); more households live on a shoestring than in great comfort. Still, half the members report that they give one hundred dollars or more each month to the church, with almost half of those giving at least twice that amount. While City cannot count on deep pockets among its members, it can count on their generosity.

The generosity of City's members is multiplied by the church's cooperative partnerships with a half dozen or so other area churches. All are conservative, evangelical or charismatic, urban-oriented congregations. They cooperate to sponsor some social ministries, have joint worship services and special programs, and provide activities for their youth. This group of churches cooperated to begin a Crisis Pregnancy Center to provide area women with alternatives to abortion. City also works with Austin's Circle Urban Ministries to serve the Austin community. And the church's youth participate in Inner City Impact and Youth for Christ activities.

City also benefits from the presence of Moody Bible Institute in Chicago. Some of the church's leaders are graduates of that historic evangelical school; some Moody students attend the church; and City often has guest musicians and preachers from the school. The thinking and experimenting fostered by a place recognized as a leader among evangelicals spills over into the congregations like City that are connected to it. Conversely, City is known at Moody as a place that is making a successful effort at multicultural ministry, and it offers a lab for stu-

Table 5.2. City Baptist Church, Oak Park

Ideas and priorities	
Christian practices rated "essential"	Prayer
	Bible study
	Living Christian values
	Sharing faith with others
Ministries rated "very important" or	
"essential"	An evangelism program
	Helping members resist this world
	Encouragement of individual witnessing
	Service to the needy
	Preparation for the next world
Resources	
Average Sunday attendance	200
Annual operating budget (1992)	$169,870
Household incomes above $50,000	17%
College degrees or more	52%
Average age	39 years
Activities (beyond worship) participated	
in at least monthly	Bible study
	Fellowship
Relationship to the community	
Live ten minutes or less from the church	59%
New to the community in the last	
five years	30%
Ethnicity	71% European
	24% African American
Participate in civic & community	
activities more than once a month	40%

NOTE: One hundred three people responded to our survey, amounting to approximately 51 percent of average Sunday attendance. This may be taken as a very good representation of all regular attenders, although it underrepresents African American attenders.

dents and faculty who are interested in practical experience. City's ministers can readily consult with Moody teachers who have thought and written about such issues, and they can tap the Moody network when they need to hire new staff members.

While the church's multiracial direction seems to have been set before Pastor Bill Smith arrived, he proved to be the skilled leader City was looking for. One of his emphases was leadership training for his parishioners, building up a strong and diverse core of lay leaders. As we have seen, many of City's members are not in occupations that have prepared them for leadership, do not have incomes sufficient to engage in culturally enriching activities, or are relatively young, none of which disqualifies them from serving the church. City has engaged in a focused effort to identify committed and promising potential leaders and provide them with the training and mentoring that will enable them to move into positions of teaching and administration in the church.[2] The program has also proved beneficial to those asked to do the mentoring—often older adults. Said the associate pastor, "We're not asking them to teach Bible studies or anything, but just to walk through life with somebody who needs someone to look up to. I don't think we listen enough to older people anymore." Lacking an abundance of members who already occupy recognized leadership roles in the community, City is developing its own leaders from the inside.

STRUCTURES OF AUTHORITY

Earlier in its history, City Baptist was an American Baptist church, with strong ties to the Northern Baptist Seminary in Chicago. However, by the late 1940s, the church was already moving in a more conservative direction and supporting the American Baptists less and less. Finally, in 1981, it severed ties entirely, becoming an independent, nondenominational church with full authority to govern its own affairs—and full responsibility for its own mistakes.

Internally, the church is governed by a board of five elders (one of whom is the pastor), responsible for the spiritual life of the church, and a board of deacons, responsible for the church's administrative affairs. The deacons report to the elders, and the elders supply key members to a pastor search committee when the church is between pastors. When the former pastor was dismissed, it was the board of elders that made the decision. The board plays a critical, central role in the church. In more recent times, the elders have been able to devote their attention to long-term goals of growth and development. They write ministry plans every year, develop a budget accordingly, and then meet quarterly to evaluate how they are doing.

The deacons are organized bureaucratically to oversee various areas of the church's program: music and worship, church staff, missions, facilities, finances, Christian education, and "bodylife" (fellowship, Christian nurture, and growth). Both men and women may be deacons, while only men may be elders, and both groups are elected by the congregation after potential candidates are examined by the current elders to determine their spiritual qualifications.

The congregation has the final say on all important decisions. They meet in quarterly business meetings for elections, budget decisions, and the like. But more importantly, when the congregation is facing critical changes, there are often extensive opportunities for discussion and participation before decisions are made. When Pastor Smith came, for instance, the church adopted a new mission statement and rewrote its constitution. "We streamlined the old forty-page one down to six pages," he recalled. "It was a very broad-based, very long process, because we involved everybody. We brought everybody in who wanted to be involved, and that takes a little longer. But it has great ownership when you get finished. Everybody feels a part of it." Indeed, this constitution has become important in ordering the church's life. Members carefully follow its prescriptions, thereby reinforcing their sense that official procedures are open and available to everyone's scrutiny. Mentoring and leadership education are bringing increasing numbers within the inner circles of decision making, but the congregation's democratic structure allows anyone with time and interest to have a say.

Until 1994, the pastoral staff of City Baptist had always been all white and all male. While the church had talked about the need for a multicultural staff for years, each new person hired had been white. However, as the church sought a new senior minister, nonwhite candidates were actively pursued. In early 1994, the church called Rev. Arthur Jackson, a forty-five-year-old African American, to be their new pastor.

CULTURE

City is first and foremost a biblically based evangelical congregation. It likes to call itself a "New Testament church." Its doctrinal statement, written into the constitution, begins by recognizing the verbal inspiration and authority of the scriptures and goes on to include all the "fundamentals" conservative Protestants usually claim. Its mission statement, however, begins to flush out those abstract doctrines in its three foci: worship, spiritual nurture, and sharing the gospel "without distinction." That last phrase most clearly describes City's particular calling. They start with a literal reading of the Bible, and in it they find a gospel that compels them to proclaim the availability of God's grace "without distinction."

They might have added that phrase—"without distinction"—to their other two mission foci. As we have seen, this congregation is engaged in spiritual nurture, mentoring, and leadership development that intentionally includes people across racial lines. It is also a congregation learning to worship "without distinction." More accurately, they are learning to appreciate each other's distinctiveness. Rather than holding separate "white" and "black" worship services, as some consultants on multicultural ministry advise, City found the Bible calling them toward inclusive worship. Each service includes music familiar to both constituencies. White members are learning a more relaxed sense of time, as well. These changes in worship style have perhaps been the hardest for older members to accept, but they seem to have created a sense of community that genuinely includes people of varying traditions.

As an evangelical church, City emphasizes personal evangelism—each individual's responsibility for inviting friends to come to church, telling them about their need for salvation, offering them care and support. Word of mouth has brought most of City's new members over the last several years. In addition, however, City does twice-yearly mailings to the surrounding community describing the church and inviting people to attend. Once a person has walked forward during an invitation hymn, declaring their desire to become a Christian or to transfer into the church from another congregation, the next step is a series of six new-member classes. Here they learn basic beliefs, the history and mission of the church, what members are expected to do, and where they can fit in. Once baptized by immersion and accepted into full membership, they are encouraged to join one of the church's "identity" groups. These small groups are organized roughly around age groups, but are diverse in ethnicity and marital status. Currently less than half the regular attenders are in one of these groups, something the pastor said he would like to work on if he were staying longer.

The identity groups meet weekly, usually in a home, and engage in serious Bible study—line-by-line exegesis and extensive discussion of the background and meaning of the texts. But also included is a healthy dose of personal sharing and prayer. It is to these groups, as well as to Sunday school groups, that people bring their concerns about job and family, unsaved neighbors, or community politics. Here they share information and resources and support each other with practical advice and material aid. The church challenges its members to live Christ's way in every aspect of their lives, and it is these small groups that often help members work out just what that means.

The theology of this church emphasizes individual salvation and individual responsibility for living Christ's way. Their traditional mission efforts have included both local evangelism and active support for overseas missionaries. The world will be changed one person at a time, they believe, through the process of individual transformation. Both through their witnessing and in the work many do for the good of the community, they try to live out that promise. The virtues they rated most essential on our survey reflect their mix of private piety and individual testimony. Prayer, Bible study, living their values, and sharing their faith are what City members rate as essential. Similarly, the ministries they rate as most important are those that bring the unchurched into the fold, that help members share their faith and resist the temptations of the world, and that prepare people for a world to come. Of all the churches we studied, this one was the most apparently "otherworldly" in its sense of mission.

Still, the practices of the church are vitally concerned with life in this world. Members also rated "service to the needy" as something their church should do, and service to the needy in this community often takes City Baptist into the world of politics and direct church activism. Sometimes members act on the side of conservative politics. Concerned about families, they work both for individual transformation and for social change, rejoicing when a father is converted and restored to his home and when the Crisis Pregnancy Center offers women alternatives to abortion. Other times, the church is genuinely ambivalent about how to respond to issues in the community. When Oak Park voted to extend health care benefits to "domestic partners" of city employees, members of City felt they ought to protest this legitimation of homosexual life-styles. Still, their stance of loving the sinner (while condemning the sin) made it hard for them to say anyone should be denied health care benefits.

Still other times City finds itself on the front lines of issues outsiders might find surprising. City's commitment to a multicultural ministry draws it into community concerns about racism, violence, and economic deprivation. Members have participated in a Unity Walk (Oak Park to Austin) that brought people from several churches and other organizations together to confess their racism and celebrate their movement toward unity. They also participated in a candlelight march to mourn the deaths of several Austin youth from gang-related violence. And as their new pastor began his tenure in 1994, concerns for economic training and opportunity were topping the mission priority list at the church.

SUMMARY

The idea of proclaiming the gospel "without distinction" has, since the mid-1980s, shaped much of the life and ministry of City Baptist Church. Taking their orders from the Bible, members have continued to engage in traditional preaching, witnessing, and Bible study. But those traditional evangelical practices have been extended to include both the middle-class white residents of Oak Park and a broad diversity of residents from Austin, as well. Through intentional efforts in leadership training, shared study and fellowship, and even alterations in worship style, the congregation has become a genuinely inclusive community. The commitment to minister without distinction has also propelled them into community concerns they might not have noticed otherwise. Now they notice, and they have the resources to begin to respond. The membership base is again solid, the budget is growing each year, and the church's lay leadership gained sufficient strength to feel confident about a period without pastoral leadership. While not officially connected to a denomination, the congregation draws profitably on connections with other evangelical churches in the area. Its sense of identity has been transformed as it looks toward a vitalized future.

A similar transformation of identity seems about to get under way in a very different congregation nearly a thousand miles away. There the cultural barriers are not racial. Gwinnett County, northeast of Atlanta and still predominantly white, is often seen as a haven from Atlanta's urban scene. The residents of Gwinnett have consciously chosen *not* to live in a neighborhood like City Baptist's. In fact, a generation ago, a trip to downtown Atlanta was a major and dreaded excursion. Today, the people who remember those days are working to get along with people for whom Atlanta is now a daily commute. The cultural divides that face Gwinnett's congregations are those between traditional small-town living and the mobile, complex life of suburban newcomers.

Hinton Memorial United Methodist Church, Gwinnett County: Small-Town Church Invaded by Suburbia

The two women I interviewed on my visits with Nancy Eiesland to Dacula, a small town in Gwinnett County, Georgia, could hardly have been more different. The first, a young mother whose husband works for an Atlanta utility company, runs a manicure studio. The family lives the typical frantic life of suburbanites, coordinating schedules, meals, and transportation around work, school, volunteer, and extra-curricular activities. The couple has chosen Dacula because they like the space they have (an acre) and the country atmosphere, but their life is an essentially urban one. The second woman has probably never even been *in* a manicure studio. Her life revolves around garden and kitchen, church and community. She and her husband met in their youth before World War II and went to church socials together. They raised their children in this small town and in the church, although her husband always had to work in a nearby suburb of Atlanta. They live on a quiet side street and have a huge garden in the backyard. Our visit was not complete until we had gotten a tour of the garden and a deli-cious piece of homemade cake. They have watched the world change around them, but their own lives have seemed rather uneventful. Al-though dependent on an urban economy, they have lived an essen-tially rural existence. Now both women share this community and the small Methodist church that has been a mainstay of community life for more than 150 years. Research team member Nancy Eiesland picks up the story.

During a decade of unprecedented growth in eastern Gwinnett County, Dacula has seemed to change very little. The business district is still home to the weather-beaten country store that has been a fixture since the early 1900s when "King Cotton" summoned local farmers to the town's gin. Straddling the railroad tracks, the downtown area reflects the retail services of many rural southern small towns, including the ubiquitous Dairy Queen, hardware, gro-

cery, and video stores. The city hall, a converted gas station, has added no new staff and few services in the last decade. In 1993 the city council authorized the paving of the last dirt road in town.

Yet this slow-paced small town is on the frontier of rapid suburbanization on Atlanta's outer rim. In the early 1980s, Georgia 316 tied Dacula into Atlanta's freeway system and provided easy access for pioneering suburban families to settle in the community. The relatively cheap land prices during the mid-1980s, the community's reputation for quality public schools, and the picturesquely rural environment attracted multitudes of new residents. Dacula itself has now been required to accommodate a slowly but steadily increasing residential population and is in the process of being transformed from a rural small town to a nascent suburban community. Today Dacula is two communities drawn together primarily by school and church activities. The old community of long-time residents whose families are buried in nearby cemeteries continues to be present, although this community represents a declining proportion of the population. Mingling with it is a rapidly growing population of young parents seeking a safe and spacious place in which to rear their children.

Founded in 1837, Hinton Memorial United Methodist is a historic congregation in the Dacula community. As Pleasant Hill Methodist Church, the congregation met on the western outskirts of Dacula until 1857 when a city father, Dr. S. H. Freeman, deeded the church four acres inside the city limits. In the frame church built on the in-town site, as in the previous facility, a slave section was marked out. A brick structure was built on the same site in 1910, and the congregation became known as the Dacula Methodist Church. The present building was constructed in 1955, and the church was renamed Hinton Memorial in honor of Dr. Samuel L. Hinton and Alice Stanley Hinton, longtime and generous members. Throughout all this history, until a full-time pastor was assigned in 1956, the congregation was a circuit stop; on the Sundays when there was no Methodist preacher they frequently alternated services with nearby Hebron Baptist Church.

During the 1960s and 1970s the congregation was heavily influenced by the branch of the Hinton family for whom the church had been renamed. In the 1980s, when the church received a "lady preacher," the Hintons expressed their displeasure by withdrawing.

Rev. Gerald Gerhard assumed the pastorate next, and under his leadership the congregation tripled in five years, from 40 to 120 weekly attenders. Reverend Gerhard came to Hinton directly from seminary, full of enthusiasm and ready to take advantage of new opportunities for church growth made possible by the suburban inflow on Dacula's periphery. His dynamic style and youth attracted many young suburban families and reinvigorated long-term members.

After two years at Hinton, Gerhard, who had come to the church a traditional Methodist, experienced the baptism in the Holy Spirit. Soon the congregation gained a reputation, depending upon factional allegiance, as either a "safe haven" for charismatics or a "charismatic ghetto." Gerhard altered the

church's longstanding liturgical practices to include charismatic praise cho-
ruses, substituted unstructured worship for the Apostles Creed and the Lord's
Prayer, and actively taught charismatic theology. Within the congregation, the
rift between traditional and charismatic Methodists grew. Finally in 1990,
the congregation experienced a schism when Gerhard and more than half of the
members left the Methodist church to found an independent charismatic congre-
gation, Trinity Fellowship.

By 1992, Hinton Memorial averaged fifty-five people in attendance, slowly
rebounding from the schism, which had taken a deep toll on the congregation
both emotionally and financially. Rev. Dean Head, a retirement-aged tradi-
tional Methodist pastor, was sent to bring healing to the congregation. The
congregation deliberately turned inward. The financial drain of a mortgaged
parsonage, built in the days when the church was rapidly growing, has been
severe. For lack of personpower and financial resources, many youth and chil-
dren's programs were eliminated or allowed to die slowly. While Hinton
Memorial has gained several committed young couples with children, the pre-
ponderance of the congregation is still elderly old-timers who enjoy each other's
company and care about their church and community.

The smell of coffee welcomes them to church each Sunday. That seductive
aroma draws early arrivals to the small old-fashioned kitchen where people
stand around chatting. The five- to seven-person choir slowly congregates in
the loft to practice hymns from the United Methodist hymnbook for the morn-
ing service. Just as people are settling into deep conversation in the kitchen, the
Sunday school buzzer shatters the ease, insisting they report to their appointed
rooms. Yet the adults often shrug off the pesky buzzer and move to their own
internal signal, proceeding to their rooms only after they have downed another
cup of coffee and have caught up on the news of the community and the congre-
gation. The children's and youth classes, generally of five to seven members,
meet in pleasantly decorated rooms. In the parlor, the senior adults engage the
United Methodist quarterly and each other with equal vigor. The adult class
that meets in the fellowship hall addresses topics of interest such as the history
of church music or areas of stress in members' lives.

The hiatus between the second buzzer that announces the end of the Sunday
school hour and the choral call to worship is a time of much meeting and greet-
ing in the sanctuary. Several old-timers can be counted upon to make the
rounds to every person, shaking hands and welcoming them to this Sunday's
service. Newcomers, quickly noted, are often the focus of special attention.

The service follows a predictable pattern of greetings, hymns, Apostles'
Creed, prayers, offertory, sermon, and benediction. This routine is punctuated
with considerable spontaneity, however, especially during the Children's Mo-
ment, fellowship time, and announcements. Fellowship time often lasts for
nearly ten minutes, with congregants wandering throughout the sanctuary in
their quest to make everyone feel welcome. Announcements, too, are a time of
spontaneous contribution of information about church activities, pleas for help

with farm work, or impromptu business meetings (negotiating menus, meeting times, and the like). The sermons by Reverend Head tend to be punctuated with many folksy anecdotes woven around an exposition of a Scripture passage that teaches the Christian duty to live moderate, disciplined lives. As the twelve o'clock hour nears, the pastor hurries to a close, so that members can share in another ten or fifteen minutes of fellowship on the front steps or the back parking lot before trundling home for Sunday dinner.

In early 1993, the congregation began considering a proposal that might alter these patterns, however. They were approached by their district superintendent about becoming a "redevelopment congregation." This program of the North Georgia Conference of the United Methodist Church is designed to enable congregations in changing communities to gain the financial resources, programming, and training to engage in active outreach. This proposal was somewhat controversial at Hinton, since it would mean that the congregation would have to vigorously pursue growth. Some congregants, newcomers and old-timers alike, pointed to the local megachurch, Hebron Baptist, whose membership numbers more than three thousand, and asserted that they joined Hinton exactly because they did not want to get lost in a large church. Hinton congregants value their warm community and are concerned that the denomination may force them to grow more than they would like. Despite these concerns, members approved participation in the conference's redevelopment program, primarily because the denomination would then subsidize the salary of their next pastor, who it was hoped would be more proactive in meeting congregational needs and reaching out to the community. In June 1993, Rev. Tom Elliott arrived, and the process of "redevelopment" began. Soon thereafter, the congregation signaled its new identity by again changing its name, becoming the First United Methodist Church of Dacula.

RESOURCES

Since the split, money has been rather tight. During Reverend Gerhard's ministry, when the church was growing, a new parsonage was built and the sanctuary remodeled, leaving the church to pay a mortgage of five hundred dollars a month. With well over one hundred regular attenders, that was no problem; with fifty, it sometimes became impossible. By the time the church paid staff salaries and its bills each month, there was sometimes not enough to make the mortgage payment, and the treasurer would appeal for some individual to take it on for the month. Fortunately, people with deep enough pockets and generous enough hearts always kept up the payments.

The members of Hinton are not poor (only 16 percent reported household incomes below $20,000), but only a few are really well off. Of those who responded to this question on our survey, 32 percent reported household incomes above $50,000 (see table 5.3). Most, however, give only modest amounts to the church. Nearly half (43 percent)

Table 5.3. Hinton Memorial United Methodist Church, Gwinnett County

Ideas and priorities	
Christian practices rated "essential"	Living Christian values
Ministries rated "very important" or "essential"	Service to the needy
Resources	
Average Sunday attendance	50
Annual operating budget (1992)	$45,000
Household incomes above $50,000	32%
College degrees or more	45%
Average age	50 years
Activities (beyond worship) participated in at least monthly	Bible study
Relationship to the community	
Live ten minutes or less from the church	84%
New to the community in the last five years	46%
Ethnicity	97% European
Participate in civic & community activities more than once a month	51%

NOTE: Thirty-eight people responded to our survey, amounting to approximately 76 percent of average Sunday attendance. This may be taken as a very accurate representation of regular attenders.

average less than one hundred dollars per month, while only one-third average more than two hundred dollars. The pattern of giving was likely to be sporadic, with large special gifts followed by months of modest gifts. The people at Hinton had always resisted regular budget pledging. Although not farmers, they were continuing the patterns typical of farm families, whose incomes are unpredictable at best. Pledging would be one of the new measures put in place when Reverend Elliott arrived.

Although cash income was a problem for Hinton in its postschism years, the church had other assets. The building itself, well situated in the town and in good repair, is ideal for a small-to-midsized congregation. Anyone looking for an old-fashioned church to match the old-fashioned town they had chosen for a home would find Hinton ideal. It provides adequate space for worship, Sunday school, meetings, and dinners with plenty of room on the property to expand.

The church also had its historic place in the community to draw on. Long the home of some of Dacula's leading citizens, Hinton continued to attract well-educated professionals. Lots of schoolteachers, coaches, retired teachers, and people who work for the school system belong to

the congregation today. Almost half (46 percent) of the church's members are in professional or managerial occupations, with the remainder spread rather evenly across all sorts of clerical, white-collar, and blue-collar jobs. Similarly, nearly half (45 percent) have a college degree or more. This level of education, along with the experience and contacts members have gained in their occupations, provides a human resource on which the congregation can draw as it plans for the future.

The church could also count on an army of volunteer labor to paint, mow the lawn, make minor repairs, and prepare for special events. The system was ad hoc, but the result was satisfactory.

STRUCTURES OF AUTHORITY

Ad hoc also describes the way Hinton has traditionally made decisions. The impromptu business meetings during Sunday morning announcements are one example. Similarly, the administrative board was as likely to gather for a few minutes after church as to call a formal meeting. Other committees suggested by the official *United Methodist Book of Discipline* simply did not function at all. Nominees for office were sometimes not consulted, apparently on the assumption that jobs and people were pretty much interchangeable, with most jobs more a matter of "Filling in the blank" than of matching expertise to a specialized task.[3] The older members of Hinton had known each other too long to worry about doing things by the book. When something needed to be done, they knew who to consult to make sure it was done.

Those informal ways, however, sometimes did not work as well with the newcomers. If nominated for a job, they wanted to be consulted so they could decide if their skills and interests matched the job's requirements. If meetings were scheduled, they wanted to know they would happen in a predictable way. Their calendars were simply too full to accommodate ad hoc meetings.[4] Long-term members, eager for the new energy the newcomers could bring, were less sure about turning responsibility over to them. There was some effort to make certain that each committee had a majority who "would know how we do things around here," as one older member put it. When Reverend Elliott came, he simply bypassed the old committee system entirely to form new task forces on worship, stewardship, and evangelism. They were able to incorporate more of the newcomers (along with long-time members), but for a specified, limited responsibility. As the congregation moves toward "redevelopment," it may take some time to establish new ways of doing business that accommodate both the informality of the old days and the energies of the newcomers.

A similar clash between old ways and new has been apparent in efforts to make Sunday morning worship a bit more formal. After the chaos of the charismatic years and the folksy informality that prevailed

under Reverend Head, Reverend Elliott's attempts to impose order have generally met with acceptance; but his attempts to rein in the fellowship time have not. On at least two occasions, when the pastor has tried to get the people back into their seats to continue the worship service, one older member has informed him, "Not yet, preacher." The old informal structures of influence remain.

All of this local activity takes place, of course, within the domain of the United Methodist system. The Methodist annual conference has both given and taken away during these troubled times. Although in the early years of growth under Gerhard, denominational networks provided a structure that encouraged his charismatic activities, in the end, it was the denomination that put an end to his ministry at Hinton. When the annual conference offered him a smaller, more remote parish as his next assignment, he left Methodism entirely, taking most of the church with him.[5] The same North Georgia Conference then sent Hinton a retirement-aged pastor and encouraged a time of hiatus. Still, the conference was eager to receive the annual apportionments assigned to the church; when the church could not pay, the conference threatened not to assign a full-time pastor. And finally, it was the conference that decided Hinton might be worth the gamble of redevelopment and sent a strong pastor who would help the church reach out to the community. Throughout all of this, the members of Hinton have felt relatively powerless. While they know that the conference can provide them with needed resources—help in growth, a good pastor, even salary subsidies—they also know that the conference expects them to keep their end of the bargain (including paying their apportionments) and makes its decisions guided by its own good wisdom.

Doing the business of the church is likely to be a delicate balancing act in the coming years. Old informal patterns will remain. Newcomers will push for more inclusion and more predictable formal structure. And the Methodist conference will have goals and resources of its own. The health of the church will very much depend on finding ways for diverse internal constituencies, plus representatives of the denomination, to pursue common goals and communicate with each other about their desires.

CULTURE

That Hinton has done its business informally over the years should not be mistaken for a lack of orderliness and decorum at this church. On the contrary, doing things in an orderly and dignified fashion is a key virtue here. Even the extended fellowship time, which might look chaotic to a newcomer, has its own order. Not only are the greetings subdued and nondemonstrative, but everyone knows who to talk with and what subjects are off limits. Likewise, the lack of a printed agenda

did not mean that committee members did not know what was expected of them. Hinton had a sense of decorum based on years of experience, rather than on a handbook of rules.

In large measure, it was this sense of decorum that was so violated by those who wanted Hinton to be a charismatic fellowship. The singing, the praying, the testimonies, and the speaking in tongues all violated what older members saw as proper. They had opened their doors to newcomers in their community only to see their church's worship utterly transformed. The new styles seemed to the older members more like the Pentecostal churches on the back roads of their southern community than like the dignified Methodist church at the center of town. Said one longtime member of that era, "It was kind of like the Methodist church was not important to those people coming in, and it was important to those of us who had been there for awhile. And we just felt like we wanted to stay a Methodist church." They bought the new Methodist hymnal when it came out, he remembered, but most of the singing was praise choruses. Even the Apostles' Creed and the Lord's Prayer disappeared from worship.

This period in the church's history forced many Hinton members into theological debates over all sorts of issues they found troublesome. While they are willing to take on most any subject in good-natured argument, the idea that the essence of the Christian life and perhaps even one's soul were at stake was alien to them. They did not like being told they were not Christian if they did not have the same gifts of the Spirit others possessed. Hinton's traditional members have a rather commonsense view about Christian living. They are convinced that they need to live an honest, upright life that will be judged worthy by God—giving more to life than they take. You should "do unto others as you would have them do unto you," follow the principles in the Bible, and do your best at everything you try.[6] Adding other, more esoteric, requirements simply did not make sense to them.

If the Christian's obligation is simply to live a good and loving life, God's role is that of a loving protector who will eventually bring his children home to heaven. The most commonly chosen images of God on our survey were savior, comforter, and father. Death was often talked about, but the promise of heaven muted any despair it might evoke. People are very aware of God's care for them in this world and look forward to God's care in the next. Said one woman, "I've got Jesus to lean on, when I have problems." They see God's presence in the natural world, in beautiful things, in the provision of rain and crops, as well. Even though they do not themselves depend on the land for their livelihoods, they remain highly attuned to their natural surroundings.

A vital part of their surroundings, of course, is the community in which they live. Hinton is the publisher of a newsletter, "All Around

Town" that is distributed to a mailing list of thirty-seven hundred addresses throughout Dacula. In effect the local newspaper, an issue may include a story on the new elementary school, a history of important people in the life of Dacula, recipes, jokes, and community news. Hinton has always been a center of community activity and a participant in the community activities of other institutions. Schools plan their calendars with churches in mind, and churches reciprocate. Annual barbeques or bake sales are attended by all, whether held at the Methodist church or sponsored by some other group. These activities, in fact, provide a meeting ground that offers newcomers a chance to participate in celebrating and recreating the identity of this southern small town.[7] Here they learn the stories of years gone by—who makes the best chocolate cake or the best peach cobbler, whose family used to own which piece of land, who is related to whom—and they contribute their own visions of what small-town life ought to be.

That the church and its members remain closely linked to that community-building process is one of many reasons people come to Hinton rather than to Hebron Baptist. Long the sister small-town church to Hinton, Hebron engaged in an aggressive effort at growth so that now people from all over Gwinnett County flock to its sprawling buildings, erected across the road from the original frame church and cemetery. Hebron offers everything suburbanites could want, from basketball teams for their youth to support groups for adults. Members arrive on the doorstep of each newcomer almost as soon as the moving van pulls in, and their programming seems to dominate the whole community. It is a style of church life utterly new to Dacula.[8] The people of Hinton, by contrast, do not want their congregation to be rebuilt in a suburban image. While they are open to change and growth, they want to preserve some of the old along with the new.

Their own methods of recruitment are in the midst of redefinition. In the past, they waited for people to indicate some interest before they ever tried to recruit them. Visitors were discovered (not tagged or signed in) in the course of all the greeting that happens on Sunday morning. They would usually get a follow-up call from a deacon and a visit from the pastor. Once they indicated an intention to join, they would be called to the front at the end of a Sunday service, at which time the congregation would recite with them the "Vows of Membership" found in the back of the Methodist hymnal. In coming weeks, new members routinely would be invited to join in the work and play of the congregation. Before long they might be teaching Sunday school, mowing the church lawn, helping with Meals on Wheels, and attending meetings of the United Methodist Women. In such a small group, it was hard to get lost.

As the new pastor guides the church in more systematic outreach into the community, some of these patterns may change. He is eager, for instance, to have lay members do home visits, noting that church growth research indicates that pastoral visits are less well received. In a group steeped in southern reserve and decorum, however, it may be difficult to convince some of the older members to make such visits. They will have to find a place for this new behavior in their code of southern hospitality. The natural friendliness and inclusiveness of the congregation bodes well, however, for its ability to absorb at least limited numbers of newcomers. Indeed, by early 1994, worship attendance had risen past seventy-five.

SUMMARY

Hinton Memorial United Methodist Church probably will find ways to incorporate more and more of the suburban newcomers flooding the northeast corner of Gwinnett County. It is unlikely, however, to become a megachurch like Hebron. Having once experienced change at a pace (and of a kind) members were unwilling to endure, its current process of change appears steady but gradual, creating an arena in which old and new can come together to recreate a small-town church that fits the dreams of both groups.

Since the North Georgia Conference has decided to invest in the congregation, not only does its resource base appear secure through this transition but its strong pastor can provide the patient leadership transition requires. Programs and structures of governance are slowly evolving, but further conflict is always possible, for the informal ways of long-term members will often clash with the formal rules and procedures, offices, and committees that newcomers are likely to feel more at home with. Still, the newcomers likely to choose Hinton are precisely those who want a small church in a small town, where they can feel at home and raise their children.

Conclusion

Each of these congregations has chosen to be the sort of place where people of difference can come together. Whether black and white, immigrant and native, or suburbanite and small-town dweller, these groups are seeking to hold together disparate constituencies around a common sense of mission, identity, and religious kinship. From the strict evangelicalism of Oak Park's City Baptist to the civic spirit of Hinton in Dacula, Georgia, to the combination of evangelism and social gospel at Brighton Evangelical Congregational, each has found resources in its own theological tradition to support efforts at sustaining diversity. While different ideas may support these efforts at adaptation and inclusion, some attention to ideas seems essential. In the midst of changing a congregation's fundamental sense of identity, members need some conscious rationale for what they are doing.

In each church, a sense of common purpose is nurtured in high levels of member commitment, intentional training of new leaders, and revised committee structures that make room for everyone. BECC and City Baptist have worked hard at getting everyone equally involved in making decisions, and Hinton appears ready to bring to fruition a similar process of structural change. Similarly, BECC and City have introduced new cultural elements into their worship practices, while Hinton is still struggling over how much of the old casual country style will remain.

The road to this point has not been an easy one for any of them. The recent past has been marked by serious conflict and the departure of large blocks of members at both City Baptist and Hinton. BECC suffered a long period of decline. All entered their period of restructuring after having been seriously depleted in spirit and resources, knowing that their membership was at a crisis level facing a declining future, all made crucial decisions to alter their courses.

These are not, however, generally high-resource congregations. They have among the lowest member incomes of those we studied, along with relatively low educational levels. Both Hinton and BECC have lived consistently on the edge of financial disaster. But all three have—now—strong pastors committed to the process of change, members who are willing to give sacrificially, and working partnerships with other community organizations. In addition, Hinton will have financial help from its denomination. Both from their own resources and from the resources of their partners, these three have put together viable bases for action.

They have transformed their demographic challenges and limited resources into struggling but growing congregations in which differences in social class and culture are blessed. All have acknowledged that difference can create conflict, that people sometimes stumble over conflicting expectations about how people behave. In each case, differences in ethnicity or culture are intimately tied to differences in social class: Middle-class churchgoers are being confronted by people whose sense of propriety and decorum differs from theirs. In attempting to find common religious ground, all three congregations often remind themselves of religious ideas that transcend differences. And in all three congregations, people pray for each other. In small groups and in worship prayer times, people learn about each other's diverse everyday foibles and promise to pray for each other nonetheless.

CHAPTER 6

Adaptation: Creating New Internal Structures

The transformations in the adapting congregations in this chapter are not immediately visible when one walks through their doors. The faces in the sanctuaries, for instance, look much like those of a decade ago. At Carmel United Methodist, one still sees affluent suburbanites; at Grace Baptist, struggling blue-collar workers; at Hope Baptist, African Americans. However, looks are deceiving. At Hope, in southwest Atlanta, attempts to reach an economically diverse community have gone hand in hand with internal changes in the way money is raised and decisions made. Grace Baptist in Anderson, Indiana, has absorbed within its constituency and in its own finances the shocks of the city's economic downturns. The whole membership is less economically secure today, and the church is more careful as a result. Members of Carmel, Indiana's Carmel United Methodist, still well-off suburbanites, are far less stable and committed to the community, far more urban in their orientation, than the suburbanites of a generation ago. The result has been a painful internal restructuring of the congregation to allow for the transience that is now a fact of life there. In each of the three churches, changes in the community have led the congregation to change the ways it carries on its internal life as a group. Members raise money differently, make decisions differently, and select their leaders differently. Without the challenges of shifting demographic and economic structures, none of those changes might have occurred.

Hope Baptist Church, Southwest Atlanta: Praising God and Serving the Neighborhood

From the outside, it is clear that southwest Atlanta's Hope Baptist Church has changed. Over the last few years, the congregation has moved to a new location, built a new building, and hired a new pastor.

229

What is still being worked out, however, are the implications of all that. The new location has brought a new mix of constituents; the new building, a new set of possibilities; the new pastor, a new set of priorities. Marcia Robinson of our research team fills in the rest of the story.

With the economic and ethnic change that began in the wake of civil rights legislation, the southwest Atlanta neighborhood where Hope Baptist Church is located has seen two shifts. The first was from white working-class home owners to black working-class home owners, and the second was from black working-class home owners to poor, unemployed, and working-class black people, many of them renting rundown houses. The older generation of white people who remained and the older generation of black people who moved into the area in the 1960s have died, leaving their property to children who either sold or rented out the old houses to lower-income people. As a part of this transition, substantial businesses and pleasant shopping areas have been replaced by fast-food restaurants, check-cashing places, and liquor stores.

In 1989, Hope left its longtime location on Northside Drive to move into this predominantly black, economically depressed community riddled with drugs, teenage pregnancy, unemployment, and other problems. At first known only as "the large church on the corner," it now seeks to become a religious community center for a downtrodden neighborhood.

There are two worship services, a Sunday school, and a class for new members every Sunday at Hope. Early morning service starts at 7:45 and was, in 1992, attended by fifty or so mostly older people from the old Northside Drive congregation who prefer the older gospel-style worship of this service. By 1994, the numbers and diversity of persons at this service had grown significantly, but the style remained. After the first service, several women from the Pastor's Aid Ministry prepare and sell breakfast in the large fellowship hall of the Sunday school wing of the church. Sunday school classes generally start promptly at 9:15, even though students continue to arrive up to the time when classes break for the Sunday school assembly in the sanctuary. Many people told me that Sunday school was one of the places where they get their best fellowship and enrichment. The new-members' class, which meets simultaneously with the Sunday school classes and is taught by the pastor, is one of the best places to learn about the mission and vision that the pastor has for this church.

The largest service of the day, the regular morning worship, begins with the deacons' devotional around 10:45. The deacons pray and sing in the old gospel style and encourage the audience to join in, though few do. They begin by "raising" a hymn, generally a slow, sorrowful tune that speaks of the struggles of black life and the faithfulness, righteousness, and providence of a God known as Father. This worship form, descended from slave experience and in marked contrast to the more contemporary style of the rest of the service, is still meaningful for the lives of black people, whose experience remains one of daily oppression. As the choir marches in, the mood shifts with their lively contemporary gospel music.

During the winter and spring, four or five hundred attend this service, about a third of the church's baptized and registered members. The sanctuary, large enough to accommodate them comfortably, is a large octagon with five broad sections of plush burgundy pews, carpeted throughout. Behind a large choir stand in front, lies a curtained baptismal pool. The imposing central pulpit is flanked by piano, organ, and other instruments. Four modern stained-glass windows are set in one wall, and the central, octagonal dome has a clerestory.

As for the preacher and the preaching that seem to be drawing all of these people, Pastor Harold Jackson is a black man in his early thirties whose primary aim is to make the Christian message "real" to the people of the church and the surrounding community. His style of preaching is a mixture of black gospel and charismatic teaching, a dynamic combination of old and new. He emphasizes worship that is Spirit-led, spontaneous praise, characterized primarily by themes of joy and victory. The congregation participates with amens and other vocal expressions, singing, clapping, dancing, shouting, and patting tambourines. The service usually lasts until nearly two o'clock in the afternoon, and the most enthusiastic stay to the end.

According to Hope's 1989 yearbook, the church began in 1925, when it was located in a storefront building on Hayes Street in northwest Atlanta. After several efforts to firmly establish the church, in 1933 the late Rev. B. R. Smith became the pastor and stayed for a little over thirty-three years. He was loved for his passionate, traditional black gospel preaching style, as well as for his devotion to the people of Hope. Under his leadership, the church moved to a larger facility on Davis Street (presently Northside Drive), where it remained until 1989, when the construction of the Georgia Dome precipitated the latest move.

During those early years, the congregation averaged two to four hundred people and felt to many members like a family. They were mostly hardworking, respectable people who found personal value and spiritual uplift by participating in the church's worship, fellowship activities, leadership, and administration. Under the leadership of Pastor Jackson, the old family environment is being transformed into a spiritual community center, significantly altered in size, style of worship, and organization.

In the old church, Hope's general theological orientation was rooted in the idea of a loving and all-powerful God who, as Father, was present with his children as they struggled with racial, social, and economic oppression and the problems of daily life. Worship focused on God's providence and God's promises for the next life. In the same tradition, Hope's organization gave its people personal and spiritual uplift by providing them with an arena for autonomy. Hope's structure was based on a conference system that allowed members to vote on issues brought before them by the deacons and pastor, along with a group of auxiliaries, or programs, which were the church's primary source of income as well as key expressions of its ministry and mission.

Pastor Jackson's theological focus, worship style, and church organization challenge and seek to transform these aspects of old Hope. His theological vision focuses on spiritual and personal victory, and he has introduced a group of ministries aimed at problems facing black youth, black men, and the black family, as well as at substance abuse. These ministries are replacing the auxiliaries of the old congregation in the decision-making process. Moreover, since Jackson's theology stresses tithing, the purpose of the ministries, unlike the older auxiliaries, is not to raise money for the church.

This transformation, along with the church's dramatic growth since the move, has been a mixed blessing to old Hope. The new Hope forming under Pastor Jackson's leadership involves people who live "victoriously" in this life, worshipping enthusiastically in a blend of charismatic and black Baptist worship patterns and reaching out to the community in their personal lives and through the church's social outreach ministries. The old church, meanwhile, has lost its family atmosphere and its old structure, both of which provided the personal value and spiritual uplift members had grown to cherish. However, it now reaches many more people with the gospel and has opened its arms to a community who needs it.

Some of the members of old Hope have adjusted to its changes and are now active members in its new life. However, there has been conflict, not over the value of social outreach—the members have long practiced that—but over a church structure and theology that no longer gave voice to their sense of striving. For a time, two different congregations existed in this church. One was the traditional congregation made up primarily of people from the old Hope. The other was the vibrant, charismatic, mostly younger congregation forming under the leadership and vision of Pastor Jackson. Hope was a church at the crossroads. Only as it came to embrace its new identity, while respecting its history, could it turn its full attention to ministry in the difficult community in which it is located.

RESOURCES

Since moving to its striking new building, Hope Baptist Church has experienced significant new growth, with attendance now at least 50 percent higher than in the old location. With a new pastor, a new building, and many new members, the church has a confident sense that it can do what needs to be done.

That confidence is enhanced by the youthfulness of the congregation, with an average age among those who completed our survey of just thirty-seven (see table 6.1). Largely attracted by a young and enthusiastic pastor, these new members are bringing renewed energy to the church. As in many churches, women outnumber men here— sometimes four to one, even with the pastor's emphasis on ministry to men. In addition, a sizable contingent of middle-aged and older persons, most of them veterans of the old church, remains highly commit-

Table 6.1. Hope Baptist Church, Southwest Atlanta

Ideas and priorities	
Christian practices rated "essential"	Living Christian values
	Prayer
	Bible study
	Attendance at services
Ministries rated "very important" or "essential"	
	Service to the needy
	An evangelism program
	Preparation for the next world
	Helping members resist this world
	Cooperation with other groups for community improvement
	Encouragement of individual witnessing
	Encouraging good citizenship
Resources	
Average Sunday attendance	600
Annual operating budget (1992)	N/a
Household incomes above $50,000	20%
College degrees or more	39%
Average age	37 years
Activities (beyond worship) participated in at least monthly	Bible study
Relationship to the community	
Live ten minutes or less from the church	45%
New to the community in the last five years	45%
Ethnicity	97% African American
Participate in civic & community activities more than once a month	52%

NOTE: Only sixty-four people responded to our survey, amounting to approximately 11 percent of average Sunday attendance. This should be taken as only a tentative representation of all regular attenders.

ted to this congregation. Many hold key leadership positions, and their wisdom and experience are as much a potential resource for the church as the energy of the youth.

Their building fits their optimistic mood. The large sanctuary is designed to draw the congregation together into an intimate circle before God, with a semicircular arrangement of the pews that allows much of the congregation to see most everyone else. A spacious open area at the front is the setting for devotionals, the offerings, and the times of prayer and healing that are central to Hope's worship. The rest of the building provides ample meeting and classroom space, with a large fellowship hall and kitchen. Outside the sanctuary, in a gathering area that includes an information desk, members greet visitors and chat with friends. Its gracious furnishings, along with the new and well-equipped look of the entire building, create an impression of a church that has arrived, surely a welcome presence in this Atlanta neighborhood.

The congregation that gathers here is economically diverse. There is a sizable contingent of college-educated professionals with ample incomes whose skills and community connections make them valuable contributors in many of the church's leadership positions. There are also many people who have stable working-class jobs in the service sector and in government. Most of them have completed high school, and some have taken courses in vocational schools or junior colleges. They have enough money to get by, but not enough for luxuries. Many are hardworking and creative, able to organize and succeed at whatever ventures the church gives them the opportunity to undertake. Finally, many people who put on their Sunday best each week to come to Hope have neither economic stability nor the education to bargain for better. The resources they bring to the church are more spiritual than material.

Still, a growing number of these folk are willing to give generously of what they do have. Since Pastor Jackson began to stress tithing, an increasing number of members are pledging 10 percent of their income. He teaches the new members that tithing is expected, and almost two-thirds of those who have been through his orientation class have pledged to tithe. If the congregation is willing to support Pastor Jackson's move away from old-style fund-raising techniques, the result could be a more stable budget, not dependent on special events and annual gifts, and greater clarity about who has authority to spend what money. The old system fosters decentralized spending, as well as unpredictable giving. The new system could bring more predictability to the church's use of its resources. The old system, of course, had significant side benefits in the leadership training and visibility afforded those who participated. A successful move to a new system will require that the energy and honor formerly generated in the old system be recreated in other places.

STRUCTURES OF AUTHORITY

What Pastor Jackson is attempting in this congregation is nothing less than revolutionary. He is asking congregants of this traditional black church to change not only the way they worship, but also the way they raise money and the way they make decisions. The old system organized the church into auxiliaries—ushers, willing workers, missionary society, mothers, nurses, junior ushers, and the like. Each provided opportunities for fellowship, offered services to the church, developed leaders, and raised money, competing with other auxiliaries for the biggest gifts on church anniversary days. They also served as a link in the decision-making process, taking concerns to the deacons and pastor, who in turn might bring them to the church in conference.

This new pastor wants to transform the auxiliaries into ministries. He has supported some new groups—a food ministry group and a substance abuse ministry, for example—and some of the old groups have gotten new names. The Usher Board is now the Usher Ministry, for instance. It is unclear, however, whether this new organizational structure will meet the multiple needs addressed by the old auxiliary system. While the changes seem to have broad support among many of the new members and the most skilled younger leaders, maintaining the support of older members, for whom auxiliaries have defined church life, will require a good deal of pastoral attention and persuasion. Pastor Jackson has actively cared for his older members, calling several people each day for a pastorly visit, but he is less eager to seek them out for consultation or advice.

In fact, there have been grumblings about how decision making is taking place in the church under this new system. Some members noted that, with few church conferences, major changes seemed to be happening without discussion and voting by the members. The pastor, on the other hand, believes his role demands clear leadership. As shepherd to this flock, he describes the church as a theocracy, not a democracy. God is in charge, not the majority. As God's servant, the pastor must articulate a vision for the church, a vision most often held up from the pulpit, not in the board or conference room. In his preaching, Jackson mentions new ideas for how the church should do its ministry, expecting that those who hear will be motivated to support that vision. Unfortunately, people in the church who are accustomed to being consulted sometimes hear such messages as announcements of what the pastor has unilaterally decided.

The most critical arena for working out such concerns about decision making is between the pastor and the deacons. Tradition gives deacons in a black Baptist church a powerful role. They recruit and recommend pastors to the congregation, and it is often they who act to dismiss pastors who fail to meet the church's expectations, something that has happened more than once in Hope's history. This pastor's ideas about spiritual leadership place the deacons firmly in the role of supporters, not directors, a role some of the current deacons were unwilling to assume. By the end of 1994, some of them, along with other unhappy members, had left the church, and the potential for conflict waned.

The organizational power structure in place at Hope Baptist Church has only a little to do with its nominal connection with the National Baptist Convention, U.S.A., Inc. The denomination is virtually invisible in the church's life, and no one except the pastor could even recount whether and at what points the church had maintained any official denominational ties. The pastor reported that after fourteen years of being independent, he had led the church back to the NBC just the previous year. There was no indication, however, that these connections will have any impact on the future direction of the church and its ministry. What Hope decides to do, how it chooses to relate to an economically diverse African American community, will depend on internal power dynamics, not external guidance or directives.

CULTURE

The people who gather at Hope each week know all too well the pains and trials of this world. Even those who have made it into respected middle-class occupations know the pain of discrimination, of subtle and not-so-subtle racism. Even those whose own lives seem relatively unscathed need only look around their neighborhood to see the scars of an economic and political neglect that strains the bonds of family and community. For more than three centuries people of African descent, brought to this country in chains, have gathered in various kinds of worship settings to express and transform their grief. The worship styles of this congregation grow out of various streams of that tradition.

The style of the early service and the morning devotion represents one of those streams. As our researcher Marcia Robinson notes, it is rooted in slave experience. "These people allow this deeply expressive and sorrowful music to permeate the whole of their being, clapping and swaying as they sing, resulting in a single expression of worship that transforms these few individuals into an embodiment of their praise and worship of God." In expressing their sorrow to God, it is transcended. Hope is found in God's promise of eternal life.

The main worship service draws upon another stream in black worship tradition, usually associated with Holiness or "sanctified" churches: lots of upbeat, contemporary music from congregation, choirs, soloists, and ensembles, keyboard and drums, and tambourines. There are no hymnals in the pews; the day's hymn is reproduced in the bulletin. More important than the hymn, however, are the spirituals and choruses that everyone can easily sing. Choir and instrumentalists embellish the familiar melodies and harmonies; members of the congregation stand and clap and dance; and the performance goes on as long as the spirit can be sustained—sometimes ten or fifteen minutes. During these times, as during the altar call, various members "get happy," sometimes dancing before the altar until they are spent, then being helped out of the sanctuary by fellow parishioners. Others speak in tongues, sometimes encouraged by the pastor. The organist and drummer often emphasize the pastor's words or pick up on a song he suggests. While a small core of people regularly participate in these praise activities, at least half the congregation joins in with enthusiasm most of the time. In boisterous, ecstatic praise, the pain of this world is overcome in the here and now. The congregation gains both an experience of momentary transcendence and a sense of energy and possibility that carries them into the rest of the week.[1] Pastor Jackson and those who support the introduction of this new style at Hope insist that people need to experience victory in their worship, not bemoan their defeats.

The members of Hope also get to celebrate victories in their Sunday school classes and other small groups. There is the new Male Ministry, a spiritual support group for men. There are ministry groups as well as Bible study groups led by the pastor on Wednesday night and by a deacon on Saturday morning and a new Friday night praise service. When people first present themselves for membership in the church during an invitational hymn, they are invited into the pastor's Intensive Care class. Meeting at the same time as Sunday school, they go through a seven-week orientation course on the church, its basic beliefs, and what it expects of them. The hope is that, having started coming at Sunday school time, they will continue in a regular class after this series is over.

Still, fewer than one hundred adults are involved in Sunday school, and many of those are also the stalwarts in mission activities, choirs, and auxiliaries. Not nearly all those who attend Sunday worship have any other experience with the church. For those who do, in groups both small and large, prayer requests include the full range of life's pain—from lost keys to crack babies. The pastor and the church encourage people to be open with each other, not ashamed to tell their fellow church members their troubles. At the same time, people are likely to share with each other the triumphs, small and large, that remind them that God is still in charge. In these gatherings, as in worship, healing and miraculous assistance, God's mercy and God's providence are talked about, celebrated, invoked. People come away convinced that God's power is theirs.

What they, individually and collectively, choose to do with that sense of power is still being worked out. Just as their organizational structure and worship styles are in transition, so their sense of mission is evolving, as well. Our survey—probably tapping only the most active members—revealed a congregation where all sorts of ministry are deemed important, from preparing for the next world and resisting this one to serving the needy and working for community betterment. No other congregation in this study rated so many ministries so high on their list of priorities. The pastor preaches that God wants folks he can use, people who don't mind going out and helping people wherever they are—children in the projects, prostitutes, drug abusers.

"Christ came into the world to deal with rotten folks, and he wants a church that will do the same," Pastor Jackson says. He sees the presence of a beautiful building in the midst of such a declining neighborhood as a miracle. He would like to see the church building used all the time to meet the needs of the community.

Increasingly, members in the church are organizing to address neighborhood and city needs. A group of a dozen or so helps out at a homeless shelter that is run by a member of the church. Hope is one of the few black churches to be involved in this ministry to mostly black people. Members are concerned about their young people and have invited a doctor in to talk to youngsters about sex and AIDS. While he stressed abstinence, he was also candid about protection. Younger kids are asked to bring in their report cards; good ones are rewarded, and kids who need help get tutors. Members are also concerned about the physical health of adults, and a health ministry group organized a health fair, open to the neighborhood, at which people could get information and screening for several common maladies. Similarly, members have been working with a for-profit food ministry that puts together baskets for sale at fifteen dollars. This arrangement, however, hasn't been entirely satisfactory, and they are hoping to change tactics. There is a clothing ministry. And members do a variety of things to combat substance abuse. As an early-prevention measure, they run a summer camp and an after-school program that attempt to build positive self-images among black youth; and they have a Boy Scouts program. A part-time minister acts primarily as a referral service for people with drug and alcohol problems, getting them into treatment and rehabilitation programs and staying in contact with them as they try to change.

SUMMARY

The congregation of Atlanta's Hope Baptist Church slowly—and not without conflict—seems to be gaining a sense of itself as a place where victories happen and are celebrated. The Sunday altar call sees victories over inner demons and sinful ways. Victories are experienced and recognized in enthusiastic worship, and victories happen in minds and bodies throughout the community as a result of the church's care. Hope has attracted significant new numbers to its new location and works hard at integrating them. The worship style introduced by this pastor seems well suited to community needs, which are also being addressed by the ministries under way in the congregation. The primary challenges facing the church have to do with internal governance. The switch from auxiliary fund-raising to tithing could easily have backfired. Not everyone has been happy with the changes in worship or excited about the new directions in missions. Some wish for a church more conservative and staid in its worship and organizational life. Most of all, there are people who want to know that their opinion matters. Integrating new and old, Baptist tradition and holiness enthusiasm, pastoral direction and congregational consultation, has been the challenge standing between Hope and a full-fledged mission encounter with its community.

While Hope seems well on its way to the sorts of restructuring that will secure its future, Grace Baptist in Anderson has largely accomplished that task. As Baptist churches, both are locally autonomous (indeed, Grace is completely independent), inventing their structures as they go. Both have a strong sense of mission to their community and the will to do what is necessary to put their financial houses in order.

Grace Baptist Church, Anderson: Financial Stability in Uncertain Times

At Grace Baptist Church in Anderson, Indiana, the part of the transformation that is most apparent to the visitor is the excellent condition of its buildings. When I visited, Pastor Leigh Crockett took researcher Connie Zeigler and me on a tour of the property, pointing out what had been done in recent years—paint here, new carpet there, roof fixed, wiring brought up to code. It was a mess when he got there—the visible signs of the financial mess they were in. Since then, Grace Baptist has discarded both old furnishings and old practices that threatened its future. As the city of Anderson underwent a wrenching economic downturn, Grace went through an economic crisis of its own. Connie Zeigler gives this account of Grace's story.

Anderson's current dilemmas are a far cry from the boom times in which Grace Baptist Church was born. Twelve laypersons and the Reverend Paul Vincent founded the church in 1956, when Anderson's future held immense promise. In November 1958, the congregation purchased two acres of land at their present location and in 1959 built a small church and hired their first full-time minister, Rev. James Puz. Two and one-half years later, church members voted to remove Puz and offered the ministry to Rev. Don Camp, an active lay leader. In 1964, during a period of steady growth, Grace Baptist added ten new Sunday school rooms to its facilities.

Located just outside the Anderson city limits on County Road 300 North, the church is identified by a sign in the parking lot as "Independent Fundamental." The main building is a one-story, flat-roofed structure with a yellow brick facade. But for the small steeple added recently to the roof, it looks more like a late 1960s elementary school than a church. To its west sits the large building that houses Indiana Christian Academy, founded in 1973 for youngsters from kindergarten through twelfth grade. Both the sanctuary and the academy were built during Camp's tenure as minister. While these additions were symbols of the mission and success of Grace Baptist Church, they brought increasing financial responsibilities. Before the congregation could expunge the debt for the church building, they added to it the huge burden of the school mortgage.

Financial problems became acute in the early 1980s as General Motors (GM) layoffs accelerated. This general recession magnified Grace Baptist's fiscal predicament. Although Camp's powerful ministry doubled attendance between 1976 and 1983, debts mounted and the facilities deteriorated. In the 1980s, Pastor Camp and his staff cut the church budget by $100,000. By 1983, when Camp decided to embark on a full-time evangelism career after twenty-three years as pastor, the church had nearly $150,000 in past-due bills, and the utilities had been turned off more than once.

Claiming that the Bible gave him sole authority in the search for a new minister, Pastor Camp kept the church members in suspense for many months as he sought the man he wanted to replace him as the spiritual leader of Grace Baptist Church. Finally, he offered the church one candidate, Leigh A. Crockett, Jr., whom 93 percent of the members agreed to support. Crockett became the leader of a church in grave financial difficulties, with deteriorating facilities, and another man's staff.

Under Pastor Camp, information about the church's economic circumstances had been kept from the laity, including its leaders, and the school administrator had near autonomy in church financial decisions. Within two years, Pastor Crockett had brought in a new school administrator and a new assistant minister/business manager charged with helping Grace Baptist meet its earthly as well as spiritual needs. Crockett drew the congregation into the decision-making process through quarterly and emergency meetings. Not long after he arrived, he informed the congregation of the extent of their money problems, asking them to pray and to fast about it. The following Sunday, the church held a special offering for reducing the debt, to which Pastor Crockett made a public donation of $1,000. By the end of the week members had raised over $56,000 and were able to pay $38,000 on the church mortgages, bringing them current in their payments for the first time in five years. Church finances slowly improved. The ministerial staff took voluntary pay cuts. Bills were paid in a timely fashion and any extra money was banked.

As funds accumulated, Pastor Crockett approached the membership to vote on physical improvements to the church. Over the next months and years, they paved the parking lot, carpeted the sanctuary and halls, redecorated Sunday school classes, added a steeple to the building, and made improvements at the school. The pastor has asked only for renovations that the church could pay for in cash, and finally in 1993, members began a campaign to eliminate their debt entirely. As the physical plant slowly improved and the debt decreased, the church began to think differently about itself. While members and staff still worry that GM plant closings would have a major financial impact on the church, their goal of operating on sound financial footing seems within their grasp at last.

Although the congregation is proud of overcoming its financial obstacles, only the staff fully appreciates the changes that have been wrought. For most members, the church is where they receive the fellowship and biblical message that sustain them. They often remark that not much has changed since Pastor Crockett came to the church, for the continuity of the message they receive allows them to view their church as enduring much as it always has.

As people arrive each Sunday morning, they are greeted by ushers at the door. The sanctuary lies directly ahead beyond a wall of clear glass, its floor covered with gray and burgundy tweed carpet, the pews upholstered in royal blue. About six hundred people, including a handful of African Americans, will fill the pews in the center of the church and in one side extension; the other extension is closed off with a vinyl folding curtain. Behind the pulpit and choir loft, directly above the baptistry, rises a ten-foot cross with a carved Bible at its top.

At 10:25, when music minister and school administrator Pastor Newton steps to the pulpit to announce the first song, he has to speak loudly into the microphone to be heard above the conversations that fill the auditorium. The congregation stands to sing from a hymnal titled Soul-Stirring Songs. Pastor Crockett, in his early forties, wearing a gray-striped, double-breasted suit (none of the ministers wears a robe), offers a prayer. After the offering, he asks members to introduce their visitors. A few people stand and introduce their guests, while others simply raise their hands to signify that they are visitors. After people greet those around them, there is more congregational singing and a selection by the choir before Pastor Crockett gives the announcements and prayer requests. When he finishes, the congregation sings again as the choir and assistant pastors exit the platform to take seats with their families.

Sermons at Grace always focus on how life is different when people believe in Jesus Christ as their personal savior. Pastor Crockett begins by reading a brief passage of Scripture, and members turn to the verses in their zippered leather Bibles and read along; some highlight the words in yellow. The pastor prays, then begins the sermon. Speaking so quickly it is difficult to catch each word, he exhorts his listeners to lead others to Jesus. The time is short; people must accept God's power and turn away from Satan. "Jesus frees us from slavery to hell," he says. Throughout the sermon Pastor Crockett gestures dramatically, sometimes stepping down onto the floor in front of the pulpit.

As he finishes, he asks the audience to bow their heads. He appeals for anyone who is not saved, or who is wondering what salvation means, to raise his or her hand. As each hand goes up, he says, "God bless you, brother [sister]." A counselor from the church goes to each person who has raised a hand and slips out of the sanctuary with him or her. After a few moments, Crockett asks for the saved persons who were especially touched by the service to raise their hands. "God Bless you, Bill; God Bless you, over there," he says. As the invitation hymn is sung, he steps down in front of the pulpit and invites anyone who is ready to "make a decision for Christ" to come forward. When the invitation is *concluded, he closes the service with prayer and walks down the aisle to stand at the rear door of the sanctuary, while the assembly sings, "He's coming again, our very same Jesus, He's coming again."*

RESOURCES

The major dilemma faced by Grace Baptist Church in the deep recession of the late 1970s and early 1980s was—not surprisingly—financial. In the 1960s, when Anderson was booming and the church was growing by leaps and bounds, anything seemed possible. Never a wealthy church, Grace simply went out "on faith," not only building a sanctuary, but launching in the early 1970s an extremely expensive full-scale Christian academy. Those in charge dreamed of equipping and running a school that would rival any competitor in the training available to its students. Tuition alone could not support the school, so the church constantly underwrote operating expenses, in addition to paying the mortgage. Since the school's administrator had full access to the church's budget, school needs often took priority over church needs. But so long as economic times were good, such practices could continue with little apparent ill effect.

When the recession hit, however, Grace Baptist could no longer keep up the pace. Bills started to go unpaid. The church was seriously behind on the mortgage. Leaks went unfixed, carpets were dangerously frayed, wires were held in place on the platform by conspicous patches of duct tape. The sound system did not work, and there were pot holes and weeds in the parking lot. The practice of going out on faith, trusting God from one payment to the next, was clearly not working in the midst of layoffs and a devastated economy. When Pastor Crockett arrived, he introduced some discipline into the church's financial practices. "I've been trying to reteach them," he said, "that if God wants us to have something, why can't he give us the faith to believe we can put it into the bank and then go buy it? And so that's what we've done." Excess spending on the academy stopped. Extra funds were raised to pay off old bills. The church had to begin to live within its means. New economic realities called for new church practices.

Grace Baptist still had considerable resources on which to draw. With about six hundred people there each Sunday, the tens and twenties in the offering plate could add up. But more importantly, this church stresses tithing. In fact, the ratio of reported giving to reported income was highest in this church of any we surveyed—an average of 8 percent of household income. Members' incomes are not high (see table 6.2). More people have household incomes under $20,000 (28 percent) than above $50,000 (19 percent). But they give generously. With

Table 6.2. Grace Baptist Church, Anderson

Ideas and priorities

Christian practices rated "essential"	Prayer
	Bible study
	Attendance at services
	Living Christian values
	Sharing faith with others
Ministries rated "very important" or "essential"	An evangelism program
	Encouragement of individual witnessing
	Helping members resist this world
	Preparation for the next world

Resources

Average Sunday attendance	600
Annual operating budget (1992)	$385,000
Household incomes above $50,000	19%
College degrees or more	21%
Average age	47 years
Activities (beyond worship) participated in at least monthly	Bible study
	Fellowship
	Recruiting converts

Relationship to the community

Live ten minutes or less from the church	44%
New to the community in the last five years	13%
Ethnicity	94% European
Participate in civic & community activities more than once a month	40%

NOTE: One hundred thirty-eight people responded to our survey, amounting to approximately 23 percent of average Sunday attendance. This may be taken as a fair representation of all regular attenders.

combined numbers and generosity, the church more than makes up for the lack of wealthy donors.

The income levels Grace's members report reflect the working-class character of the congregation, which includes few professionals or managers (16 percent) and a vast majority in either clerical and sales positions (27 percent) or·blue collar occupations (50 percent). Not surprising, given this occupational picture, is that fewer than a quarter of Grace's members (21 percent) have college degrees. Two-thirds have finished high school or done some post–high school work, but 10 percent are not high school graduates. Such folk are, of course, particularly vulnerable to the sort of economic downturn Anderson has experienced over the last decade. With minimal education and skills and without the security of union jobs in stable industries their parents enjoyed, people often have to improvise, piecing survival together by holding multiple jobs, getting some support from their families, and learning to get by on less. Some have come to Anderson from elsewhere, following family or friends or rumors of job openings.

The resources Grace Baptist has at its disposal, then, are not the gifts of wealth and status earned in the outside world. Rather, Grace multiplies small gifts into large ones, using loaves and fishes to feed a multitude. Everyone seems willing to give what they can, recognizing that at some future time they themselves might be in need. By combining lots of small gifts, the church has been able to get back on its feet. And by regular disciplined and generous giving, the families of the church have pooled their resources to make the church building a more attractive place. Both those feats—paying their bills and fixing up their building—have given them a sense of confidence that they can continue to provide ministry to the community, that they will have a place from which to preach and teach the gospel.

The building is now in reasonably good repair, but in 1992 broken-down air conditioners created a crisis. The church is still operating close enough to the financial edge to be affected by such events. In addition, a fleet of buses causes a continuing drain on the church's budget. Maintaining aging buses and saving toward new ones, plus the air conditioning repair, took slightly more money than the church received in 1992, requiring the use of some of its hard-won reserves.

Much of what has been possible at Grace has happened because of capable pastoral leadership, supported by a competent staff that works well as a team. That Pastor Leigh Crockett (yes, a descendent of Davy) believes both in big dreams and in careful organization has been apparent in his response to the church's financial difficulties and in his approach to decision making. He has tried to draw a wider circle of people into the process, while keeping lines of authority and spheres of responsibility clear. His parishioners are not well equipped by education and experience for leadership, but the pastor has engaged in persistent leadership education from the pulpit and in the committee room, offering them opportunities to participate and learn at church what they do not get from their jobs or other training.

As an independent, nondenominational church, Grace has had to rely largely on its own resources for getting through this time of restructuring. The wider fundamentalist network is available for guest speakers and musicians, retreat leaders and evangelists, because the pastor's experience teaching in fundamentalist colleges has given him exposure to that resource. Within Anderson, the church uses the services of various community organizations to extend its help to people in need. Still, with no ready denominational reserve on which to call, Grace Baptist knows that its survival depends on homegrown ingenuity and persistence.

STRUCTURES OF AUTHORITY

As an independent church, Grace is accountable to no outside authority. The school participates in the Indiana Association of Christian Schools, more an advisory body than an accrediting one, and the pastor belongs to the Indiana Baptist Fellowship, which is essentially a pastors' conference. The structure of the church's internal decision making, then, is a local matter, and despite the strong denominationlike culture that pervades U.S. fundamentalism, patterns of authority are quite diverse.[2] Some churches are essentially run by the pastor, with minimal advice from anyone and no democratic participation. Other churches are thoroughly democratic, while still honoring the pastor's leadership. Grace Baptist has experienced both.

Pastor Crockett has adopted the more participatory style. Important issues are taken to the whole congregation for a vote, and there are regular church business meetings. Not that the pastor exercises no influence or that there are no clearly delineated spheres of authority—Pastor Crockett talks about authority as the umbrella each person operates under. His is the big umbrella over the whole church, but deacons, staff, and other leaders have smaller umbrellas, and underneath those umbrellas they are in charge. As long as all the umbrellas stay in right relationship with each other, individuals have a good deal of freedom to work—within the confines of their particular "umbrella." Each person is accountable, finally, to the whole body for the task they do.

When Crockett has an idea he wants to implement, he begins by talking with his staff and the deacons. These bodies serve as sounding boards for what is necessary and feasible. Only with their approval does the idea go to the congregation as a recommendation. By then, the pastor, staff, and deacons are likely to be convinced that this idea is God's will for the church. When they present it, a sense of divine urgency often accompanies the proposal, and the pastor may remind the congregation of the importance of a spirit of unity. Members are given a full plate of information and offered ample opportunity for questions and discussion, but they are very likely to agree that this is God's will for their church. Never since Crockett has been pastor has the congregation turned down one of his suggestions that has come through this process. He told us that he has had to train the congregation to participate in decision making. He recalled that at first they were uncomfortable with this, since it was different from how things were under the previous pastor. But now they are glad to have a voice in decisions.

CULTURE

The central experience for the members of Grace Baptist Church is conversion. Most who join Grace come as new converts, and for many conversion is no empty theological word. They have known lives of degradation, and now they know what it is to be redeemed. The congregation has a rich lore of stories about drug use and alcoholism, unstable marriages and sporadic employment, even brushes with the law—stories about how life *used to be* before being transformed by religious faith and religious community. This is a community that specializes in forgiveness, but it is a forgiveness leavened with a healthy dose of accountability. No matter what one's past life, one can be accepted here. But once accepted, one is expected to change, and that very expectation makes enduring change more possible. The pastor says that the mission of the church is to evangelize and to edify. Both are necessary to sustain the transformations this church seeks.

Grace employs all the usual evangelical methods for recruiting lost souls into the kingdom. An extensive bus ministry brings unchurched children to Sunday school and worship services. In an organized visitation program, teams from the church call on people who have attended or expressed some interest in the church. And church services are televised. Each of these efforts brings a slow trickle of inquirers into the church. However, most converts come because a neighbor, friend, or family member has brought them. When visitors are recognized in services, often a church member introduces them.

Once they have walked the aisle to declare their faith, have been baptized by immersion, and have thus become members of the community, their "edification" consists largely of the Bible study and prayer that dominate church life. The three most important Christian virtues, according to the people who completed our survey, are praying, studying the Bible, and attending church services. At Grace, those ideals are also reality. In Sunday school classes, people get new Bible lessons each week; they study the Bible again in women's groups or at Wednesday night prayer meeting; they are encouraged to read the Bible at home every day. No wonder that the stories and lessons of the Scripture become the stuff of everyday conversation.

But the Bible is not the only source of the lessons people learn at Grace. Recognizing that many of his parishioners are not widely read, the pastor takes every opportunity to teach them about history, politics, and everyday practicalities. His newsletter columns and sermons often include stories about world events past and present, and the Civic Leaders Sunday each fall offers Grace's members current information they might otherwise not have. In this congregation, members who formerly read little are encouraged to study for themselves and to share their insights with each other.

They are also encouraged to pray for each other. Many church functions include a time for prayer requests, and people freely share the joys and sorrows of their lives. This is a church where tragedy seems never far from the door. During the time we were there, there were several cases of cancer, accidents that endangered jobs, a fatal car crash, and a murder—all directly touching the lives of this working-class congregation. All were shared and prayed over.

While some situations are unlikely to be changed by the prayers of church members, prayer here is not a passive activity for those resigned to their fate. One of the members, head of a United Auto Workers local, got up during a praise service one evening to report that his back was stiff from riding in the car. He had just gotten back from Detroit, he said, where he had asked a vice-president at General Motors what was going to happen to Delco and Inland Fisher Guide and the other area plants where he had workers. When asked, "Are we gonna be here five years from now?" the vice-president told him they were asking themselves if GM was going to be here in five years. The union official was appealing to his church to pray about this. "There's a lot riding on these plants, they could affect 200,000 to 300,000 people in the spin-off plants. Please pray for this situation, it's critical."

Did praying with his fellow church members make a difference? At the very least, praying offered an opportunity to frame their economic dilemmas in something other than market terms.[3] He and others in his church often reminded themselves that "God is not spelled GM." In their scheme, God is infinitely greater than GM. Rather than face GM in quiet resignation, they invoked that higher power, daring to presume that God might be concerned about their work. No matter what else happened to those prayers, the very act of praying afforded an opportunity to critique the social order of this world and envision a social order in which people have work to do. Such a critique is often the precursor to action. This union official was active in leading his organization to make changes that would minimize their risks of massive cuts. He later told Connie Zeigler that "they came in and did a study, and it didn't come out too favorable for our work habits and managerial staff and stuff like that, so we took the bull by the horns and got some things turned around. When GM made the announcement a couple of weeks ago about the last of the plant closings for this round, we were supposed to have had some plants on that list. But because we were able to get out in front on the thing and turn some things around, they actually used us as an example of how not to lose your plant." For him, as for others at Grace, prayer, Bible study, and the everyday conversations of church members combine to form a cognitive map that can remake the everyday landscape.

The congregation is also the central location on the social map of many church members. Of those who completed our survey, nearly all (87 percent) said they participate in Bible study at least weekly, nearly two-thirds (62 percent) participate in fellowship activities more than once a month, and almost half (47 percent) participate in recruiting new members at least once a month. Three-quarters said that at least three of their five closest friends are in the congregation, and an even larger percentage (83 percent) have at least one other member of their household in the congregation. For those connected to the school, the round of church-related activities is even more all-pervasive.

This network of friends and activities can also become a network of concrete mutual aid. The deacons and the pastor coordinate assistance to church families that fall on hard times. A birth or a death brings the women of the church with food and household assistance. And when a church member starts a new business, that fact is likely to be advertised at church. The church itself has even provided space in an unused barn for one fledgling business (although it was careful for tax purposes to ask for some services in return). Members are encouraged to patronize each other's stores, and they understand when high start-up energy keeps someone away from services more than they might like. These people value hard work and are willing to be creative, improvising new economic solutions in the midst of hard times. While there are no deep-pocket capitalists in the congregation, this is the sort of economic community Max Weber described in his observations about Protestant sects in America.[4] Like those nineteenth-century groups, the church encourages asceticism and hard work and also serves as a mutual aid society, credit reference, and pool of customers.

SUMMARY

Because the members of Grace Baptist expect the world to be a hostile place, they band together for comfort and assistance. Their community provides not only spiritual support in the face of secular adversity, but also material and social support. As with South Meridian Church of God on the other side of town, the practices of Christian fellowship and piety serve this congregation well in economic hard times. Unlike South Meridian, however, Grace did not enter this downturn in sound financial condition. While members' practices of mutual sustenance were well poised to sustain them, their church's financial practices had to be transformed. The "on faith" unplanned spending of good times had to yield to careful planning, frugality, and increased generosity. As all gave according to their means, the combined effect was a congregation able to survive and thrive. Those who could, gave sacrificially;

those who could not knew they could depend on the church for assistance. In this congregation, all sorts of miracles seem very real.

The congregation—and its community—stands in sharp economic contrast to its Indiana neighbor Carmel. As Anderson congregations were attempting to discover ways to live with scarcity, Carmel churches were swimming in abundance. Yet that abundance did not guarantee tranquility. The changing economic circumstances of Carmel's residents (from long-term resident professionals to mobile managers) also necessitated congregational change.

Carmel United Methodist Church, Carmel: Choices and Loyalties in a Pillar of the Community

Neither Grace Baptist in Anderson nor Carmel United Methodist in nearby Carmel, Indiana, fully realized the implications of community change as it was happening; neither adopted new strategies as a conscious response to that change. Grace tried new fiscal strategies when the economy made old strategies unworkable. Carmel United Methodist has come up with new administrative strategies to make the church more responsive to Carmel's latest round of residents. While Grace accomplished this transition with no overt conflict, Carmel was not so fortunate. Michelle Hale recounts Carmel's history.

Methodists were early residents of Carmel, Indiana, and started meeting informally in 1838. After occupying several locations, the Methodist Episcopal Carmel Church constructed its first building in 1850 and went on to build a concrete-block church near the center of town in 1905. This building became a center of local activity. Reflecting the rural nature of Carmel throughout the 1800s and early 1900s, members then were mostly farmers, and baptisms were held in the nearby White River.

A key turning point in this congregation's history occurred with its designation as "station charge" in 1948; which brought the church's first full-time minister; it had previously shared a preacher with several nearby churches. In the aftermath of World War II, the village of Carmel was beginning to attract Indianapolis professionals who wanted to raise their children in a safe, small-town environment. From 1930 to 1958, Carmel grew from six hundred residents to six thousand. Some of these people commuted to Indianapolis and the surrounding area to work, but they still identified with Carmel as their home.

As Carmel began to grow, so did its Methodist church, reaching a membership of eight hundred by the end of the 1950s, including many of the newly arriving professionals and business people. The congregation soon ran out of space in the old cement-block church and launched a communitywide fundraising drive for a new facility. They built the present sanctuary south of the center of town in 1958 on an acre of land bought from one of the members.

The 1960s saw an initial growth spurt in the community, but the real boom came in the 1970s, when Carmel surpassed both state and national population growth rates. During this period, as the church continued to mirror the community's growth patterns, it was constantly pressured for space, adding an educational wing in 1966 and a second addition in 1979. By then, Carmel United Methodist Church (CUMC), having changed its name to reflect the merger and name change in its denomination, had become the second largest Methodist congregation in the state, with a membership of nearly two thousand. Situated on one of the main thoroughfares in Carmel, the church building was an imposing steepled brick colonial structure surrounded by an expansive lawn and a huge parking lot.

CUMC's 125th anniversary, in 1971, was a high point in the church's history. Rev. Warren Saunders had been senior minister since 1964 and helped guide the congregation through its numerical and physical expansion. He was adept at personally ministering to his congregants, and under his direction the church maintained a friendly, caring, and inclusive atmosphere. During these years, the church staff increased, as did programming. The Christian Youth Fellowship was very active, as were the choirs, the United Methodist Women, and many other groups, including workers trained in conservative evangelism techniques. By 1980, key lay leaders were planning for even further expansion of the church facilities. However, Reverend Saunders retired in 1982, electing to remain in Carmel and stay active within the community and congregation. At about the same time, the phenomenal growth in the community leveled off, as did the congregation's growth.

The appointment of Dr. Joe G. Emerson in 1984 as senior minister spelled change for CUMC. Dr. Emerson was more interested in preaching the social gospel than in maintaining Saunders's conservative evangelism programs. In earlier years, as one of only three churches in town, the congregation had included people from a broad range of theological persuasions. Now, with over forty churches in Carmel, no one church needed to meet everyone's needs, and Emerson felt justified in moving CUMC back toward liberal Methodism. In addition to this theological shift, Emerson thought that leadership should be rotated more frequently and shared by a greater number of members than in the past. As Carmel had become populated with professional but rather overinvolved residents, churches like CUMC now had many experienced leaders from which to choose; but these leaders had less and less time to devote to the church.

Many longtime CUMC members were unhappy with this turn of events, while newer members disproportionately supported Emerson. The internal conflict came to a head in 1989–1990, when an expansion committee authorized by some of these same former core leaders recommended a new building. Longtime members claimed that the committee did not consult with the entire congregation and tried to build "Joe's Palace" behind the congregation's back. The committee realized too late that the former core members might have been overlooked in the planning process since they were, by that time, largely out of the official committee structure. The dispute involved styles of both administration and *theology. Some disaffected members felt that Dr. Emerson was trying to chase out all conservatives in favor of his brand of liberalism. They also assumed that his different personality and leadership style meant that he was trying to take over personal control of CUMC. Less accommodating and communicative than Reverend Saunders, Emerson was at a loss as to how to make peace without compromising his convictions. His attempts at conciliation failed, and a large bloc of the more conservative members eventually left the church.*

Today, amidst remnants of this feud, the staff and membership generally feel that the worst is behind them. These events have helped to arrest the congregation's growth and hurt the church financially, although CUMC always managed to keep its head above water. Today most new members are only vaguely aware that there have even been any bad times. In fact, CUMC has successfully restructured its debt and is again planning for the future. Goals for the 1990s and beyond include focusing more on providing quality programming and Sunday services and less on membership numbers and facility expansion.

Sunday services are already a central focus for the church. A few mostly older couples trickle into the nearly empty parking lot just before 8:00 A.M. for the first service. These early worshippers make their way to the small chapel for an informal version of what will be repeated—twice—in the main sanctuary. Activity picks up as nine o'clock approaches. The pace of new well-kept family cars pulling into the parking lot mounts to a high pitch by 8:55. Young families and older couples in fashionable dresses and suits emerge from their cars. After depositing their children in Sunday school, the adults rush off to the sanctuary in the center of the building—only a few adults attend Sunday school classes themselves. Greeters, who smile and shake hands with most people, usually have little idea which are visitors, which members. Most of the roughly three hundred present sit in couples, clustered in the front half of the pews. The long, narrow sanctuary is high ceilinged, plain but elegant. Aisles carpeted in powder blue lead to the platform area with its large central choir loft, organ, communion table, lectern, and raised pulpit. A large white cross hangs on the wall behind the choir. Four sets of huge arched shuttered windows let in a little natural light, but the sanctuary is subtly lit so that all attention focuses on the front.

The service begins as Dr. Emerson appears in the center of the chancel to read some of the announcements from the four-page insert in the bulletin. Two young acolytes then lead the choir and ministers up the central aisle for the processional. After everyone is seated, chimes ring several times and the choir stands to sing the introit. Dr. Emerson reads the short invocation, followed by an associate pastor who leads the congregation in reading the affirmation of faith. Next comes the prayer of confession and finally the pastoral prayer. Each message gently reminds the congregation to open their souls to God and be loving, in order to have the courage to face hectic lives peacefully. In between, the congregation sings classic Protestant hymns, which the choir embellishes; and the choir offers a dramatic offertory anthem. The service is wonderfully orchestrated so that each element foreshadows and reinforces the central theme of the upcoming sermon.

Dr. Emerson, a thoughtful-looking man in his early sixties, illustrates his message with many stories and anecdotes from religious and secular life. He skillfully brings the biblical text alive, interpreting its stories in light of current dilemmas. His message is ideally suited to the busy, demanding lives of his parishioners.

The service ends with another unison prayer and a short hymn. Dr. Emerson reads a benediction, again keyed to the themes of the day, and the ministers recess to the back of the sanctuary to greet the exiting congregation.

As members file out of the sanctuary, some rush off to collect their children from Sunday school rooms, and others stream past the parlor into the social hall for coffee and doughnuts. The social hall is usually full, but those present represent only a fraction of those attending the two services that sandwich this hour. While many people catch up with friends and acquaintances, there are always some couples left standing alone.

After the 10:30 service, basically a duplicate of the earlier one, the church parking lot and facilities are usually empty within about fifteen minutes of the benediction. Most people will not return to CUMC until the next Sunday, when another equally well-planned worship service will provide a break in their busy suburban lives.

RESOURCES

In many ways, Carmel United Methodist Church is the most resource-rich congregation in our study. It is first of all a very large congregation. Despite recent defections, the number of new members continues to keep pace with the number who move or drop out, and by 1993, modest growth had returned. With Carmel's growth having leveled off, the church is unlikely to expand rapidly in the coming years, but it will probably continue to hold its share of the Carmel churchgoing population. With a beautiful building in a location everyone passes, well-crafted worship services, and lots of activities for children, CUMC is in an advantageous position for attracting Carmel church shoppers.

In this congregation full of well-educated, well-paid people, Carmel's affluence is evident. Over one-third (38 percent) reported household incomes above $80,000 (the highest category on our survey), with only 20 percent having incomes below $35,000. Well over half (60 percent) are professionals or managers, with almost no one in blue-collar occupations. Only 9 percent of those who responded to our survey have never taken classes beyond high school, and fully 44 percent have degrees beyond the B.A. Skills, experience, and money are abundant here (see table 6.3).

Yet contributions per member here are barely half the amount donated, on average, at tiny, struggling Brighton Evangelical Congrega-

Table 6.3. Carmel United Methodist Church, Carmel

Ideas and priorities	
Christian practices rated "essential"	Living Christian values
Ministries rated "very important" or "essential"	Service to the needy
Resources	
Average Sunday attendance	600
Annual operating budget (1992)	$745,000
Household incomes above $50,000	66%
College degrees or more	76%
Average age	52 years
Activities (beyond worship) participated in at least monthly	None
Relationship to the community	
Live ten minutes or less from the church	79%
New to the community in the last five years	25%
Ethnicity	97% European
Participate in civic & community activities more than once a month	53%

NOTE: One hundred ninety-seven people responded to our survey, amounting to approximately 33 percent of average Sunday attendance. This may be taken as a fair representation of all regular attenders.

tional or working-class Grace Baptist. With average incomes less than half Carmel's, Grace Baptist's members manage double Carmel's average gifts. Carmel's regular annual budget in 1992 was about three-quarters of a million, having dropped with the departure of significant givers. By 1994, it was back up over a million again. More significantly, Carmel's members seem willing to give to projects outside the regular budget. When the church restructured its debt, a bond issue was chosen as the best method of refinancing. Over one million dollars in bonds, offered at a competitive rate of interest, sold out on the first day of issue. When the church decided that its nursery and the surrounding area should be renovated, it raised a million dollars in one Sunday for this project, as well. The availability of resources seems less the problem than motivating members to give.

Levels of giving at Carmel United Methodist are symptomatic of the amount members are willing to give of their other resources, as well. Probably the most precious commodity in a busy suburban community is time. Precisely because families are so privileged, multitudes of activities vie for time on their calendars. Children are in Scouts and on sports teams; dads play golf and travel on business; moms volunteer at school and for various other good causes, in between managing car pools and households and perhaps a job of their own. Church activities are unlikely to make it onto the calendar except for Sunday mornings, and even those sacred times are often crowded out by family and leisure activities. The people who responded to our survey can be assumed to be among the most active in the congregation. Still, they were more likely to participate in civic and community activities than in any church activity beyond worship. Over one-third of them reported that they do not attend worship weekly, which indicates that the normal pattern in the church is probably attendance a couple of times a month, with large numbers attending rarely, if at all. Only a small portion of the church's twenty-four hundred members are more than nominally involved. One in six of our survey respondents is in a regular Bible study group. One in four participates in any sort of fellowship activity more than a few times a year. And barely more than half ever participate in any social ministry activities. Again, given that these numbers probably overrepresent activity, actual proportions are probably considerably smaller.

Where members *are* involved in the life of the church, they bring considerable skills and experience with them. Financial decisions have the advantage of advice from investment bankers; educational decisions are guided by professors, administrative changes by managers. Beyond this specialized knowledge, the sheer levels of education, along with experience organizing and managing everything from the PTA to multimillion dollar corporations, give this congregation a marvelous pool of creative talent to draw from.

Where members are *not* involved, there is an equally talented and creative professional staff to do most of the work of the church. They write the prayers and responses and craft the worship services that are the central focus of most members' experience of the church. Joe Emerson is able to create literate and funny sermons that meet people where they are and challenge them to reach beyond themselves. The children's staff and the music staff not only run an impressive program for the church's children, they also write music and create whole musical productions. Not satisfied with existing Sunday school curricula, they are writing their own. With recent cutbacks in the number of staff positions, they feel overworked, but Carmel United Methodist's staff remains a very valuable resource to a church short of time of its own to give.

STRUCTURES OF AUTHORITY

On the surface, the question of authority is easy to answer in a Methodist church. A bishop, a district superintendent, the pastor, and a *Book of Discipline* are available to fill in all the details for how the local congregation should organize. Yet no hierarchical blueprint ever reveals the dynamics as they are worked out in a given local situation (recall St. Matthew's reshuffling of the hand dealt it by the Catholic hierarchy). As Carmel United Methodist Church acknowledged its shift from small town to suburb, its internal structures of authority had to shift, as well. That shift has not taken place peacefully but has emerged only after a monumental clash of wills, finally resulting in a major exodus.

As Carmel first began to grow in the post–World War II period, the people who arrived wanted to live in a small-town atmosphere. They quickly got to know the old-timers and demonstrated their commitment and loyalty to the community. They moved in and planned to stay indefinitely. They were, for the most part, powerful—doctors and lawyers and business people who knew how to get things done. One of the things they determined to do was protect the small-town way of life they had adopted. While it was to their advantage to have good roadways, sewer systems, and the like, it was not to their liking to share their space with people who could not afford large lots and single-family dwellings. Through a combination of investment in Carmel itself and careful zoning laws, they were determined to maintain what they had come to value.

These same people arrived in the Methodist church in the 1940s and 1950s. They were soon occupying positions as trustees and youth leaders and chairs of key committees. But more important than those official positions was their role as an unofficial power structure in the congregation.[5] Highly committed to the church, they gave generously of their money and time. They cared deeply about having a viable, growing church that could play a formative role in the community; and they expected to be involved in making key decisions about its future. One of these leaders described to us the close personal friendships he had always enjoyed with the pastors of the church. Over dinner or on the golf course they talked about new ideas for ministry or new building plans or what to do with their youth. If something important was happening at the church, he would surely know about it.

All that changed when Joe Emerson came to town. Whether because of a shrewd reading of the changing times or because of his own personal dispositions, he wanted a different kind of administrative structure. He saw that his congregation was beginning to be populated by a different kind of Carmel resident—more transient, but nevertheless highly skilled—and he wanted to move these newer people into congregational decision making as expeditiously as possible. It was probably no accident that the newer people Emerson wanted to empower were more likely to share Emerson's liberal theology, while the older Carmel stalwarts were often conservative in both politics and theology. From what we can tell, the election of new people to positions of authority in the congregation seems to have provoked little dissent. What provoked dissent was the elevation of those *positions* of authority over the *influence* of unofficial power brokers. Powerful people seem not to have minded being moved out of official committee positions so long as they thought they would still have influence.

The facilities-planning fiasco revealed, however, that decision making had moved out of those unofficial channels and into official committee structures. The planning committee had undertaken a careful process of consultation, asking people involved with all the programs of the church and people involved in every major committee to offer their advice and desires. Whether this process intentionally excluded the older power brokers or whether they were inadvertently left out of the loop, the result was the same. A major recommendation emerged without their advice and consent. They saw the process as "secretive" and under the manipulative control of the pastor. And compared to the relationship they had always enjoyed with pastors, their perception is understandable. Decisions were being made in committee meeting rooms at officially scheduled times, rather than in the informal conversations to which they had always been privy. A new arena of discussion had been created in the church, open to the many new skilled leaders in the congregation. The older leaders were not overtly excluded from this arena, but it was not their natural home. While they managed to create enough dissension to prevent the adoption of the building plans, they could not undo the transformation in authority structure that had taken place. Even their personal appeals to the bishop were to no avail. All the old modes of influence were gone, leaving exit as their only form of protest.

The by-the-book administrative structure of the official United Methodist system actually fits this highly mobile, upper-middle-class congregation very well. It facilitates orderly turnover in leadership, allowing skilled and willing people to participate with a minimum of start-up time. It fits the management mentality and experience of much of the congregation, as well. Many of Carmel's current members will not be in the congregation long enough to develop the deep informal ties that formerly defined the core. Under this system, they are able to take on a well-defined task, work on decisions through official channels, and pass their leadership roles along to others when they have invested as much as they can.

This transformation has taken place under the watchful eye of the official Methodist hierarchy. Without at least its tacit support, Joe Emerson could never have survived the fury of so large a group of powerful members. As a close friend of the bishop, Emerson had more than tacit support. So long as Emerson could define his actions and changes as falling within the parameters laid out in the *Book of Disci-*

pline, and so long as the episcopacy was willing to grant his actions legitimacy, there was little any group of laity could do. Not by coincidence, most of those who left Carmel United Methodist have also left Methodism. Although many were lifelong Methodists, they could no longer tolerate a system that seemed to them to ignore the wishes of the laity. Most have joined a local Presbyterian church.

CULTURE

The episcopal support Emerson has enjoyed is probably mostly a result of the Methodist Church's desire to bring Carmel back to the theological middle from its flirtations with evangelical programs and loyalties. The bishop may not have realized that the internal structure would become untenable, but he did realize that CUMC was starting to look rather un-Methodist. When large groups of lay people were being trained in fundamentalist James Kennedy's "Evangelism Explosion" techniques, more liberal potential members were unlikely to feel at home.

Now that the overt evangelicalism is gone, however, just what it means to be Methodist in this congregation remains ambiguous. The one characteristic cited most frequently in new-member classes and hallway conversations and interviews was tolerance.[6] The members of Carmel like being Methodist because it is a church that will let them believe anything they want. One person put it this way: "Most definitely I'd consider our identification as Christian first and denomination much less important." Methodists, he said, are "supposed to be a pluralistic church that would welcome Christians of any background, any interpretation." And CUMC has welcomed Christians of all backgrounds. Two-thirds of those who responded to our survey said that they have belonged to some other denomination, mostly other mainline groups such as the Presbyterians or Lutherans.

The result is a congregation of distinctly nondoctrinaire participants. The Bible is not a literal or inerrant document, only a guide to living a moral life. One in five say they pray no more than once a month. And few (on average 20 percent) would insist on *any* belief or practice as *essential* to being a Christian. Most members rated Bible study and sharing one's faith as "somewhat important"; prayer, seeking justice, attending church, and caring for others as "very important"; but only living out one's values in everyday life as "essential." Those rankings were reflected in conversations we had with adults whose grown children no longer attend church. What they consistently said was that what was really important was that their children believe in God and try to live a good life.

Trying to do a little good in the world might also sum up the church's sense of mission. This is not a place where deep social policy debates are prevalent. Members are involved—either through donations or sending volunteers—with a variety of programs aimed at the physically needy, those less well off than themselves. These include a women's shelter, inner-city ministries, a home for the elderly, and the like. In addition, their building is used by several community groups, including three AA groups, another twelve-step group, two TOPS (dieting) groups, a Boy Scout troop, a mental health support group, and a chorus. A Shepherd Center meets in the building, providing daytime activities and care for senior citizens. United Methodist Women, the women's missionary organization, runs a consignment shop, and church volunteers stock and run a food pantry in the building. Members who are individually involved in nonchurch charitable activities sometimes ask the church to support their work. There is a constant stream of announcements about opportunities to give money or get involved in work that benefits the community. Probably their largest investment of resources, however, is in a ministry of counseling. A full-time staff minister provides psychological and spiritual counseling to members and community alike.

The kind of one-on-one private counseling offered by the minister is far more common here than dependence on groups in which sharing of life's concerns might take place. The small group that gathers for Adult Minister Jane Voelkel's Bible study during the week is one exception. In addition, the United Methodist Women sponsored a day of prayer and denial that allowed for some quite profound exploration of God's presence in the lives of the members who attended.

The few adult Sunday school classes are also quite close, taking a good deal of responsibility for their own learning and planning regular social events together. The choir is a tightly knit fellowship, and many committees are quite supportive, enjoying each other's company and sharing concerns with each other. If a person chooses to seek communal support, it can be found; otherwise this network of fellowship can be nearly invisible.

Indeed, individual initiative is a common theme at CUMC. In the new-member classes (a four-week series, now reduced to two required meetings, with a formal dinner at the end), teachers stress that the church is unlikely to come looking for them. It will be up to them to say how and where they would like to be involved. To have chosen this church in the first place also represents an individual selection from among the many options available in Carmel. The congregation makes its programs available and assumes that those for whom they meet a need will seek them out.

The kinds of programs that seem most attractive to Carmel residents—and that now shape the life of CUMC—are worship for adults and music and Sunday school programs for children. A 1993 Wednesday night addition to the routine has succeeded by featuring a dinner and family-oriented activities. Kids Express, a choir that includes some signing for the deaf, draws over one hundred elementary age children. Its leaders have gained a level of commitment from children and parents that enables this group to hold its own against the demands of soccer and Scouts and all the other things that could pull kids away from a church activity. The group puts on major productions, including several public events outside the church. The kids are excited about having such a visible role, and their parents and grandparents flock to the church whenever they perform.

Besides the worthwhile activities for their children, the worship service is the force that draws adults in. Many people mention the choir and the other musical offerings as essential for setting a mood for worship. One woman talked about how she comes to worship because she needs to be "in the presence of something." Several mentioned the physical space of the sanctuary and the chapel as helping them to find some quiet, gain some perspective. In addition, the sermons get nearly universal praise. Said one young man, "I really enjoy the church services. I think that Dr. Emerson is just such a terrific speaker." Those who choose CUMC from among the forty congregations in Carmel do so because its worship offers them a needed respite and occasional challenge and because its programs for children help them to instill a sense of morality and citizenship in their offspring.

The church is today attempting to provide the moral grounding for children who will, in all likelihood, not be a part of this congregation or this community as adults. This marks a significant change in focus. Older members (often the ones who have now left the church) describe the church as an important influence on the community, and going to church as something everyone ought to do for the greater good of all. One man said, "You just wouldn't feel right if you didn't go to church every Sunday and participate." Another said, "My mother would say, 'Where else would you be on Sunday morning? I don't understand where you'd go. What would you do? Just sit in a chair? Everybody goes to church.'" Those kinds of assumptions no longer apply. Nor can people assume that the church will be at the center of community life. For some who participate in the activities offered by Carmel United Methodist Church, the church is an organizing influence in their lives; for most, it is one item on a busy calendar of family and community activities.

SUMMARY

In the transition from small town to suburb, much has changed at Carmel United Methodist Church. In the old days, the church was the center of town activities, its members the chief powers in the community. Today, it remains a visible presence in the community, but many more churches and many more activities vie for the allegiance of busy Carmelites. The dominant pattern of association at this church is individual choice, not communal loyalty. As the church has moved to accommodate that pattern, it has experienced a major shift in forms of authority and administrative structure, which precipitated major conflict. In addition, programming has become a smorgasbord dependent on individual initiative, rather than a community bound by long ties of family and shared experience. This is a congregation with more than ample resources of people, money, and talent for accomplishing whatever it might choose to do. But its individualist focus means that few projects catch the imagination of the congregation as a whole. Its programmatic and administrative transformation have left it with both the strengths and weaknesses of Carmel's privileged, mobile culture.

Conclusion

Hope Baptist, Grace Baptist, and Carmel United Methodist undertook major internal restructuring more as a result of the strong leadership of a pastor than as a planned response to community change. At each, a pastor sought to put his imprint on the congregation by reorganizing its administrative system. Hope's Pastor Jackson implemented tithing and ministry groups and supplanted the older system of auxiliaries. Grace's Pastor Crockett imposed financial accountability and opened the policy process to wider participation. CUMC's Joe Emerson went by the book (the *Book of Discipline*, that is) in bringing new leaders into official church positions. How much each pastor understood of the gaps between the congregation's existing ways of doing business and the constituency most likely to populate the church in the future we really cannot say. Each may simply have followed the promptings of his own favored administrative style. The result, nevertheless, was adaptive change. Hope Baptist is better equipped to meet the challenges of an economically mixed constituency. Grace Baptist has its financial house in order and can weather the vicissitudes of future economic downturns. And Carmel United Methodist can integrate mobile suburban professionals with dispatch, offering them modes of low-commitment religious involvement to fit their demands. This rather incidental form of adaptation has taken place across different polities, different theologies, different cultures, and different levels of resources. The most clear common denominator is a strong pastor, willing to weather conflict in the pursuit of a new way of doing the congregation's business.

CHAPTER 7

Innovation: Birth and Rebirth

The voluntary religious system in the United States allows for the possibility of religious innovation by creating a space in which religious entrepreneurs can promulgate their messages, in which religious collectivities can organize to pursue their goals. That voluntary system by no means guarantees such innovation, however. Were no religious entrepreneurs to appear, no religious messages to take hold, no religious collectivities to gather, religious institutions would simply wither away. (As we saw in chapter 3, many congregations do just that.) But in the midst of changing communities, it should not be surprising to find whole new religious institutions, just as we might find new ethnic businesses or new social service agencies. In this chapter, we turn to the stories of congregations either born or reborn in the changes their communities have encountered.

Assessing the rate of congregational founding is difficult. The first few years of life are by far the most precarious for organizations of any kind; how many are founded and fail within a matter of months or a few years is impossible to count without data gathered regularly over a long period of time. In addition, these new congregations are precisely the ones most likely to escape detection in our canvasing of the community and to be unavailable by phone for the gathering of detailed data on their programming and history. Of the 295 congregations on which we have historical data, 62 reported that they had been founded in 1980 or later, and an additional 22, founded before that date, had moved to their present location since then. While there are surely more new congregations in these communities, these can tell us a good deal about what sorts of congregations are being founded and how they are faring.

First, they tell us that new congregations are not distributed evenly across our nine communities. Not surprisingly, communities experiencing demographic growth and expansion also have more new congregations, compared to communities experiencing decline. Anderson and Oak Park have fewer new congregations than average, for instance, while Gwinnett County and Carmel have more. Second, they tell us that new congregations are not distributed evenly across denominational traditions. More than 60 percent of the new congregations are evangelical or Pentecostal (compared to 38 percent of the older congregations). Very few (six) new congregations are affiliated with the mainline Catholic and Protestant denominations, white or black, and three of those are Catholic parishes in formerly Protestant-dominant areas. In these communities, new congregations are founded almost exclusively outside the established religious denominations to which half of the older congregations belong. On this score, Northview Christian Life Church is typical. It is a new evangelical congregation in a community formerly dominated by mainline churches.

Most of these new congregations are still small; half report average attendance at less than one hundred. They also have not yet developed extensive programming—one-third have no internal programs beyond their worship services, and two-thirds have no programs oriented toward serving the community (compared to 16 percent and 48 percent respectively among the older congregations). In this respect, the two new congregations we will look at here are atypical. Both were founded in rapidly growing suburban communities and have quickly established themselves as some of the largest congregations in our study. Future attention to small new congregations is clearly needed if we are to understand fully this sector of the religious ecology.

New congregations start with a blank slate; reborn ones do not. However, unlike the more gradual adaptations we have observed in earlier cases, reborn congregations have either a more radical break between past and future, a more thorough eclipse of their old identity, or both. Sometimes a congregation reaches a crisis point and either moves or dies (as did the churches in chapters 2 and 3). At other times, a similar crisis becomes the catalyst for the creation of something new. Having reached the limits of their existing mode of being, reborn congregations gamble on starting anew.

Of the four cases we will examine here, two involve the "resurrection" of a nearly dead congregation, with the aid of both a strong pastor and a supportive denomination. One of these resurrections is complete; the other is just under way. The third case is a new congregation sponsored by a denomination, while the fourth is a new congregation "planted" by an entrepreneurial pastor. In each case we see the interplay of external support structures, internal determination, and individual initiative. Each has resulted in a new institution peculiarly fitted to the constituency it serves.

Good Shepherd Lutheran Church, Oak Park: Rebirth of a Community Church

Oak Park, Illinois, is the sort of family-oriented liberal enclave where people are forbidden to park on the street overnight and the hours when children can trick-or-treat on Halloween are strictly regulated. That does not mean Halloween is ignored—far from it. On the weekend I was there in 1992, nearly every house was extravagantly decorated with pumpkins and scarecrows and haystacks, and children were elaborately costumed for the occasion. When the appointed time arrived, they took to the streets like children everywhere, their safety carefully guarded by watchful parents and town regulations.

As in other suburban communities, children's activities are the focus of much energy here. Good Shepherd Lutheran Church is no exception. The children's time in each Sunday's worship is a lively and anticipated segment of the service, and the noises of restless children are simply part of what people have come to expect here. But this is not just a child-oriented church. Parents and other adults enjoy the service, as well. The Oak Park residents who have rediscovered this church in recent years have come to expect that they will go away inspired and informed. Penny Edgell Becker tells the rest of the story.

Oak Park's record of integration and outstanding community services gives today's residents a great deal to be proud of, and Good Shepherd Lutheran is very much a part of that progressive community. Founded around the turn of the century, Good Shepherd has always been in its present location, on a large corner lot in south Oak Park. It is a neighborhood church, built in an Early American style, red brick with a small bell tower. The long-term members speak of familylike attachments to people in the congregation reaching back over a lifetime; they note how hard it is to separate their memories of Good Shepherd from the fabric of their everyday lives of working, making friends, and raising a family.

Not many long-term members remain, however. The community's changes in the 1960s and 1970s took a toll on Good Shepherd. When, during the 1960s, a socially activist pastor became an advocate for civil rights and particularly for integration in Oak Park, some members left. When integration became a reality in the village, more moved out. One long-term member reports that by the time housing prices started to stabilize and people realized that integration would work, Good Shepherd had lost about half its members to white flight. By 1981, fewer than fifty members were available to consider whether they should keep the church doors open.

That vote to stay open was a turning point in the congregation's history. In 1984 when the denominational office realized that the congregation was serious about wanting to stay alive and to grow, they sent in Jack Finney, designated

Good Shepherd a "mission redevelopment congregation," and provided modest financial support for the next five years.

The key to surviving, according to Jack Finney, is to put down roots in the local community. From census data he discovered that the most common household type in south Oak Park was the two-parent couple with children. Nationally, this type of family was returning to the Church in droves, looking for spiritual nurture for the adults and a Christian education for the children. Jack Finney advertised, and he went out visiting. People started to come in. One woman remembers the change this way: One spring there were six people in the choir, and in the fall there were twenty-five.

Today, on a typical Sunday 185 people come to Good Shepherd, out of just under 400 baptized members. Some wear suits or business dresses, but many come in jeans and a sweater. Most of the congregation is white, although one may see four or five African American adults and nine or ten African American or Hispanic children. There are many young children in the congregation, but few teenagers. From September to May, people begin to arrive around nine o'clock for children's classes and the Adult Forum. (In the summer the service is at nine, and once a month it is held outdoors, on chairs set up on the side lawn.) There is much talk and laughter; some members are getting the altar flowers and communion items ready, and in the kitchen the coffee has already been put on. A little before 10:30 the classes break up, and people go into the sanctuary for the service.

Light and airy, the cross-shaped space in which they gather would probably seat three hundred with its balcony. The stained-glass windows—pale earth-tone shades of olive, grey, light brown—depict New Testament scenes, with phrases like "He is Risen." Behind the altar hangs a large cross that has flames on each arm, one for every founding member.

The format of the Sunday service varies. The Lutheran Book of Worship is used quite frequently, but red binders contain alternative forms of the liturgy. These are usually more informal, with contemporary (gender-inclusive) language and folk melodies. After the opening prayers and scripture, there is a children's lesson, called a mini-meditation. The pastor tries to include the children in some activity—a reading or role-play exercise—often without great cooperation, but always with good humor.

The sermon lasts perhaps ten minutes. The pastor stands front and center, often on the floor in front of the altar rail, not in the pulpit. Sometimes he focuses on a social issue, for example, the persistence of racism or other forms of intolerance. But more often he speaks of the dilemmas of personal life and relationships, with an emphasis on healing and hope. He is not particularly demonstrative, but most of his sermons radiate an intensity to which people respond quite positively.

During one of the hymns, ushers pass down the aisle and collect the "Yes" sheets that have been placed in the bulletins. On them people record their attendance, sign up for an upcoming event or activity, and write prayer requests.

During the Prayers of the People the liturgist and pastor pray for these requests, providing an immediacy of communication about the congregation's needs.

There is also communion every Sunday, true to the Lutheran tradition, followed by a hymn and closing announcements. The announcement time breaks the formal mood of the service and usually involves laughter and questions or comments from the congregation. That finished, the pastor strides out, saying "Go in peace, serve the Lord," and the congregation replies, "Thanks be to God." For at least fifteen minutes after the service people are chasing each other down, making connections and plans for the coming week's activities. They are busy people, and most will not return to the church building until the next Sunday.

Jack Finney says it is important for a congregation to be able to name its story. He calls Good Shepherd a resurrection congregation, and the members agree. Starting from the vote to stay open, the congregation has grown 300 percent since 1984. It is also a qualitatively different congregation than before the vote. The current mission statement defines the congregation's core purposes in five paragraphs: openness to all people, dynamic corporate worship, ministry to the poor, spiritual nurture of members, member commitment of time and money. The church has developed a letterhead slogan that encapsulates its mission: "Embracing the diversity of God's creation and celebrating our oneness in Christ."

This commitment to openness is manifested in stands on specific social issues. An open and affirming congregation, Good Shepherd's openness to gays and lesbians is known throughout the community. It is also known for its racial tolerance, although it has only a small percentage of minority members. Although it has no official inclusive-language policy, there is de facto use of gender-inclusive terminology in references both to God and to humanity. And the congregation complained loudly when the photographer sent to take pictures for the church directory insisted everyone name a head of household and made disparaging remarks about nontraditional household arrangements.

While the growth and change have not been totally without tension between old and new members, they have successfully weathered the generational transfer of leadership and the change in the culture of the congregation, largely by relying on a very open decision-making process. It also helped that many of the people most opposed to change left earlier on. Making the decision to engage in a major building renovation project took more than a year, but eventually a consensus was built that included the vast majority of members. Undertaking this project signals an end to Good Shepherd's "resurrection" process and the beginning of a new stage of established prosperity.

RESOURCES

Today Good Shepherd is a resource-rich congregation, but a decade ago, that was not the case. The current members of Good Shepherd are mostly well-paid professionals; more than a quarter of the households have incomes above $80,000 (see table 7.1). In 1992, the church undertook a $500,000 renovation campaign and confidently raised the money. Levels of giving are steadily on the rise. Still, more than half the "giving units" contributed less than fifty dollars per month in 1991. While the members seem very well off, their obligations are high, as well. With a recession on, and rising mortgage and tax burdens on young families, this congregation feels grateful to comfortably support its staff and program and give consistently to various benevolent causes. After years of growth, the budget is reaching a plateau.

Good Shepherd's building, the church's home long before the current growth in membership, sits in a quiet residential section of town, which has historically marked it as a neighborhood, family-oriented church. Today, almost three-quarters of the members live within a ten-minute drive, and from the reports of older members, the situation was similar in earlier decades. While the church does not have a large population of elderly or handicapped persons, it welcomes such people. The renovation project undertaken in 1992 made the building accessible by adding an elevator and wheelchair ramp. When the town recently redid the curbs and gutters in the area, curb wheelchair cutouts were also placed near the ramp. More important for the congregation's immediate needs, the project created new classroom space in the basement to better handle the growing church school population. Minor remodeling in the sanctuary included opening up more space around the altar, so the pastor can stand facing the congregation as he presides over communion each Sunday. Each change has made the building more hospitable to the current and potential constituency of Good Shepherd. Combined with an excellent location and virtual absence of debt, the church's material resources seem more than adequate for the task at hand.

At least as impressive are the human resources the church has accumulated. Over half the members have some education beyond college. When the congregation needs to do strategic planning or provide services, when they want to make a difference on a community issue, they have the skills and connections of their members on which to draw. The managers and professionals who have made this their church home seem eager to put those skills at the disposal of their congregation. In addition, several members of Good Shepherd who work at the national Evangelical Lutheran Church in America denominational headquarters in Chicago bring their special expertise and church experience to the congregation, as well.

While the congregation is now resource rich, the important question for our purposes is what resources enabled Good Shepherd to make the transition from its old identity to the new. To answer that question,

Table 7.1. Good Shepherd Lutheran Church, Oak Park

Ideas and priorities	
Christian practices rated "essential"	Living Christian values
Ministries rated "very important" or "essential"	Service to the needy
Resources	
Average Sunday attendance	185
Annual operating budget (1992)	$218,000
Household incomes above $50,000	54%
College degrees or more	88%
Average age	45 years
Activities (beyond worship) participated in at least monthly	None
Relationship to the community	
Live ten minutes or less from the church	72%
New to the community in the last five years	52%
Ethnicity	95% European
Participate in civic & community activities more than once a month	40%

NOTE: Eighty-three people responded to our survey, amounting to approximately 45 percent of average Sunday attendance. This may be taken as a good representation of all regular attenders.

one has to begin with the thirty-five or so people who voted to keep the place open. Their determination, their ability to convince the denomination to support them, and finally their willingness to become a part of the new Good Shepherd have made the change possible.

The single most critical resource in this congregation, however, the one that has made the difference between the old Good Shepherd and the new, is its pastor. The money the denomination contributed in the early days made a difference, but it was nowhere near as important as the denomination's vote of confidence in connecting the church with Jack Finney. It is not that Finney did all the work—although in the early days he did a great deal. It is that he had the skills to identify the congregation's potential constituency and both the energy and determination to seek out and convince that constituency that Good Shepherd could be a spiritual home for them and their children.

Finney has an uncanny ability to make connections—to see a need and imagine who and what could meet that need. In this case, he discerned the most prevalent spiritual needs in this affluent, progressive suburb, and he worked with his recruits to create a church that would meet those needs. He is also well-connected with the denomination and with lots of training and consultation resources on which he can call for advice and new ideas. When asked about the strengths of the church, people in the congregation still point to his ability to create a network of care, to lead them in making decisions, and to preach in a way that meets their needs.

STRUCTURES OF AUTHORITY

In some ways, the most striking thing about Good Shepherd is the *way* they do what they do. This is a very participatory place. When the idea of renovating the building was broached, it went through nearly a year of discussion and modification before final plans were made. During that time, small groups talked face-to-face about what they most wanted in a renovated facility and what they most wanted to save. They talked about finances and argued over budget. The committee in charge listened and modified their proposals accordingly. Only as near consensus emerged was a final decision made. One member recalled another issue on which a very deliberate process of participation was put in place.

> For example, when they were going to develop a new mission state-ment, and that was the one that included 'Reconciled to Christ' [the open and affirming statement], there were neighborhood gatherings all over the place. And I know I went to one, and I was put in a group that was of very diverse opinions. But it was a group in which I felt safe. And I think that's a key. So there was just dialogue all over the church, around the mission of this church. Our vision for it. And he [Pastor Finney] was in our group—and I'm sure he was in the others, taking notes and being very serious about it.

Part of the pastor's ability to make connections and meet needs rests in this ability to listen—and to help others listen. He is aided in this pro-cess by the social-class position of his parishioners, whose education and professional experience have amply prepared them for talking, de-liberating, planning, visioning, and otherwise arriving at participatory decisions.

The congregation also participates in the initiation of business. Not every new idea comes from the pastor. Finney notes that Lutherans are supposed to believe in the priesthood of all believers, and this church practices it. When members have an idea for a new program or minis-try, they can take it to an existing committee or work toward creating some new committee to sponsor it. Asked how that process might work, one younger member said, "I might talk to other people that I think would have a similar interest and see if a group of us wanted to present that to Jack, and then ask him where we needed to go from there. I have a feeling that Jack would say, 'Hey, great idea! Why don't you write it up and take it to council?' . . . I get the impression that new ideas are not only welcome, but they are sought after. New ways to serve, to rally, to congregate, to tie people in and together. I have the impression that those ideas are constantly being sought." With a congregation full of talented, involved people, Good Shepherd encourages that involvement by taking their suggestions seriously.

Effective communication further encourages involvement. Each Sunday's announcement period is a lively exchange of information. A variety of lay people make their way to the lectern to remind others of upcoming events, work that needs to be done, causes that need their support. The same young woman noted, "This church communicates well. You know, you could get up and make an announcement. There's just a real openness about it. If two or three people had an idea, you can make an announcement in church, you can write something for the newsletter. . . . That's one of the newsiest newsletters of any church that I've been to. I mean, you read it because you *want* to be aware of what's really going on." Communication also happens in the dashing about after Sunday services and in the computerlike memory (his metaphor) of Jack Finney's. Now that the congregation has grown, that task has become more formidable. Both its size and its entrepreneurial quality mean multiple projects, myriad committees, and a batch of good ideas percolating at any given time. Each interest group is likely to work largely in isolation from others in the church, pursuing the project or cause that has captured its passion.

Besides the announcement and newsletter forums and the pastor's memory, the one formal place for these diverse interests to come together is the church council. It is composed of thirteen people, including chairs of nine standing committees, and meets once a month to discuss plans, give reports, air new ideas. The elected president of the congregation presides, and the pastor reports like everyone else. Council members and committee chairs are elected by the membership each year. While there is a nominating committee (and the pastor certainly makes suggestions), it is also possible for members to volunteer to serve in various capacities as their skills and interests allow. One member recalled that he volunteered *not* to be on anything property related, since that is what he does all week at work. Others are eager to match their vocational skills with positions in the congregation. While this congregation values an open, egalitarian style, it also recognizes that council positions are powerful ones. Closeness to the information flow and to the shaping of the congregation's agenda makes the council an admittedly influential body. When two older members lost seats to newcomers in the late 1980s, it was clear that the transformation of the congregation from old identity to new was nearly complete. Its habit of operating with an open, democratic polity made that transition possible.

While the congregation's internal structure is highly participatory, its external ties lie with the Evangelical Lutheran Church in America, a denomination created by merger in 1988 whose actual power over the congregation's affairs is relatively slight. About 60 percent of the congregation grew up Lutheran, while the rest have switched from some other denomination (a percentage close to the national average).[1] Most of the switchers come from other mainline traditions, rather than from evangelical, Pentecostal, or non-Protestant groups. With a strong contingent of lifelong Lutherans and a group of members who work for the denomination, there is a clear Lutheran presence here. When the congregation needs a pastor, the denomination helps make the connection and must ultimately approve the placement. In the case of Good Shepherd, that consultation and ratification proved quite benevolent. In day-to-day affairs, the denomination is as present as the congregation chooses to make it. At Good Shepherd, there are frequent phone calls, requests, and suggestions. The denomination is seen by the pastor (and most of the congregation) as a resource more than as a hindrance.

CULTURE

The new culture of the Good Shepherd congregation is heavily influenced by the quests and concerns of its new baby-boomer members, the sorts of people Wade Clark Roof has dubbed a "generation of seekers."[2] While many have spent time in their young adulthood away from religious participation, they see life as a spiritual journey of which this congregation is now a part. One woman, now a very active member, told us that she was raised in a rather conservative, evangelical Methodist church, and she still misses some things about that tradition—the eloquent preaching, the music, the spirit, and the emotional intensity. But when she visited Good Shepherd, she was moved by the liturgical form of the service and came back. She asked her husband to come with her, but he was not interested at all. When she told him it wasn't "like a typical church," he agreed to try it just once, and they have been attending together ever since. She says that at that time in her life, she felt it was "time to come back," that "God spoke" through the neighbor who invited her to come. Her husband could come because, like her, "his war with the church was over." She says she cried every Sunday for two years, it was so moving. Like many others in the congregation, she had found a spiritual home that touched her deeply, providing a new sense of orientation and belonging.

When we asked Good Shepherd members what gives them this sense of spiritual connection, they mentioned what happens both on

Sunday morning and in the small groups the church sponsors. Most say they like the liturgy, but also the variety from Sunday to Sunday. The "alternative liturgy" notebooks offer a change from the routine, balancing tradition and innovation. At the initiative of one of the small groups, these notebooks have been edited to use inclusive language, a change that deeply pleases some of the members. Many also enjoy the good music and fine congregational singing. Sometimes, playful rituals ask the worshippers to see things anew. One member recalled, for instance, "One Sunday we sang 'Jesus Loves Me,' and we sang it out of doors, to the neighborhood, to the community. Now that seems almost childish, but it's profound." She went on to add that Pastor Finney has "somehow fostered a sense of intimacy in the church." That intimacy is especially apparent in his sermons. They often strike deeply resonant chords for these seekers. The image of "journey" is prevalent, and the pastor encourages it. He takes them along on his journey, talks about things that bring him great pain or joy, shares his struggles and doubts along with the things about which he is sure. He creates a sense of intimacy with his hearers, and in that intimate space they all sense that they encounter God.

Intimate spaces are also created in the covenant groups the congregation fosters, groups of eight to twelve persons who gather—usually weekly—in someone's home for conversation about issues that concern them. The groups set their own agendas and design their own ways of operating. Leadership usually rotates. Those in the group make a "covenant" with each other about their commitment to participation, and the level of sharing is often quite deep. Other small groups who meet on a more informal basis, with less commitment and permanence than the covenant groups, offer a similar opportunity for support and spiritual exploration. At any given time, nearly a dozen such groups may be operating. In them, people ask hard questions about life and death, explore their images of God, talk about their evolving sense of vocation and frustrations with work or family. They share with each other times of divorce and job dislocation, as well as celebrations of new work and family ties. These are not just "private" concerns. The spiritual advice given in these groups has far-reaching implications for the very "public" lives of the members in the economy and in the larger community. Their investment in each other makes possible investments beyond their immediate circle.[3] As one member suffered through the pain of her husband's death from AIDS, she was able to share his story with her covenant group, with the congregation, and, through a Lutheran-produced videotape, with people in churches all over the nation.

Some of what makes these small groups work spills over even into the business of the church. Jack Finney never begins a meeting without asking people to "check in." Members routinely share with each other the significant events of their days and weeks before addressing the business of a committee or council meeting. He describes the process of getting involved at Good Shepherd this way: "You can begin by having the courage to pass the peace, and a lot of people don't come back here because we hug and touch and move. . . . That's the first step. The second would be to chat with people afterwards. The third would be to come to coffee hour. Coffee hour is very important at Good Shepherd. Then the next is to come to social groups like the choir and young adults or something like that. And if you still want to go deeper, you're in a covenant group." Human connection, caring for one another, is central to what makes Good Shepherd thrive.

Members learn this, in fact, from their earliest days in the congregation. When they go through new-member orientation classes, by the second session Jack is already asking them to "check in." They hear about worship at Good Shepherd and about opportunities for service, but they learn by experience how the congregation sustains its common bonds.

Maintaining those bonds takes a little more intentionality these days. For the first few years of the congregation's rebirth, the excitement and intimacy were sustained in part by the common mission of reestablishing the congregation and in part by the relative smallness of the group. Their will to survive and their pastor were the chief rallying points. Now there are too many people for the pastor to remain such a central figure, and no one doubts that the congregation will survive. (Having been influenced by various congregational workshops, they describe this as their transition from "pastor centered" to "program centered.")[4] The small groups are now all the more important for creating the sense of belonging and intimacy that these Oak Park residents have found at Good Shepherd.

They found it in very Oak Park fashion—by "shopping," doing research on their own, or both. Few of the new members came because they were invited by a friend or because extended family members already belonged. Instead, they looked in the *Yellow Pages*, saw the signs in the neighborhood, called to find out about services, and simply visited to see if they would like it. Finney estimates that the church hosts more than three hundred visitors each year. If a person visits twice, they get an invitation to a brunch at Finney's home and from there an invitation to explore church membership. The congregation initiates contact, then, simply by being present in places where people in the community can stumble across it. Those in the community who are searching for a spiritual home have to take the next step. But once they have made a step in Good Shepherd's direction, they are welcomed warmly and systematically urged toward membership.

The community they join is not only a place of worship and a place for intimate fellowship, but a place that tries to make a difference in the world. They aim toward spending at least a tithe of their budget on causes outside the congregation, a commitment more important to some members than to others. They provide financial support for a variety of ministries, from health and hunger to justice and ecology, in Chicago and beyond, through the denomination and through independent agencies. Many members also spend volunteer time working for political causes, helping to build Habitat houses, serving in soup lines and shelters, and the like. Congregational leaders try to match the causes to which the church gives money to those in which church members are involved. They do not always succeed in supporting all the good ideas they generate, however. Some hoped that the renovation would include showers and other facilities that would allow the church to serve as an overnight shelter in Oak Park's Community of Congregations shelter program, but cost and logistics stood in the way.

The renovation project highlighted much of what has changed at Good Shepherd, much of what has stayed the same, and the tension between the two. Nowhere was that more visible than in disagreements about what to do with the founders cross, which has the names of the founding members engraved on flames covering the arms of the cross. Younger members, who had no particular attachment to it, were willing to see it disappear in the renovation of the altar area. Older members saw this attitude as a repudiation of them and of the church's past. One woman recalled, "Some older members were convinced at first that it was a plot by the newer members to destroy the last vestiges of the old congregational identity." But when the remodeled altar area was complete, the cross was still there—more prominent than before. While this congregation may have been "reborn," a symbol of its old identity remains visible. In this cross, the new congregation honors the determination of those who stayed and midwifed it into being.

SUMMARY

An established identity, a good location, and an adequate building helped Oak Park's Good Shepherd Lutheran begin again. Drawing in members with high levels of income and education has helped to sustain it. Those material and human resources are significant in themselves, but more important is the fact that young, well-educated, well-paid professionals *are* Oak Park, and that by building a core of such folk, Good Shepherd began again to mirror the community from which it could draw members. Good Shepherd had done just that in the old Oak Park, but as the community changed, the congregation lost much of its old constituency and resource base. It has now successfully reconnected with the changed community, reestablishing the reciprocal relationship between community and congregation and building a participatory style and sense of community that fit the folk who today call Oak Park home. Even the church's attempts to make the world a better place fit the liberal impulses of the community. A spiritual home for people already very involved in work and community betterment, Good Shepherd enables them to put their lives in perspective and share their journeys with others who care.

Oak Park is not unlike the Candler Park neighborhood in Atlanta. In both places young professionals have discovered charming older homes and have created something of a liberal enclave. In Candler Park, a diverse community has grown up in recent years that includes a sizable number of gays and especially lesbians. Each community had been a "traditional family" close-in suburb at its height in the postwar era. Each was threatened by the racial transitions of the sixties and seventies. Unlike Oak Park, Candler Park made no efforts to integrate, with devastating effects on the congregations in the neighborhood. As the community has taken on its new "gentrified" character, many of the congregations left in the community were barely hanging on. Epworth was one of those.

Epworth United Methodist Church, Candler Park: Blending Traditional Values and Alternative Life-styles

On the Sunday I visited Epworth United Methodist in Atlanta's Candler Park, I was sitting in the church basement with researcher Tammy Adams, visiting the older adult Sunday school class, a long-standing group full of traditional southern Methodist ladies and gentlemen, when about half an hour into their Sunday routine, a young woman wandered in. Dressed in a manner typical of the neighborhood—granny glasses, Walkman, baggy pants, sweatshirt—she was clearly "in her own space." The teacher didn't quite know what to do, but he welcomed her and asked how she was, to which she replied, "I'm so-o fine!" After about twenty minutes, she wandered out as mysteriously as she had wandered in, but she showed up again in worship. In fact, she kept coming back. It turns out that an older member had spotted her in the park across the street and casually invited her to come—and she did. Epworth is that sort of place. The members have always thought of theirs as a friendly neighborhood church. People are willing to invite even the most unlikely prospects to attend. Dealing with the changes they introduce, however, is a more difficult process that has only recently begun. Tammy Adams tells the story of how Epworth has come to this place of strange contrasts.

Epworth United Methodist Church was started in a sitting parlor in Candler Park in 1890 by members of the Edgewood Methodist Church. It immediately took root in a growing middle-class residential area. When the first building burned to the ground, struck by lightning in 1897, members rebuilt, only to have that building struck by lighting on two other occasions in 1902. Edna Kitchen, a parishioner of ninety-two, recalls being taken from Sunday school and people scrambling to retrieve valuables such as the altar Bible as the building was catching fire. After refurbishing, that building continued to serve the ever growing congregation until 1925, when new property was purchased on McClendon Avenue. Men from the church helped to dig the foundation for a building Epworth has occupied since 1928.

The early members of Epworth were blue-collar residents of the Candler Park neighborhood, as well as some successful businessmen in the area. The local elementary school, Mary Lin, is named after a beloved member of Epworth. Hard times came as Epworth struggled through the Depression, but by the end of World War II, church membership had grown so much that a new sanctuary was needed. In September 1952, Epworth moved into its present sanctuary. When asked to reflect upon the church's heyday, older members almost always point to this time under the leadership of Dwight Nysewander, their longest-serving pastor.

The sanctuary they built is a traditional red-brick Georgian-style building with four large white columns and a large white steeple. Inside, it is equally traditional, with wooden pews and red-velvet seat cushions, a choir loft behind the pulpit, and a large stained-glass window of Jesus kneeling in the Garden of Gethsemane above. Almost every piece of furniture, window, and liturgical object has been memorialized to a loved and remembered parishioner.

By the time the church moved into this sanctuary, however, membership numbers fallen from their peak, reached in 1949. From then until the late 1980s, the church lost one hundred members about every five years, finally stabilizing in the low two hundreds, with attendance and active membership substantially below that. Multiple problems fed this trend. As African Americans moved to nearby areas in the 1960s and 1970s, some white flight occurred, but mostly people were just moving into new suburban homes. A good number of Epworth's members stayed, but the church's old neighborhood base was clearly gone.

While the surrounding neighborhood changed, however, Epworth did not, continuing to maintain its identity as a working-class congregation espousing 1950s ideals. Its ministers during this period were either on their way to retirement or otherwise about to exit from the ministry. That pattern finally changed with the appointment of Art O'Neill and Melissa Sexton O'Neill as co-pastors in 1990.

Still, Epworth did not receive Art and Melissa with open arms. It took some time for the congregation to get used to the idea of a woman pastor and a male pastor with a beard, especially when they were married to each other and going to share the pastoral role. The O'Neills spent two years establishing their credibility in the congregation and in the community; then things began to change.

During 1992, Epworth was able to start a children's choir, build a new playground, hire a part-time children's worker, have a substantial Christmas program, baptize a number of infants, rework the administrative council, begin a coffeehouse program, continue renting to Atlanta Cooperative Preschool, remodel rooms for classroom space and children's library, and start a number of spirituality groups and a long-term Bible discipleship group—all while the church's ministers birthed their first child.

The congregation also looks different today. While the average Sunday attendance has not changed significantly, the mix of old and young has. Epworth is losing a significant number of its elderly members to illness or death, and those persons are being replaced by young adults and families. Where the congregation was one-third young adult, two-thirds elderly in April 1992, those numbers had reversed a year later.

When this contingent gathers on Sunday, two Sunday school classes date to the heyday years of Epworth—the Worker's Class and the J. B. Allen-Utopian Class. (A third, the Pairs and Spares Class, contains a mix of ages.) There are also a number of graded youth classes from nursery to high school. The only class that does not start at 9:45 is the new Young Adult Class. In the words of Jim Pelot, offical Sunday school attendance taker and bell ringer, "The Young Adult Class . . . why that would be the 10:10 class."

To the Worker's Class come retired blue-collar workers, people who built Candler Park and Epworth United Methodist church with their own hands. Their class begins with a traditional opening exercise. They have a hymn sing, followed by announcements, hear a lesson (more typically a mini-sermon), and then take an offering. When they have finished for the morning, many of these parishioners leave, not attending the regular Sunday worship. Although their numbers are dwindling, they remain a powerful presence in the church.

As people finish Sunday school and others arrive for worship, younger members strike up conversations in the sanctuary, while children run up and down the aisles among the gathering congregation. Dress is casual for the younger adults, while older members tend to stick with the traditional suit and tie and Sunday dresses and enter the sanctuary much more quietly. Seating tends to follow a very consistent pattern.

After the organ prelude, the O'Neills enter the sanctuary through doors on opposite sides of the congregation. Whichever of them is preaching enters from the left. Whichever of them is not preaching serves as liturgist. The choir, numbering fifteen or so, enters directly above them. The general order of worship is not unusual Methodist fare, although Art and Melissa have been known to try out new liturgical components. The minister of music often introduces a new hymn from the 1989 United Methodist hymnal with a short description about its history or author.

Laity are becoming increasingly involved in the services, delivering community announcements, reading scripture, and serving the elements during communion. During the Ritual of Fellowship, everybody is urged to sign the *friendship folder, visitor or not, and to shake somebody's hand. During the last stanza of the final hymn, people are invited to come forth to unite with the church by profession of faith or transfer of membership. When they do, a reception line forms at the front of the church following the service.*

After the service, people generally mill around inside the sanctuary, greeting one another and talking about church and family activities. Members will return to a busy round of family and professional activities, looking forward to the community and spiritual renewal they will find when they return the next week.

RESOURCES

Epworth's buildings have always reflected the health of the congregation. To erect the first building on their McClendon Avenue property, men of the church dug the foundation with their own muscle and sweat. The move into a new sanctuary, more than a generation ago, marked what today's older members remember as a high point in the church's history. That the church has begun to repair and remodel the buildings in recent years is a sign of better days. Fixing up old places is, after all, what most of the new members of Epworth like to do; they have bought houses that are "fixer-uppers" themselves. Restoring the church's fine architectural details of bygone years and making the old building functional for today seem natural.

That the first room completed in Epworth's renovation is the History Room says a good deal about the value this church places on memory, on maintaining a story about their past. Members remember the fun they had together and the ways people invested in the church and in each other. Some of that investment is tangible, in the form of small memorial gifts for special projects around the church. Drawing on the intangible heritage—and helping people come to terms with the underside that always exists in a community's past—has been a task consciously undertaken by the O'Neills. Even as they recognized the need to move into the future, they were sure that they needed the resources of the past. Melissa mused one day, "There will never be another Epworth, in my opinion, where people have known each other for fifty years. That will never happen again. And that's sad to me. Even though this is as much of a grounded community as I would expect you would find in Atlanta, it's not going to happen again. So what does that mean for us as a church? How are we going to continually readapt to the new faces that come and try to build community when they're going to be gone in two years?" As each of the older members passes away, there is a keen sense of a history lost, and those who are moving into leadership positions at Epworth now do not want that history to be lost forever.

The History Room is, of course, not the only thing happening in

Epworth's building. The church derives rental income from commuting seminary students who occupy rooms on the top floor during the week and from a co-op preschool. The buildings that for so long were open only on Sunday are now busy every day of the week. In addition, there is space for a Boy Scout troup and for the neighborhood association meetings. The church is slowly working on remodeling other areas of its educational wing to make it more hospitable to the children and young families who are beginning to come. A new playground out back is used mostly by the co-op preschool kids, but also by the church's families. Yet the changes come slowly. The boiler still gives out from time to time, leaving the building without heat. The two buildings, seventy and forty years old, will continue to be a financial drain in the years ahead.

Epworth's budget was up about 20 percent in 1992, and the church paid its apportionments to the North Georgia Conference in full. Still, this is not a congregation with deep pockets. Only 23 percent have household incomes over $50,000, virtually none over $80,000 (see table 7.2). While not all of the older adults are on a tight budget (a third have incomes over $35,000), many of them are. In addition, a substantial segment of the membership is still in school, especially seminary and graduate school, with little cash to spare. It is perhaps not surprising, then, that only 20 percent give two hundred dollars per month or more to the church, while twice as many (42 percent) give less than fifty dollars per month. While some older members think that younger ones are not pulling their financial weight, our survey found no difference in giving patterns between older and younger members. There are both old and young among the top givers and both old and young among those who give the least.

Very real differences exist, however, between the old Epworth and the new in occupation and education patterns. Longtime members were mostly blue-collar workers during their employed years, and fewer than a quarter (23 percent) held college degrees or higher. Of those under forty-five, in contrast, only 8 percent reported not completing at least a college degree. About half (46 percent) are in professional occupations. These new members are bringing to Epworth both needed financial resources and a reservoir of skill and experience on which the church can draw in the years ahead.

Bridging the differences between older Epworth members and people coming in from the new Candler Park has been a major challenge facing the O'Neills. Not only have they been concerned about preserving the heritage represented by the older members, but they have also made aggressive efforts to reestablish Epworth in the Candler Park community. Their youth and energy have been valuable assets in this process, and that they, too, fit the urban pioneer mold has made recon-

Table 7.2. Epworth United Methodist Church, Candler Park

Ideas and priorities	
Christian practices rated "essential"	Living Christian values
Ministries rated "very important" or "essential"	Service to the needy
Resources	
Average Sunday attendance	100
Annual operating budget (1992)	$120,000
Household incomes above $50,000	23%
College degrees or more	41%
Average age	50 years
Activities (beyond worship) participated in at least monthly	Bible study
Relationship to the community	
Live ten minutes or less from the church	42%
New to the community in the last five years	30%
Ethnicity	87% European
Participate in civic & community activities more than once a month	55%

NOTE: Forty-five people responded to our survey, amounting to approximately 45 percent of average Sunday attendance. This may be taken as a good representation of all regular attenders.

necting easier. When, in December 1993, they moved on to another assignment, the conference assigned the church another experienced in-town pastor, the Reverend Elaine Puckett.[5] By giving Epworth strong pastoral leadership tailored to the new Candler Park neighborhood, the conference has provided a necessary resource for the church's potential transformation.

STRUCTURES OF AUTHORITY

At Epworth, we have a reprise of the role played by church hierarchies at Berean Seventh-Day Adventist, Hinton United Methodist, and Incarnation Episcopal. In each case, relatively small, declining congregations suffered when assigned retirement-aged, mismatched, or otherwise less desirable pastors. When assigned pastors that fit the profile of the potential congregation rather than the declining one, these congregations took on new life. In no case can the pastor do it alone; committed lay leaders are essential, as well. But those lay leaders can rarely provide the energy and build the bridges without solid pastoral leadership. In denominations with episcopal polities, pastoral placement in not in the congregation's hands.

Epworth has been a loyal part of the North Georgia Conference. At its annual charge conference—a business meeting where all the church organizations report to the visiting district superintendent—older members respectfully submit their reports of mission projects and gifts, attendance at special events, and the like. Some of the younger members, however, have yet to learn this routine. Nearly two-thirds (64 percent) of them come to Epworth from traditions other than Methodism, and many share remnants of the antiauthority ethos of the sixties. They are much less likely to honor those in office out of sheer loyalty.

Blending the tradition and loyalty of the older members with the egalitarian experimentation of Candler Park's urban pioneers is the challenge of governing Epworth at this stage in its history. At the annual barbeque and bazaar, when younger members wanted to introduce some new activities aimed at children, older members objected. The next year, the younger members just did the new activities without asking. When the bazaar was a tremendous success anyway, everyone seemed to forget that something new had been added—without permission.

When the O'Neills arrived in 1990, they found few functioning committees and an informal system of communication much like Hinton's. A few longstanding families formed an informal executive committee, making key decisions for the church. Everybody knew who traditionally did what job. There was a newsletter, but the grapevine was a more effective means of communication about church issues and activities. Since 1990, a dozen or so committees have been put in place, and they are becoming actively involved in planning the church's activities. An official Administrative Council draws together the heads of programs and committees into a churchwide decision-making body. Financial decisions always go to the trustees first. Both trustees and Administrative Council are fairly well balanced between old and new members. But, like Hinton, Epworth will continue for a while longer to find points of conflict between the informal ways of the longtime members and the more formal order preferred by the younger newcomers.

Experimentation is further straining the bounds of tradition in the role of women at Epworth. The new chair of the trustee board is a woman, a first for the church. Women as official leaders has been a somewhat difficult concept for some of the older members to accept. They were not at all sure they liked the idea of a woman co-pastor, and some never got past thinking of Melissa as her husband's assistant. Faced with a *pregnant* woman co-pastor, a couple of older women left the church. But by the end of the O'Neills' tenure, the congregation had grown so used to the idea of women in the pulpit that getting a female senior minister barely caused a ripple.

CULTURE

The energy and care Epworth's members have invested in their church over the years is still visible. In the months leading up to the annual bazaar and barbeque, women in the Share Group gather regularly to make the crafts that will be sold to raise money for the church. During Advent, a lovely Christmas tree is erected in the sanctuary and covered with ornaments made by Epworth members. These "Chrismons" are delicately covered in gold braid and sequins and made in the shape of crosses, mangers, stars, and the like.

When Epworth's longtime members heard that they were being assigned a clergy couple, they faced a dilemma. On the one hand, it looked like Epworth's best chance in a long time to reverse its decline. On the other hand, neither O'Neill met their definition of an acceptable pastor. Both Art's beard and Melissa's gender challenged these faithful members to accept leadership they were not sure they could trust. They decided it was worth a try. For many of the older leaders, the gamble has been worth it; they are delighted to see the church growing and care deeply about the O'Neills (a feeling that is clearly reciprocated).

For many of the others, however, the result has been a congregation they increasingly do not recognize. The lack of decorum in the sanctuary, the lack of respect for who has always done what, the fact that others are now in charge—all of that has left them feeling increasingly alienated. As a result, they come to Sunday school, where things are predictably the same, and then they go home. When the church planned a Christmas program immediately following worship and put up sets for the pageant in the fellowship hall space the Workers Class uses, the class protested. Their last undisturbed space was being invaded. On that day, the sets stayed, but the Workers Class did not. It remains to be seen how long these members will stay with this emerging new congregation, if they do at all.

The God who sustains these older members provides places of comfort, strength, and safety; loves his children but expects them to obey and punishes them when they do not. The younger members also find comfort in God's presence; they, too, trust God to hold the world together. But their God is a much more amorphous reality. One woman described God as a "presence" and an "ultimate" explanation. Theirs is a struggling, questioning, journeying faith that is willing to tackle tough theological issues—again, they are the "seeker generation." They read Karl Barth and talk about Bill Moyers's series on myths. They contemplate God on hikes in the Sierras and think about how small each person is in the grand scheme of things—yet God loves us all.

One Sunday, as the service was drawing to a close, Melissa announced that she wanted to change the closing hymn. Printed in the bulletin was "Pass Me Not, O Gentle Savior." But based on a midnight revelation she asked if people would mind singing the old Shaker song "Lord of the Dance" instead. Everybody smiled and laughed a little. She said that she could not get the song out of her head, and people could even dance while singing, if they wished. It was the sort of moment of spontaneity that Candler Park residents would relish. Many of the younger members sang it without their books, having learned it sometime in their youth, but most of the older members could only stumble through what for them was an unfamiliar song (and they certainly were not dancing).

While most of the time, there is enough commonality in the congregation to make worship together possible, there are enough differences to cause occasional awkward moments. Multiple small groups help to meet the diverse spiritual needs of the congregation. The older adult Sunday school classes, United Methodist Women's groups, and the like provide places of study and fellowship for more traditional members. The younger members—many of whom spent time away from church in their teens and twenties—have found the new spirituality groups, the young adults Sunday school class, and the Sunday evening discipleship class to their liking. One of the members of the discipleship class told the congregation one Sunday morning about what they had done—thirty-six weeks of committed Bible study with daily study times required, plus two and a half hours of study on Sunday evenings. They read the Bible cover to cover during that time, trying to find connections between the Scriptures and their personal lives.

These new groups put a premium on becoming a cohesive community by openly sharing one's questions and doubts, as well as one's joys and certainties. Just how open one should be, and about what, is another of the issues on which Epworth is seeking a new middle ground. Older, traditionally southern members live with high expectations for respectable behavior, along with a willingness to look the other way when otherwise respectable people fail. Younger members are likely to accept a wider variety of life-style alternatives, but they too think such matters are best not discussed in public. Older members might accept the homosexuality of an otherwise respected friend, for instance, but would view it as a serious failing that should be kept strictly quiet. Younger members who might not see it as a failing are no more eager to make it an open issue in the congregation. If gay and lesbian persons choose to come to Epworth, current members will not protest, but neither do they want to take this issue on as a crusade.

What they do want to take on is not yet clear. They routinely raise money for a variety of mission causes, United Methodist and otherwise. In addition, the United Methodist Women help various local agencies with money, goods, and occasional volunteer effort. No sustained sense of commitment to any given mission or outreach effort has yet arisen. Mostly, people simply know that they want to reestablish Epworth as a presence in the Candler Park neighborhood.

Art and Melissa began that task by becoming something of a ubiquitous presence themselves. They hung out in local coffee shops, went to neighborhood association meetings, and began to invite local organizations to use the church's building. They were received well. One neighborhood association official said, "Art and Melissa were just willing to do anything for us. We have not only our monthly meetings there, but a lot of other meetings as well. They always have lots of meeting space, and they're just wonderful to work with. And they've really done a lot of outreach into becoming a part of the community." When the first younger persons began to show up at worship at Epworth, however, they were often uneasy about being the only people under sixty in the congregation. As more came, that problem faded. Those who come today are very likely to be from Candler Park or some other nearby neighborhood. Of the members under forty-five, 70 percent live within ten minutes of the church. Within that radius, the ethnic, life-style, and economic range is quite wide. Which of those people will make Epworth home in the years ahead is still not clear.

Anyone who shows up at Epworth gets a warm welcome. When a homeless man appeared in the services one day, he was greeted by old and young alike during the passing of the peace, despite his disheveled appearance and unpleasant odor. There are, however, few systematic efforts either to recruit or to nurture new members. People seem to be coming because they hear about Epworth in the neighborhood or from friends. They stay because they find in this congregation people who are enough like themselves, who share spiritual struggles enough like their own, who value similar virtues of community and family, that they choose to make this congregation a part of their lives. Epworth is thus likely to grow along the lines of its emerging constituency: young, well-educated, professional, community-oriented, innovative, and free-spirited. Some are likely to be gay and lesbian, but Epworth does not appear likely either to seek them out or to make their presence an issue. It is even more unlikely that Epworth's new members will look like the older people who used to populate the place. The congregation emerging here represents a whole new start, a new church built on the original foundation.

SUMMARY

Epworth United Methodist appears well on its way toward reestablishing itself as a community church. Just as the old Epworth served the old Candler Park, so the new Epworth appears poised to serve the urban pioneers who now make this in-town neighborhood home. The primary question remaining is just how open the new Epworth will be to which segments of the Candler Park community. The church's resources of persons and money, still somewhat precarious, are sufficient to support a growing program of activities. With the commitment of the North Georgia Conference to providing strong pastoral leadership and the growing cadre of well-educated professionals in the congregation, Epworth has what it needs to move ahead.

That movement has not, of course, been easy. Some older members have found the congregation's new direction alienating. Balancing the expectations and needs of older and younger members is a major task in these years of transition. There are differing ideas about God, about how people should live their lives, and about how the church should run. Newer members live in Candler Park; many of the older members no longer do. It has taken the commitment of both constituencies to bring Epworth back to life, but now many of the older members are being lost to illness and death. Within a few years, all that will be left of that old identity will be found in the History Room—and in the vision it took for that late 1980s remnant to dream again about connecting congregation and community.

Just as denominations have played a key role as partners in the rebirths of Good Shepherd and Epworth, so the denomination was critical in the birth of St. Lawrence Parish. The Roman Catholic Church makes decisions about new parishes in its centralized hierarchy and organizes new parishes as new Catholic populations emerge. The growth of Gwinnett County, northeast of Atlanta, has presented the Church with just such an opportunity.

St. Lawrence Catholic Parish, Gwinnett County: New Catholics in a New Setting

In 1970, a band of eight to ten Catholic families made up the fledgling St. Lawrence Parish in Gwinnett County, northeast of Atlanta. The county was still largely rural, with only about twenty-seven thousand persons in the wider area surrounding Lawrenceville, the county seat. And it was also traditionally southern in its religious composition, with 62 percent of its religious adherents Baptist, 22 percent Methodist, and most of the remainder members of conservative Protestant denominations. A mere 2 percent of the county's population was Catholic.[6] Still, the archdiocese of Atlanta placed a mission there and over the next two decades watched it grow into a parish with over fourteen hundred families enrolled. Today, almost as quickly as the archdiocese can place another priest and build another building in Gwinnett County, it is filled to capacity with Catholics, pouring into the area from all over the country. For their southern evangelical neighbors, Catholic parishes are a part of the much altered landscape of the county. But for Catholics from traditional older parishes in other parts of the country, St. Lawrence is as much a new experience as the southern culture itself. It neither looks nor feels like the parishes "back home." One of the earliest members of the parish noted that "there were no traditions established here; we didn't have to fight that." Over the years, St. Lawrence has reveled in starting from scratch. Our research team member Barbara Elwell introduces us to the way this suburban, post–Vatican II parish carries on.

The history of St. Lawrence begins in 1965 when the archdiocese established a mission in Lawrenceville at the request of the four or five Catholic families living and worshipping in the area. For its first two years, the congregation celebrated Mass in the basement of one of the founding members. It spent two more years worshipping at a nearby funeral home and another two years renting space at a small downtown appliance store. In 1969, members of the steadily growing congregation purchased ten acres of land and began planning the construction of their own building, which they finally occupied in 1973 after pitching in to do the bulk of the construction work themselves. In 1974 the church received canonical status as a parish.

The property St. Lawrence occupied is located about one-half mile east of downtown Lawrenceville on a major thoroughfare in an area that includes several strip shopping malls, the Lawrenceville Church of God (which is remarkably similar in size and appearance), and a small neighborhood of older modest homes. Parishioners park behind the main building in a large lot, at the very back of which are a small shrine to the Virgin Mary, a satellite dish, and the rectory. Between the parking lot and the church are four portable buildings used for religious education classes.

The story of St. Lawrence Catholic Church is one of humble beginnings and continual growth. Membership in the parish grew to three hundred families in 1985 and to well over fourteen hundred families today. While these numbers suggest that the bulk of the parish's growth occurred in the late 1980s, the membership of St. Lawrence was actually split twice in the 1970s when the archdiocese founded new parishes in neighboring Lilburn and Snellville. The archdiocese is presently in the process of creating several more parishes in the area, and the prospect of being broken up again is welcomed by both the leadership and the laity at St. Lawrence. Despite a certain measure of pride stemming from their undeniable success story, there is widespread concern within the congregation that the parish has grown too big too fast.

While one of St. Lawrence's neighboring parishes has to hold nine weekend Masses to accommodate the growing multitude of Gwinnett Catholics, St. Lawrence manages to get by with four: one on Saturday night and three on Sunday morning. On Saturday evening and Sunday at ten o'clock, the sanctuary fills with 250–300 adults and 100–200 children. Sunday's 8:15 and 11:45

Masses each attract another 200 worshippers (including adults and children). The 11:45 Mass is slightly more traditional than the others and is not interrupted by dismissals for religious education classes or other special events.

The most attended Mass is Sunday at ten o'clock. Parishioners generally arrive just in time for Mass and file into the church through the "gathering area," a spacious room just outside the sanctuary that was added to encourage people to hang around for a while before and after Mass and get to know each other. The sanctuary itself is large and full of light. The walls to one's right and left as one faces the altar are made up almost entirely of tall windows. The altar area is slightly elevated and very open; the altar and lectern are made of glass. Four main sections of pews form a half circle around the altar. There are also a balcony and a small glassed-in chapel in the back. Inside the church, the atmosphere is bustling. A few folks kneel and pray briefly before Mass begins; most roam in search of seats, greeting one another briefly but warmly. Children are everywhere. (One longtime member says that "church on Sunday is like a giant nursery.") Ushers keep the balcony closed until it becomes clear that there will not be enough seats for everyone on the main floor. On crowded Sundays, the chapel in the back of the sanctuary fills up and extra chairs are added in the gathering area (where one can see, thanks to the glass walls, and hear, thanks to the sound system).

Before Mass begins, the music ensemble often tries to teach the congregation new arrangements, but despite the upbeat prodding of the music minister, the singing at this church is consistently unenthusiastic. Undaunted, the music minister invites the congregation to join in the "gathering prayer," and Mass begins. After the opening section of the service, the priest leads the congregation, with everyone's hands extended outward, in a prayer dismissing the children to go to their religious education classes. (They return in time for the celebration of the Eucharist.) The children process out, leaving Reserved signs on their seats.

After the dismissal, Father Martin Kopchik (Father Marty) begins welcoming newcomers and visitors. He roams the congregation, equipped with wireless mike, for as long as necessary, warmly chatting with each visitor and handing out a necklace with the symbol of St. Lawrence on it, a personalized version of a visitor's nametag.

The Mass continues with the communal confession of sin, which Father Marty almost always prefaces with an exhortation to ask forgiveness "for the times we have been selfish." Following Scripture readings by one of many lectors, Father Marty reads the gospel and gives the homily. His homilies almost always begin with a story of the life of an exemplary person (various saints, Albert Schweitzer, a garbageman in Toledo) and go on to encourage the congregation to learn from that person's example, highlighting virtues of individual sacrifice and devotion, generosity, and service to those one meets.

The celebration of the Eucharist proceeds in typical Catholic fashion, except that the congregation, for the most part, does not kneel at the customary points. The practice of standing rather than kneeling was instituted by Fr. Ken Bayer in the 1980s. His reasoning was that kneeling is a penitential gesture and should be reserved for penitential seasons. "The rest of the time," Father Marty says, "we reflect the resurrection community we are by standing." Father Marty takes his time celebrating the Eucharist, occasionally chanting the eucharistic prayer. Six to ten eucharistic ministers (men and women) help out with communion and are themselves served last. After receiving communion, folks pray quietly until all have been served.

The Mass ends with well-wishing from Father Marty—"May this be the best day ever for you and your family"—and with an upbeat recessional song. As the song concludes, folks file back out into the gathering area, pick up a bulletin from one of several ushers, and exit through the fellowship hall. Some linger briefly to pick up a doughnut and coffee and to chat with friends and family, but, in general, folks move out very quickly.

St. Lawrence's basic character and identity were decisively shaped by Fr. Ken Bayer, who served the congregation from 1980 to 1989. Under his leadership the church's main building was built, described by one member as "the showcase of the archdiocese." Although quite modern in appearance, unlike most of the other Catholic churches in Gwinnett County, it looks like a church, thanks largely to an unusual but rather striking bell tower. It was also under Father Ken that the congregation developed a "progressive" liturgical style (kneeling only during penitential seasons, baptism by immersion, and the like). The glass altar, the baptismal pool, and the openness of the worship space reflect his leadership. Since his departure, Father Marty has carried on in the same spirit. His ministry is marked by a concern to shape the life of the congregation in keeping with the reforms of Vatican II. In particular, he is trying to move away from an authoritarian or hierarchical style of leadership toward greater collaboration and participation, in the hope of getting as many people as possible involved in the life of the parish.

Getting people involved in the parish is perhaps the greatest challenge facing St. Lawrence at this point in its history. Given its rapid growth and a limited number of opportunities for involvement, the vast majority of members simply attend Mass on Sunday. Many have enrolled their children in religious education classes (more than seven hundred kids enrolled in all) but are otherwise uninvolved in the institutional life of the parish. The leadership hopes to remedy this through the establishment of Small Faith Communities—groups of eight to twelve parishioners who meet outside the confines of the church itself to cultivate the life of faith together. Given both the size of St. Lawrence and its makeup (young professional couples with children, whose lives revolve around work and family), the effort to involve more people in the life of the parish is likely to be a struggle for some time to come.

RESOURCES

St. Lawrence's building is one of its greatest resources. Its distinctive exterior, especially the bell tower, makes it a landmark on a busy street in Lawrenceville. As new Catholics move into the area, they are quite likely to notice this attractive new building and to find it handy. But more than visibility, the building gives St. Lawrence the sense of identity and involvement that lie at the heart of this parish's life. Its large gathering area is reminiscent of the living rooms of its suburban parishioners. When people enter, they feel at home. When they progress into the worship space, its very appearance signals the nontraditional form of this parish's worship life. Pews arranged in a semicircle, no visible statues of saints, and a pastor and deacon who sit in the congregation until time to preach or celebrate Mass give expression to the post–Vatican II notion of the church as "people of God." Rather than remote and awesome, the feel of this church is intimate, as if worship depends on the worshippers as much as on the celebrants.

As impressive as are the exterior, gathering area, and sanctuary, the remainder of the building serves the parish less well. Office and classroom spaces are cramped, with little space for gathering groups of any size for activities other than worship. The church must rely on portable classroom buildings (trailers) for its vast catechetical program. If St. Lawrence had high levels of participation in parish activities, there would simply be no place to put people.

Because of its membership numbers, St. Lawrence can almost always muster enough personpower for the things it chooses to do. However, its vast flocks of parishioners are typically harried suburbanites whose time is at a premium. Their average commute is thirty minutes each way to work, and 13 percent of those who are employed work more than fifty hours per week. Eighty percent of the married women in the parish work outside the home, but even the housewives are likely to spend their days carpooling and otherwise occupied with the busy round of family activities. While most of St. Lawrence's members have fallen into the patterns of their southern neighbors as faithful Sunday morning (or Saturday evening) churchgoers, only a core of a couple of hundred members participate in other parish activities with any regularity (see table 7.3). Still, with such a large parish, it takes only a small percentage of participation to carry on an impressive array of activities.

St. Lawrence's financial resources reflect that same mix of immense potential and limited commitment. The parish's median household income is about $50,000, but the members are spread rather evenly over the range from 20,000 to 80,000. Most are quite comfortable, then,

Table 7.3. St. Lawrence Catholic Parish, Gwinnett County

Ideas and priorities	
Christian practices rated "essential"	Living Christian values
Ministries rated "very important" or "essential"	Service to the needy
Resources	
Average Saturday/Sunday combined attendance	1,000
Annual operating budget (1992)	N/a
Household incomes above $50,000	49%
College degrees or more	53%
Average age	43 years
Activities (beyond worship) participated in at least monthly	None
Relationship to the community	
Live ten minutes or less from the church	43%
New to the community in the last five years	48%
Ethnicity	97% European
Participate in civic & community activities more than once a month	39%

NOTE: Two hundred thirty-six people responded to our survey, amounting to approximately 24 percent of average Sunday attendance. This may be taken as a fair representation of all regular attenders.

but a sizable number have incomes low enough to make careful budgeting a necessity. Still, the parish is apparently not high on the priority list for most members. Only 260 families turned in pledge cards in the fall of 1992. Of those who responded to our survey, almost two-thirds (64 percent) give less than one hundred dollars per month to the parish. Given the sheer numbers of households contributing, this seems sufficient to support parish programming.

One of the consequences of a relatively limited financial base is that St. Lawrence's staff is barely adequate to the needs of such a huge parish. In addition to the pastor, Father Marty, there are a half-time associate, a lay minister for youth, a lay Christian education minister, and an office staff. Sometimes they simply reach the limits of their ability to meet the needs of the parish. When some parents lamented that no children's Bible school was planned for the summer of 1993, for example, the Christian education minister said, "I cannot and will not take it on. . . . I'm willing to help, but not to be responsible for it." The youth minister supported her, saying that he too was overextended. He even acknowledged, "I get angry. Something worthy comes up, and it gets dumped back in my lap." At this point in the meeting of the Christian Education Committee, a lay member responded, "Maybe it's time for the laity to take responsibility." Another member agreed. "It's our church; we're responsible for making it work. For too long we've been used to having the church do for us." The Christian education minister suggested putting a blurb in the bulletin asking for volunteers. "If people want to, they'll come forward." The second member agreed. "People need to be empowered. They need to know there's an opportunity." As a result, a week-long summer Bible school, called Summer Safari, was held at the church that summer, with a lay person in charge. Nearly one hundred elementary age children were enrolled.

Probably the most ambitious project this parish has undertaken was the construction of its first building. One member provided a generous financial guarantee while the funds were raised and spent. But most impressively, members of the parish did virtually all the construction work themselves. Only on the few items for which they did not have the expertise did they hire contractors. Parishioners there at the time remember it as a time of pride and strong comraderie. The parish was much smaller then. Everyone knew everyone else, and there was a keen sense of being pioneers together. That depth of commitment is much harder to engender now that the parish is overflowing.

Volunteer labor is still present, however; for example, most of the pastoral counseling is handled by volunteers. Stephen Ministry, a national organization of lay ministry training, teaches listening skills and how to offer advice and comfort, including when and how to refer people to professional assistance. St. Lawrence has an active corps of volunteers who have received this training, and as a result Father Marty reports that he does very little counseling himself. This sort of volunteer ministry is possible in part because of the high skill level of this parish. Over 80 percent have some education beyond high school, and half (52 percent) have a college degree or more. Almost half (42 percent) of those employed are in professional or administrative occupations. Many of them have been transferred to the Atlanta area by large corporations and bring with them what they have learned about getting things done. St. Lawrence, then, has both the strength of numbers and the potential strength of members' skill, experience, and connections—as well as material resources. Its potential is limited only by the willingness and ability of its members to commit those human and material resources to the parish.

STRUCTURES OF AUTHORITY

But for the authority of the Roman Catholic Church, St. Lawrence would not exist. The diocese sanctioned the beginning of the mission, designated it a parish in the early 1970s, okayed the purchase of land,

and has sent pastors and otherwise guided the parish's life. The larger Catholic network, in turn, provides additional resources and training both for staff and parishioners. Whether it is videotapes for the Rite of Christian Initiation for Adults (RCIA) class or workbooks for starting Small Faith Communities, the institutions of the Church have a clear impact here.

Many of St. Lawrence's parishioners, however, keep the Church's authority at arm's length. Like the lower-level participants in many large bureaucracies, they shake their heads in dismay at pronouncements from "headquarters" that seem to have no relevance for their lives. They especially keep their distance from Church teaching on the role of women and on sexuality.[7] When a nearby bishop was widely quoted as saying that "women can no more be priests than men can have babies," various parish members were appalled and said so. For these more progressive Catholics, individual conscience is to be weighed alongside Church authority. Others in the parish take Church authority more seriously. The members of the pro-life group, for instance, assume that good Catholics should take Church teaching on abortion to heart. Some of them admit that the Church's "consistent pro-life ethic" (in which opposition to abortion is linked to opposition to war and capital punishment) is difficult to accept. Still they struggle to do so, feeling that it is their obligation as Catholics to understand and support Church teaching.

This tension between tradition and innovation shows up on a variety of issues. One group in the parish, for instance, is proud that theirs is among the first parishes to implement Lectionary Based Catechesis (LBC). This new program uses the lectionary Scriptures for the day—and their own experiences of God's presence—to teach children about the faith, rather than beginning with a set of doctrines to be explained and mastered. Another group at the parish, however, finds this new program vacuous. Without a firm grounding in Church doctrine, they worry, children will be left to drift. Some felt strongly enough to leave their places on the Christian Education Commission over this issue. Enough others agreed to cause the staff to bring in a mediator to help heal the wounds. These more conservative members also worry that so few parishioners practice the older traditions of devotion to Mary, praying the rosary, and the like. Not everyone is happy with the kinds of autonomy and participation encouraged by Vatican II and embraced by most of this parish.

All the church's decision making is geared toward efforts at consensus and lay involvement, tapping the "wisdom of God" that is resident among the people, as leaders are likely to put it. The staff's typical style of leadership might be described as "facilitation," although they still exercise a good deal of guidance and initiative. They are quite skilled at presenting ideas and winning the support of the lay leadership. The Parish Council is the principle coordinating body for the congregation. In addition there are five commissions, coordinating and governing bodies with responsibility for organizations and activities in a given area—spiritual life, education, service, administrative services, and community life. All the parish's various organizations fall under one of these commissions. And as we have already seen, those who participate in these bodies can sometimes take major responsibility for what happens in the parish.

Of the three Roman Catholic parishes in this study, St. Lawrence has by far the most well developed structures for member participation. Having begun its life since Vatican II, its traditions are shaped by that council's pronouncements about the role of individual conscience and the Church as the people of God. While the priest is ultimately in charge, everything about his relationships with his parish—from the way he greets visitors on Sunday to the way he runs a meeting—communicates the importance of lay involvement. The way the parish does business is shaped by these theological factors, but it is also shaped by the educated, skilled, and mobile people who make up the congregation. Nearly everyone in the parish can offer the perspective of at least one other parish; no one can get away with saying "we've always done it this way." While there are some for whom Church authority is a consideration, most of St. Lawrence's constituents have the skills and experience to make their own plans and decisions without waiting for permission.

CULTURE

Everything about St. Lawrence reflects the attempt to balance new and old, tradition and innovation. The community itself is, of course, just such a mix. Lawrenceville was, until the last generation, a sleepy southern county seat. Now it has built a huge, ultramodern county office complex, and it has restored the old courthouse square. Subdivisions are rapidly squeezing out the last of the farm land. What remains, too expensive to farm, is dotted with For Sale signs. But people move to this remote section of the Atlanta metropolitan region at least in part because it still feels small town and rural. Still, this parish's balance between new and old is not, as in Hinton United Methodist's case, cultural—Catholics, after all, are part of what has displaced the old Lawrenceville. Theirs is a struggle to combine the disparate elements of Catholic tradition they all bring with them into something that makes sense in this place where everything—material and cultural—seems to be newly constructed. Building a new kind of Catholic parish seems only natural here.

One of the most obvious aspects of St. Lawrence's attempt to construct new things out of old traditions is its liturgical innovation. Constant experiments with new practices have to be explained to the parishioners. The altar table and lectern are made of glass, we are told, because they should not distract from the actions that take place there. The baptismal font is big enough for an adult to be baptized by immersion, and at Easter that routinely happens. The semicircular arrangement of the pews and the openness of the altar area reinforce the sense of equal participation among all who gather here. Partly as a result of this arrangement of their worship space, St. Lawrence members participate more intimately than may be usual in the communion service, experiencing it as a communal ritual, not just an individual one. Lay eucharistic ministers serve in pairs (usually a man and woman, one with bread and the other with cup), offering both elements to everyone who comes forward. Recently, it became the custom for these ministers to be served last (instead of first), thereby emphasizing that they are servants. There are often new songs to learn, although the congregation is not enthusiastic about singing. People kneel much less often than is traditional. Various rituals of blessing—for those who will teach catechism classes, for new members, for the children who leave each Sunday for a portion of the service to be taught in their LBC classes, for RCIA participants, who also leave for classes until they are received into the Church at Easter—involve gestures and sentences that most of the congregation have learned for the first time at St. Lawrence. Each of these innovations draws on the history and tradition of the larger Church but also modifies those traditions on the experience of these Catholics in this place.

My favorite of St. Lawrence's liturgical innovations was the way the sanctuary was decorated for Advent in 1992. Taking a cue from the familiar New Testament reference to Jesus coming "from the root of Jesse," a huge stump was placed between the altar and the baptismal font and adapted for use as an Advent wreath. Each Sunday during the season candles would be lit here, rather than in the midst of the usual circle of greenery. The symbolism, of course, had to be explained to the worshippers. But I saw in this odd liturgical decoration a potent symbol of this parish's life. It was not hard to find a stump in this rapidly growing suburban area. Just look for the latest pasture and woodland being blasted clear for another few hundred houses. While the liturgical symbolism pointed worshippers to the ancient roots from which Jesus came, the more contemporary symbolism pointed them to the uprootedness of their community and their own lives.

In the midst of that uprootedness, St. Lawrence provides a place of spiritual strength and a kind of extended family for those who worship there. Three-quarters of the members have lived in the community less than ten years; half, less than six years. New arrivals are a regular occurrence, and Father Marty's routine of walking the aisles to greet them personally destroys any notion of this as an anonymous place to worship. When researcher Barbara Elwell first observed this routine, she wrote in her field notes, "This is highly unusual in a Catholic church. I have never, ever, ever even heard of such a thing." For most of the visitors it was probably a first, as well. It provided a glimpse of this parish's efforts to create a Catholic community in unconventional ways.

While half of these newcomers have no more than one relative living anywhere nearby, 80 percent are married, and 60 percent have children living at home. Heavily invested in work and in raising children, members find the friends and activities of the parish a welcome support system. At the ten o'clock Mass, nearly two hundred children fill the church with a constant undertone of whimpers and fidgeting. When they return from LBC, marching two abreast, they are an impressive sight. The entire congregation is committed to providing these children with a loving, Christian environment and high-quality religious education.

But the parish is more than just an extension of home for the adults there. They find in their weekly sojourn to Mass a time of reflection, an infusion of spiritual energy, a moment of healing. When a group of parish women gathered to talk about prayer, they were asked what draws them to prayer. Their answers included anxiety, helplessness, hopelessness, desperation, need, gratitude, habit (this offered by an older woman), and the need for comfort. Father Marty's homilies are often infused with therapeutic language, translating the gospel message into words of personal comfort for busy and distracted souls. Sin, he says, is a matter of wrong attitudes and selfishness, of doing things that aren't loving. Confession is, then, a kind of counseling; the priest is the representative of the community, helping the confessing sinner see how to do better. Experiencing forgiveness (and being forgiving) can be powerfully transformative, he preaches. When people really allow themselves to experience what happens in the Mass, it can change how they live their lives. Father Marty prays, "Fill us to overflowing in the Eucharist today so that we may share you this week wherever we go."

This rather modern interpretation of sin and salvation does not fully describe the spiritual life of St. Lawrence Parish, however. As we have seen, there are also very traditional people here, engaged in traditional Catholic piety. A group gathers to pray the rosary every Friday night. The St. Vincent de Paul Society and the pro-life group both close their meetings by reciting the "Our Father." For many of St. Lawrence's adults, the traditions of the church are etched firmly in habit and memory. For others, newer experiences of intense spirituality are important, as well. A group from St. Lawrence regularly journeys to nearby Conyers for the monthly appearance of an apparition of the Virgin Mary, joining thousands of other pilgrims to the farm of Nancy Fowler, who claims to receive these regular messages from the Virgin. Still others have participated in Cursillo (an intense spiritual renewal retreat) or in Marriage Encounter weekends. Others have participated in Catholic (and non-Catholic) charismatic services. "In the Catholic Church there is room for different kinds of spirituality," says the religious education minister. Only rarely does this spiritual diversity seem to bother anyone at St. Lawrence.

That diversity may thrive at least in part because of the relatively diverse backgrounds of the members. Not only do they hail from all over the country, but not all are lifelong Catholics. Twenty percent grew up in some other religious tradition (mostly Baptist, Methodist, and other mainline Protestant groups). In many cases, Catholics from elsewhere are marrying native southern Protestants and bringing them into the Church. In addition, many in this baby-boomer parish spent a good portion of their youth and young adulthood away from the Church. We have no way to know exactly how many, but both national studies and conversations around the parish would suggest that having dropped out for a time is a common experience.[8]

Those from other traditions (and some of the returning dropouts) find themselves in RCIA classes. where they learn about Catholic traditions and doctrines and how Catholics govern themselves. But mostly, they are encouraged to explore and claim their own experiences of God. When they are formally welcomed into the community they are asked what they are seeking, and most speak of spiritual guidance and support. That rite of welcoming is another instance of St. Lawrence's liturgical flair. Researcher Barbara Elwell describes what happened the day she witnessed this event.

Father Marty began the Mass by announcing that "five men and women want to become part of our family, our community." He explained that the ritual would begin out in the gathering area and asked the first three rows of each section of pews to join them as representatives of the community. He encouraged any others who wished to join in to come along as well. We processed out into the gathering area behind a man carrying a nine-foot cross, all chanting, "Come and see, come and hear, come and bear the cross of Christ." Out in the gathering area, the "inquirers" who were to be welcomed stood in a group with their sponsors. They were identified by heart-shaped name tags. Father Marty began by explaining who they are: candidates (three of them), persons who have been baptized in another tradition; catechumens (one of them), persons who have never been baptized; and baptized Catholics who have not been confirmed (one of them). He faced them as he spoke, but because he was wearing a microphone, those who were still in the main sanctuary could hear what he was saying.

Next Father Marty addressed each pair of sponsors and candidates individually. He began by introducing the sponsor and saying something about how much they mean to the church. The sponsor then introduced the candidate. Father Marty spoke warm and encouraging words to the candidate while hanging a symbol of St. Lawrence around their neck and asking two questions: What do you ask of God at this point in your journey? And how can the community help? He then told them that their journey would require that they "embrace the cross of Christ." The man with the cross stepped forward, and the candidates placed their hands on it as the crowd chanted again, "Come and see, come and hear, come and bear the cross of Christ."

Baptized Catholics, of course, get no such elaborate ritual welcome, and it is sometimes hard for new members to find a place in this large congregation. With forty to fifty new families registering in some months, it is easy to get lost in the crowd. Those who participate in one of the ministries or get involved in a commission or council often find in those groups a community of support. For others, the parish is characterized by the momentary intimacy of the Mass. It is partly to counter this tendency toward anonymity that the Small Faith Communities experiment was undertaken. Drawing on materials created by Fr. Arthur Baranowski, St. Lawrence's staff hopes to offer a series of home-based small groups where parishioners can share their struggles and joys, providing a forum in which faith and everyday life intersect.[9]

The primary focus for St. Lawrence's ministry is, then, the diverse individual spiritual needs of its members, most of whom are relatively unconnected to populations whose material needs go unmet. They are vaguely aware that homelessness is a problem in Atlanta, but Atlanta seems a long way away. Even those who commute into the city every day manage to keep it at a psychic arm's length. As newcomers, most are also not especially rooted in Lawrenceville. Their primary focus is family and neighborhood, with only a general awareness of the problems of poverty or injustice or war that plague the rest of the world. As a result, the several attempts to begin a peace and justice group in the parish have fizzled. One of the parish's most active ministries is an addiction counseling program, which serves mostly nonmembers.

The St. Vincent de Paul Society and the new pro-life group are the two points where St. Lawrence members attempt to reach out to problems and issues beyond their experience. Both are relatively small groups. The pro-life group is concentrating its energies on educating the parish, and theirs is a message many parishioners would rather ignore. The SVP Society manages a thrift store in Lawrenceville that is among the very few resources for people in that part of the county who find themselves in need. They group raises $30,000 to $40,000 per year for aid to local people, with about half that amount coming from sales at the thrift store. A monthly "second collection" at Masses supplies the remainder. The regular corps of volunteers associated with this ministry, aware and concerned about the needs in their community, are relatively successful at devising manageable projects for their busy suburban fellow parishioners. Through small contributions of time or money, at least some of St. Lawrence's members attempt to make a difference in the world beyond family and church.

SUMMARY

Planted in the 1970s among the rapidly growing suburbs of Gwinnett County, St. Lawrence Catholic Parish reflects the diversity of the population drawn to this southern metropolis and the newness of just about everything in the community. With its constituency growing exponentially, St. Lawrence has grown as well, creating in the process a new kind of Catholic parish. It reflects not only the strong influence of Vatican II, which had just concluded as the parish was founded, but also the newness of Catholicism in this community and the diverse traditions from which its members come. With no single tradition of its own and no local tradition to draw from—and permission from the Church to experiment—St. Lawrence has shaped its liturgies and created new forms of governance to fit the family-oriented, mobile, well-educated people who populate Gwinnett County. They find in the parish a spiritual haven and an extended family, a place to nourish the soul in the midst of busy suburban lives.

Northview Christian Life Church, Carmel: Joyful Praise in the Stressful Suburbs

In Carmel, a very similar suburban community outside Indianapolis, another new church has done its own kind of innovating. Starting with a different theological tradition—the Pentecostalism of the Assemblies of God—Northview Christian Life Church has arrived at forms of church life that in their own way also modify tradition to meet the demands of a mobile, well-educated, family-oriented community. Even the name of the church distinguishes it from its more traditional Assemblies of God cousins. Here pastor-founder Tommy Paino has planted a congregation that he hopes combines the best of the Pentecostal tradition from which he comes with the best of a more subdued evangelicalism. The result is a mix many of Carmel's residents have found appealing. Joan Cunningham of our research team tells us more.

Carmel's transformation from a small town in a rural area to an affluent, suburban edge city happened within the lifetime of most residents. Most members of Northview Christian Life Church, however, do not come not from Carmel but from surrounding areas, including Indianapolis and Noblesville, and do not believe they share the materialistic life-style that typifies Carmel. The church says that it wants members who are "people with an infilling of His Spirit and life that reveals His character in the fruit of the Spirit—love, joy, peace, patience, kindness, goodness, faithfulness, gentleness, self-control—and the gift of the Spirit, particularly faith, wisdom, knowledge, discernment, prayer, healing, and servanthood."

Church members are further distinguished from many area residents in their acceptance of charismatic practices, present in the church since its founding by Pastor Tommy Paino III in 1980. While associate pastor at Lakeview Christian Center, his father's church, Pastor Tommy "wanted to start a church from scratch." To announce the new church, he sent a letter to the entire Carmel zip code. In it he noted his training at Fuller Theological Seminary and explained the balance he envisioned between Pentecostal practices and mainstream evangelicalism.

That letter got enough response for the church to begin. Like many young churches in Carmel, Northview began meeting at a local school. With the help of Lakeview Christian Center, it broke ground for its current building at 131st Street and Gray Road a year later, in a residential area across the street from a Lutheran church. (Such corner locations are typical for churches in the Carmel area.) A small sign bearing the church's name and a dove marks the entrance to the rather plain brick building, which is surrounded on two sides by a large parking lot. A fountain and pond grace its south side. Those passing on Gray Road can see the partly glass wall of Northview's two-story sanctuary.

Although Lakeview bought the land and financed the original construction, Northview assumed the financial obligations in August 1983. By the time construction finished in November 1983, average attendance had reached 770 and membership had increased from slightly under 200 in 1982 to over 300. Just two years later, Northview purchased another piece of property—eighty acres on the edge of town, including the highest point in the area—hoping someday to build a new church there.

By 1986, with combined attendance for the two Sunday services averaging over a thousand, an ambitious attempt was made to build on the new land. When sufficient support and money for construction could not be raised, the effort was dropped. The church did, however, renovate the barn on the property to include a large dining area, kitchen, living room, patio, and basketball court.

Since that time attendance has remained around twelve hundred, but membership has grown to approximately five hundred. Since the church does not stress membership, many regular attenders have not joined. Two additions have been made to the original church building, once to increase the size of the sanctuary and again to add office space. The limited number of classrooms in the current building have to serve a variety of purposes for the church's extensive program of activities.

On a typical Sunday, the parking lot is almost full. The pastoral staff and greeters hand programs to worshippers as they enter one of the three entrances to the sanctuary, whose 750 seats are almost all filled. The interior is decorated only with two banners and a few plants; a large cross hangs on the wall behind an old-fashioned wooden pulpit. Instead of pews, there are cushioned chairs that can be rearranged for different occasions. The crowd that gathers is mostly parents with children of all ages, dressed more casually than in some "Sunday best" churches. There is much talking and laughing as people greet friends before the service.

Singing draws their attention to the front, and congregants stand, often raising one arm heavenward as they join in opening the service. Some songs are favorites, and many attending do not refer to the printed refrains. The tempo is at first upbeat, and everyone claps in time. The beat of succeeding songs gradually becomes slower and quieter. During these songs it is not unusual to see couples, arms around each other, swaying slightly to the music, or parents holding their children. The last songs, which create a peaceful, worshipful mood, are interspersed with times of prayer. Most of the worshippers join in, praying softly but audibly in their seats. A few pray quietly in tongues. This joyful participation in song and prayer is much of what draws so many to worship here each Sunday.

The offertory prayer and collection follow, while music plays. Worshippers are reminded to fill out attendance forms and greet their neighbors after the offertory. Announcements may include special church events or a visiting pastor. When Pastor Tommy announces that it is time for children sixth grade and under to attend Sunday school, they are escorted out of the sanctuary by their parents, who take a few minutes to return; in the meantime everyone moves about, greeting each other and chatting amiably.

The service resumes with some additional singing and Pastor Tommy's sermon. Many times the message is part of a series that will continue over several weeks, relating the Bible to contemporary life. When the pastor reads from his Bible, members of the congregation follow along in theirs.

After the closing prayer, worshippers who wish to are invited to come forward for an additional prayer time. Members who have participated in Caregivers classes are available for support, as are the pastors. People can come to pray for help with spiritual, physical, and other problems in their lives. While they pray, most of the worshippers leave, crowding into the small narthex and hallways. Parents retrieve their children from Sunday school and then chat with other adults in small groups. Others move to the information counter, picking up literature or looking for sign-up sheets. Even after fifteen or twenty minutes a large number of members remain at the church.

Northview's dramatic growth has challenged the pastoral staff, the members, and the building. It has been hard, for instance, to accommodate both the need for the prayer and healing time at the end of the service and the need for gathering and visiting. During the week the building houses a music outreach program, a twice weekly mother's morning-out program, and a counseling center. On a typical Sunday the chapel doubles as a Sunday school classroom and a choir break room.

In the fall of 1992 the congregation voted again to begin plans for a new building, scheduling a pledge drive for the spring of 1993. The new building will dramatically increase the number of classrooms available, while only slightly increasing the size of the sanctuary, enabling the church to more effectively emphasize education. If funds can be raised without the sale of the current building, Pastor Tommy would like to keep it as a community center.

The church hopes a new building will alleviate the crowding in the current facilities. Additional classrooms will also allow for adult Sunday school classes, not currently available on Sunday morning. In addition, the new location places the church outside Carmel and closer to the latest suburban boom community, Fishers. With the new church building and the renovated barn, the church feels it will have something unique to offer.

RESOURCES

When Northview members compare themselves to the rest of Carmel, they feel surrounded by people significantly better off than themselves. That is only partially right. Compared to our survey respondents at Carmel United Methodist, for instance, Northview's respondents are slightly less well off (see table 7.4). Fourteen percent have household incomes above $80,000 per year, compared to CUMC's 38 percent. Northview's median income, while comfortable, falls about $15,000 lower than CUMC's—in the $35,000 to $50,000 range. Probably as a result of this income difference, more of CUMC's wives can afford to be full-time homemakers. Both congregations are made up primarily of professionals and managers, but Northview's respondents are, on average, slightly younger (forty-six compared to fifty-two), which may help to account for part of the income difference. On balance, then, Northview may have slightly less-affluent participants, but they are by no means financially strapped.

More importantly, Northview Christian Life Church has established a tradition of financial commitment among its members that enables them to sustain a much larger budget than their richer Methodist neighbor. With an almost equal number of regular participants, Northview has twice as much money to work with. Almost half our respondents reported giving more than two hundred dollars per month (the highest category on our survey), and judging from the church's 1993

Table 7.4. Northview Christian Life Church, Carmel

Ideas and priorities	
Christian practices rated "essential"	Prayer
	Bible study
	Living Christian values
	Attendance at services
Ministries rated "very important" or "essential"	An evangelism program
	Helping members resist temptation
	Service to the needy
	Helping members share their faith
Resources	
Average Sunday attendance	800
Annual operating budget (1992)	$1.39 million (plus building fund)
Household incomes above $50,000	43%
College degrees or more	63%
Average age	46 years
Activities (beyond worship) participated in at least monthly	Bible study
Relationship to the community	
Live ten minutes or less from the church	29%
New to the community in the last five years	18%
Ethnicity	96% European
Participate in civic & community activities more than once a month	36%

NOTE: Only seventy-three people responded to our survey, amounting to only approximately 9 percent of average Sunday attendance. This may be taken as only a tentative representation of all regular attenders.

revenue of $1.7 million, it probably amounts to considerably more. That budget figure included almost $1 million in regular offerings and $384,000 to the building fund, plus several thousand dollars each for benevolence offerings, missions gifts, scholarships, and the like. None comes from endowment, grants, or other outside sources. In addition, the church has so far received $1.7 million in pledges toward its new building. While its resources are not unlimited, this congregation has more to work with than any other in our study. Its membership has all the ingredients: numbers, relative affluence, and commitment to giving.

The single biggest consumer of those resources has been Northview's continual search for adequate facilities. Building-fund drives are always challenging congregants to give more, and they have constantly dreamed about having a building that would really meet their needs. By late 1993, with the walls going up at their new hillside location, those dreams seemed more nearly a reality. Having mushroomed in the early years, the congregation had outgrown the current building almost as soon as they moved in. While the worship space is fairly adequate, space for dozens of other kinds of meetings is severely limited. Although the current location appeals to Carmel residents, the church has correctly determined its constituency as larger than Carmel. Whereas 79 percent of Carmel United Methodist's members live less than ten minutes from their church, only 29 percent of Northview's worshippers live that close. The new location will capitalize on their regional, north-suburbs identity and put them closer to the most rapidly growing sections of those suburbs.

Like other Carmel residents (and indeed like residents of Gwinnett County, Georgia), Northview's members are well educated. Nearly two-thirds (63 percent) have college degrees or more. They are not, however, terribly well connected in the larger community. The average member participates in community organizations only occasionally (compared to CUMC, where the average member is actively involved in at least one community organization). Most of Northview's members' time is occupied with family, work, and church activities. Their best friends are likely to be in the congregation, as well. As a result, the church gets "first rights" on the skills and time of many of its members, but is less able to connect through them to resources in the larger community.

Yet not everyone who attends has made such a total commitment. Over half of those in church on a given Sunday have not officially joined, and it is fairly easy to remain anonymous in such a large crowd. People can come for the inspiration and comfort they receive, making little commitment to further support or participation. It is significant that our lowest survey response rate was in this congregation. In this relative anonymity, Northview is like most other large churches. In an attempt to counter it, Northview passes registration pads down the aisle each Sunday morning for visitors and members to record their attendance. That information is entered into the church's computer system, and people who have not attended recently are contacted. (This is just one of several ways the church combines volunteer labor and technology to good advantage.) The church works hard to get and keep people involved, but even those who are involved do not always become members. Membership is a big and serious step here. Those who *do* join have expressed an uncommon level of commitment. With a core of nearly five hundred members, along with another five hundred or so regular attenders, Northview has a sizable reservoir of human potential available.

Its most striking human resource, however, is its pastor. Tommy Paino, following in the footsteps of his father, wanted to found a new church. In 1980, he chose rapidly growing Carmel as the location, sent out letters to everyone in town, found a school in which to hold services, and launched the effort. Correctly guessing that traditional "holy roller" Pentecostalism would not catch on in such a place, Paino has guided the congregation to create a style of worship suited to its needs. He has recruited members, assembled a staff, dreamed up programs, and provided much of the energy for the building campaigns. He has remained remarkably attuned to the needs of those who come through his doors, sometimes employing professional survey consultants to help him hear those needs. Never content to rest on a plateau, Pastor Tommy continues to adapt and push forward.

STRUCTURES OF AUTHORITY

While this congregation is nominally affiliated with the Assemblies of God, it exercises a great deal of local autonomy. It supports not only some Assemblies missions causes, but independent work, as well. It now uses Assemblies Sunday school materials but used to buy from David C. Cook. One could attend here for quite a while without ever knowing the church's affiliation. In fact, in a survey of the congregation, more people chose "nondenominational" than "Assemblies" as a description of the church. No bishop can move their pastor, and no outside agency can tell them what to do with their property. Begun as an entrepreneurial effort, the church continues to survive (and thrive) by its own devices.

Inside the congregation, most routine decision making takes place in the staff and in the boards of elders and trustees. Elders are primarily concerned with spiritual matters, trustees with the more mundane needs of the church. Elders are appointed by Pastor Tommy—seven men (no women), including himself and two other staff members. Eight laymen serve with the pastor as trustees. There is also a missions committee that screens requests for missions funds and promotes missions awareness in the congregation. And, of course, there is now a building committee. Whenever big decisions need to be made, the whole congregation is called into a business meeting; otherwise, the congregation meets only once a year to hear reports and approve a budget. By 1994, Pastor Tommy and other church leaders had realized that the number of people involved in leadership roles was in fact rather small, and they began to devise plans for training and deploying dozens of small-group leaders who could better connect grass-roots concerns to the program planning of the church.

Building plans, not surprisingly, have been the occasion for several congregational meetings and much discussion. Even with several hundred people in the room, there is lively debate, with extensive questions of the pastor, trustees, and building committee. The pastor sometimes wishes they would just trust their leaders, but he is very good-natured about encouraging the debate. When the first meeting in August 1992 did not resolve all the congregation's questions, the decision to build was put off until October. At this stage in the process, the congregation seemed to feel included, but there have been a few grumbles that most of the church's business is remarkably "top down." Indeed, with a core of only about a dozen laymen involved in decision-making bodies (and no regular newsletter that reports on issues and decisions facing the congregation), the remaining hundreds of members and regular attenders are remarkably uninvolved in governing themselves. The pastor's engaging, casual, and open style helps to alleviate these worries, but with a congregation full of skilled and educated members, plans for more leadership opportunities make sense.

CULTURE

If Northview's members are uninvolved in governing themselves, it may be because they are so busy attending Life Groups and going to church parties, going on mission trips and teaching Sunday school, learning to be Caregivers and going to prayer meetings, that there just is no time for committee meetings. This church's range of available activities for children, youth, and adults is so vast that it has published a directory. Adults, can choose from numerous Bible study classes, various fellowship groups and events, prayer groups, seminars on family life issues, a women's group, and opportunities to spend intensive time building up one's spiritual life. Of these latter, Discipleship Walks are probably the most popular. Similar to Cursillo weekends, they provide a place to talk with sympathetic others about the deepest joys and pains in life; people often find a strong sense of divine presence and healing in the prayer and testimonies and rituals of these weekend retreats.

Northview also offers ample opportunity for giving and receiving all sorts of care. The Counseling Center employs three full-time and two part-time counselors in a fee-for-service professional operation. Help in more routine matters is provided by the Caregivers, who have been trained to "apply the healing love, grace, and truth of Jesus Christ into hurting areas" of people's lives. The Healing Grace ministry offers those who have the spiritual gift of healing a chance to exercise it, while other groups simply mobilize to call visitors, pray for people in need, or take in food at times of family crisis. Others work with the benevolence group to hand out aid to needy families (mostly from outside the church). And there are at least three recovery and support groups—for women dealing with sexual abuse, for people with food addictions, and for codependents. While the language of therapy is superceded here by the language of spiritual discipline and healing, modern concerns for the psyche are as present at Northview as at any of the more liberal churches we studied.

The people at Northview, like suburbanites everywhere, experience the world as a stressful place. They are distressed by the materialism that surrounds them and the busyness of life—too many things, too much to do, too many places to go, too little time. For many, worship at Northview offers a window of calm in the midst of that busyness, a time of comfort and joy in the midst of stress. The singing, praying, and physical expressiveness of worship here help to create that sense of joy and calm and hope. When the pastor described the kind of world people live in, he named

> the fears of parents raising their kids in a society that's kind of like, "Hey, there are no rules out there!" Just the overwhelming nature of parents dealing with kids, people who are working in situations where their jobs are not secure, their marriages are under tremendous stress. I would say just the complexity and the level of stress that have all combined to create a rather crazy world system. That's what people carry in here. And Pentecostalism has traditionally provided an escape . . . [but] hopefully we're not doing that here. Hopefully a message is being preached that tells people, "Yeah, the world's tough and life's tough, and it's going to get tougher. But there is a hope here that sustains us, that we can find in our faith. Our *faith* gives us a hope that there really is a meaning here to all of this, and we can muddle through."

The pastor's sermons and the Bible study classes (and the Life Groups and all the other prayer and study opportunities) offer the chance to think through many of life's dilemmas. This is not the sort of place that emphasizes unbending old-fashioned rules for living (Thou shalt not's), but it is the sort of place that expects a high degree of spiritual discipline and offers the support for achieving it.

Being saved not only means an eternal reward in heaven but also God's presence and grace in this world. Northview participants often talk about what God does in the most mundane aspects of their lives, noting God's guidance in decisions large and small, even God's intervention in the circumstances of their lives. God, of course, has the help of a very active, well-organized congregation. For almost any need that arises, someone in the church can help. Even such secular activities as looking for jobs or buying and selling property are posted on the church's bulletin boards. But more than impersonal bulletin boards, the many small groups in the church are forums where everyday needs are shared and prayed over. Researcher Joan Cunningham's notes on one singles' group meeting included this description of their prayer requests. (The names have been changed.)

> Melissa has a problem at work with a superior who wants to get her fired, and Steve is worried about a meeting next week at work. Susan said this is her first-year anniversary with Bob, which is a record for her. At this time they are really looking for the Lord's guidance in their relationship. Jill is also having problems at work; she works at a day care, and the kids are driving her crazy. She doesn't have any money, and she hates where she lives. We all laughed at that one. Bonnie mentioned her surgery. Agnes had attended her best friend's wedding and said that she felt like she was losing a friend and that her friend might be moving away. She had tears in her eyes.

Each participant then prayed with one person next to them, asking especially for God's blessing on their concerns. God's calming presence is found, then, in the church's worship, but also in the support of fellow church members, and in everyday encounters with the Holy Spirit. Even if this congregation plays down its Pentecostal roots, the Holy Spirit is nonetheless central to its members' experience.

Worship at Northview draws on enough of the Pentecostal heritage to engage the feelings and imaginations of those who attend, although not enough to please those who, for instance, have the gift of tongues and wish they could more visibly exercise it. Traditional Pentecostals sometimes find this church too tame and go elsewhere. From both Pentecostalism and evangelicalism, Northview draws its strong emphasis on conversion and on sharing of faith. The emphasis on Bible study and on biblical preaching comes more from the evangelical side of the family, the pastor says. And there are even some high-church elements here. When communion is celebrated, for instance, the worshippers file forward to a pair of servers—one with bread, the other with a cup. They take the bread, then dip it into the cup. In liturgical churches, this is called *intinction*. Northview does not use the term, but it has borrowed the method. The pastor is also intent on introducing other practices and symbols from the larger church community, infusing them with new meaning as they are practiced in this charismatic congregation.

He is able to do this, in large part, because his congregation comes from a broad mix of denominational backgrounds. Only one in five grew up in Assemblies or other Pentecostal churches. About two in five grew up in Baptist, Methodist, or other evangelical churches, and another one in five grew up in more mainline Protestant churches. The remainder mostly had Catholic upbringings. As at St. Lawrence, a mobile suburban location has brought together a mix of people in a setting that has allowed them to draw freely on a variety of traditions, sometimes inventing their own.

Like other evangelical and Pentecostal congregations, Northview is very focused on missions. Each year, congregants spend a good portion of time listening to visiting missionaries tell their stories, especially during the week-long missions emphasis. They try to give 10 percent of their budget to various missions causes, and in 1992 they came close to achieving that goal, although other needs at the church always seem to cut missions giving somewhat short. Northview contributed toward the support of thirty mission families, as well as supporting a variety of social action agencies ($3,100 to World Vision, for instance) and carrying out its own mission efforts. At least once each year a team from the church embarks on a trip to Latin America, sometimes to help build church buildings, sometimes to teach Bible classes, help to recruit people, do puppet shows with children, and the like.

This mission work outside the United States is a curious parallel to members' work in their own community. Here too they focus on building church buildings and offering opportunities to engage in spiritual learning and disciplined living. Even people who come seeking a handout discover that this congregation wants to do more than offer a temporary fix. Through job counselors, legal counsel if necessary, and financial planners, those who receive immediate monetary aid also are helped to achieve the personal discipline and social support that will enable them to escape their misfortune for good. Beyond benevolence and counseling, however, Northview is relatively uninvolved in local community concerns. A few people have participated in some area pro-life activities, and the church serves as a polling station on election day. Otherwise, there is little mention of social issues or politics around Northview. The strong sense of these believers is that social change comes one person at a time.

SUMMARY

Northview Christian Life Church combines the entrepreneurial vision of its founder-pastor with the skills and resources of its members and participants. Together they have crafted a worship experience that draws on a variety of traditions to create the sort of calm and inspiration these busy suburbanites long for. Together they have developed a vast array of programming that meets social and spiritual needs. They provide especially for the personal spiritual and psychological needs of the members through counseling, other sorts of care giving, and multiple opportunities for retreat and renewal. The stresses of work and family and resisting a materialistic world are brought to the church, where they are reinterpreted by the experience of worship and the discipline of study and prayer with fellow believers. While this congregation may emphasize personal well-being, theirs is not an individualistic or self-sufficient message. It is in dependence on the church and on God that people find the inner strength to live in a difficult world.

Conclusion

Integration and an influx of liberal young professionals transformed Oak Park, Illinois. The alternative businesses located in Little Five Points and the affordable housing of the neighborhood transformed Candler Park, in Atlanta, Georgia, into a hospitable place for lesbians, gays, and others who want a diverse neighborhood. And explosive suburban growth transformed the small-town landscapes of Carmel, Indiana, and Lawrenceville in Gwinnett County, Georgia, into magnets drawing together people from every region and tradition. All four of these "new" congregations have been built in the midst of the growth and change that surrounds them and clearly reflect the character of those changes. Good Shepherd Lutheran and Epworth United Methodist each serve their new communities in the way their former incarnations served the old. St. Lawrence Catholic and Northview Christian Life were both created by the disparate, mobile suburbanites who found themselves in a new place in the 1970s and 80s. St. Lawrence serves its immediate "parish," while Northview has created a suburban niche that draws on a somewhat larger geographic region.

These congregations share a sense of being something new and a sense of freedom to experiment with ways of worshipping and ministering that draw on the various traditions people bring to the place, as well as meeting the needs they find when they get there. All engage in liturgical innovation, ranging from St. Lawrence's glass altar to Good Shepherd's alternative liturgies, Northview's combination of evangelical and Pentecostal styles, and Epworth's occasional moments of spontaneity. All have mobile constituencies who bring a variety of traditions into the mix. None have to contend with a single tradition that locks it into "the way it's always been done here."

They stand in varying relationships to an official denomination, but all have carved out space in which to work. Even St. Lawrence and Epworth seem to have more support than interference from their hierarchies. Good Shepherd is in a very similar position, and Northview works essentially on its own. Each has received some sort of boost from a group that believed in it. In Northview's case, it was a sponsoring congregation. In the other three, it was some initial sponsorship and support from their denomination. But in each case (except Epworth), that initial sponsorship has long since ceased to be essential.

All four of these congregations are remarkably focused on personal well-being, including therapy, and each supplies its own form of spiritual renewal. Good Shepherd is more focused on social issues and political action than are the two new-suburbs churches or Epworth. But all four are busy places, offering a wide range of opportunities for involvement. They are also well-resourced places. All have very well educated congregations, and on average the highest family incomes of any group of congregations in the study. They differ most in the degree to which they are able to call on the resources of their members. The intense commitment of Northview stands in contrast to the very low levels of giving and participation at St. Lawrence and Good Shepherd, now that they have achieved stability and success. Epworth stands midrange, apparently calling on extra energies as it engages in its rebuilding process.

With resources and freedom—and a setting that called forth innovation—each of these congregations has created a ministry attuned to the needs of a constituency brought together out of social change. Individual religious entrepreneurs and resourceful denominations have both contributed to the remaking of the religious landscape in these changed communities. While some congregations were moving, others adapting, and others declining, new congregations were completing the picture. The demographic changes that transformed Oak Park, Carmel, Candler Park, and Gwinnett County also generated the need for the communal spaces invented and reinvented by these congregations. Although each is highly attuned to the individual needs of its seeker constituents, each is also creating a community in which those needs are expressed and often transformed, in which individuals join with others in reaching beyond themselves.

CHAPTER 8

How Congregations Change

As the ebb and flow of demographic and economic change reconfigure urban neighborhoods, the institutions anchored there inevitably change, as well. Both the social dislocations and the social energies of urban life are channeled through congregations. As old communities disperse, so do the congregations that served them. As new communities coalesce, it is often around congregational life that they form a sense of identity. Whether in the immigrant parishes of earlier days (and today) or in the parishes serving stressed-out suburban managers, the concerns of everyday life lie at the heart of what happens in a congregation. As those concerns are redefined by shifts in the economy or the population, the array of religious organizations in a community will be altered, as well.

Shifting Religious Ecologies

Having looked intensively at twenty-three congregations that have faced such dislocations, it is time again to take the larger view of these nine communities, to remind ourselves of the larger patterns of change in which the twenty-three are lodged. The story of each community's religious ecology is bigger than the stories of the few congregations we selected for study.

In Long Beach, California, for instance, the struggle to rebuild the downtown did not begin soon enough to head off strong out-migration, which had a dramatically negative impact on all of the area's large urban churches.[1] Most have been through at least two decades of decline, and many have fewer than one hundred in weekly attendance. They fit the same patterns we saw in chapter 2—scattered members, a younger generation moving away, little programming, and no outreach. They have little energy for responding to the lesbian and gay presence in their community (or to the growing immigrant population—not the focus of our study, but nonetheless an important reality here).

As Long Beach's gay community gained visibility and confidence, its members began to press the religious economy for a viable, integrated religious life. Two new congregations were formed: a Metropolitan Community Church founded in 1971, a gay congregation especially active in supporting gay causes, and Christ Chapel, more Pentecostal in worship style and less visible in political style, but no less committed to supporting lesbian and gay persons.[2] These new congregations did not, however, meet everyone's religious needs. Many gay and lesbian people wanted to worship alongside straight people, and to be a part of the religious traditions in which they grew up. Congregations like First Congregational and St. Matthew's have responded to this need. Many gays and lesbians had been in the churches all along, simply invisible. One gay man described what happened when he began attending a mainline Protestant congregation in the area. "We first started going there, my lover and I, about seven, eight years, a little over seven years ago. We, you know, literally after church, during coffee hour, just sort of stood there and talked to each other. No one came over to talk to us. But we could look around, and just our sixth sense said, well there's plenty of gay people here, it's just that they're not very open. And that turned out to be true, actually." Over the years, that congregation came to treat these two men as a couple. They were included in all aspects of the church's life, even though some members continued to refer to them as "nice young bachelors."

Except for the routine protests at the Gay Pride Parade, overt religious opposition to gays and lesbians in Long Beach is almost nonexistent. We had a hard time finding anyone who wanted to publicly condemn gay people. Most congregations have not openly acknowledged the presence of gays and lesbians in their midst, but most do not openly condemn them either. First Congregational is certainly more activist than most, and even St. Matthew's is more open than most.

Congregations that choose to move toward more openness have the support of the local ecumenical body, the South Coast Ecumenical Association. With support from most of the mainline religious bodies in town, this association serves as a vehicle for many community concerns, especially poverty and homelessness. An association official recounted, "About a year ago . . . [we] decided to form a task force or subcommittee on gay, lesbian, and bisexual persons to help increase dialogue and understanding. . . . We've also been gathering a list of churches that are open to gay people so that when people call the council we will be able to give out a list of churches."

The congregations in Long Beach are confronted by a community vastly different from the Protestant, white, family-oriented "Iowa by the Sea" of years gone by. With more ethnic diversity, more uncertainty in the economy, and a visible gay and lesbian community with which to contend, many have not survived, while others have been formed as specific responses to the new populations in the area, and still others are slowly acknowledging the changes within their own walls.

In Candler Park, Georgia, the starting point for response to a lesbian and gay population was not so much a collection of mainline downtown churches as the typical array of southern evangelical Protestant alternatives. In 1970, Baptists, Methodists, and Presbyterians accounted for half the congregations in the neighborhood, with Lutherans, Episcopalians, and Catholics, a Maronite congregation, and the Salvation Army rounding out the mix. But since 1970, many of those congregations have undergone the same sorts of decline we have seen elsewhere—constituents moving away, a younger generation not recruited, loss of contact with the immediate neighborhood.

In the midst of that decline, however, there has been tremendous religious innovation. An ashram of Krishna followers has been organized, as has a congregation of the Metropolitan Community Church (the same gay/lesbian-oriented denomination that established a congregation in Long Beach). Two black churches have moved in, as have white churches as diverse as Primitive Baptist and Church of God, Cleveland, on one side and Anglo-Catholic and Orthodox on another. A Friends meeting has recently built a new building in the area, and a gay and lesbian Reconstructionist Jewish group uses the building, as well. When First Existentialist moved into its building across from the park, it was but a small part of this growing diversity. Between First Existentialist, the Metropolitan Community Church, and the Reconstructionist Jewish gathering, there are three dominantly gay congregations. In addition, a few of the mainline Protestant congregations are quietly open to those in the gay and lesbian population who wish to attend more traditional services. A nearby Catholic parish also has a gay outreach, somewhat similar to that at St. Matthew's in Long Beach.

When the Atlanta Gay Pride Parade is held each year, numerous religious groups participate—although they complain about being stuck at the end of the line of march. In 1992, more than 250 people gathered at the Shrine of the Immaculate Conception for an interfaith celebration during Pride Week. Although many, perhaps most, lesbian and gay people feel alienated from religious communities, in Atlanta, including the Candler Park neighborhood, those who wish to join in have a good deal of religious activity to choose from.

The religious starting point for Allston-Brighton, Massachusetts, differed from that in either Long Beach or Candler Park. That Boston neighborhood had been dominated by Catholic parishes for more than a century, with St. Columbkille's the largest at twelve hundred families.[3] With recent immigration, both it and St. Gabriel's have one Spanish-language Mass each weekend, and St. Columbkille's has a ministry to the new wave of Irish immigrants. St. Catherine's, as we saw, is the site for the Boston archdiocesan apostolate for Salvadorans. Other non-English-speaking groups are encouraged to find equivalent apostolates in their language in other parts of the city.

The few mainline Protestant churches in Allston-Brighton are, without exception, small, and only Brighton Evangelical Congregational has any significant non-Anglo membership. Several, however, house immigrant congregations in their buildings, although the immigrant groups tend to be aligned with a denomination other than that of the sheltering church, generally an evangelical group. Even though there was virtually no evangelical or Pentecostal presence in Allston-Brighton before about 1980, all the new immigrant congregations are either Catholic or evangelical Protestant. Altogether, since 1980, the community has birthed at least two Hispanic, one Chinese, one Korean, three Haitian, three Brazilian, and one African congregation, only one of which has its own building.

One new consortium of six congregations shares converted commercial space, one of the more innovative arrangements we encountered.[4] The Anglo congregation in the mix is as new as the others. Its pastor and his ordained wife are the primary staff for the effort, but each congregation has its own leadership, and all are represented on a decision-making body that determines financial arrangements, times of building use, and the like. All the congregations are basically evangelical in focus, but no single denominational identity binds them together. As each grows, its position in the consortium can be reevaluated. By sharing resources, each congregation gains strength (and autonomy) it might not otherwise have.

Some of the immigrant congregations in Allston-Brighton also get help from the Emmanuel Gospel Center (EGC), an urban ministry group that serves the entire Boston region. EGC's staff includes a minister for Hispanic churches and one for Haitians. The Hispanic minister described his work of networking and support this way: "Everybody comes [to new congregations] mainly because of the language barrier first—secondly, because they do not know the Anglo system, or English system, the way the city is run. So a pastor will need some information; if he doesn't have it he will tend to call the Gospel Center and say, 'Do you know anybody who can help me with this?'" EGC supports immigrant congregations of all types (not just evangelicals) and tries to help them stay in touch with each other. It is challenging work. In the last five years, the number of immigrant congregations has nearly doubled in the city. While in Allston-Brighton congregations like St.

Catherine's are in serious decline, many others are being founded, and a very few, like Brighton Evangelical Congregational, are integrating the immigrants into existing congregational structures.

Still another configuration of religious organizations was the starting point in Los Angeles's West Adams neighborhood. Here were African American congregations from the full array of Baptist, African Methodist, and Pentecostal denominations, along with several churches from predominantly white Protestant groups that had changed hands during the sixties. A handful of West Adams's African American congregations were beginning to lose significant numbers of members by the early 1990s, but others were as strong as ever and consistently active and visible as political, social, and economic advocates. Large congregations that serve as rallying points in the community, along with Holman United Methodist, include, First A.M.E., Trinity Baptist, and First A.M.E. Zion. When violence broke out in April 1992, these churches were on the front lines of the salvage operation. First A.M.E., in fact, became a familiar sight to television viewers all over the nation, as community leaders gathered there to try to discern how to respond to the destruction that years of frustration had finally wrought.

None of these congregations, however, has a significant immigrant presence. Traditionally, *Hispanic* has meant *Catholic,* and three of the four Catholic parishes in West Adams have added Spanish-language Masses as the immigrants poured in. (The fourth, a Polish parish in the neighborhood since soon after World War II, is a niche congregation serving a large, scattered, Polish-immigrant constituency.) The equation of Latino and Catholic no longer holds, however; and established black churches have been joined in West Adams storefronts by an equal number of churches where Spanish is spoken. A few established congregations rent space in their buildings to new immigrant congregations, as well, often mirroring the pattern of "sheltered" congregations we saw in Allston-Brighton.

In West Adams, the array of new alternatives was considerably wider than that in Boston, however. Recent additions included two Buddhist temples and two Islamic centers (one Black Muslim and one Middle Eastern). By the time we were trying to count congregations in 1992, about half of the forty-seven we could find belonged in the African American tradition, one-third were predominantly Hispanic, and the remainder were mostly Asian. Although we have founding dates on only nineteen of those congregations, at least 20 percent of those had been founded or moved into the neighborhood since 1980. While some congregations are in decline, then, and some are adapting, the most prevalent response here is religious innovation. New congregations are being founded rapidly, taking advantage of whatever transfer of resources they can manage from existing congregations.

The disturbances of April 1992 posed a real challenge to the congregations in this neighborhood. Cooperation and voluntary action were widespread in the immediate aftermath; in the weeks that followed, some congregations added job programs and gang reconciliation efforts. As a symbol of the efforts to rebuild—and an endorsement of the cooperation this crisis called forth—religious and civic leaders organized "Hands across L.A." On 14 June, six weeks after the uprisings, people from community organizations across the city made a human chain running the length of Western Avenue through South Central. They came to demonstrate their solidarity with the neighborhood and with each other, forming a striking tableau indeed. Researcher Bob Pierson and I drove up Western as the crowd was gathering and then joined the line with the people from First A.M.E. Among the groups we saw along our drive were representatives of several Jewish temples, a couple of groups of Buddhists, at least one contingent of Krishna followers, and Korean women in long, brocaded, pastel dresses. One group of Asian women stood in dramatic traditional white hats and long dresses in front of a three-story burned-out building, like delicate flowers sprouting from the rubble. Across the street, a huge group of Mormons in white shirts and black skirts or slacks gathered next to a group with a Sri Lanka–America sign. Nearby stood a small Episcopal group with an elegant banner and a U.S. flag, several religious science groups, one group apparently in fervent prayer as we drove by, and an occasional Roman Catholic sister. Ministers had worn their most spectacular attire—everything from stoles of African weaves to long black robes and plain clerical collars. There was even one small group of Sikhs. And, of course, there were hundreds of people from all sorts of African American churches and people with no visible affiliation at all. At three o'clock, we all joined hands and sang "We Shall Overcome." This rainbow of religious and ethnic diversity represented both challenge and hope for this troubled neighborhood, a dramatic example of the central role of congregations in generating the social capital necessary to sustain a troubled community.

While West Adams is part of a community that often feels powerless in the face of injustice and deprivation, Oak Park, Illinois, sits firmly within the old Establishment, and its religious ecology reflects that position. Forty percent of the community's congregations are white mainline Protestant.[5] The vast majority were founded before World War II, and several occupy impressive Gothic or romanesque buildings on the town's main street. In fact, the Protestant establishment was strong enough well into this century to prevent the building of a Catholic church on that thoroughfare. Today, however, there are four Roman Catholic and two Orthodox churches in town, along with a Baha'i congregation and three Jewish synagogues—two Reform and one

Conservative; the Catholic and Jewish congregations are among the biggest in the community. Many of the Protestant churches, including some in the center of town, have experienced significant decline in the last two decades and now have congregations of less then one hundred worshipers. Those who have sought out the liberal, integrated community that Oak Park has become are more religiously diverse than were its former residents.

Few of the congregations in Oak Park have achieved the level of integration of the community as a whole, however. Most, if not all, are theoretically open to nonwhite members, and over half the white congregations reported at least some minority participation; but in only about one in five is that participation higher than 10 percent. African Americans who have moved into Oak Park have evidently not joined the existing congregations in any great numbers. City Baptist is definitely an exception, not the rule. Nor are African Americans attending the four predominantly black congregations in Oak Park. Integrating the church population has been less a priority than integrating the housing stock. As late as 1988, the village board resisted the efforts of a black congregation to purchase a building on the main street. The African Americans we spoke with said that most black Oak Park residents simply do not go to church in the community. They may travel back to an old neighborhood or not go to church at all. Oak Park's pattern of religious change, then, has included some decline, as old Oak Parkers moved away, and a small amount of religious innovation, fitting the needs of the more religiously varied residents who now make Oak Park home. There has been less adaptation, however, than might be expected in this liberal enclave.

Anderson, Indiana, was anything but a liberal enclave when economic disaster struck there. Like Oak Park's, its history is overwhelmingly Protestant, but Anderson is also distinguished by its impressive number of churches—121 Christian congregations, 113 of them Protestant.[6] As the world headquarters for the Church of God, Anderson is home to nine congregations from that denomination, but at least forty other denominations have congregations here, many of them within the broad stream we usually identify as evangelicalism. Anderson is a church-building town, and most of the churches it builds are conservative and evangelical.

In the midst of the city's economic woes, those congregations survived but did not thrive. Fewer new congregations were founded than in some other communities, and most old ones are simply holding their own. The declining population and economic fortunes of Anderson seem also to have precipitated a certain amount of jockeying for position relative to limited resources. We focused on three congregations that were moving from one part of town to another, and they will join at least seven others that have moved since 1980. Where adaptation took place, it was mostly of the rather invisible sort we saw at Grace Baptist. There is little to indicate that the overall conservative religious ecology has been altered by Anderson's economic hard times.

The story is similar in southwest Atlanta, whose religious ecology, revolutionized in the 1960s, shows few signs of changing in response to recent economic shifts. In the midst of the earlier residential and commercial transition that swept the neighborhood, religious institutions were transformed.[7] Some white churches simply sold their buildings and left. Other white churches (especially those in denominations with buildings owned by the hierarchy) more or less quickly evacuated their old membership, leaving a new black constituency to represent the denomination. A few congregations, like Incarnation Episcopal, tried to establish an integrated constituency. At the same time, black congregations from elsewhere in the city moved in. Some bought the buildings being vacated by fleeing whites, and others built new buildings of their own. Our information on the seventy-one congregations we found in this neighborhood is quite sketchy. About one-fifth are affiliated with traditionally white denominations and used-to-be-white congregations. Another third (37 percent) are affiliated with traditionally black groups, and most of them moved into the neighborhood since the 1950s. Of the remainder, mostly independent evangelical and Pentecostal groups, we know less about when they arrived or who they currently serve.

Within this array of congregations are both tiny storefronts and well-established churches with a reputation as centers for the black community, Ralph David Abernathy's West Hunter Street Baptist being the most prominent. There are newcomers on the religious scene, as well: a Black Muslim mosque, the Hillside International Truth Center, and the Pan African Orthodox Christian Church (the latter two with very large congregations). That combination of established black churches with nontraditional religions is unlikely to change in the near future. Both traditional and nontraditional groups are confronting the economic diversity of the community with the full gamut of responses, from decline to successful adaptation to the birthing of new congregations.

While economic declines seem to challenge congregations to hold on, offering them little in the way of resources for growth, the economic boom that accompanies suburbanization is the opposite. Indeed the communities with proportionately the most new congregations were Carmel, Indiana, and Gwinnett County, Georgia. As Carmel began to grow, people in various denominational headquarters tagged it as a promising place to "plant" a church.[8] At the turn of the century, Carmel had five churches, at the end of World War II, eight. Since 1980, at least fourteen new churches have been founded, bringing

Carmel's total to forty-two. That rate of growth, however, does not correspond to population growth. At the end of World War II, there was a congregation for about every one hundred citizens. Today, the ratio is about one to every six hundred. That does not necessarily mean that fewer Carmelites attend church, only that the churches they attend are bigger than those of half a century ago.

Like Anderson, Carmel is overwhelmingly Protestant and dominantly conservative. The two Catholic parishes are, however, quite large, as are several of the liberal Protestant churches. At least half a dozen churches in Carmel—of all types—average more than five hundred in Sunday attendance. One of the newest, an independent evangelical fellowship founded in 1991, is already putting over seven hundred people into its rented warehouse space each week. Although other Carmel congregations have used rented school space in their early days, as soon as they can afford it (which usually is not long), each new congregation builds a building. People report that Carmel's churches seemed to be in a continual "building campaign." Homes for congregations are being built almost as fast as are homes for the town's residents.

The same is surely true in Gwinnett County. Local school buildings are often full on Sunday mornings, in use by whatever new congregation has most recently been birthed.[9] But the new additions are still largely of the same varieties that have always characterized the small-town South. As growth began to occur, denominational church planters targeted this county, as well. The Southern Baptists had a full-time person working at the task, and between 1980 and 1992, the denomination went from twenty-nine to sixty-one churches in the county. In 1970, the section of the county we studied was populated exclusively by traditional southern evangelical denominations—eight Baptist, seven Methodist, one Presbyterian, and one Disciples. Since that time, the Baptists and Methodists have added new congregations, and they have been joined by several nondenominational churches, a Lutheran congregation, and a new Cumberland Presbyterian church that is meeting in a movie theater. The only real variety comes from the new Unitarian church—and three large new Catholic parishes.

That seeming continuity masks, however, the changes going on inside Gwinnett's churches. Many realize that the county's growth presents them with an unprecedented opportunity, but they have no idea how to take advantage of it. A visit to their services is a step back in time. (Several still sing from shape-note hymnals.) A country Pentecostal church, at the end of a long unpaved driveway, continues its traditional revival services with their antiworldly messages. Another Pentecostal group that holds its revival under a tent has continued run-ins with the local police over neighbors' complaints about noise levels.

A small-town Baptist church planning to build a new building does not want to grow "too big." As one longtime member described his congregation, "We're good-hearted country folks just trying to do right."

When these church members say they do not want to grow *too* much, they undoubtedly have in mind the several "megachurches" that have joined the religious landscape of Gwinnett County. In the area we studied, the most prominent was Hebron Baptist, which has posed a significant challenge to every other church around.[10] Like mom-and-pop businesses competing with WalMart, they feel embattled. But some congregations are surviving nicely, growing apace. The old downtown Baptist church in Lawrenceville has retained much of its small-town establishment character, while growing at a moderate rate. The new Church of God, on the other hand, has adopted a distinctly uptown flavor, with its beautifully furnished new building dubbed a "Worship Centre." The message still sounds antiworldly, but the setting would put the most comfortable suburbanite at ease.

The Church of God, one of five area congregations that boast more than 750 in attendance each Sunday, sits next to one of the others—St. Lawrence. Twenty years ago, a large Catholic church in the heart of Lawrenceville would have been as unimaginable as the upscale Pentecostal church next door. Yet Gwinnett County has learned to imagine all sorts of new things; there is no escaping the suburban sprawl, although lots of people and a fair number of congregations are trying to do just that. Almost without trying, however, new congregations are being born, an above-average number are growing, and many of the old ones have significantly changed their styles of worship and modes of operation. Some of Gwinnett County's churches will decline and fail, but far more will take advantage of the abundance of human resources pouring into the area to construct and adapt congregations for the future.

In all nine communities, the organizational responses of congregations include maintaining the status quo, resistance, relocation, and various forms of internal and external alterations in programming. The results range from severe decline to growth and transformation. While our data on the 449 congregations we surveyed in these communities are admittedly incomplete, we can extrapolate from them to estimate that 21 percent of the congregations that existed in 1992 had been founded since 1980. An additional 7 percent, founded earlier, had moved into their current location since 1980 (see table 8.1). We cannot estimate how many of those currently in the community will move elsewhere.

Of the congregations in existence before 1980, the best measure we have of adaptation is their reported growth in membership; those that were growing were also likely to have new programming in effect.

Table 8.1. Changes in Congregational Ecologies by Type of Community Change

	Percentage in suburbanizing communities	Percentage in other communities	Percentage in all communities
Congregations founded since 1980	33%	17%*	21%*
Congregations moved in since 1980	6	8	7
Older congregations that are growing	38	15	21
Older congregations that are stable	16	31	27
Older congregations that are declining	7	28	23
Total	100%	99%**	99%**
(Number of cases)	(70)	(225)	(295)

*In West Adams, southwest Atlanta, and Candler Park we have reason to believe that there are more new congregations than these numbers reflect.
**Column does not add to 100% due to rounding.

These growing congregations constitute about 21 percent of the total. However, more than half of them are located in Carmel and Gwinnett. When those two resource-rich suburbanizing communities are excluded, only about fifteen percent of all the congregations on which we have information seem to have adapted and grown in the face of population shifts and economic adversity.

In those same challenging communities, declining congregations constitute 28 percent of the total, with the remaining 31 percent holding their own, stable in membership at least for the time being. Most of these have added no new programming and show few signs of attempting to adapt. We can guess that their days of membership stability may be numbered. Fully 59 percent of the congregations whose communities have undergone population and economic shifts, then, appear to have chosen to maintain their existing identities. About half of them are already in decline, while many of the remainder will likely begin to decline in the years ahead.

In contrast, only 7 percent of Carmel and Gwinnett County's congregations have declined. As we saw, suburbanization does not guarantee success; the integration of urban newcomers can pose serious challenges.[11] However, the influx of large numbers of child-rearing families provides most congregations with exactly the constituents they can most easily pursue. Indeed, only 16 percent of the congregations in these suburbanizing communities are merely stable.

These nine communities, then, began with very different arrays of religious institutions. In every case, the social changes experienced have meant shifts in the array. In most cases it has become more varied. In many cases one kind of religious group has lost strength, while others have gained. The types of change present in the community affect the range of responses likely to be seen among the congregations. Growth of new populations, for instance, leads to the establishment of new congregations, while economic decline leads to reshuffling, both within and among congregations. Cultural immigrants, rather than the geographic kind, are more easily absorbed into existing structures. Race and ethnicity, however, remain major barriers that sexual orientation and exurban migration are not. Congregations are more likely to establish "sheltered" congregations or simply rent out their buildings than to set up integrated ministries.

While the ratio of congregations to population has declined in some instances, that change seems more a matter of increased congregational size than of declining overall participation. It appears that new congregations are being founded at a pace likely to offset the slow deaths of old congregations and likely to reflect the shifts of populations from declining neighborhoods to growing ones. Both suburban growth and the influx of non-U.S. immigrants has resulted in congregational growth, adaptation, and—especially—entrepreneurship. While we found many congregations in the throes of decline and many others biding their time, we also found tremendous organizational vitality. When we consider the religious ecology as a whole, adaptation and innovation are at least as visible as decline and death.

Explaining Adaptation

In the long view, the question of congregational health may best be answered by looking at the whole population of congregations, assessing how the entire array best fits a changing environment. In the shorter view, we may also ask how any given congregation survives such challenges. How are new and adapting congregations different from those that merely hold their own or decline? What factors in their available resources, their ways of making decisions, and their internal cultures make some congregations good candidates for surviving major environmental change, while others become part of the cycle of organizational decline and death?

With the twenty-three cases we have examined, some patterns and tendencies are apparent. Perhaps the most striking pattern in the summary of responses and outcomes presented in table 8.2 is the relationship between *trying* to change and achieving change. Of those currently experiencing serious declines in membership and resources, all have

Table 8.2. Responses and Outcomes among Study Congregations

Outcome	Congregational Response		
	Active resistance	No change	New programs attempted
Decline	Brighton Avenue Baptist, Allston-Brighton Gray Friends Meeting, Carmel	Carmel Wesleyan, Carmel St. Catherine's, Allston-Brighton	*Berean Seventh-Day Adventist, West Adams*
Relocation	First Baptist, Anderson East Lynn Christian, Anderson	South Meridian Church of God, Anderson	
Niche identity		*Holman United Methodist, West Adams* *Incarnation Episcopal, Southwest Atlanta*	
New constituents and/or structures			St. Matthews, Long Beach First Existentialist, Candler Park First Congregational, Long Beach City Baptist, Oak Park Brighton Evangelical Congregational, Allston-Brighton *Hinton United Methodist, Gwinnett County* Carmel United Methodist, Carmel Grace Baptist, Anderson Hope Baptist, Southwest Atlanta

Table 8.2. *(Continued)*

	Congregational Response		
Outcome	Active resistance	No change	New programs attempted
New or reborn congregation			St. Lawrence, Gwinnett County Northview Christian Life, Carmel Good Shepherd Lutheran, Oak Park *Epworth United Methodist, Candler Park*

NOTE: Congregations in italics are ones about whose future we are uncertain. They are placed here based on our best estimate of the outcome they face.

either actively resisted change or have continued with existing patterns, apparently unable to envision how things might be different. While we cannot say whether congregations outside our study population also tried new programs and failed, we can say that congregations that do *not* try new programs and new forms of outreach when they are faced with environmental change are not likely to survive past the life spans of their current members. Four of our study congregations persisted unchanged and now find themselves in serious states of decline that put their near-term survival in question.

The one congregation that may break this pattern is West Adams's Berean Seventh-Day Adventist. It does seem to be trying to adopt new programming that will appeal to the neighborhood (Spanish translators and the like) but may not succeed. A pattern of decline has been in place, and an older leadership seems reluctant to let go. They are already in effect a niche congregation, drawing black Seventh-Day Adventists from a wide area. However, there are other competitors in their niche, and there may not be enough of that specialized population to go around.

It is, however, possible for a congregation to keep its essential identity and programming intact through other, more active survival strategies. Those that seek out a new location and those that create an appeal to a nonneighborhood population are engaging in strategies designed to protect their organizational survival. While establishing a niche identity appears to be an increasingly effective strategy in a mobile and cosmopolitan society, it is not an entirely new one. H. Paul Douglass describes similar congregations in the 1920s, and Gaylord Noyce lists such magnet congregations as among the responses to urban change in the 1960s.[12] The ability to sustain a congregation that is not identified with its immediate neighborhood depends on both the particular identity chosen and the resources available to sustain it. The chosen identity must be specialized enough to distinguish it from others, but not so specialized as to have no possible constituents.[13] The niche may be defined by all Swedish Lutherans in an area with no other Swedish Lutheran congregations, for instance. Should all the Swedish Lutherans become so assimilated as to make their ethnicity irrelevant, however, the congregation may have lost the resources necessary for sustaining its life in that niche. People are willing to drive out of their immediate neighborhoods to attend congregations that offer programs and styles of worship that are not widely available and are especially suited to their own particular needs. They must, however, know about them, which requires a well-connected membership. Niche congregations need members who have extensive connections in the community by way of which they can recruit persons who occupy the same population or categories of identity.

Sustaining a long-term identity in a given place, transferring that identity to a new place, or transforming it into a regional magnet are three very different responses to neighborhood change, but all maintain a congregation's historic character and programming. In that way, they stand in contrast to new and adapting congregations. It is time to look more closely at that contrast.

RESOURCES

When we compare the membership and budget sizes of the congregations that have adapted with those that have not, stark differences emerge. The congregations that have begun new programs have today, on average, far larger memberships and far bigger budgets than do the congregations that have maintained existing patterns. However, this difference is much more a *result* of their response to change than a predictor of it. Brighton Avenue Baptist, First Baptist of Anderson, and St. Catherine's in Allston-Brighton, which all used to have stable memberships and ample budgets, were not prevented from changing by numerical or monetary weakness. In fact, both the rebirth of Oak Park's Good Shepherd Lutheran and the active ministries of tiny Brighton Evangelical Congregational demonstrate that the decision to adapt can come in spite of radically depleted coffers.

Obtaining monetary support from a denomination to replenish those coffers is a mixed blessing. In no case was denominational support sufficient to make the difference between death and survival. Some congregations received support when they were already in desperate straits. Carmel Wesleyan and St. Catherine's in Allston-Brighton are examples of this pattern. In both cases, hierarchical denominations made decisions about providing subsidies that the congregations themselves felt little control over. Most members at St. Catherine's did not even know such a subsidy was being provided. In these cases, denominational money increased a feeling of helplessness, even as it staved off immediate financial disaster. Good Shepherd Lutheran and Hinton United Methodist in Gwinnett County, on the other hand, received money as "redevelopment congregations." The money, which came as part of each congregation's decision to seek change and growth, increased the congregation's sense of powerfulness when it was ready to act. It appears, then, that when denominational money is an expression of a partnership with the congregation (and when the congregation's own budget is still reasonably sound), this material resource can be quite useful.

The material resource that plays a more consistent role in the process of responding to change is the congregation's building. A building that places high demands on the congregation's other resources seems to be an impediment to creative adaptation. Carmel Wesleyan, St. Catherine's, Brighton Avenue Baptist, and East Lynn Christian and First Baptist in Anderson have all had excessive recent costs for repair, rebuilding, heating, security, and the like. These are also congregations whose strong attachment to their buildings is often out of touch with the church's current needs and uses. They return each week to buildings that hold sacred memories, rather than using their property as an asset for current needs. They have neither the resources to restore the buildings to their former glory nor to turn them into new centers for ministry activity. Old buildings directly effect the ability of congregations both to engage in certain activities and to imagine what those activities might be.

Potent here is the combination of the material drains imposed by deteriorating buildings and the way the congregation interprets its material situation. Material resources do not have an unmediated force of their own. Even severe difficulties with a building can be overcome. Among the congregations that have engaged in significant adaptation and innovation, Anderson's Grace Baptist and First Congregational in Long Beach faced material challenges equal to any faced by those that have remained unchanged. Both had buildings in serious need of repair and renovation and found in those projects tangible ways to express their commitment to renewal. Still, serious building costs have faced proportionately more of the congregations now in decline than of those that have changed in more positive ways. That some congregations overcome such liabilities does not negate the larger pattern of difficulty.

Unlike business organizations faced with changing markets, voluntary organizations can operate with a reduced resource base, drawing on human investments to compensate for and transform the material resources they may lack. Church members are not there, after all, primarily for material rewards or to provide material goods to a market, but for social and spiritual rewards that can be generated with relatively small investments of actual capital. What seems far more important than material resources for the survival of these voluntary organizations are the human resources that make it possible for change to be imagined and planned for. Someone has to see the connections between the congregation as it now exists and the congregation as it might someday exist. Someone has to imagine that it might remain spiritually and socially rewarding for its participants. Such human resources involve both the clergy and the laity, both those who provide leadership and those who must lend their energies to any effort for change. While lay leadership is important, pastors emerged here as critical players in the process of change.

The key role played by pastoral leadership can be seen in the stories of congregations like Oak Park's Good Shepherd Lutheran, where new pastor Jack Finney spearheaded efforts to make the congregation known in the community and to provide worship and support for newcomers who began to visit. It can also be seen in the story of Long Beach's First Congregational, where Mary Ellen Kilsby's energy, persistence, vision, and political savvy made it possible for the church to embrace their new lesbian and gay constituents. It can be seen in the dynamic worship, new decision-making structures, and innovative ministries introduced by Pastor Jackson at Atlanta's Hope Baptist, and in the entrepreneurial strategies of Tommy Paino, founding pastor of Northview Christian Life in Carmel. It can be seen in the patient educational and organizational work of Pastor Crockett that turned around the financial morass at Grace Baptist in Anderson. It can also be seen in the multicultural skills brought to Oak Park's City Baptist by Pastor Bill Smith, whose commitment to community involvement, integrated worship styles, and aggressive lay leadership training has been the catalyst for the successful integration of that congregation. And in spite of the conflict he precipitated, an equal measure of leadership strength can be seen in Joe Emerson's breaking up of the old elite at Carmel United Methodist so as to open the church's structures to more mobile newcomers.

For all of these pastors, strong leadership also meant strong lay participation. In some cases, highly educated professional congregations would hardly have stood for less. They expected their pastors to be effective managers and visionary leaders, but they also expected to be consulted, to be involved in shaping policy, to exercise their own managerial and planning skills. In other cases, less well educated congregations were intentionally trained and included by pastor-educators. Pastor Crockett and Pastor Smith are both notable for their efforts to train a corps of lay leaders from among people without the obvious status credentials prevalent at someplace like Carmel United Methodist or Good Shepherd Lutheran. The members at Grace Baptist and City Baptist are smart people. Although most do not have graduate degrees, and most do not engage in planning and managing in their secular work, they have a kind of practical wisdom the churches needed. Their pastors offered them opportunities to learn management skills so as to place their wisdom in the service of their churches.

Not every congregation that has adapted has a strong pastor, but most do. Pastors in the status quo congregations, by contrast, tended not to introduce new ideas and programs. Most provided excellent care for the people in their congregations and performed well the duties expected of them. Most fit nicely with their parishioners, working hard to maintain the pattern of church life all of them expected. If they perceived any need for change, they were unwilling or unable to undertake the difficult (and often conflictual) work of dislodging old routines. A few expressed to us their sense that their leadership skills were simply not up to the challenges they knew the congregation faced. Others simply pastored the best they knew how.

A few of the declining congregations, however, had at some point in their histories had strong pastors who attempted to lead them toward change. Brighton Avenue Baptist and Gray Friends Meeting in Carmel both forced out pastors who tried to push them in directions they did not wish to go, which makes clear that strong pastoral leadership alone is not sufficient to create organizational adaptation. Also essential are responsive, imaginative, and energetic lay persons willing to participate in the necessary processes of change and to alter a rewarding pattern of involvements for something they hope will be better. For the members of these congregations, participation in a worship routine they have long valued with people who have been friends for decades is a reward they are reluctant to forfeit. New programs and new constituents promise more strain and difficulty than immediate reward.

Ironically, nonadapting congregations have far higher levels of commitment than do adapting ones. If commitment is measured in terms of regular attendance and giving high percentages of their personal incomes, the members of declining congregations are, on average, the most committed. They are giving sacrificially, knowing that with only small numbers everyone's dollars count.[14] This is true across theological traditions—at moderate East Lynn Christian in Anderson, as much as at evangelical Carmel Wesleyan. Their commitment is more a matter of size and survival than of theological orientation. These small bands of survivors are often very attached to each other and willingly gather for Bible study and worship with their friends. In fact, their very commitment to each other and to the memories their congregation represents may be among the major obstacles preventing congregational adaptation to new circumstances.

While commitment is clearly affected by theological and cultural expectations, it seems also to be affected by the stage at which the congregation finds itself on the road toward transformation. People at Good Shepherd, for instance, recall the heady early days of their rebirth. Everyone knew everyone else. Everyone was involved and working hard. Now that they have firmly established their new place in the community, such intense effort is no longer needed, and some of the early pioneers miss it. Today, for instance, both Hinton and Epworth United Methodist Churches find themselves on the cusp of change, with higher levels of participation than one would expect for mainline, liberal churches. Since that participation includes a variety of new programs in both cases, theirs does not appear to be the intense inward-looking commitment of the declining congregations but the commitment of a corps of members willing to be pioneers. In the early stages of change, commitment *does* make a difference. In the later stages, however, the congregation's resources of personpower and money have reached levels sufficient to require less of each individual member.

Across theological traditions, and across the stages of change, one human resource that makes a difference is education. Congregations that have adapted have higher average levels of education than congregations that are declining or moving; and new and niche congregations have the highest levels of all. Why should this be the case? Here it may be helpful to look specifically at the kinds of changes these congregations faced. Three of the most educationally advantaged congregations—First Existentialist, First Congregational, and St. Matthew's—faced an influx of lesbians and gay men in their communities. They were able to make the new population welcome in part because they and the newcomers were alike in so many ways. While the newcomers differed in sexual orientation, they shared with existing church members the sorts of tastes, outlooks, and skills that come with higher education and professional jobs. A somewhat similar situation may exist at City Baptist. There the new ingredient is not sexual orientation but race. And again, education may help to smooth the way for integration to occur. Higher education provides a ground of common experience for black and white members, and it creates higher degrees of tolerance that make this sort of adaptation more possible.[15]

Four other high-education congregations are in locations where college degrees are the community norm—Oak Park, Carmel, and to a lesser extent Gwinnett County. Three of the four are the new or reborn congregations. To survive in these mobile, professional, highly educated suburban enclaves, such new congregations had to attract highly educated members. Finally, the two niche congregations also have high levels of member education at their disposal. Both appeal to a highly educated African American professional class, and that is part of what will make possible the establishment of a recognizable niche in their respective communities.

Where there has been change without high *average* levels of education in the congregation, we can nevertheless see the work of well-educated key leaders and the teachableness of others. We have already noted the efforts of Pastor Crockett at Grace Baptist. In addition, at Atlanta's Hope Baptist, many of the emerging young congregational leaders are college- and graduate-trained professionals, who join a core of older teachers and nurses in providing both guidance and inspiration in the congregation. These are people with connections and skill and the determination to see their community improve. Similarly, Brighton Evangelical Congregational would not have the same level of engagement with its community without the foresight and skill of Eunice Taylor.

We see a strong relationship between education and adaptation, then, for at least two different reasons. In some cases, high education in the congregation represents a response to a particular high-education population. Congregations build high-education memberships in high-education communities, even when those "communities" are scattered. In other situations, education bridges cultural barriers, offering common ground on which people of different sexual orientations and different races can stand. It also encourages the sorts of tolerance that may help congregations welcome at least some populations that others might deem alien, changes how people look at the world, and offers them skills necessary in planning for change. And as can all voluntary organizations, congregations can use the basic skills members learn in higher education (not so much *what* they learn, but what they learn about *how* to learn). Congregations can survive with very few material resources of their own if they have the connections and imagination to find partners and creative uses for the resources they do have. While educated lay and clergy leaders do not guarantee such imagination, they do help.

STRUCTURES OF AUTHORITY

We have already implied that a key ingredient in adaptation is strong clergy in creative partnership with lay leaders and members who see that leadership as legitimate.[16] In the cases examined here, that legitimacy was earned in the particular local interaction of the congregation, rarely conferred by any outside denominational authority. In fact, in most cases denominations are either hindrances, irrelevant, or—at best—supporting players.

The supporting-player role was most evident for the two Long Beach congregations in their responses to the gay and lesbian population. At St. Matthew's, it was the archdiocese that suggested beginning the Comunidad ministry and that supplied key leadership in the early days. At First Congregational, the United Church of Christ supplied important educational resources and moral support for the open and affirming process in which the congregation engaged. In both cases, the congregation could feel assured that what it was doing had denominational approval and support. (The case of St. Matthew's is, of course, complicated by the Catholic Church's opposition to homosexuality. While parishioners are very aware of living in tension with the Vatican on this issue, they nevertheless feel supported by their own archdiocese in ministering to gay and lesbian persons.)

Besides resources and legitimation for new programming that enable a congregation to adapt to new circumstances, denominations can provide more dramatic aid to congregations that need a complete transformation. We saw that most clearly at Good Shepherd Lutheran in Oak Park. Especially in supplying the congregation with a "redevelopment" pastor, but also in providing some financial relief, the denomination helped to make that church's rebirth possible. As our study was coming to a conclusion, a similar course was being charted by Hinton Memorial United Methodist in Gwinnett County. A new pastor and financial relief were being supplied by the denomination in exchange for the congregation's commitment to devise new ways to reach its suburban neighbors. In Candler Park, where Epworth United Methodist's case is not as dramatic, the denomination now appears ready to supply strong pastoral leadership as well, beginning to play a supporting role to the congregation's new efforts at outreach and ministry in the community. In these cases, the denomination's role is genuinely important.

The other example of creative denominational support is the role the Catholic Church has played in birthing St. Lawrence Parish. Catholic lay people cannot start a church on their own, nor can an entrepreneurial priest set up shop without Church approval. The diocese draws parish lines and supplies parish priests. Therefore, when the Atlanta Diocese decided that Gwinnett County was ready for another Catholic parish, it supplied crucial initial resources of personnel and legitimation. Hordes of incoming Catholics took things from there. Now the role of the diocese is simply the periodic redrawing of parish lines, adding yet more churches to serve this growing Catholic population.

In none of these cases, however, would denominational support have been sufficient. Only as the local members decided to take initiative did change actually happen. It would do no good for the diocese to start parishes without Catholics to fill them. The aim of redevelopment efforts is to make the denomination's aid again unnecessary. And denominational program support has to be locally appropriated. Comunidad did not really thrive at St. Matthew's until local members took it over. And First Congregational took denominational resources and then designed its own plan of action. That partnership between local and denominational bodies presents a sharp contrast to the situation at East Lynn Christian in Anderson. There the denomination offered its support and approval for outreach into an increasingly diverse community, but the congregation refused. Even in the hierarchical system of the Roman Catholic Church, St. Matthew's was not obligated to respond, but chose to. In the best of cases, denominations can create a climate that encourages change and provide resources to assist that change, but denominations—even hierarchical ones—cannot force a local parish to become something it does not want to be.

The converse of that proposition is that denominations—especially hierarchical ones—can ignore local congregations that need their help, withhold important resources from congregations that might otherwise be willing to adapt, and drain those congregations of locally needed money by insisting on payment of denominational "dues." All of the congregations about whose future we are uncertain are in denominations that make them dependent on outside authority, especially for their pastoral leadership. All have suffered from an imbalance of resources received from the denomination in proportion to the resources expected back from them. Holman United Methodist simply fell behind in their payment of "apportionments" to their conference. Hinton United Methodist and Berean Seventh-Day Adventist, on the other hand, paid large portions of their meager budgets to their conferences at times when that money was needed at home.

Most problematic of all are pastoral placements that fail to meet the needs of the congregation. Pastoral placements are likely to reflect both the denomination's confidence in a congregation's future and the direction in which the denomination wishes a congregation to go. The assignment of white priests to Episcopal Church of the Incarnation, for instance, reflected a view of the parish as integrated, while the assignment of an African American priest reflected a new perception. Had the Los Angeles district assigned a Spanish-speaking pastor to Berean Seventh-Day Adventist, it would have represented a major impetus toward a type of change that Berean might have resisted. As these two examples illustrate, congregations can be ahead of their denomination as well as behind it, eager for a change the denomination does not recognize or preferring more gradual change than the denomination might push for.

The situation at St. Catherine's illustrates the dilemma of denominationally vulnerable congregations. First the nuns were withdrawn from the parish, leaving a large gap in the pastoral ministries that could be offered. Then Father Jim was taken, as well, leaving even the Never Too Old Club without its sponsor and guide. With no staff to support outreach into the community, change at St. Catherine's is extremely unlikely.

St. Catherine's, along with Carmel Wesleyan, shows how denominational dependence can have pernicious effects on a local congregation. Both these churches feel at the mercy of the denomination, utterly subject to someone else's decisions about what their budget will be, who will lead them, and therefore what sorts of programming they will be able to offer. They do not perceive themselves as powerful enough to initiate change on their own. Other congregations in hierarchical denominations are able to counter the power of the denomination through various resources at their disposal. Their size, the longevity of their pastor, the money they contribute, the visibility of their ministries, the skills and connections of their members—all can provide local congregations with bargaining power.[17] At the same time, they provide those congregations with human resources for initiating change. Congregations low in such human resources *and* also in hierarchical denominations are doubly disadvantaged. They cannot avoid being neglected by the denomination, and they do not have the ability to act on their own. The opposite is true in Carmel United Methodist and St. Matthew's in Long Beach, dramatic examples of the way a high-resource local parish can turn the power of a hierarchical denomination to its benefit, becoming doubly advantaged by combining its own strength with the resources and legitimation of the denomination.

In seven of the thirteen new and adapting congregations the denomination was a supporting player, but in six others, denominations were simply irrelevant. Only two of those—Grace Baptist and City Baptist—are genuinely independent, nondenominational churches. The other four are in denominations with "congregational" polities, and the ties binding the local body to anything beyond it are extremely weak. These congregations have drawn on a variety of resources in adapting to their communities, but they have been quite without obligation to anyone in either staff or programming. They have sought out the leaders they needed and the programming they felt would best serve their communities. They have not had to ask for anyone's permission or wait for anyone's approval. They have used their autonomy to good advantage.

However, local autonomy is a double-edged sword. Just as it can allow a flexible response to change, it can also leave floundering congregations to engineer their own demise. Of the seven congregations that are declining or moving, five are in denominations that allow them the same local discretion enjoyed by a thriving Hope Baptist or a First Congregational. Brighton Avenue Baptist, Gray Friends Meeting, and First Baptist Anderson—like East Lynn Christian—have exercised their autonomy. Whatever difficulties they are now encountering have been of their own making.

The role of denominations, then, while varied, is nonetheless real. The one clear message here is that when congregations and denominations act in concert, the results can be quite positive. Where congregations seek advice, legitimation, and support, denominations can be very helpful. Where congregations see such advice as imposed and refuse it, no amount of hierarchy can force change.[18]

If the efforts of outside authorities depend on the receptiveness of the congregation, what of the decision-making processes inside the congregations themselves? In almost every instance, the congregations that have been newly born, reborn, or significantly changed have also had to work hard at creating and recreating their decision-making structures.

- Carmel United Methodist has dislodged an old elite, reorganized its committees, and opened the process to a wider range of newcomers.
- Grace Baptist in Anderson has instituted strict fiscal policies, and members have been brought into the decision-making process through the educational efforts of the pastor.
- First Existentialist in Atlanta engages in a rather constant round of retreats and debates about how best to include new people and maintain sufficient levels of commitment.
- Long Beach's First Congregational organized an elaborate educational and decision-making strategy before its vote on becoming open and affirming. Pastor Kilsby has also created several ad hoc groups as forums for new ideas.
- City Baptist in Oak Park has created an intentional leadership training program that brings diverse people into key positions.
- Brighton Evangelical Congregational Church has reorganized its committee structure and brought new constituents into those committees.
- Hope Baptist in Atlanta is creating mission groups out of its old auxiliaries and moving toward a financial system based on tithing instead of special offerings.

- St. Lawrence Parish in Gwinnett County has created a complex system of committees and experimented with how members would be nominated to those bodies.
- Carmel's Northview Christian Life Church trusts much of its decision making to the pastor and a small group of elders but has recognized the need to expand its leadership base.
- Good Shepherd Lutheran in Oak Park went through an extensive series of roundtables, forums, and educational activities before deciding whether and how to remodel its building.
- Epworth United Methodist in Candler Park has been activating committees long dormant and inviting new people to participate. For instance, a woman chaired the board for the first time.

The one clear exception to this pattern of structural change is St. Matthew's in Long Beach, where there has never been appreciable lay participation in decision making for the parish. There the Comunidad group itself has labored to create effective governance and planning mechanisms. The other temporary exception is Hinton United Methodist in Gwinnett County, where structural changes are only beginning to get underway. In every other case, these congregations have recognized that lasting change will necessitate broad-based involvement by all the constituencies represented in the congregation. Where old structures protected old elites, new structures have been invented.

Inventing new structures that dislodge old elites often means conflict. Sometimes the conflict is prolonged and serious, leading to significant loss of membership, the case at Carmel United Methodist. The process at Atlanta's Hope Baptist was similar, although not quite as severe or open; and Atlanta's Epworth United Methodist, whose future is still uncertain, has also seen the slow exodus of older members unsympathetic to the congregation's apparent new directions. It appears unlikely that many of them will remain, making Epworth's story a somewhat painful rebirth. In each of these cases, the transformation of the congregation into the sort of association that would meet the needs of a new population has meant significant alienation and anger for constituents already in place and in power. Not changing would likely have meant the sort of slow decline that has faced First Baptist Anderson or Carmel Wesleyan; but changing meant conflict.

Sometimes the conflict that accompanied change was chronic and contained, a constant tug-of-war between older interests and newer ones. Brighton Evangelical Congregational and Good Shepherd are in this situation. While their older members sympathize with the changes that have occurred, old habits die hard. When someone suggests moving a revered object or changing the order of worship or perhaps contributing to a controversial cause, the congregation is suddenly reminded that those who are now the majority are different from those who used to be. Such conflicts are rarely life threatening. These older members have long since made their peace with being a minority. But they are not a silent minority. The very drive that made it possible for them to change also makes them unlikely to stifle their disgruntlement. The new members, in turn, recognize the valuable contribution of these "church fathers and mothers." Accommodation is not out of the question. Still, change has not come without conflict.

Sometimes, as at First Congregational and First Existentialist, conflict is simply assumed. It comes and goes, forming and re-forming around various issues, but not threatening the stability of the congregation in any significant way.[19] These highly educated, highly participatory people expect to disagree with one another. There are strong democratic traditions in these congregations, and democracy does not mean, for them, routine unanimous votes. Occasionally someone gets unhappy enough to leave, but even that is seen as the natural outgrowth of persons finding their own best place to worship (or not worship). These are friendly divorces, not acrimonious ones.

Other conflicts have been devastating and painful in ways that may not immediately seem related to issues of responding to a changing community. When a tongues-speaking pastor and his followers were finally forced out of Hinton United Methodist in Dacula, the longtime members just wanted to return to "normal." And when City Baptist's earlier pastor and his followers were similarly pushed out, the congregation felt more tired and wounded than anything else. Yet both these painful church splits prepared the way for the decisions that would make change possible. Both congregations looked at the remnant remaining and recovered a sense of their own goodness. With troubling elements in the congregation gone, they could turn their energies to other, equally pressing, matters.

This pattern of conflict—in all its varied forms—stands in remarkable contrast to the peacefulness of the declining, moving, and niche congregations. None of them has experienced any significant conflict in the recent memory of the congregation. Even when Gray Friends Meeting and Brighton Avenue Baptist kicked out the pastors that tried to introduce new habits to them, the conflict lay not within the congregations, but between them and their pastors. This pattern makes absolutely clear that attempting significant changes will involve conflict, and congregations unwilling to engage in conflict will not change.

Exactly what sort of internal organizational change happens will vary from one situation to the next, but congregations that manage to incorporate new constituencies will also have to change how they do things. Some may be able to work in partnership with a denomination, gaining both resources and legitimation from that body. But changes can rarely be imposed from the outside. It is in the internal structures of the congregation itself that the life and death decisions will be made.

CULTURE

Having listened to the unique stories of each of these twenty-three congregations, what can we say about the common patterns of culture, of ideas and practices, that unite those that have adapted and set them apart from those that remain relatively unchanged? While there is indeed enormous variation, there are also common themes in the way they define their physical space (their artifacts), the things they do together (their activities), and the ideas that give them their sense of direction and identity.

Church buildings, as has been noted, are both resource and artifact. They provide the congregation with the ability to carry on certain activities, to be a presence in the community; but they also symbolize that presence, sending messages about who worships there and who is welcome. Most visibly, the congregations that are declining or moving differ from other congregations in that their church buildings sit as silent, empty witnesses most of the time. While in some of the evangelical churches a small group returns on Sunday night and Wednesday night, Sunday morning is the only time during which most of these buildings are visibly alive. First Baptist, Anderson, stands as a lonely, secured sentinel, subject to repeated vandalism. St. Catherine's cannot afford to turn on the heat during the week, leaving the Never Too Old Club often in the cold. Carmel Wesleyan is simply off the beaten track, invisible to most of the community even when it is occupied.

In contrast, the doors of St. Matthew's, in Long Beach, are always open. And across town, First Congregational is a beehive of activity at nearly any time of any day. Brighton Evangelical Congregational's food and clothing ministries keep neighborhood people coming in and out of the building in a steady stream. And there are nearly always cars in Holman United Methodist's parking lot. While the buildings of the declining congregations often hold precious memories for the members, the buildings of the adapting congregations symbolize their openness and their willingness to use their spaces for multiple purposes.

Inside, things have changed, as well. Instead of morning coats, one sees a variety of modest dresses and even jeans at Brighton Evangelical Congregational. Grace Baptist's repaired and remodeled building symbolizes the church's fiscal health. At First Existentialist, a sculpted figure of a child joins numerous other pieces of art in the sanctuary. St. Lawrence's Advent stump symbolizing the "root of Jesse" also symbolized the congregation's uprootedness and newness. And at First Congregational, the frequently used baptismal font came to symbolize the congregation's success in attracting "straight" young families, alongside their new gay and lesbian members. On a walk through any of these buildings, the rooms and furnishings will remind congregation members not only of days gone by, but also of new ministries and newcomers. This reappropriation of symbols is dramatically illustrated in a story Carl Dudley tells about a Norwegian church that sold its building to a black congregation. The Norwegian congregation had placed a boat in the vestibule as a symbol of its oceanic heritage and planned to take the boat to their new building. The black church, however, had immediately adopted the boat as part of *its* heritage and refused to let it go. The same boat meant something very different—and no less important—to this new constituency.[20] None of these churches has as dramatic a reappropriated symbol as the Norwegian fishing boat transformed into African slave ship, but each has given its old surroundings new meanings.

More than surroundings have changed, of course. We have already examined in earlier chapters the myriad changes in activities and practice that have characterized the adapting congregations. Worship and eating, two of the activities most common to all congregations, deserve to be highlighted again here. Church members gather in their sanctuaries to celebrate their connections to God, and they gather around tables to celebrate their connections to each other. All congregations do these things, but for congregations that have incorporated new populations these functions are crucial in the process of transformation.

Changes in worship may include the style of preaching, the sorts of hymns sung, the length and timing of the service, the sorts of language and symbols used. Such changes are especially critical for congregations attempting to cross significant racial and cultural lines. City Baptist is the most notable example of this, combining "white" and "black" styles of music in its services. Brighton Evangelical Congregational has made similar efforts to acknowledge the diversity of the congregation in the symbols used for worship. At Carmel United Methodist, sermons routinely incorporate the sorts of stories a mobile suburban congregation would understand. To succeed with its incorporation of a similar suburban population, Hinton United Methodist, in Gwinnett County, will have to do the same.

In contrast, congregations incorporating lesbian and gay constituents seem required to change little in their worship. In addition to sharing high levels of educational attainment, gay and straight members seem to share similar aesthetic sensibilities, as well.

But like other congregations incorporating new populations, the three who have included lesbian and gay members have developed important rituals that involve the sharing of food. Coffee hours, fellowship dinners, soup suppers, potlucks, and free meals for the community abound among these adapting congregations. Neither new nor niche congregations approach the frequency and intentionality with which adapting congregations gather around tables laden with coffee and food.

Many of the declining and moving congregations, on the other hand, also share meals with each other, but for them the result is the reinforcement of existing ties. What adapting congregations seem to do well is to create opportunities for different constituencies to eat together. They have after-church potlucks, holiday picnics, and well-attended coffee hours. Just as they intentionally alter their styles of worship, so they also pursue the informal, interpersonal sharing that occurs in the context of a common meal. Both are instrumental in building the new culture necessary for an adapted congregation.

In addition to these changes in the use and meaning of space and changes in the most highly charged ritual events, adapting congregations are distinctive for the way they approach what a church is supposed to be about. The authors of *Varieties of Religious Presence* posit four typical ways congregations orient themselves toward their communities.[21] Congregations with a "civic" orientation work at being good, cooperative citizens of the community, helping out where they can, without significantly challenging the status quo. Their emphasis is on individual citizenship, in contrast to the corporate action of "activist" congregations. Activist congregations, who also want to be good citizens, see that goal as requiring advocacy and change. The "sanctuary" orientation is the most otherworldly in seeking to shield members from this world's temptations and prepare them for the world to come. The "evangelist" orientation sees the church as an agent for changing individual lives. Our questionnaire contained slightly modified versions of the questions used to identify these orientations.[22] In each congregation, we found the average member score on each of the four clusters of items and determined which orientation(s) was most typical for that congregation (see table 8.3).

"Civic" congregations are by far the most numerous, and they are found in roughly predictable numbers in each category of response. The civic orientation in itself is uninformative for understanding responses to change because it does not specify the community to which the congregation should relate or how it is to accomplish that task. One can endorse the goal of being a good citizen without any clear sense of which needy people should be served or how to work with others toward community betterment. When congregations are already well focused on their constituencies, these mission goals give shape to their action. But when the constituency itself is in doubt, the ideas of service, cooperation, and citizenship are not sufficient to motivate adaptation.

Only two of our congregations are primarily activist in orientation, and a third is a mixture of activism with civic and evangelistic goals. Still, those two activist congregations are among those that have adapted to their new environments. And Holman United Methodist, where activism is a secondary orientation, is poised between adaptation to its disparate neighbors and service to its regional constituency. With its particular orientation toward advocacy for the African American community, Holman's combination of civic and activist ideas is shaping its emerging niche identity. These activist congregations see their mission as centered on seeking this-worldly change. As they themselves have been surrounded by change, they have been relatively well prepared for the work of adaptation. At least among this sample of congregations, being activist has *not* led to decline. The activists have an openness to new populations and to new ways of serving old ones that has allowed them the sort of creative flexibility they needed.

Almost as rare as the activist orientation is the sanctuary one. Indeed *none* of our congregations is *primarily* oriented toward protecting its members from this world and preparing them for the next. This orientation is, however, paired with evangelistic fervor in three congregations, and with a civic orientation at St. Catherine's Parish in Allston-Brighton. Two of the four occurrences of the sanctuary orientation are among the declining congregations. Such an otherworldly orientation here seems to reflect a kind of escape from this world, an inability to imagine that it might be a friendly place in which the congregation and its members could thrive. The other two occurrences of strong sanctuary orientations, both in Anderson, are in congregations whose changes have been largely internal (Grace Baptist) or who are establishing themselves *as* a haven in a hectic, demanding, difficult world (Northview Christian Life). Both have a very clear sense that people in their community *need* sanctuary, and these congregations actively seek to construct it and make it known. Their sanctuary orientation represents engagement with their world, not escape from it.

Five of the eight congregations that are maintaining their existing program and identity are evangelists in the way they approach the mission of the church (compared to four of the thirteen adapting congregations). They think congregations should have an active evangelism program and encourage members to share their faith on their own, as well. That emphasis on recruitment, however, has mixed results. In two cases—East Lynn and First Baptist in Anderson—the endorsement of evangelistic emphases is not matched by actual activities in the church. Finding themselves stuck in neighborhoods in which they feel out of place, these congregations have largely put their evangelism on

Table 8.3. Summary of Factors Affecting Congregational Responses

	Trajectory	Attendance	Average age	Building
St. Catherine's	Declining	300	65	High cost Underused
Brighton Avenue Baptist	Declining	15	65+	High cost Underused
Berean Seventh-Day Adventist	Declining	250	47	Minimal cost Moderate use
Gray Friends	Declining	50	n/a	Minimal cost Moderate use
Carmel Wesleyan	Declining	50	n/a	High cost Moderate use
First Baptist	Declining/moving	150	61	High cost Underused
East Lynn Christian	Declining/moving	60	69	Minimal cost Underused
South Meridian Church of God	Moving	400	48	Minimal cost Moderate use
Holman United Methodist	Niche	600	53	High investment High use
Incarnation Episcopal	Niche	100	51	Minimal cost Moderate use
St. Matthew's	Adapting	450	54	Minimal cost Moderate use
First Congregational	Adapting	300	55	Moderate investment High use
First Existentialist	Adapting	75	38	Minimal cost High use
Brighton Evangelical Congregational	Adapting	50	52	Minimal cost High use
City Baptist	Adapting	200	39	Minimal cost High use
Hinton United Methodist	Adapting	50	50	Moderate cost High use
Hope Baptist	Adapting	600	37	High investment High use
Grace Baptist	Adapting	600	47	Moderate investment High use
Carmel United Methodist	Adapting	600	52	High investment High use
Good Shepherd Lutheran	Rebirth	185	45	High investment High use
Epworth United Methodist	Rebirth	100	50	Moderate investment Moderate use
St. Lawrence	New	1000	43	Moderate investment Moderate use
Northview Christian Life	New	800	46	High investment High use

% College educated	Mission Orientation	Polity	% Living < 10 minutes away	% Civically active
11	Civic/sanctuary	Hierarchical	91	16
N/a	N/a	Congregational	N/a	N/a
41	Evangelist/civic/ sanctuary	Hierarchical	33	31
N/a	N/a	Congregational	N/a	N/a
N/a	Evangelist	Hierarchical	36	30
34	Evangelist	Congregational	49	42
21	Evangelist/civic	Congregational	25	27
40	Evangelist/civic	Congregational	53	38
64	Civic/activist/ evangelist	Hierarchical	30	55
81	Civic	Hierarchical	31	47
60	Civic	Hierarchical	79	40
75	Activist/civic	Congregational	33	50
83	Activist	Congregational	55	44
44	Civic	Congregational	67	64
52	Evangelist	Independent	59	40
45	Civic	Hierarchical	84	51
39	Evangelist/civic	Congregational	45	52
21	Evangelist/ sanctuary	Independent	44	40
76	Civic	Hierarchical	79	53
88	Civic	Modified Hierarchical	72	40
41	Civic	Hierarchical	42	55
53	Civic	Hierarchical	43	39
63	Evangelist/ sanctuary	Congregational	29	36

hold. In two other instances—Berean Seventh-Day Adventist and Carmel Wesleyan—efforts at evangelism continue, in spite of frustrations caused by a changing constituency. Both are continuing long-practiced evangelistic methods of revivals and "visitation," but both are finding those techniques less successful than in the past.

Evangelistic orientations are not, then, guarantees of success. In many cases, congregations think of evangelism primarily in terms of recruiting people like themselves (including their own children) into the congregation. That formula works nicely for a new congregation, like Northview Christian Life. Indeed, of all the new congregations in these nine communities, the vast majority have been started by evangelicals, with just such a strategy of planting churches in fertile soil. An evangelistic orientation seems to be a highly effective organizational strategy when the tasks are innovation and new congregational development.

But when the supply of potential recruits moves away and becomes difficult to find, the emphasis on evangelism is not by itself sufficient to motivate congregational change. Only when evangelism includes a strong emphasis on inclusion can it be a powerful aid in the process of adaptation. When the message is that God loves everyone equally, that the message of salvation is for everyone, then new constituencies can find their way into a congregation, as City Baptist's emphasis on ministering "without distinction" shows. Congregations that see their task as saving souls can adapt to changing circumstances only so long as they are willing to deal with the diversity of cultural and physical packages those souls come in.

This description of the very mixed effects of mission orientations makes clear that ideas do not always have predictable effects in the midst of congregational attempts at adaptation. Believing that congregations should be good citizens and servants of the community only helps when a congregation has also understood the nature of—and is willing to welcome—the community in which it is located. Believing that the congregation should be about the business of saving souls is no more helpful in the process of adaptation, if the congregation does not understand and welcome the diversity those souls represent. Being oriented to activism in the community *does* seem to assist the congregation in adapting, and being oriented to sanctuary from this world *does* often seem to stand between congregations and change.

But other ideas thought to be important for understanding U.S. religion today proved less helpful. If ideas about the Bible can be taken as rough theological indicators, theology does not predict responses to change. Congregations with a predominantly conservative view of Scripture differed little from congregations with a predominantly liberal view. Although we did not ask extensive questions about social and political views, we were able to observe the programs and rhetoric of these congregations, and only a few of them can be put neatly into any ideological camp. It *is* possible to identify most of them, imperfectly, as either liberal or conservative, but those identifications are nearly useless in explaining how they responded to change. There are only three—two activist and one evangelical—for whom the issues of abortion, gay rights, and the like are at all live issues of conversation.[23] The two activist congregations, as we have noted, are among those that have adapted; but the population to which they have adapted is telling. Both have included lesbian and gay people in their membership. Their orientation toward social change and their liberal political orientation are clearly intertwined with their ability to undertake this particular kind of congregational adaptation. If the challenge had been different, their response might have been different. On the other side of the presumed ideological divide, Grace Baptist's militant conservatism seems to have had little to do with the way in which it responded to Anderson's economic woes or to its own need for financial restructuring.

Having said that congregational adaptation is not well explained by theological and ideological factors, it is also important to note that ideas do matter. Each of these adapting congregations had to do some ideological work. They had to discover elements in their own theological heritage that could be turned to the task of explaining and encouraging change. City Baptist turned to its evangelistic heritage and learned to value ministry without distinction. Many of the more liberal groups brought an emphasis on God's inclusive love to the fore. Sermons and slogans reinforce and give expression to changing congregational practices. New congregations like St. Lawrence in Gwinnett County and Northview Christian Life in Carmel spent a good deal of energy working out new rituals and ideas that would give expression to the life experience of new populations. The careful arrangement of St. Lawrence's worship space reinforced the presence of God in the midst of the worshippers. The old pulpit, saved from earlier buildings, combined at Northview with contemporary surroundings to symbolize the congregation's unique blending of old and new. In each case, the store of theological stories, symbols, rituals, and ideas was plenty rich enough to allow the construction of new cultural patterns. What matters is not *which* ideas congregations draw on, but whether they engage in the work of reshaping those ideas for their new situation.

SUMMARY

Confronted with a changing environment, congregations seem to draw on the stock of activities they already know and the resources they have at hand more than on any ideological blueprint. Even ideas about the Bible do not necessarily guide a congregation in its decisions about whether to move or stay, whether to change or remain the same. Those decisions are best understood in the matrix of resources and structures that shape the ongoing life of the congregation. Almost no material deficit is so great that it cannot be overcome by the determination of a group of people who decide they want to survive and are willing to change.

Congregations that have the good fortune to be located in a usable building that does not overtax their other resources are better able to make that decision, but even old buildings can become assets. Having a strong pastor who is willing and able to lead the congregation in imagining its future seems to be a key additional ingredient. Likewise, the educational resources of the congregation itself can be called on to aid in that imagination and to bridge cultural gaps of various sorts. Because congregations are voluntary organizations, based in the needs of and rewards generated by their members, these human resources of determination and skill seem to be the necessary components of congregations that establish new relationships with their changed environment.

Congregations do not, however, adapt all on their own. Most are part of a larger denominational structure that can help or hinder the process. The key factor is not the official authority structure of that denomination, but the ability of the denomination to strike up a creative partnership with the congregation. Hierarchical denominations have little ability to force changes on congregations that do not want to change. Conversely, locally autonomous congregations can almost always seek out resources from their denominations or other agencies, if they so choose. Both kinds of denominations can start new churches, although the hierarchical systems do not allow for the additional possibility of efforts by individual entrepreneurs. The most discernible effect of hierarchical denominational structures is that they can sometimes create dependency and vulnerability in congregations. Financial subsidies to a struggling congregation can leave the local body without a sense of control over its destiny. Financial demands *on* the congregation can be equally pernicious. And the failure to appoint strong pastoral leadership for a congregation otherwise ready to change can leave that local body feeling abandoned and powerless. Congregations not located in such hierarchies have the advantage of greater potential flexibility, but they can use their autonomy for either adaptation or resistance to change.

Perhaps most striking in the processes of change we have observed is the association of conflict with change. Most congregations are accustomed to thinking about conflict as a sign of distress, perhaps even as a sign that they are drifting from their proper mission. Quite the contrary. Congregations that systematically avoid conflict are also very likely to avoid changing. So long as they have a stable constituent environment, that may be perfectly healthy. But in any situation that disrupts the congregation's relationship to its constituents, calling into question its location, its structures, and its ministries, conflict is nearly inevitable. Part of the need for a strong pastor and educationally skilled participants is the need for persons willing and able to engage in debate and conflict. In the larger scheme, the rich and diverse ecology of congregations in a community makes division within a given congregation less onerous, perhaps even welcome.

Adaptation can take many forms, but it is not an easy process. It requires determined effort at finding resources, establishing new partnerships, and developing new leaders, new programs, and new ideas, and often involves fighting among people who love each other. Most congregations do not choose adaptation. They choose not to fight and thus not to change. They may be aware that the ecology in which they were born no longer exists, but they continue doing what they know to do. This may be a determined and principled decision that the identity and mission of the congregation must be preserved for as long as possible, or it may be the result of a prolonged failure to decide. After a period of slow decline, these congregations are likely to disappear from the scene, perhaps making way for utterly different congregations to sprout up in their stead. As with any other ecology, death is an inevitable part of the life cycle.

CHAPTER 9

Congregation and Community: Conclusions

This project set out to understand the role of congregations in the midst of community change. We wanted to know how they fare, by what processes they adapt (when they do), and even what the process of decline and death looks like. While we have focused detailed attention on the individual stories of twenty-three congregations, we have also insisted that these stories be seen as part of a constantly changing institutional environment. Congregations are a part of a community's institutional infrastructure, a part of the structures and connections that make social life possible. Those structures and connections are not neutral shells into which any given group can be placed. They are, rather, living networks of meaning and activity, constructed by the individual and collective agents who inhabit and sustain them.[1] As such, we can expect that new actors and new circumstances will precipitate new patterns of organization and connection.

The metaphor of an ecology has been helpful here. As with any ecology, new life forms are constantly emerging, as old ones fade from the scene. As the resources of the environment change, some species find they already have the adaptive mechanisms needed for survival. Others evolve new ways of garnering necessary resources, and still others whose habitat needs are not met by the new environment must move or face extinction. Organizations, of course, are not species, but they still need resources to survive. For economic organizations those resources include innovative entrepreneurs, skilled participants, the ability to generate new technologies, available unexploited markets, and sufficient capital.[2] For congregations, as for all voluntary organizations, many of the same resources apply, but the most crucial resource is membership. Voluntary organizations must be able to mobilize sufficient time, energy, and goodwill (as well as money) to carry out their mission. Therefore, the primary environmental changes likely to affect

346

the well-being of voluntary organizations are changes in the number and types of persons available to them.

We can think about the community in which a congregation is lodged as an ecology of resources and organizations in which people seek out social support for everything from the most basic survival needs to sociability, aesthetic pleasure, meaning making, and community improvement. To understand what is happening in a community, in fact, it may be more useful to observe the stock of skills and connections it comprises than to inventory the organizations themselves. This "social capital" is the essential stuff of our lives together, the network of skill and trust that makes civic life possible. Social capital, writes James Coleman, "inheres in the structure of relations between actors." It consists, in part, of trust and mutual obligation, in part of information gathered and available, and in part of norms that encourage prosocial and discourage antisocial behavior. Once groups are organized, the relationships they generate may remain available for future organizational endeavors.[3] Social capital is the raw material out of which new organizational species can be created, the residue left when old organizations die.

We should pay attention, then, not so much to the decline of any given organization but to the whole inventory of organizations and the available social capital that may lie dormant outside officially organized structures. As Carl Milofsky writes, "Organizational death may be a viable solution to certain problems as long as it contributes to the overall well-being of the community. . . . The death of a particular neighborhood association matters only if new organizations are not spawned and if former activists no longer participate in community affairs. . . . The system is healthiest when unproductive units fail, allowing their resources to be recycled into other, healthier units."[4]

We should not have been surprised, then, to find that congregations geared to a community of middle-class home-owning families fail when that community fills with transient singles and immigrant newcomers.[5] Nor should we have been surprised that changes in the economy of a community had little direct effect on congregations, except as those changes resulted in losses to the available population of members. That some congregations find ways to adapt in the face of such shifts in their environment is far more remarkable than that some congregations die. What Milofsky points toward, however, is the question of net gains and losses for a community from changes in its organizational population. Are the skills and contributions represented by a given organization (or species of organizations) really disappearing, or are they simply going dormant or being recycled into other organizational forms?

In this case, I think we can say that some of the types of social capital represented by given forms of congregational life do indeed disappear in some community transitions.[6] Transitions can mean that there is no one left in a community who remembers how to organize a ladies auxiliary or run a vacation Bible school. *But* there may also not be any ladies who need an auxiliary or children who need a vacation Bible school. That is, those skills may have died for lack of a clientele, or they may have migrated to where they are, in fact, needed. Transitions may also result in the disruption of patterns of connection *among* congregations and between them and other institutions. As congregations change in constituency and program, their networks of connection will change. Where a given community experiences widespread changes, it may find itself temporarily without the social capital necessary for making connections and establishing trust. The leaders of new immigrant congregations may not belong to the same civic clubs and ministerial associations that facilitated the coordination of activities among an earlier community population.

Does that mean that communities must expect to experience net long-term loss in the religious social capital available to them (this being another way of asking whether transient modern urban life means the inevitable secularization of society)? In some cases, perhaps the answer is yes, but most often, outmoded forms of belief and practice seem to get replaced by new forms. The temporary depletion of social capital precipitated by periods of transition seems to be remedied with time, as new congregations generate their own connectional resources. Indeed, as one set of congregations, born to mobilize the religious and social energies of one population, declines and dies, another set is being born in its stead, mobilizing the new religious and social energies of a new population. Each new population group is free to form religious bodies to suit its own sense of value and mission and identity. The voluntary and particularistic character of religion in the United States makes the process of religious births and adaptations both possible and likely.

It does not, however, make it necessary. It is certainly possible to imagine that new populations might channel their associational energies in new directions, even destructive ones, that religious organizations might not survive. That they do survive as a vital part of U.S. society is an important piece of the story this project has told.

While we have seen in these pages congregations that have completed their missions and are unlikely to find new ones, we have also seen an enormous amount of associational energy spent to found, move, and transform congregations and to found, shelter, and support new congregations. More than 20 percent of all the congregations we located in these communities had been created since 1980.[7] While at least that many are likely to die within the next ten years, it appears that the overall population of congregations is at least stable, if not growing. At least as impressive as this entrepreneurial energy is the adaptive energy that other congregations expend in finding more suitable locations and moving, recycling their property into an altered community religious ecology and investing their own social and monetary capital in a new place. Similarly, congregations that choose the path of internal adaptation invest tremendous human and material resources in remaking themselves. If these communities can be taken as indicators and their congregations as barometers, the religious institutional sector seems to be thriving. Not all religious organizations are thriving, but the sector as a whole exhibits remarkable vitality.[8]

Congregations and Modern Community Life

This vitality flies in the face of a long tradition of sociological theorizing. Almost from the moment cities appeared, analysts predicted that their diversity, density, and sheer size would bring both the loss of "community" and the decline of religion. For at least a century, sociologists have been preoccupied with the transition from gemeinschaft to gesellschaft, as Ferdinand Toennies put it, worrying and theorizing about what forms of association would bind complex modern societies together. In his influential 1938 essay, "Urbanism as a Way of Life," Louis Wirth took Toennies's categories as "ideal types" from which he built his contrast between urban and rural forms of social life.[9] Urban social relations are "impersonal, superficial, transitory, and segmental," he argued. In cities, family, neighborhood, and church would lose their binding and ordering influence. Even ethnicity was expected to lose its orienting capacity. Talcott Parsons's model of social relations, while more subtle, embodied a similar contrast between modern and premodern polar types. On the premodern side were affectivity, particularism, ascription, and diffuseness. In such communities, relationships had emotional depth, were idiosyncratic, were lifelong, and had functional breadth across many aspects of daily life. On the modern side, by contrast, stood affective neutrality, universalism, status achievement, and specificity. Here, social relations are coolly rational and to the point, and all people are treated with equal (dis)regard, according to the particular place they have earned for themselves.[10] The expectation of much of this century's social theory has assumed, then, the loss of community and the rise of atomized individuals.[11]

Where religion retained a place in these expectations about modern life, it either disappeared into universal moral principles (as in Parsons's system),[12] or it assumed a place as segmental as the rest of urban existence—a small niche in the complicated lives of urban persons and communities—or it became an internal, individual meaning system.[13]

Sociologists of religion often followed this line of theory by positing contrasts between rural and urban churches that emphasized the latter's loss of a tightly knit, geographically defined constituency. In the plurality of religious offerings, the dispersion of potential members, and the segmenting of urban life, the modern religion they described was a shadow of its former self.[14]

Many of these same theorists lamented the decline of community and rise of individualism they were describing, noting that without the guidance of fixed social roles or tight-knit communities, the individual has the monumental task of constructing a self alone. As much as modern communities are liberating, they are also alienating and disorienting.[15] Atomized individuals, to the extent that they really exist, pose a threat both to individual well-being and to the well-being of the social world they inhabit. With the declining power of "communities of memory," perhaps we have no moral compass beyond the utilitarian individualism of the marketplace.[16] Even the most important decisions can be guided only by individual utility and market preferences. The implicit contrast to such dangerous individualism was a nostalgic, ill-defined sense of "community."

It seems to me that the persistent positing of dichotomies—individualism versus community, for instance—has hindered our ability to understand both modern urban life and the role of religion. By beginning with evolutionary assumptions (that tradition inevitably gives way to modernity), our theoretical models have too often been unidirectional and unilinear. More of one meant less of the other. With each step along the way, more of traditional, communal, and religious life is left behind, to be replaced only by the modern, rational, world of strangers described by modernization theories. Yet we know that this story is not unilinear. It does not begin at a fixed point in time and proceed inexorably toward the present. Historian Thomas Bender points out that if we were to believe every historian who has written about community breakdown in the United States, we would not know whether to place the critical turning point in the 1650s, 1690s, 1740s, 1780s, 1820s, 1850s, 1880s, or 1920s.[17] (More recent observers would surely add the 1960s to that list.) A unilinear evolutionary story does not fit our history very well.

Nor does the bipolar view fit our current reality. Urban life has not weakened kinship bonds, and religious participation is higher in cities than in small towns.[18] That city people may have fewer close relationships with their immediate neighbors does not mean that they have fewer relationships—only that those relationships are more dispersed.[19] Dozens of case studies have demonstrated the persistence of ethnicity and neighborhood, as well. Somehow the communal life that was supposed to disappear in the face of the modern urban world has simply not gone away, sociological theories to the contrary. The lament for its presumed demise seems both to obscure the present and to misread the past. Claude Fischer writes, "Confined together by barriers of geography, poverty, illness, ignorance, law, prejudice, and custom, most old-world people lived out their lives in a small group, shared a common fate, and knew one another intimately. This familiarity, by the way, did not necessarily mean affection. In contrast, Americans have more typically found their fellowship in voluntary association, be it clubs, churches, or neighborhoods."[20]

In this positing of polar opposites, the reality of modern social life has, in fact, been obscured from the very beginning. As is the case for all dichotomies, the dominant pole tends to silence the subordinant one. Assume a trajectory toward "progress," and any evidence that old ways remain or that the road is not entirely straight disappears in the blinding light of progressivist categories and predictions. With society's move from benighted tradition to enlightened modernity established as the official story, the voices telling other stories have been relegated to the margins.[21]

In recent years, the voices of outsiders have increasingly challenged this dominant story, however. While what people mean by "postmodern" varies enormously, it seems at least to mean the breaking apart of assumptions that we can all agree on a single telling of our history. Feminist and womanist sociologists such as Karen McCarthy Brown and Victoria Erickson have reminded scholars that the first step in reconstructing what we think we know about the world is listening to the voices—the stories—of those at the margins.[22] Patricia Hill Collins has written about the interpretive advantages of being an outsider.[23] Outsiders see things insiders do not. While the outsider, too, has a particular location, a particular filter through which the world is seen, the presence of the outsider's perspective in itself calls into question the universality of the supposed center, a process Dorothy Smith has also written about.[24] All of these writers warn of the dangers in any theory that begins with dichotomies. Life is much more a both/and proposition than an either/or one. Either/or theories too often exclude and obscure realities that do not fit the "positive" end of the theoretical continuum.

The primary difference between modern urban life and earlier folk society is not, then, the presence of community in one and its absence in the other. Urban life is not best characterized by a decline in the number and closeness of a person's ties, but by the fact of their chosenness and their embeddedness in a larger matrix of the very sorts of segmented relationships that are indeed a new feature of life in modern cities. It is not that community has disappeared, only that it now exists alongside other types of relations and can be (indeed must be) constructed by the persons involved.[25] While it may be that an understanding of the social systems of modern life must start with the individual's network of relations (rather than with a given set of enduring institutions), that does not imply that urban life has begotten a hopeless individualism. We may begin with the individual, but we immediately see that individuals are still very much embedded in networks of social relations that supply the social capital necessary for community life. Those individuals may live in an anonymous world, but they have carved out spaces of sociability in the midst of that anonymity.

One of the most prominent of those spaces of sociability is the congregation. Only when we move beyond the dichotomies of modernization theories that predicted religion's demise can we appreciate the enduring character of these local religious gatherings. They are neither the "lifestyle enclaves" of individualistic religious consumers nor traditionalistic throwbacks to an earlier time.[26] They are social creations of the modern world, encompassing the both/and quality of modern social life, not an either/or accommodation. They are gatherings of individuals who choose to be there. Where religious identities are not fundamentally ascribed, individual choice is fundamental to congregational life. In this system of choice (and the pluralism it implies), congregations are thoroughly modern institutions. Yet they are communal gatherings, collectivities, that afford their members an opportunity for connections with persons, groups, divine powers, and social structures beyond their own individuality. The substance and depth of those commitments are no less real simply because an individual is committed to other institutions, or because this commitment may not last a lifetime.[27]

Following Parsons's scheme, Stephen Warner notes this both/and quality of congregations. They are characterized by patterns from both sides of Parsons's set of dichotomies.[28] They are affective, calling people beyond the calculating rationality of the state and market. They are diffuse, arenas where persons deal with each other in some measure of wholeness, not merely as role incumbents. And they are particularistic, highlighting the things that set them apart rather than looking for underlying universalisms. On those three dimensions, congregations belong to the world Parsons would have called traditional. But on the fourth, ascribed versus achieved statuses, congregations belong largely on the modern side of the ledger. While family tradition and social class and ethnicity (ascribed statuses all) still help to define the range of congregations a person may consider, decreasing numbers of members stay in a single congregation for a lifetime. Powerful ascriptive forces still mark the larger religious picture with discernible traditional patterns, but mobility and education increasingly blur those lines.[29] Elsewhere, Warner has written about "elective parochialism" as a characteristic of people who have the educational and life experience skills to qualify as "cosmopolitans," attuned to the larger social world in which they live, yet invest themselves in a particular locality, becoming "parochials" by choice.[30] In both these conceptions, Warner points us toward the way in which congregations become a space for sociability alongside other, more anonymous, modern structures. Although chosen, they still may involve intense social commitment.

That balance between chosenness and commitment is at the heart of the story Robert Wuthnow tells about the role of small groups in U.S. society. He, too, points out that in a modern, fragmented society, people are capable of banding together into communities. He notes, like the others, that these bonds are not ascribed, that they are chosen and relatively easily changed. This, he says, makes such small-group communal attachments fitted for the sort of mobile and diverse society in which we live. They free us to follow the pulls of vocation from one location to another and allow the needs of very diverse populations to be served. They are neither the impersonality of work and governmental structures nor the intense personalism of the family. As a result of standing between these extremes, such commitments shield us and help us to adapt but do not, he says, fundamentally change us.[31]

Here I would disagree. No commitment fails to change the person who makes it. It is one of the ironies of social life that individualism and communalism are utterly intertwined.[32] We only know who we individually are as we build that identity out of the attachments in which we are embedded.[33] It is the multiplicity of those attachments—not their absence—that produces the celebrated individual freedom of the modern world.[34] The small groups Wuthnow studied are clearly among the attachments—the spaces of sociability—that create the web of modern community. His research shows that nearly half of those who belong to small groups have been members for five or more years, giving fairly generously of their time and energy to the group. While their participation may sometimes seem utterly self-absorbed, it cannot truly be so. As he shows, people who do not conform are pushed out; the power of groups to shape behavior remains strong. In addition, people who belong to such groups are more likely to contribute time and money to other civic causes in their communities. He reports that "small groups generate a substantial amount of caring and interest that extends beyond the boundaries of the group." "Small groups," he says, "are strengthening community attachments rather than encouraging their members to focus only on themselves."[35]

Many small groups (over half, by Wuthnow's count) are associated with congregations, have religious content, or both. They are a growing part of the local religious institutional infrastructure, another example of the religious associational energy that pervades U.S. society.

While Wuthnow worries about the "domestication" of the religious faith he finds in such groups, their concerns with everyday realities of gift giving, kitchen work, termites, child care, and friendship reflect the sorts of integration (diffuseness) of lives not neatly divided into institutional roles.[36] This everyday domestic faith, and its support in thousands of small groups, is another illustration of why the modern story of institutional differentiation is not the only way to describe social life. Such diffuse involvements are not a remnant of the past but a modern invention, existing alongside more specialized roles. They are "segmental" attachments in the degree to which they are limited, involving neither the whole person nor the whole of a lifetime. But they are also "core" attachments in that members have intrinsic worth, trust each other with diffuse and open-ended obligations, have a sense of belonging, and the like.[37] Such spaces of sociability have been historically more available to women than to men, for whom the modern story came closer to reality. For both men and women, however, modern life can include religious (and other) commitments that involve both emotional depth and a breadth of concern for life issues.

Religious congregations, including the small groups they house and sponsor, are then a space of sociability where real commitments are made (even if temporary and partial) and where persons are thereby formed and transformed. Congregations are not best described as *merely* the product of individual choices. They are social realities sui generis. While people may shop for the congregation that best fits their individual tastes, the resulting group is not merely a collection of individual consumers but a community, a public, a collective, a piece of the larger societal whole. The choice to join represents a real choice and an implied commitment. It is different from the taken-for-granted belonging of earlier times and places. It is weaker in the sense that we are conscious of our ability to choose (and by implication to unchoose).[38] But it is stronger in its consonance with individual identity and purposiveness.[39] The necessity of choice is both a modern reality and (ironically) part of the ancient wisdom of the Jewish and Christian traditions. Peter Berger points out that both begin with paradigmatic stories of individual choice: Abraham's choice to leave his "father's house" and Paul's choice to leave the community of Pharisees in which he had been a leader.[40] That believers might make radical individual choices resulting in strong communities is a truth long cherished by religious reformers.

Today, we join groups that hold out the promise of self-transformation and nurture and that multiply our individual efforts at influence in the world. Precisely because of this concentration of social energy, voluntary congregations can carry at least as much weight as the established churches of yore. They may not be able to muster troops or tax the citizens for their support, but they can channel the energies of those same citizens in ways that equally affect the world.[41]

Congregations as Particularistic Spaces of Sociability

It is in the nature of this focusing of social energy that congregations are relatively homogeneous and particularistic. Warner argues, as we noted, that congregations are more often particularist than universalist in their orientation. He then adds Parsons's fifth pattern variable to note that congregations are also "collectivity oriented."[42] That is, they direct the participants' attention toward a group larger than themselves and their immediate kin in a way that avowedly asserts this group's difference from every other. It is this combination of collective public commitment with particularistic belonging that gives U.S. congregations an important place in society. Drawing people to a public space beyond the household mobilizes collective sentiments. And in their very particularity, congregations allow the full range of U.S. pluralism to be expressed.

This acknowledgement of the particularity of congregations calls into question both political theories and theologies that have emphasized the need for religion to embrace a universal message, emphasizing the "fatherhood of God and the brotherhood of man" (to use a phrase prominent in the early days of the ecumenical movement). H. Richard Niebuhr, social theorist and theologian, looked at the denominational diversity of the early twentieth century and declared it a sin. At the end of his chapter titled "The Ethical Failure of the Divided Church," he declares denominations to be emblems "of the victory of the world over the church, of the secularization of Christianity, of the church's sanction of that divisiveness which the church's gospel condemns. . . . [U]nless the ethics of brotherhood can gain the victory over this divisiveness within the body of Christ it is useless to expect it to be victorious in the world."[43] That religious communities should be formed around social divisions seemed to him contrary to the Christian gospel.

In Niebuhr's and earlier times, as analysts faced the move from traditional to modern society, the diversity of those traditional, parochial groups seemed both mind-boggling and threatening. The analysts' proposed solution was the modern liberal nation-state, alongside modern "rational" bureaucracies.[44] Economic and governmental organizations would run by predictable, written rules, universally applied. The structures of the state would affirm universal citizenship and suppress rival tribalisms.[45] Benevolent representatives of all the people would impose order on the chaos. In the United States, the image was both the Statue of Liberty and the melting pot. All were welcomed to citizenship; all were expected to merge their particularity into a national identity that would only hint at the diverse flavors that went into the soup. Such modern national entities have thrived for much of this century, but now, at century's end, the idea of uniting diverse groups into a single cultural whole is becoming increasingly untenable. Despite more than a century of "melting," parochial languages and customs remain alongside common languages and cultures that allow diverse groups to communicate. Increasingly, peoples throughout the world are claiming that the subordination of their language and customs has occurred in the service not of a universal ideal but of another group's language and culture, masquerading as a universal ones. Whatever the merits of these claims, the reality of political universalism has fallen far short of its ideals.

In social theory, as well as in politics, a universally practiced "rational discourse" has been taken as an ideal made possible by the modern world.[46] Decisions could be reached by rational actors, based on universal principles, in a conversation theoretically open to all. Such "public" discourse, in contrast to private ones, could pursue "the common good." While such an ideal has much to commend it, Nancy Fraser identifies a number of difficulties inherent in its assumptions.[47] Those who argued for such rational and accessible public spaces rarely included the public work of women or marginal ethnic groups in their models.[48] Indeed, the "public" activities of men depended on the existence of women's support work and the infrastructure of bourgeois family life. The line between public and private is not a given, but always a matter of contesting interests. Nor is "the common good" a given. It, too, conceals differing, but silenced, concerns. The notion of "the public" always conceals the extent to which there are many publics contending for access and power. So long as inequalities remain, devalued groups will be at a disadvantage in competing for a role in the conversation. They will have devalued participatory styles and will get interrupted, silenced, and subsumed into someone else's universal "we." Such devalued groups are not well served by an insistence that only one public exists. In reality, they have always formed what Fraser calls "subaltern counterpublics," places where minority collective interests are given voice and mobilized.

The division of the world into public and private spheres has, as Fraser noted, been a gendered division: Men belong in the public realm of rational discourse; women belong in the private realm of affective and particularistic interests. The same division, however, has been used to describe the changed role of religion in its disestablished and plural (modern) state.[49] Religion became, according to these arguments, "merely" private. That designation is echoed in current assumptions that if congregations are not directly involved in "public" projects such as political organizing or the provision of social services, they must be irrelevant "private" institutions.[50] However, at the same time that nineteenth-century religion was supposedly retreating into a feminized private sphere, church women were taking to the streets, legislatures, and saloons in pursuit of political, moral, and economic reforms they thought would make the society more livable for all its members.[51] And "public" men were gathering in secret societies to perform ancient mystical rituals and affirm their solidarity.[52] Neither men nor women were living in the neat public/private dichotomy to which they had been theoretically assigned. Recent research on participation in voluntary organizations confirms the inadequacy of gendered public/private distinctions. Thomas Janoski and John Wilson conclude, "Women have as high a rate of participation in community-oriented associations as men. This suggests that women care as much about the public household as the private, that they have as public a role as men, albeit of a different kind, a role born of their frequent role as mothers."[53] Neither women's work nor religious values and gatherings are well analyzed as "merely private." Again, a dichotomy disguises reality.

The larger point, however, is that while the modern world pretended that a single, universal public was possible, the postmodern world recognizes the plurality and contestation among publics that has been present all along. It also recognizes that moral judgements of all kinds require an intimate knowledge of particular situations as much as they require universal principles.[54] While modernist social theory took pains to relegate religious gatherings to the margins and to "private" life, a newer paradigm can include religious communities as among the "publics" present in a complex society. Just as the either/or dichotomy of communal versus urban life is better described as both/and, so the either/or dichotomy of a single "common good" versus warring particularisms is better described as a both/and web of multiple publics, collectively constituting the whole. Even those who formerly thought of themselves as the "mainline" can take their places alongside the other "subaltern counterpublics," recognizing that no one community can define the whole.

It is important to note that these contesting particularities need not threaten the social order. Elective parochialism is not the same as the ascribed kind.[55] People who have chosen a particular way of life may shun the ways of life they have chosen against, but they cannot view them as utterly alien. Although the potential for conflict is still very real, mitigating factors abound. The complexity of social life increases the likelihood that cross-cutting loyalties will exist, that no single attachment will prevail to the exclusion of all others.[56] Connections to diverse persons, made through association at work and school, in neighborhoods, clubs, politics, and the marketplace, keep identities and loyalties from polarizing. Even the most dedicated conservative churchgoer is part of a larger web of relations that make a monolithic conservative worldview difficult.

While the rhetoric of some political ideologues makes polarization and "culture war" sound like apt descriptions of life in the late twentieth century, everyday reality is far more complicated. It is not that ordinary people are "muddle-headed" about ideas they ought to think through and get right, as James Hunter argues.[57] People whose lives are defined by everyday troubles and joys feel much freer than do professional ideologues to put together ideas and practices from a very large cultural tool kit. Those ideas may not appear to form a coherent intellectual system, but they contribute to workable strategies of action. Just as Ann Swidler reminds us that ideas function differently in settled and unsettled times, ideas also function differently inside and outside contested arenas.[58]

Among the congregations described here, the great majority represent just such arenas of everyday practice, rather than ideologically-defined camps. Support for an evangelical view of the Christian life is not systematically opposed by those who see social activism as more important, or vice versa. Most of the people we met have simply not learned the ideological lesson that if they believe in promoting social justice, they should place less emphasis on witnessing; or—at the other pole—that if they believe in witnessing, they should be wary of calls for social justice. They were perfectly willing to affirm that *both* social justice and evangelism are important, or perhaps that neither of those things is as important as a life of prayer, Bible study, and high moral standards.[59]

I would worry that we might have stumbled onto peculiar congregations, but the evidence for the middle ground of everyday practice goes beyond our twenty-three examples. In their study of a wide range of denominational officials, Daniel Olson and Jackson Carroll report a similar large middle ground in which people are drawing on elements from both evangelical and liberal traditions (as well as some who fit neither).[60] Carroll and Marler report that even at two seminaries that ought to represent the two poles, there is little evidence of a raging war and a good deal of evidence that much middle ground exists.[61] In his study of congregations and social action, Carl Dudley found a similar lack of polarization.[62] And Penny Becker insists that "liberal" and "conservative" do not adequately describe the conflicts and decision making of the larger group of congregations she studied in Oak Park.[63] In short, a variety of people doing research in a variety of settings have failed to uncover the cultural divide that has been hypothesized. While such a divide may exist for national lobbyists and in media images, it does not explain the everyday life of religious organizations as they face the everyday difficulties of survival. As Robert Wuthnow has

modern society. As I argued earlier, modern society is best understood as containing anonymous relationships and bureaucratic structures *alongside* overlapping pockets of communal solidarity. Voluntary organizations—from choirs to PTAs to ethnic heritage societies to congregations—are the places where relationships of trust are formed, where a sense of identity is nurtured. Social capital in its most basic form, these relationships of trust facilitate communication and coordination of activities in society and provide well-being to their participants.[75] Both individuals and society as a whole benefit from the act of belonging, in all its particularistic multiplicity.

The benefits of belonging are enhanced, however, by the legitimacy accorded to recognized forms of voluntary organization, especially congregations. Warner speaks of congregations as being "presumptively legitimate."[76] Groups recognized as congregations receive, by definition, a measure of acceptance, and the social identities enshrined in those congregations are therefore recognized. For First Congregational in Long Beach, a respected downtown church, to openly incorporate gay and lesbian persons into its membership and to further sanction their presence with a church entry in the Gay Pride Parade is to lend the church's legitimacy to a new social group, helping to bring it into the civic arena. Congregations are places of belonging, but belonging to a religious community has a moral weight not always granted to other memberships.

In addition to the basic social capital generated in the associative arenas of congregations and other voluntary organizations, such groups bear the special responsibility of convening the "subaltern counterpublics" Fraser describes. They are the places where otherwise voiceless people have a voice, where those denied leadership learn to lead.[77] Recall the intentional leadership training programs at both City Baptist and Grace Baptist. Before granted participation in the social arenas dominated by elites, nonelite populations create their own social organizations. This has long been true for immigrant groups, creating parallel societies in the midst of an alien culture. And it has most emphatically been true for African Americans, especially as they have gathered in black churches.[78] When no one else seemed to hear the voices of pain, black churches were communities of solidarity and comfort. When no other public spaces were available, church sanctuaries became organizing halls. Here the music and stories and art and language of a people have been preserved and celebrated. Here the conversation "behind the wall" has continued, offering to the conversation "at the wall" both the richness of its heritage and the depth of its critique.

Among the many accomplishments of such subaltern counterpublics—as of all voluntary organizations—are the creation and enhancement of civic skills. If social capital is the basic stuff of organization and connection, civic capital is the repertoire of skills and connections necessary for political life. Beyond association and trust, civic skills involve especially the arts of communication, planning, and decision making. In the research of Sidney Verba, Kay Schlozman, and Henry Brady, civic skills are measured in terms of the concrete activities of letter writing, participating in decision-making meetings, planning and chairing meetings, and giving presentations or speeches.[79] These skills, often learned in school and on the job, can also be learned through participation in voluntary organizations. Every club that plans a special event, every society that needs officers, and every congregation that asks its members to teach classes and chair committees provides opportunities for the development and exercise of civic skills.

In his study of Latin American Pentecostalism, David Martin argued that such processes also work in societies not yet fully democratic. The Pentecostal emphasis on the gift of tongues means that everyone is given a voice, anyone can participate. Even the custom of testifying, Martin speculated, provided a kind of school for democracy. By establishing "lay and unmediated channels of communication," evangelicals in these repressive societies effect a "revolutionary reversal of all social order." In the sheltered space of the sect, each person can be remade and can "give 'tongue' to [both] frustrations and aspirations."[80] The practices established in such communities then lay down a cultural pattern that can gradually "leak" out into the rest of society.

Martin's hunches are, in fact, confirmed by the research of Verba, Schlozman, and Brady. Civic skills are not specific to the organizations in which they are developed and used. Their research demonstrates that—over and above background characteristics like income and education—civic skills are directly related to participating in the political process, especially to activities beyond voting.[81] While advantaged people are more likely to have jobs that give them skills and more likely to join voluntary organizations, *anyone* who joins an organization gains the advantage of membership and participation. People who are relatively disadvantaged in background and job characteristics gain proportionately more from participation in voluntary associations. Because people of all economic and educational levels belong nearly equally to congregations (whereas other voluntary organizations are disproportionately middle and upper class), congregations are the single most widespread and egalitarian providers of civic opportunity in the United States.

The centrality of congregations in the civic and political process is not, of course, new. The first congregations of European settlers on these shores were church and government rolled into one, and the meetinghouse saw debates about both doctrine and civic duty. On the

U.S. frontier, churches often provided the first social anchor for a community, instilling necessary skills and providing structure for the growth of a stable civilization.[82] Some congregations still have a keen sense of their meetinghouse role, hosting community gatherings and political debates. The larger denominational bodies to which they belong also provide arenas for civic debate around important issues of the day.[83] But the research on civic skills suggests that even when congregations are at their most "private" and "sectarian," they may be facilitating the political process. The same person who learns to write letters to missionaries and collect money for new hymnals can use those skills to participate in local and national political life.

The importance of participation in voluntary associations has also been recognized in the work of Robert Putnam, especially in his influential article "Bowling Alone." He traces over the last generation both a substantial decline in U.S. political participation and a persistent, sometimes precipitous, decline in membership and participation in various voluntary organizations. "The most whimsical yet discomfiting bit of evidence of social disengagement in contemporary America," he says, is that "more Americans are bowling today than ever before, but bowling in organized leagues has plummeted in the last decade or so."[84] They are, he concludes, bowling alone and thereby missing out on the social interaction and occasional civic conversations that coincided with the Tuesday-night bowling league.

Perhaps Putnam is right to be worried about the associational health of the United States, but his central example is a telling one. That people are not bowling in leagues does not tell us that they are necessarily bowling alone. They may be bowling with informal friendship groups, their families, or their Sunday school classes. The decline in one form of associational participation—while disconcerting to those with an economic investment in that form—does not signal a decline in association, as such. Putnam is unconvinced by the countertrends he sees, but the congregational ecologies we have examined would lead me to think otherwise. While old congregations are dying, new ones are being born. As older forms of congregational life are suffering, new forms are thriving. Putnam is right to be concerned for the continued vitality of face-to-face voluntary organizations where civic skills can be learned. Our evidence would simply suggest that he should look more closely for the new spaces of sociability that may be replacing old ones.

Congregations and other voluntary organizations, then, generate the basic social capital of association, along with the civic capital of communication and organizational skills. They do this especially well for those least advantaged in other sectors of the society, acting as subaltern counterpublics. Voluntary organizations also benefit their communities in more tangible ways. They provide not only human resources for the work of sustaining modern social life, but material resources as well—meeting space and vehicular transportation, bulletin boards and public address systems, copying machines and paper. Just as the human resources amassed for the good of the organization itself can be recycled for the good of the community, so the material resources of congregations and other voluntary organizations provide an infrastructure for doing the work of the community, an infrastructure often most visible in times of crisis. In the days after the 1992 uprising in South Central Los Angeles, the normal flow of food into the area was seriously disrupted. Supermarkets had been burned and looted, but the churches were still standing, and nascent distribution systems swung into action. Everyone from the Episcopal diocese to the Salvation Army to Catholic Charities activated their food and clothing networks, and soon eighteen-wheelers were arriving at church doors, and neighborhoods were getting food. As John Orr and his associates note, "Inventories were already in place. Volunteers were already recruited. The distribution mechanism had already been charted. The distribution sites were already identified—religious institutions, located on almost every square mile of the affected area."[85] The material infrastructure of gymnasiums and kitchens and telephones and vans is a critical part of the social capital contributed to the rest of society by voluntary organizations, especially by congregations. Robert Wuthnow reports in his study of how Americans use their money that "religious organizations tell people of opportunities to serve, both within and beyond the congregation itself, and provide personal contacts, committees, phone numbers, meeting space, transportation, or whatever it may take to help turn good intentions into action."[86]

As the Los Angeles example illustrates, voluntary organizations often contribute quite directly to the well-being of society by channeling resources and volunteer energies toward arenas of need. Nearly all congregations report providing some sort of human service activities; more than 60 percent report social benefit programs, such as promoting civil rights; half report educational programs that reach beyond their own congregation; and nearly that many support arts and cultural programs. In many cases this is support given through coalitions, rather than directly provided, but the extent of congregational involvement in the provision of social services is broad indeed.[87] From affordable housing to shelters for abused women, from food pantries to refugee resettlement, congregations are often the organizational vehicles for the ameliorative work that needs to be done in a community. Our culture sees helping the needy as a religious virtue and expects religious organizations to be engaged in service activities.[88] The people in the congregations we studied were no exception. Eighty-eight percent said that helping the needy is very important or essential to living the Christian life, and 92 percent said that service to the needy is very important or essential to the ministry of their congregation. Part of the cultural definition that surrounds religious institutions is that they will provide direct services to people who need their help. That same cultural definition makes it likely that people in need will seek out congregations as sources of help.

That constellation of cultural expectations also makes congregations a likely vehicle for the volunteer energies of those who want to help. Even people who are not members may join in a congregation's tutoring program or help out at the shelter once a week. Like other voluntary organizations, congregations create helping roles. They construct opportunities for doing good that allow for a bounded exercise of compassion—one that is recognized as legitimate and honorable, but one that allows us to do good without being absorbed by the effort. In his study of how we care for each other and for society, Wuthnow made this very basic point. "Without soup kitchens, the role of soup-kitchen helper could not exist. Thinking of something as a role is contingent on having organizations that institutionalize these roles. . . . [T]hree-quarters of the activities people mentioned that involved giving of their time to help others were linked to various organizations such as charities, churches, service clubs, health organizations, and neighborhood centers."[89] Congregations are able to expend social capital in service to the community because they are recognized as legitimate places for investment by people with social capital to spend.

In this as in many other civic functions, congregations take their place alongside other voluntary organizations as providers of services, arenas of public discourse, supporters of civic well-being, and the like. In each of these functions, the work of congregations is similar in kind to the work of other groups, although congregations often have a certain edge. They are more egalitarian in membership, taken as a whole, and therefore more accessible to disadvantaged groups than are some other voluntary organizations. They carry more moral weight in legitimizing the community membership of new populations, and they have the most pervasive infrastructure for meeting community needs, along with the expectation that their provision of such services is to be trusted. Put simply, the recognized moral character of congregations sets them apart from other civic organizations, giving them a place of special honor and responsibility.

The Moral and Spiritual Capital of Congregational Life

Congregations create some kinds of social capital, then, that differ from the contributions of other associations. More than any other organizations, congregations are expected to represent the community's moral order, to hold up the best human values while condemning human fault. When politicians indulge in idealistic moral rhetoric, we are never quite sure that it represents anything beyond their own partisan interests. We expect religion, on the other hand, to hold up the highest ideals for their own sake. This becomes especially important in the upbringing of children. The tie between congregational membership and family formation remains strong in U.S. culture.[90] Those who sow wild oats as young adults often return to the fold when their children reach school age. At least since the Halfway Covenant, in the seventeenth century, parents have sought the protection of faith and the good graces of the Church for their children—even when they themselves were less than enthusiastic believers.[91] Many adults see religious training for their children as part of their obligation to the world. They would not be doing good or making the world a better place if their children were denied the training provided by the church. While other institutions may participate in the moral upbringing of children, none take on this task quite so explicitly as do religious bodies.

This concern for inculcating moral standards does not end with children. Congregations also want their adult members to live by the principles of the faith. Even members who are less than orthodox in their beliefs are encouraged by congregations to practice the faith by living the Golden Rule.[92] In these twenty-three congregations, we often heard from adults who especially valued worship each week as a time for reflection and priority setting. The set-aside time, the sacred space of the church, perhaps the inspiration of the music reminded them of what should be most important in their lives, almost regardless of the preacher's message. For others the teachings and doctrines are much more thoroughly and articulately incorporated into everyday life. But for both the theologically well versed and the theologically inept, congregational membership had been consciously sought out as a way to support virtuous living. Conservatives often make the point that disaster awaits those who stray from regular church attendance, but liberals seem to intuit the same thing. They may not come as often, but they know that this particular organization plays a key role in their lives. There may be other community organizations concerned with upholding moral virtues, but congregations retain a central role in that task.

One of the reasons congregations hold such a key position must surely be their linking of moral virtue with sacred presence. Congregations are not just places to be reminded of what one ought to do. They are spaces where "ought" is put in cosmic perspective. While people may encounter transcendent realities in all sorts of places, congregations bear the weight of cultural expectation. The spaces and rituals of congregational life invite transcendence. We expect to meet God—at least on occasion—when we go to church or synagogue or mosque.

This linking of moral instruction with transcendent presence is often powerfully conservative, resulting in "bad faith" (to use Sartre's term). Peter Berger describes the way in which religious legitimation can prevent human action. People "live in the world they themselves have made as if they were fated to do so by powers that are quite independent of their own world-constructing enterprises. . . . By means of the 'otherness' of the sacred the alienation of the humanly constructed world is ultimately ratified."[93] God's stamp of approval can be an alienating force, convincing us that the world is as God would have it be, out of the reach of mere mortals. In that sense, congregations are often seen as bastions of status quo conservatism.

Yet such is not always the case. This same sense of transcendence can "de-alienate" as surely as it can alienate. It can reveal the world to be "merely" human constructions, susceptible to human intervention. This accounts, Berger notes, for the recurrent use of the biblical tradition against those who would appropriate religion for oppressive ends. "False consciousness and bad faith, widely legitimated by means of religion, may thus also be revealed as such by means of religion."[94] Extraordinary encounters with divine forces—whether through direct experience or mediated through sacred stories—create a perspective that makes critique and action possible. In the cosmic conversation that takes place in worship, divine actors can enter the human drama as partners for change.

As places of religious ritual, congregations are potential sites for social and personal transformation. Victor Turner captured the transformative power of ritual in his notions of "anti-structure" and "communitas."[95] Ritual intentionally alters the usual social arrangements and allows the envisioning of a different state of being (communitas). Durkheim called the ritual state "collective effervescence" to denote its volatile potential.[96] More recently, a number of researchers have noted the power of religious experience as motivation for individual and collective action in the world.[97] And anthropologists and historians have chronicled the ways in which colonial peoples have appropriated the symbols and stories of their colonizers as their own tools of transcendence and resistance.[98] Whether candlelight vigils in East Germany, or the strains of "We Shall Overcome," or the sight of a sinner repenting at the altar, the gestures, sights, and sounds of religious ritual are experienced as powerful by the participants. In writing about community sources of social capital, Carl Milofsky notes that "spiritual well-being is an important intrinsic value [as a] source of enthusiasm for community building."[99] Stephen Warner, among others, has emphasized the sense of power often generated by religious experience, and theorists since Weber have noted the power of religious ideas to motivate action in the secular world.[100] Even religious events that seem only to direct the worshipper toward some future world are nevertheless linked to this one by their enactment in a concrete place by a definable group of people.[101]

What happens in congregations is different from what happens in other social gatherings, then. Because they are religious, transcendent experiences and ideas about God are central to the values congregations protect and disseminate among their members. Describing the Latin American Catholics he studied, political scientist Daniel Levine wrote that "*religious* motives and values undergird other aspects of group life and keep them going in the face of possible adversity. . . . The continuing power of religious belief and commitment provides a basis for enduring solidarities and the construction of meaningful vocabularies of moral concern."[102] Yet even these "purely" religious elements are not without community significance. Congregations are both sacred places, making claims for the power of a transcendent Other in the midst of this world, and civic places, mobilizing all sorts of resources for the sake of the community. The ideas and ways of life nurtured in congregations can shape other aspects of everyday life in both direct and indirect ways. In congregations, we voice collective grievances, envision solutions, seek divine sanction, gather material goods, build networks, invest time and energy. As an ongoing institutional presence in the community, congregations provide the stability within which cultural traditions are preserved and sometimes created anew.

That modern urban Americans are expending considerable organizational energy to create and transform local religious collectivities testifies to the centrality of these collectivities in the larger social system. In the midst of places where social capital is being strained to the limits, people are gathering to worship and to pray, to eat together and to debate, to distribute aid to the community and to organize protests. Each congregation gives expression to the yearnings of very particular people in a very particular place and in so doing reflects the enormous diversity present in U.S. society and in any community. Collectively, they represent a vital element in the civic culture. They are public forums to which individuals choose to commit some portion of their time and energy. No one religious institution stands at the center of any community, and proportionately few stand at the center of individual lives. Still, taken together, they provide a sense of transcendence and integration for their members and a similar point of transcendence and human concern for the community. As people construct and reconstruct urban neighborhoods, they have not neglected to build religious institutions that will sustain them. The religious associational energy we have seen expended in nine communities is a window on the continuing importance of religious gathering places in the nation's cultural landscape.

Focus Questions

This set of questions was worked out in consultation with the research team to guide the observation and interviewing of the researchers. Suggestions for specific methods of data gathering are included for each set of questions.

Focus I. Questions about the Congregation

Primary questions:
What does the congregation do, how does it give meaning to what it does, and how is it related to the community, to other institutions, and to the individuals in it?

How, if at all, has this congregation's life been altered by social change?
How have they acted to protect and/or adapt their activities and meanings?

Specific things to consider:
1. History. How does this congregation tell its "story"? What are the high points and low points in their reading of their history? Are there recurring metaphors or myths? Who keeps this history, and who is ignorant of it? What does their story say about why they exist, why the institution is worth preserving? How has recent change precipitated revisions of this story?

- Gather a "focus group" of 3–6 longtime members.
- Do a "time line" (see *Handbook*) with a small group.
- Gather commemorative and other descriptive documents.
- Interview longtime members.

2. The sacred. How does this congregation invoke the sacred? What does it do that points beyond itself to some larger reality? What language and image does it use to describe this sacred reality? What are their key symbols? What do they say about how people ought to relate to the sacred? What is the implicit (and explicit) theology? How is this related to what they say they should do (their norms)? What is the balance between sacred and secular in their language?

- Listen to sermons and observe worship.
- Attend church school classes.
- Tour the building with a guide(s) who can explain its special places and meanings.

3. Norms. What does the congregation expect of the persons in it? Are there behavioral boundaries beyond which they may not go? What levels of participation and investment in the congregation are expected? What behavior is visibly rewarded? What surprises people?

- Observe and listen.
- Find out whether anyone has ever been expelled.
- Ask interviewees questions about their agreements and disagreements with "church policy" (letting them define that term).

4. Membership. How does the congregation recruit and socialize its new members? What assumptions are made about what sorts of people "fit" (their target audience)? What is their perception of the community? How are these assumptions shaped by class consciousness (and actual class position)? Recognizing that they will probably claim to be "diverse," what are the limits to that diversity?

- Find out about recruitment drives.
- Attend a new members' class.
- Observe the visible and oral signs of class (use of language, dress, allusions to "culture").
- Interview someone who has recently visited for the first time.
- Ask interviewees to describe the typical person who lives in the church's neighborhood. Ask whether they themselves ever lived in the neighborhood and why they left (if they did).

5. Balance between individual and community. Where are the zones of anonymity and intimacy? What aspects of people's lives are seen as "their own business"? In what contexts, if any, does the congregation encourage discussion about one's everyday life?

- Listen to sermons.
- Attend small-group meetings and social occasions (church school classes, women's or men's groups, etc.).
- Ask interviewees about who their closest friends are and about what sorts of things they talk about with church people.

6. Mission and "programs." What is the congregation's stated (and/or implicit) "mission"? What is it about "this world" they wish to affirm or change? What are their goals and central activities? What activities give people energy? What activities have they changed or discontinued and why? How does their official version of their "mission" compare to what they actually do?

- Gather official documents—mission statements, weekly bulletins, flyers, newspaper articles or ads, etc.

372

- Listen to sermons and church school lessons.
- Listen for announcements and informal communication about events, paying attention to "tone" (excitement, pleading, resignation, etc.).
- Ask interviewees about their participation (past and present).
- Ask interviewees what makes them proud of their church.

7. Power. How does the congregation make decisions (formally and informally)? What assumptions are made (or stated) about who can do what? How is this related to resources of money and time? What role does the pastor play in leading the church? Who are the key lay leaders, and how are they identified and nurtured?

- Attend "business meetings" or administrative board meetings.
- Ask interviewees about some recent decision—whose idea was it, who was consulted, who decided, who's involved in carrying it out, etc.
- Ask interviewees about persons they see as *potential* leaders in the congregation.
- Ask the pastor about his or her "style of leadership" and watch for examples (or contradictions).

8. Agency. (a) Perceptions. What, if anything, does this congregation think it has the power to do? What forces are seen as beyond their control? What actions or responsibilities are "delegated" to other institutions in the community (seen as not the congregation's business)?

- Listen for the assumptions behind what people say about their mission and activities.

(b) Resources. What internal resources (material and ideal, money and conviction) does the congregation draw on to accomplish those things? What personpower, skills, equipment and facilities, and *money* are they willing and able to utilize? What ideas are used to motivate and justify action?

- Listen to sermons and announcements.
- Find out about the budget and endowment.
- Attend events or observe ministries in which the church is involved, observing who is there, doing what.
- Ask interviewees about their involvement and contributions.

(c) Partnerships. With what other institutions (denomination? community agencies? sister church? ecumenical community organizations?) is this congregation allied? What is the strength and nature of the partnership? What do these organizations do in behalf of the congregation? With what institutions is the congregation allied by virtue of its members' connections? What material and other resources are available from these outside sources?

- Watch for references in church literature, announcements, etc.
- Ask key leaders.
- Interview someone from the partner organization or denomination.

9. Issues. How does the congregation talk about the most important issues facing it (remembering that this may simply be week-to-week survival)? How, if at all, are those issues related to changes in the community? What language is used to discuss these issues—pragmatism? rights? duty? calling? theological or secular?

- Attend planning meetings.
- Listen to sermons and announcements.
- Ask key leaders about what they think these "key issues" are.
- Listen to informal conversations over coffee, etc.

10. Differences and conflict. What are the significant divisions and conflicts within the congregation? How are the story and purpose told differently in different sectors? How are norms of behavior and participation different? How are those differences handled—avoidance? open conflict? debate?

- Ask interviewees how they think people in the congregation are different and to "map" these differences (what kinds of people go together, what they agree on, etc.)
- Attend business sessions.
- Attend a variety of different events, groups, etc., observing differences in who is there and who leads.

Focus II. Questions about Individuals

Primary questions:
What do individuals do, in what relationships are they embedded, and how do they give meaning to what they do?
  How, if at all, have individual meanings and actions been altered by social change?
  How, if at all, has their involvement in this congregation played a role in their (re)construction of meanings and patterns of action?

Specific things to consider:
1. Individual biography. How do they tell their life story? Are sacred forces active in it? Do sacred symbols frame or interpret the story? What "stages" or periods do they describe? When is/was religion most important? Has their relationship to organized religion changed at different stages in their lives? At what point did this congregation become a part of their lives? How did they come to it and why did they join? What keeps them coming? What could (or does) drive them away?

- Ask interviewees to tell you about their lives—perhaps beginning with some fairly recent transition (moving, job change, child's birth) and working back and forth from past to present.

2. Decisions and issue definition. How do they describe the most significant decisions facing them (or recently made) individually (or as a family)? Do they

see their own lives as related to larger community issues? What sort of language do they use for describing issues and solutions—cost-benefit? moral obligation? sacred duty? submitting to God's will? Where do they seek out information for making decisions? Whose advice do they seek?

- Ask interviewees for a concrete example of a major decision and find out how they made it.
- Ask interviewees about the significant issues facing some group that does not include themselves (e.g., ask elderly about problems youth face, ask people who don't live in the neighborhood about problems the neighborhood faces).

3. Nature of and relationship to the sacred. How do they describe or envision their primary sacred reality (their god)? What are the key attributes? What power do they think this god has in life? And how do they describe their relationship to sacred reality, i.e., what must one do to "be saved"? How do these individual experiences and meanings relate to congregational norms and rituals (i.e., how does the individual's account relate to the "stock stories" of the congregation)?

- Listen for what people pray about.
- Ask interviewees about what they like best in the church's worship services and when they feel close to God.
- Attend catechism classes.
- Learn to use their religious language and ask them to define terms for you.

4. Purpose. What are their most important activities and relationships—their sense of what gives them purpose?

- Ask interviewees how they introduce themselves.
- Ask interviewees what they would want in their obituary.

5. Activities. What things in fact consume most of their time and energy? Where do the activities and relationships of the congregation fit into this pattern? What are their patterns of "investment" of time, money, energy?

- Ask interviewees to walk you through a typical week.
- Ask about memberships in various organizations.
- Watch for evidence of their activities (bumper stickers, when they are unavailable for church activities, phone interruptions, etc.).

6. Relationships. What are the most significant relationships in their lives? Which, if any, are connected to the congregation?

- Ask interviewees to name their 5 closest friends. Note especially which, if any, are members of the church and/or of neighborhood organizations.
- Ask interviewees about close relatives who live nearby.
- Ask how these things have changed in the last 5 years and why.

7. Fellowship. What activities of the congregation facilitate and nurture relationships? In which congregational contexts, if any, do people talk with each other about their lives?

- Talk to people responsible for inducting newcomers about what they think is most important.
- Attend social gatherings, work groups, study sessions, and the like.
- Talk to people who seem to be on the fringes about what they wish the church would do.

8. Status and power (outside). Where do these people fit in the larger social order? What resources (economic power, "connections," influence, and experience) do they have and where do those resources come from (job, education, etc.)? Remember that status simply means "place," and everyone has one.

- Ask interviewees about their jobs and their educational background.
- Observe their surroundings.
- Ask about who they might call to help solve some personal or community problem.

9. Leadership. Where does this person fit in the congregation? What influence do they have, on what issues, and with whom? For what are they honored?

- Ask interviewees who they think of as the most exemplary members and the most influential members.
- Observe who speaks, from what position, on what.
- Watch newsletters and bulletins for items naming persons for honor, concern, contact persons, etc.

10. Interdependence. Do they use their power in behalf of the congregation or of individuals in it? Do they depend on the congregation or individuals in it for help? If so, what kinds of assistance do they expect from the congregation? What kinds of needs do they express in congregational contexts (prayer requests, announcements, and the like)?

- Listen for what requests (prayer and otherwise) are made.
- Ask interviewees whether they have ever gone to the church for help of any kind.
- Ask interviewees whether they have ever helped someone in the congregation in any way (brought in food, contributed money, helped paint a house, etc.).
- Ask interviewees whether the church has ever asked them to help a person or organization in the community.

Congregational Survey

CONGREGATIONAL SURVEY

This congregation is part of a national study of "Congregations in Changing Communities." As part of that study, we would like to have information from as many individuals in the congregation as possible. Please take a few minutes to respond to these questions--in most cases you can just check (X) the response that fits you best or fill in a brief answer. Where we ask for your belief or opinion, we really want to know what you think. There are no "right" answers. Where you really can't answer, just skip on to the next item. Since lots of different kinds of churches are being studied, some questions may use unfamiliar terms--just do your best to answer in a way that makes sense to you. *Note that your responses are completely anonymous; the code number on this questionnaire only identifies your congregation.* When the questionnaires have been tallied, your congregation will get a summary of everyone's answers.

FIRST, QUESTIONS ABOUT YOUR CHURCH AND COMMUNITY ACTIVITIES

1. How long have you been attending this congregation (parish)?_____
   Are you a member here? [ ] yes [ ] no

2. Have you ever belonged to a congregation of a different denomination? [ ] yes [ ] no
   If so, which denomination(s)?_____

_____

3. About how often do you participate in each of the following church and community activities?

	Daily	Weekly or more	2-3 times a month	once a month	a few times a year	never
Worship services (or liturgies)						
Sunday School or Bible study groups						
Choirs or other music groups						
Community/social ministries						
Seeking converts and new members						
Church fellowship activities						
Church building upkeep						
Private prayer and meditation						
Civic, school, political, professional or other community groups						

4. Go back to the list above and place a check to the left of any of the activities in which you have leadership responsibilities (teaching, committee membership, etc.).

5. How many members of your household are regular attenders in this congregation?_____

6. Think for a moment of your five closest friends (outside your family)--how many are members of this church?_____

7. How long does it take you to travel from home to church (one way)?_____

8. About how much does your household contribute to the congregation <u>each year</u>?
    [ ] less than $100 [ ] $100 - $599 [ ] $600 - $1199 [ ] $1200 - $1799
    [ ] $1800 - $2399   [ ] $2400 or more

NOW, SOME QUESTIONS ABOUT YOUR BELIEFS AND VALUES

9. Which best describes your view of the Bible? (check one)

    ____ It is an important piece of literature, but is largely irrelevant to our lives today.

    ____ It is the record of many people's experience with God and is a useful guide for individual Christians in their search for basic moral and religious teachings.

    ____ It is the Word of God and its stories and teachings provide a powerful motivation as we work toward God's reign in the world.

    ____ It is the inspired, authoritative Word of God that is without error in all that it says about faith and morals.

    ____ It is the inspired Word of God, without error not only in matters of faith, but also in historical, scientific, geographic and other secular matters.

10. When you think about the qualities of a good Christian life, how important are each of the following to you? (rate each one)

	Essential	Very Important	Somewhat Important	Not at all Important
Reading and studying the Bible regularly	____	____	____	____
Spending time in prayer and meditation	____	____	____	____
Actively seeking social and economic justice	____	____	____	____
Taking care of those who are sick or needy	____	____	____	____
Attending church regularly	____	____	____	____
Receiving the sacraments	____	____	____	____
Avoiding worldly vices	____	____	____	____
Seeking to bring others to faith in Christ	____	____	____	____
Seeking to bring beauty into the world	____	____	____	____
Practicing Christian values in work, home and school	____	____	____	____

11. When you imagine what God is like, which of these pictures is likely to come to mind?

	Very Likely	Somewhat Likely	Not at all Likely
Father	____	____	____
Mother	____	____	____
Deliverer	____	____	____
Judge	____	____	____
Comforter	____	____	____
Liberator	____	____	____
Savior	____	____	____

Congregational Survey

12. When you think about priorities for <u>your church's activities in the community</u>, how important are each of the following to you? (Rate each one)

	Essential	Very Important	Somewhat Important	Not at all Important
Supporting social action groups in the church	___	___	___	___
Encouraging members to share their faith	___	___	___	___
Providing aid and services to people in need	___	___	___	___
Helping members resist the temptations of the world	___	___	___	___
An active evangelism program, inviting the unchurched to attend	___	___	___	___
Fostering a sense of patriotism and good citizenship	___	___	___	___
Cooperation with other religious groups for community improvement	___	___	___	___
Preparing people for a world to come, where the cares of this world will be absent	___	___	___	___
Congregational participation in social and political issues	___	___	___	___
Helping members, as individuals, to be good citizens	___	___	___	___
Encouraging the pastor to speak out on social and political issues	___	___	___	___

FINALLY, SOME BACKGROUND INFORMATION ABOUT YOURSELF

13. How many years have you lived in this community?_____

14. How many other close relatives of yours live nearby (less than 1 hour away)? _____

15. What is your highest level of formal education?

[ ] less than high school   [ ] high school diploma   [ ] some post-high-school work
[ ] 4-year college degree   [ ] post-college graduate work or degree

16. What is your approximate total <u>annual</u> household income?

[ ] under $10,000   [ ] $10,000 to 19,999   [ ] $20,000 to $34,999
[ ] $35,000 to 49,999   [ ] $50,000 to 64,999   [ ] $65,000 to 79,999   [ ] $80,000 or more

17. What is your occupation (or what was it before you retired)?_____

18. How long does it take you to travel from your home to your job (one way)?_____

19. About how much of your working time is (or was) spent working with each of the following?

	Most	Some	None
objects (merchandise, machines, buildings, etc.)	___	___	___
people (managing, selling, teaching, etc.)	___	___	___
ideas (writing, programming, planning, etc.)	___	___	___
the land (farming, forestry, etc.)	___	___	___

20. About how often do (or did) you get instructions from and report to a supervisor?
[ ] at least daily [ ] at least weekly [ ] at least monthly   [ ] a few times a year
[ ] annual evaluations only [ ] never

21. From what part(s) of the world do you trace your family tree? For example, most people who think of themselves as "white" have ancestors from Europe. (check all that apply)

[ ] Africa [ ] Asia [ ] Europe [ ] North America (i.e. American Indian)
[ ] Latin America [ ] Caribbean [ ] Pacific Islands [ ] Middle East
[ ] Other_____

22. About when did the first of your family (or ancestors) come to North America?_____

23. In this last section, please fill in information about each person living in your household. You will be person #1, and any others living with you can be listed in any order.

In the **"Relationship"** column, put that person's relationship to you
(spouse, partner, child, etc)
In the **"Age"** column write each person's age.
In the **"Gender"** column, please write "M" (male) or "F" (female) for each person.
In the **"Ethnicity"** column, use the categories in #21 above for each person.
Use the **"Employment"** column for each person aged 16 or over. Write the approximate number of hours per week that person works for wages. If the person is not employed for pay, please write "student," "retired," "homemaker," "unemployed," etc.

	Relationship	Age	Gender	Ethnicity	Employment
Person #1 (you)	self				
Person #2					
Person #3					
Person #4					
Person #5					
Person #6					

Notes

1. Introductions

1. Tocqueville 1835. For a more recent review of the role of congregations in democratic life, see Watt 1991.

2. Hatch 1989; Butler 1990.

3. Harry S. Stout and D. Scott Cormode (1995) point out that understanding religious organizations as organizations requires acknowledging that they are both cultures and structures, indeed that neither would be possible without the other.

4. Cormode 1995.

5. Finke and Stark 1992.

6. See Warner 1993 for a review of recent arguments on the relationship between pluralism and religious vitality. Historian Timothy Smith, in "Congregation, State, and Denomination: The Forming of the American Religious Structure" (*William and Mary Quarterly* 25 [1968]:155–176), argues that U.S. religious diversity made any sort of state-supported system impossible and necessitated our system of denominations.

7. On the pervasive public role of religion, see Casanova 1994 and Ammerman 1993b.

8. This emphasis on the importance of voluntarism in the creation of congregations is a central thesis of Warner 1993.

9. James Luther Adams (1986) offers a cogent critique of this assumption. He notes that a voluntary system can distort and silence and misrepresent no less efficiently than totalitarianism.

10. Hall 1995.

11. These attendance trends are summarized in Holifield 1994. See also Roger Finke and Rodney Stark, "Turning Pews into People: Estimating Nineteenth-Century Church Membership" (*Journal for the Scientific Study of Religion* 25[1986]:180–192).

12. Hadaway et al. 1993.

13. Adams 1986, 193.

14. Douglass 1927. Another pioneering study was Kincheloe 1989.

15. Even before the crises of the 1960s, both sociologists and theologians had lamented the perceived inability of churches to adapt to the urban environment. For a review, see Lewis 1994.

16. Wilson and Davis 1966, 54.

17. Knight 1969. See also Driggers 1977.

18. Roof et al. 1979.

19. Leanne Rivlin (1987) notes that a neighborhood, to exist, must be acknowledged by residents, merchants, and users as having boundaries, identifying marks, and a name.

20. See the account of Chicago's parade and the way it has adopted the "ethnic neighborhood festival" as its structural and symbolic model in Herrell 1992.

21. Gorman 1992.

22. Lynch 1992.

23. This narrative of Long Beach changes incorporates some material written by Brenda Brasher.

24. Claritas, Inc., 1994; Bureau of the Census 1991.

25. Long Beach *Press-Telegram*, 1–5 March 1981.

26. Larry Bennett would like this place. He says that the primary urban virtues are surprise, tolerance, innovation, and participation. The public spaces necessary for these things to thrive are undermined by structures that aim for stability and security (skywalks and the like). However, "city residents are constantly improvising in their use of urban spaces" (1990, 127).

27. Edmonston and Passel 1994.

28. African Americans had, in fact, constituted a major "wave" of migrants to the Los Angeles area, especially during World War II and soon thereafter. For a discussion of Los Angeles patterns of immigration, see Muller and Espenshade 1985.

29. This history of the community has been compiled from our interviews with community leaders. The text combines sections written by Mary Beth Sievens and Gini Laffey with material written by me.

30. Bureau of the Census 1991.

31. Claritas, Inc., 1994.

32. This history has been constructed largely from an account provided by researcher Bob Pierson. In addition, it is informed by interviews with community leaders.

33. These and other population figures in this section are from Bureau of the Census 1972, 1982, 1991.

34. The process by which this was achieved is described in Goodwin 1979.

35. Farley and Frey 1994.

36. Schneider and Phelan 1993.

37. This summary of the effects of plant closure on workers is taken from Bluestone and Harrison 1982.

38. On the effects of plant closings on community infrastructure, see Perrucci et al. 1988, especially 52–63.

39. This history was compiled and partially written by Connie Zeigler and Stacey Nicholas. Information in this section has been drawn from our interviews with community leaders in Anderson.

40. Bureau of the Census 1972.

41. Bureau of the Census 1991.

42. This trend is also noted in Peter Key, "Anderson on the Rebound," *Indianapolis Star*, 16 May 1993, I-1, 2.

43. Blackwell 1991, 166–167.

44. Ibid., 276–277.

45. Even these gains are misleading. James Blackwell (1991) points out that, measured against the total population of persons now in middle- and upper-class occupations, African Americans are still critically underrepresented. Likewise he notes that blacks in suburbia are unlikely to find their closest friends or primary social activities there. Across classes, housing and social life remains largely segregated. The illusions of progress, including the case of Atlanta, are taken up in Burman 1995.

46. W. Wilson 1987.

47. Blackwell 1991, 183–185.

48. Ibid., 192–193.

49. This account is informed by White 1982.

50. James Hudnut-Beumler (1994) does a masterful job of describing the postwar suburban way of life. He opens *Looking for God in the Suburbs* by saying that it is about "the social, moral, and religious problems of a people who got nearly everything they had ever dreamed of" (ix). The success, optimism, and sense of progress that dominated the fifties are certainly reflected in Carmel's history.

51. Vidich and Bensman 1958. The description of "Springdale" reflects the way an expanding urban culture and economy may affect people unaware.

52. Eiesland forthcoming: "Mapping Faith."

53. Garreau 1991; 1994.

54. Sources for population statistics are the U.S. censuses. This section draws on our interviews with Gwinnett residents and community leaders. It has been compiled from materials written by Nancy Eiesland and by Barbara Elwell, as well as by me.

55. Leanne Rivlin (1987) argues that people have varying strengths of contacts and identification with a neighborhood. We need a new vocabulary of attachment, she says, that reflects the way chosen, circumscribed attachment is nevertheless formative. That network ties are both spatially bounded and spatially diffuse in most urban neighborhoods is the conclusion of Wellman 1979.

56. Robert Wuthnow provides a concise history of the congregation and its relationship to its place and immediate public (1994b, 40–43). See also Miller 1981 along with Melvin 1985 for the ways in which our definition of "neighborhood" has emerged since the nineteenth century and changed in recent years. Urban neighborhoods as particularistic communities emerged most clearly in the early years of this century, but reemerged as potent political units in the 1960s. Claude Fischer (1991) provides an overview of the pushes and pulls of

locale. He notes the pervasiveness of "community" in our cultural and political rhetoric and the way in which that ideology serves the privileged more than the poor. He also documents the pulls away from locality (smaller household size, increased female labor force participation, and increasing geographic separation of home from work, along with the communication and transportation technologies that make it possible to sustain relationships over longer distances) and the way they are balanced out by forces increasing the importance of locale (increased home ownership, reduced residential mobility, dispersal of the population, especially into suburbs, and the growth of class-homogeneous neighborhoods).

57. Carlos 1970. The particularism of suburbs means, of course, that there is no such thing as "suburbia," but rather many suburbias. On this point, see Newman 1975.

58. Robert Wuthnow (1994b) notes three kinds of relationships between congregation and community: the small, localized congregation that is very tied to its place and the issues of that place; the small, niche congregation that may pay little attention to the issues of its immediate context; and the megachurch that is regional in character and may be involved in urban or national issues or both. Avery M. Guest and Barrett A. Lee (1987) report that the congregations most involved in their local communities were those that had been there the longest and whose members were most like the surrounding community. They appear to be documenting the older, "parish" model of congregations solidly tied by tradition and place to a particular community. For a fascinating look at the links between family, community, and religion in an urban ethnic neighborhood, see Orsi 1985. In other research, the connection between congregation and immediate locale has often been assumed. In Walrath 1979b (as in other articles in the same volume), factors affecting local congregations are taken to be connected to their immediate location. Douglas Walrath notes, however, that "mid-town" churches cannot be so analyzed, since they tend to draw their members from throughout an urban region. The term *niche congregation* will be used here in a slightly different way from the use of *niche* in organizational theory. There the niche is the position an organization occupies relative to the array of resources needed and the array of services rendered. In this sense, every organization has a niche (see Baum and Singh 1994). In the sense in which the term is used here, a niche congregation is one that successfully garners enough resources from a large institutional environment to be able to offer a distinctive array of services with little competitive overlap.

59. On the liabilities of newness, see Stinchcombe 1965.

60. Theologians and social scientists have been examining congregational life for most of this century, and schemes for classifying congregations abound. Among the earliest (and most pervasive) was Ernst Troeltsch's distinction between *church* and *sect* (1931). More concrete data on congregations came first from H. Paul Douglass, who, as head of the Institute of Social and Religious Research, amassed during the 1920s and 1930s an impressive body of research on American churches. His analysis of the internal structure of the congregation largely followed the outlines of the programs and functions he found the

churches engaged in—from clergy roles to educational activities to social ministry. In addition, he paid attention to such external factors as region, neighborhood changes, and general cultural climate (see Douglass and de Brunner 1935). In the decades that followed, congregations fell into some disrepute among both social scientists and sociologically minded theologians. There seemed a pervasive feeling that congregations were irrelevant to the great issues of the day (see, for example, Berger 1961; Winter 1961). In addition, social scientists were perfecting survey research methods, and their unit of analysis was likely to be the religious individual, not the institution to which that individual might be attached. Theologian James Gustafson (1961) argued, however, that organized communities of faith were the primary bearers of the Christian tradition; he focused on the human, political, linguistic, and other social dynamics of congregational life. Sociologist Earl Brewer and his colleagues (1967) argued that the church should be understood sociologically by giving attention to its patterns of human relationship, its characteristic structures and systems, and the intrusion of culture and tradition on the internal workings of the congregation. Work sponsored by the World Council of Churches resulted in Mady Thung (1976) bringing sociological and organizational theories to bear in formulating a model for a "missionary church." Thung divided the relevant social factors up into external pressures and internal structures. Internally, she gave attention to modes of organization and communication, along with structures of authority and leadership.

By the 1980s, creative new work was underway. Theologian James Hopewell's enthusiasm for the congregation helped to galvanize a number of new efforts, and he proposed an anthropological and literary framework for understanding the culture of congregations (Hopewell 1987). Hopewell was part of the Congregational Studies Project Team, which produced the *Handbook for Congregational Studies* (Carroll et al. 1986), proposing identity, context, program, and process as the key dimensions along which congregations could be analyzed. By the early 1990s, Joseph McCann (1993) could recount dozens of models, typologies, images, and dimensions of church organization and offer a multidimensional model of his own.

61. Noyce 1975.

62. Writing at about the same time as Douglass, Samuel Kincheloe (1989) noted some of the same patterns. He names the "institutional church" as one alternative. It offers services to those nearby by drawing on the resources of members who come from a wide area, not quite the same pattern as that adopted by niche congregations. The other types he names are the "downtown" church, which serves a large metropolitan area, plus those that move, federate, or die.

63. Douglass 1927.

64. Kanter et al. 1992, 15.

65. Swidler 1986.

66. Erving Goffman is helpful in providing categories of analysis for these everyday patterns. He emphasizes just how precarious they really are and how essential to reinforcing the social structures in which they are embedded. See Goffman, *Interaction Ritual* (Garden City, N.Y.: Doubleday, 1967).

67. See Bourdieu 1991.
68. Kanter et al. 1992.
69. Hawley 1950.
70. DiMaggio and Powell 1983.
71. Freeman 1982.
72. Feldman and March 1981, 177.
73. Morgan 1986.
74. Bolman and Deal 1991.
75. This is approximately the framework being employed in the forthcoming *New Handbook for Congregational Studies* (Carroll et al. forthcoming). As a member of the Congregational Studies Project Team, I have participated in the plans for revision of the *Handbook* during the same time that I was carrying out this research. My thinking has obviously influenced how the *Handbook* is being developed, and, even more, my thinking has been influenced by my colleagues on the team.
76. This way of thinking about organizational culture was suggested by Dvora Yanow (personal communication, 27 June 1994). Similarly, James Spradley (1980, 5–12) admonishes ethnographers to study cultural behavior, cultural knowledge, and cultural artifacts.
77. Hodgkinson and Weitzman 1993. Paul Douglass and Edmund de Brunner (1935) included financial resources among the factors they examined in the 1920s and 1930s. More recent data are reported in several studies on patterns of giving in Hoge 1994.
78. Economist Robert Stonebraker (1993) reports that larger churches experience economies of scale—their costs per member are lower. But they also suffer from "free rider" problems—more people participate without giving. The former actually outweighs the latter, meaning that larger congregations actually have more excess revenue to spend on outside ministries.
79. Peter Steinfels has written about the many ways in which secular economic demands can affect local churches. Rising insurance rates, for instance, can make it impossible to maintain staffing levels ("Churches Are Caught in Economy's Grip," *New York Times*, 20 June 1991, 1, 11).
80. See Yanow 1993 for an excellent discussion of the way buildings function as conveyors of meaning. James P. Wind (1990) has given attention to the role of buildings in shaping the identity (internal and external) of a congregation.
81. James Gibbs and Phyllis Ewer (1969) attribute this size effect, in part, to the ability of larger congregations to support larger staffs, which in turn enable them to engage in more outreach activities. J. Kenneth Benson and Edward Hassinger (1972) report that among rural churches in Missouri, increments in size result in both more informal activities (revivals, weeknight worship services, and the like) and more formalized activities (vacation Bible school, training programs, etc.). Ironically, however, increases in size also mean lower average levels of participation (Wilken 1971). In fact, Robert Wilson (1977) notes that in contrast to the deficiencies small churches may have in money and facilities, they are likely to be strong in their "people resources" of fellowship and commitment.

82. Robert Wuthnow (1994a, 239) found, for instance, that about one quarter of the labor force has done some volunteer work in their church or synagogue in the past year; among those already active (who attend services weekly) the number is 64 percent.

83. Valuing "planning" and having the skills for it are both products of modern, Western, bureaucratic culture. Those most "modernized" are most likely to expect their congregations to be "rational" about decision making. On this symbolic function of planning, see Feldman and March 1981.

84. Robert Wuthnow (1994b, 47–48) points out that with increasingly complex governmental regulations impinging on congregational life, political skills are among the resources necessary for congregational survival.

85. Jackson Carroll (1991) says that the primary leadership tasks for clergy are interpretation, community building, and empowerment. Drawing on Donald Schoen in *The Reflective Practicioner* (New York: Basic, 1983), Carroll calls for pastors to engage in "reflective leadership," learning to analyze situations, draw on and invent necessary resources, and call forth adaptive responses that are faithful to the identity of the congregation as a Christian community.

86. The *Handbook for Congregational Studies* (Carroll et al. 1986, 51–52, 69–74) contains a helpful discussion of networks as potential resources.

87. Edward Laumann, Joseph Galaskiewicz, and Peter Marsden (1978, 458) define a network as "a set of nodes (e.g. persons, organizations) linked by a set of social relationships (e.g. friendships, transfer of funds, overlapping membership) of a specific type." Sally Johnson (1992b) describes the various forms of partnership in which congregations involved in social ministry participated. Such partnerships, she argues, provide expanded resources, ecumenical awareness, and greater visibility in the community. In another paper from the same project (Johnson 1992a), she points out that some potential partners are also competitors. Agencies already providing social services in a community may see congregations as interlopers on their territory. Joseph Galaskiewicz (1979) reports that organizational networks are built out of exchanges of money, information, and support. The organizations that control the most money are the most central to the networks, but positions that offer access to information and support are also critical in determining centrality.

88. Robert Wuthnow (1988) has written about the growing prevalence of such groups.

89. This is argued most clearly in Iannaccone 1988.

90. Kanter 1972.

91. On cultural resources, see Williams 1992.

92. Among the studies that examine the role of denominations and their authority over local congregational life are Harrison 1959, Ammerman 1990, and Farnsley 1994, along with James Wood's study (1991) of the impact of denominational civil rights policies. Mike McMullen (1994) offers a very helpful analysis of how polity affects the ways in which denominational policy is communicated to local congregations.

93. Warner 1994.

94. This is a variation on the categories proposed by Randolph Cantrell,

James Krile, and George Donohue (1983). They ask whether congregations have control over (1) their legal status and property rights, (2) ministerial careers, and (3) fiscal procedures.

95. James Hougland and James Wood (1982) found that member satisfaction was strongly influenced by a perception of appropriate patterns of control.

96. Steven Cohn (1993) uses Michels's Iron Law of Oligarchy to explain the concentration of power in the hands of pastors.

97. On this interpretive role, recall Carroll 1991.

98. See Wood 1981, especially chap. 5.

99. Larry Ingram's reflections (1980) on the power of Southern Baptist pastors have informed my discussion of pastoral authority. Philip Hammond, Lewis Salinas, and Douglas Sloane (1978) note that conservatives are more likely to claim the "charismatic" aspects of their authority, that is, to rely on divine authorization. Less conservative pastors tended, in their study, to rely on a variety of forms of authority.

100. It is interesting to note that even in the very participatory Church of the Three Crosses described by Michael Ducey (1977), the ideas and experiences of the co-pastors were critical in changing the congregation's internal and external patterns of interaction.

101. Amitai Etzioni (1961) noted that power could be based on coercion (something rarely available in voluntary organizations), remuneration (positive sanctions of all sorts), or normative grounds such as prestige, esteem, and solidarity. John French and Bertram Raven (1968) posited five bases for power in organizations: reward, coercion, legitimation, referent (identification), and expertise. Jeffrey Pfeffer (1992) distinguishes between personal sources of power (sensitivity, popularity, and the like) and structural sources that come both from legitimate authority and being in a strategic location for communication and brokering. In emphasizing the cultural and informal structure of the congregation, I am departing from some older analyses that attempted to study the congregation as a goal-oriented bureaucracy (see, for example, Hinings and Foster 1973). I do not think that the actions and structures of congregations can best be understood by giving causal priority to stated goals and official structures. An interesting application of network analysis to a local congregation can be found in Herman 1984; the author demonstrates how informal connections of esteem create the social ties around which a congregation clusters, communicates, wields power, and divides.

102. David Mechanic has noted (1962) the importance of information as a source of power for people without the authority of office.

103. The practice of sanctioning members has declined precipitously in this century. For a brief discussion of earlier practices, see Holifield 1988.

104. Hopewell 1987, 5. Another helpful treatment of the congregation as a culture is Grierson 1984, which suggests that pastors pay attention to, among other things, the congregation's remembered history, hero stories, artifacts of significance, symbols, rituals and gestures, myths of destiny, and images of hope.

105. Pierre Bourdieu (1990) argues that much of the content of a culture's symbolic and hierarchical structures is embedded in everyday practices. Every

small routine assumes the social places of those enacting it, the institutions in which they are embedded, and the history of action that has made that routine sensible.

106. Michael Ducey (1977, chap. 6) discusses the temporal ordering of worship events. The effect of cultural expectations on organizational form is elaborated by Paul J. DiMaggio and Walter W. Powell (1983). Robert Wuthnow (1994b) also notes these elements of isomorphism in congregations' forms of organization.

107. Pierre Bourdieu (1990) points to the many ways the structures of the social system are "embodied." Keith Roberts (1993) has written about the different ways in which congregations acknowledge and highlight the sensual aspects of their rituals.

108. Day 1991, 63.

109. Clark 1991, 53.

110. Cf. Cheal 1992.

111. Pierre Bourdieu (1991) argues that classifying schemes create boundaries, defining most basically "us" and "them." An excellent collection of studies that follow that lead is contained in Lamont and Fournier 1992. Such categories of difference can be reinforced in religious ritual. Melvin Williams's (1974) study of a black Pentecostal church in an urban neighborhood pointed out how the use of farm imagery betrayed the rural origins of the members and limited the appeal to a second generation of urban-born residents.

112. Pierre Bourdieu (1991, chaps. 3–4) notes the way in which legitimate religious authority is constituted in the ability to say the right words, use the right gestures, occupy the right space, and in so doing represent the whole institution, rather than merely oneself.

113. Michael Ducey (1977, 86–89) discusses the ways in which rituals subtly signal the tensions facing a group. Joanna Gillespie (1993) describes the generational differences among Episcopal women that include differences in how they relate to the experience of worship, its symbols, and its leaders. Stephen Warner (1988) provides a vivid description of a congregation in which ritual and constituency changed, leaving multiple layers of (contested) meaning in a small-town Presbyterian church. Even what it meant to be an evangelical turned out to be contested.

114. Samuel Heilman (1973) describes in careful detail the "cast of characters" and their predictable roles in the synagogue he studied. Melvin Williams (1974) even provides a map of "who sits where" in the church he studied.

115. The pervasiveness of social-class divisions in U.S. religion was decried by H. Richard Niebuhr (1929) and has been documented in countless studies since, but perhaps none more carefully argued than Pope 1942.

116. James Fowler (1991) declares internal diversity one of the marks of "the public church." Carl Dudley (1993) observes, however, that seeking diversity may be counterproductive, that diversity emerges most vibrantly when it is the by-product of commitment to other goals.

117. Joel Baum and Steven Mezias (1992) report that competition among organizations is actually very localized and specific, and we might infer that the same is true for congregations. Their study concerns Manhattan hotels and the

way size and price establish the bounds within which hotels actually compete. Size and social class, along with broad theological "families," may be the criteria defining the populations of congregations actually in competition with each other for a given group of potential members (cf. Hoge et al. 1994 on the way Presbyterian baby boomers switch only within restricted bounds).

118. Robert Wuthnow (1994b, 56–58) makes this point about cultural expectations surrounding congregations as locations for encountering sacred things.

119. Stephen Warner has also made the distinction (1985) between what he calls "monistic" and "dualistic" modes of religious experience. The latter has highly formalized routines at set-aside times for invoking God's presence. The former sees divine presence permeating everyday time and ordinary objects. No special ritual formulae are necessary; ordinary speech and everyday dress will do.

120. I have argued, for instance (Ammerman 1994), that prayer is an experience of an "alternative reality" that relativizes the pains and authorities of this world.

121. Geertz 1973. L. R. Pondy (1983) has also noted this both/and character of myths and especially of metaphors. By juxtaposing two nonequivalent elements, they make possible both change and conservation of tradition.

122. Indeed, Robert Wuthnow (1994c, 66–68) reports that adult Sunday school classes are the single most common form of support group in American society, with perhaps twenty-five million adults participating.

123. Daniel Olson (1993) reports that more conservative congregations, because of their distinctive view of the world, have denser networks of affiliation. As I have suggested (Ammerman 1987), that connection between relationships and worldview is probably reciprocal. Kenneth Wald, Dennis Owen, and Samuel Hill (1988) find conservative churches quite effective, for instance, at creating an attitudinal consensus around political issues.

124. Daniel Olson has written extensively about the nature and importance of congregational friendships. See for example Olson 1987. In addition, Donald Smith (1990) has written about factors enhancing retention in congregations, and several of those factors center on paying attention to assimilation and to nurturing relationships, especially in small groups. James Ashbrook (1966) has reported that commitment of church members in the congregations he studied was most affected by shared values and relationships; commitment meant feeling part of the church as a whole. Even the way congregations fight reveals the importance of relationships. Penny Becker and her associates (1993) found that preserving relationships ranked ahead of defending principles in most congregational fights. Recall also that Rosabeth Kanter's theory of commitment (1972) includes, along with the instrumental and evaluative dimensions, an affective dimension that recognizes the importance of relational bonds to the strength of the group as a whole. Similarly, Robert Wuthnow (1994b) says that what congregations do is draw people into an intimate community, encourage them to worship, and provide them and their children with moral instruction. Following Talcott Parsons, Stephen Warner (1994, 63) defines congregations as "collectivity-oriented, functionally diffuse, affective, and particularistic social

grouping[s]." Each of these writers has recognized the centrality of relation-ships to the reality of congregational life.

125. For a discussion of the ways in which these bonds of mutual aid consti-tute a system of "pastoral care" in the congregation, see Browning 1988.

126. Robert Wuthnow (1988) has written about some of the causes (such as increased education) and consequences (such as increased religious tolerance) of increasing religious mobility. The most complete data on patterns of switch-ing among denominational traditions is in Roof and McKinney 1987. That in-formation has been updated by Hadaway and Marler (1993), who find that switching has increased, but not necessarily between "families." That is, while people might switch from Lutheran to Methodist, they may be less likely to switch from Episcopal to Assemblies of God. Paul Sullins (1993) agrees that there is a great deal of overall stability (switching close to home) but argues that there has actually been no increase in switching over time. Dean Hoge, Benton Johnson, and Donald Luidens (1994, chap. 3) report that among baby-boomer Presbyterian confirmands, only 29 percent are still Presbyterians, with another 10 percent in other "mainline" Protestant groups. Wade Clark Roof (1993a, 174–181) reports very similar numbers: 39 percent of those reared in mainline Prot-estant groups are still in (or have returned to) similar groups; most who have left their home tradition currently participate in no religious institution. Among those who have written with some despair about this move from ascribed religion to choice are Jon Stone (1990) and Penny Marler and David Roozen (1993).

127. Edward O. Laumann (1969) found that urban friendships tend to fall within (a) broad religious groupings of Protestant, Catholic, and Jewish; (b) social class; and (c) ethnic groups. These homogeneous social groupings and their relationship to congregations will be a recurring theme in this book. It also accounts for the consistent finding in "church growth" research that change in the population of one's neighborhood is the biggest factor precipitat-ing membership decline. See, for example, Hadaway 1981.

128. See Marler 1995. Mark Chaves (1991, 512) says, "As the fortunes of that family/household type [two parents with children] rise and fall, so will the fortunes of mainstream organized Protestantism." The larger the supply of "traditional" families in a given context, the greater a congregation's chances for growth (see, for example, Hadaway 1981 and Roof et al. 1979).

129. See Ammerman 1987, chap. 9. In addition, see Davidman 1991 for a description of recruitment patterns among converts to Orthodox Judaism. There is a vast literature on conversion, especially to new religious move-ments. Most appropriate to this point is John Lofland and Rodney Stark, "Be-coming a World Saver: A Theory of Conversion to a Deviant Perspective" (*American Sociological Review* 30 [1965]: 862–875).

130. Some religious educators recognize that children learn by participating in events and activities—official and unofficial—that give the tradition its iden-tity and substance. See, for example, Westerhoff and Neville 1974.

131. Pasquale Gagliardi (1990) argues that organizational researchers should pay more attention to these artifacts, both for what they communicate and for the ways in which they shape the behavior of the organization.

132. See Michael Ducey (1977, 94–97) for a discussion of the uses of sacred space in the churches he studied. Samuel Heilman (1973) also offers a very instructive look at the physical setting of the synagogue.

133. Robert Wuthnow (1994b) notes the way special clothes have helped to maintain a sense of the sacredness of congregational activity. He observes that professionals, who dress up everyday, may have a different sensibility, however. Both he and I have noted that some congregations of professionals seem to "dress down" as a sign of the set-apartness of the worship time (personal communication, 27 December 1994).

134. See Berger 1969, chap. 1, and Berger and Luckmann 1967.

135. James Hopewell (1987, 5–9) discusses the importance of the congregation's "idiom." See also Michael Ducey's description (1977, 116–122) of the use of language, music, and styles of speaking. I have noted (Ammerman 1987, 86–88) the way language helps to maintain the boundaries of a conservative congregation. James Gustafson (1961) also includes language as a primary category of analysis.

136. Joanna Gillespie (1993) found that many of the older Episcopal women she interviewed had little explicit theological language but often related a strong sense of emotional and spiritual connection to the church that seemed to transcend language.

137. Witten 1992.

138. Richard Wood (1994) provides an intriguing theoretical explanation for how religious symbols work in changing and ambiguous environments. Any organization needs symbols that take the environment's ambiguity into account, while maintaining enough coherence to create stability. Because religious symbols are so multivalent, they may be especially useful in this task. A. Donnellon, B. Gray, and M. Bougon ("Communication, Meaning, and Organized Action," *Administrative Science Quarterly* 31 [1986]: 43–55) report, similarly, that metaphor is a particularly effective form of communication in arriving at a consensus group action, even when members disagree on why they are pursuing the action. The ambiguity of the metaphor allows individual interpretation and collective action.

139. Samuel Heilman (1973, 9) notes that the story of Kehillat Kodesh's beginnings is known by every member, and "the very knowledge of these facts seems often to be the best evidence of one's membership in the group." He goes on to include gossip and joking as modes of story telling that shape that community's life, alongside the prayer and study that are at the heart of a synagogue's identity. Peter Manning (1992) emphasizes the importance of narrative in understanding the workings of any organization. Embedded in the everyday stories people tell each other are the rules for how things get done, how people are related to each other, and the like. James Hopewell (1987), in turn, uses literary theory to identify four modal "worldviews" that characterize how congregations tell their stories. Others who have emphasized the importance of understanding narratives include Bartunek (1984) and Roof (1993).

140. Dvora Yanow (1992) writes about the power of metaphors to shape organizational life. Carl Dudley and Sally Johnson (1993) talk about "images" that shape how congregations think about how they confront the world. They iden-

tified "pillar," "pilgrim," "survivor," "prophet," and "servant" as the images that described and shaped the churches they studied. In addition, Jackson Carroll and David Roozen (1990) discerned six typical "identities" among Presbyterian congregations, which were effective predictors of such things as program emphases.

141. George Lindbeck (1984) proposes that Christian doctrine should be understood as "communally authoritative rules of discourse, attitude, and action" (18). Being religious, he says, is like learning a language; it is communal and shapes the subjectivity of the individual. "To become a Christian involves learning the story of Israel and of Jesus well enough to interpret and experience oneself and one's world in its terms" (34). Curiously, Lindbeck's theory takes almost no account of the communities necessary for the preservation and inculcation of these stories. Stanley Hauerwas (1981) argues that every social ethic involves a narrative and that the Christian life is about orienting oneself to the story of Christ. Without a story, there is no community, he says, and without a distinctive community the story will be lost.

142. Among the most useful attempts at this task by theologians are Chopp 1989 and Schreiter 1985.

143. Susan Harding (1992, 54) has written about the way fundamentalists enact and fulfill the scriptural stories they believe to be true. "Their Bible is alive, its narrative shape enacts reality." It is a discourse "which effects the world it speaks by constituting subjects who bring it about."

2. Persistence in the Face of Change

1. Hannan and Freeman 1984.
2. Dudley 1978.
3. St. Catherine's is not the actual name of this parish. Some details of its history and program have been changed to protect the confidentiality requested.
4. Daniel Golden tells the poignant story of a fatal encounter between two Allston residents—one Irish and one Cambodian—in "Neighbors," *Boston Globe Magazine*, 7 February 1993, 12–13, 27–34. The young Irish American man killed in a traffic dispute was a lifelong Allston resident and former student at St. Catherine's school. Always a bit rowdy, he began to experience serious troubles when assigned to be bussed across town to Roxbury.
5. Jeffrey Burns's description (1994) of St. Peter's parish in its Irish heyday mirrors what we heard from members of St. Catherine's. Burns describes that era at St. Peter's as "insular." In the face of a hostile native culture, Irish immigrants constructed an entire world in which they felt at home and safe.
6. Jeffrey Burns (1994, 403) notes a similar function for Catholic fundraising activities at St. Peter's parish in San Francisco. These activities raise morale as much as money.
7. When a mini-study congregation has few potential respondents, we have not tabulated congregational survey data.
8. See the discussion of Hinton Memorial United Methodist Church in chapter 5. The establishment of a niche is one option for congregations not well

equipped to compete on the same terms as others in their community (Eiesland 1994).

9. On evangelical culture, see Ammerman 1987; Hunter 1983; and Balmer 1989.

10. These styles correspond to what Steven Tipton (1982) labeled authoritative, regular, expressive, and consequential ethics. While one can observe some social class differences in this congregation in the use of these ethics, it is interesting to note their pervasiveness and near interchangeability.

11. Kincheloe 1989.

3. Relocating: New Places, New Identities

1. H. Richard Niebuhr (1929) is perhaps the most eloquent spokesperson for this point of view.

2. Daniel Olson's work on networks (1989) confirms the difficulty in integrating new members into long-established networks in congregations.

3. The Church of God's founding vision was that denominational differences would be shed, and all Christians would unite under one banner. Still, over the years, it has come to resemble other denominations in function and style. For that reason, I will use the term *denomination* to refer to the agencies to which South Meridian is related.

4. This argument is made by R. Stephen Warner (1993), building especially on the research of "rational choice" theorists such as Laurence Iannaccone and Rodney Stark.

5. Roozen et al. 1984.

6. On the role of information gathering as symbol, see Feldman and March 1981.

4. Adaptation: Integrating Gay and Straight

1. Long Beach researchers Brenda Brasher and Tom Clark were the first to use this phrase to describe the congregations they were visiting.

2. While all the people who attend St. Matthew's—English and Spanish speaking—are clearly part of that parish, our work has concentrated exclusively on the English-speaking parishioners. At present there are virtually no points of connection between the two populations. There is a priest to serve the Spanish-speaking community, and there are separate activities for the two groups. Our decision to focus on the English-speaking portion of the parish was dictated by our conceptual focus on change. This constituency represents the original population in the neighborhood, the population that has had to respond to change.

3. D'Antonio et al. 1989.

4. Both the individual focus and the spiritual eclecticism of this congregation are reminiscent of a large segment of the baby-boom population as described by Wade Clark Roof (1993).

5. Lee 1992.

6. It is a "subaltern counterpublic" in the terms defined by Nancy Fraser (1990). For more on this dynamic, see chapter 9.

5. Adaptation: Integrating across Cultures

1. Weber 1947.

2. In chapter 9, I explore the larger implications of these opportunities for leadership training. City's members are developing "civic skills." See Verba et al. 1995.

3. Charles Foster in a personal communication points out that over the last generation, Methodists have increasingly trusted local churches to train their own leaders, rather than providing training at the district or conference level. The lack of concern for expertise at Hinton is perhaps partly a result of this absence of denominational attention.

4. Note again the contrast between traditional and "rational-legal" authority. See Weber 1947, 329–358.

5. Eiesland forthcoming: "Irreconcilable Differences."

6. Elsewhere I have called this "Golden Rule Christianity" (Ammerman forthcoming).

7. Eiesland 1995.

8. Mark Silk, "The Church That Swallowed Dacula," *Atlanta Journal and Constitution*, 13 February 1993, E6.

6. Adaptation: Creating New Internal Structures

1. See Alexander 1991 for a discussion of the way such worship can be empowering. A similar argument is made by R. Stephen Warner (1993).

2. On fundamentalism's denominationlike culture, see Ammerman 1987 and Carpenter 1984.

3. A further discussion of the functions of prayer is found in Ammerman 1994a. See also Martin 1990.

4. Weber 1946.

5. The Methodist system is inherently a modern, urban, bureaucratic, cosmopolitan system. It assumes a congregation where division of labor and systematic decision making are routine. Not surprisingly, the thousands of Methodist congregations that are rural and small town in setting find this system alien. Most of my Methodist seminary students told me that the rural churches they serve find ways to create the prescribed structure on paper, while continuing to operate with an informal, essentially patrimonial system of power in reality.

6. When Emerson announced his retirement in 1994, the staff parish committee members drew up lists of things they were looking for in a new pastor. High on the list was "liberal theology," which they defined as "not limiting" and accepting of more than one theology.

7. Innovation: Birth and Rebirth

1. Roof and McKinney 1987, 165.

2. Roof 1993a.

3. Robert Wuthnow (1994c) discusses the impact of participation in small groups on activities in the larger community. Even though many such groups appear quite privatist, they nevertheless have a public impact.

4. The scheme they were referencing originates with Rothauge n.d.

5. The church's growing success in the neighborhood has been touted in the Atlanta press. See Patti Puckett, "A Congregation of Contrasts," *Atlanta Journal and Atlanta Constitution*, 3 March 1994, JN3.

6. Johnson et al. 1974.

7. In these opinions about Church teaching they are not alone. See D'Antonio et al. 1989.

8. On patterns of leaving and returning, see Hoge et al. 1994 as well as Roof 1993.

9. On the role of small groups in Catholic life, see D'Antonio 1995.

8. How Congregations Change

1. An original draft of this account of Long Beach's religious history was written by Brenda Brasher and Tom Clark.

2. On the Metropolitan Community Church, see Warner 1995.

3. An original draft of this account of Allston-Brighton's religious history was written by Gini Laffey and Mary Beth Sievens.

4. This arrangement is similar to that adopted by First Nazarene Church in Los Angeles (which was near, but not in, our study area). The difference there was that the Anglo congregation predated the others.

5. An original draft of this account of Oak Park's religious ecology was written by Penny Becker.

6. Stacey Nicholas and Connie Zeigler wrote the original draft of this material on Anderson.

7. Daphne Wiggins wrote the original draft of this account of changes in southwest Atlanta.

8. Michelle Hale and Joan Cunningham wrote the original draft of this account of Carmel's growth.

9. Nancy Eiesland and Barbara Elwell wrote the original draft of this account of Gwinnett County's changing religious scene.

10. On Hebron, see Eiesland 1994.

11. William McKinney (1979) says suburban churches may grow, but they are not easily satisfied.

12. Douglass 1927; Noyce 1975.

13. On competition within niches, see Baum and Singh 1994. Michael Hannan and John Freeman (1977) speculate that specialized organizations have to compete with the subunits of generalist organizations (the boutique with the

department store, for instance). Since congregations are more likely to establish niches on the basis of constituency than on the basis of services, this distinction seems to make less sense for niche congregations. More helpful is the application to voluntary organizations found in McPherson 1983.

14. Although he does not emphasize the role of size in generating commitment, the link between sectarianism, commitment, and small size is implied in Laurence Iannaccone's theorizing (1988, 1994).

15. Ilsa Lottes and Peter Kuriloff (1994) found, for instance, that higher education resulted in more liberal attitudes on a number of measures, especially acceptance of homosexuality.

16. Wood 1981.

17. On the balance between the congregation's power and the denomination's, see Hougland and Wood 1979.

18. This is evidence of "de facto congregationalism," as described by R. Stephen Warner (1994).

19. See Carroll et al. 1986 for a helpful discussion of diversity and conflict in the congregation. One important point to be made is the difference between fixed, non-overlapping coalitions and shifting, overlapping ones. When the same people stick together on every issue, permanent schism is much more likely than if the alliances shift with each new issue.

20. Personal communication.

21. Roozen et al. 1984.

22. Respondents were asked to rate each item as "essential," "very important," "somewhat important," or "not at all important" to their congregation's ministry. The "activist" orientation included supporting social action groups in the church, congregational participation in social and political issues, and encouraging the pastor to speak out on social and political issues. This scale had a reliability coefficient (alpha) of .78. The "evangelist" orientation included encouraging members to share their faith, helping members resist the temptations of the world, and an active evangelism program, inviting the unchurched to attend. This scale had a reliability coefficient of .82. The "sanctuary" orientation includes preparing people for a world to come, where the cares of this world will be absent, and fostering a sense of patriotism and good citizenship. The reliability coefficient for this scale is .66. The "civic" orientation included providing aid and services to people in need, cooperation with other religious groups for community improvement, and helping members, as individuals, to be good citizens. The reliability coefficient on this scale is .58.

23. This lack of polarization contradicts the picture painted by James Hunter (1991).

9. Conclusions

1. Emirbayer and Goodwin 1994.
2. Freeman 1982.
3. Coleman 1988.
4. Milofsky 1987, 278.
5. Cf. McPherson 1983.

6. While we have not seen it in these communities, it is certainly possible for totalitarian governments to make traditional forms of association very difficult in an effort to appropriate social capital for themselves.

7. This is slightly higher than the proportion reported by the Independent Sector survey of 1992, which estimated that 20.1 percent of American congregations had been founded after 1970 (see Hodgkinson and Weitzman 1993).

8. Warner 1991.

9. Wirth 1938.

10. Parsons 1951, 58–77.

11. Robert Holton and Bryan Turner (1986, 211) have written, "The project of reconciling individualism and secularisation with community and moral order remains fundamental to sociological inquiry." They see Parsons's theory as an answer to the nostalgia of communitarian critiques of modernity. I think Parsons still drank too deeply from the well of modern/premodern dichotomies.

12. Parsons 1964.

13. On religion retreating into enclaves, see Berger 1969; on religion as an individual meaning system, see Luckmann 1967.

14. Nelson 1971.

15. Riesman 1950; Whyte 1957.

16. Bellah et al. 1985.

17. I am, in fact indebted to Bender 1978 for the thrust of this argument. He clearly points to the need to understand community as containing *both* primary and secondary relationships.

18. On kinship bonds in cities, see T. Wilson 1993; on religious participation there, see Finke and Stark 1988.

19. Fischer 1991. See also Wellman 1979.

20. Fischer 1991, 80.

21. These are themes I develop more fully in Ammerman 1994b.

22. Brown 1991; 1993.

23. Collins 1985.

24. Smith 1979.

25. Ahlbrandt (1984, 136) has shown that strong neighborhoods need both a strong social fabric of personal (family and friendship) and institutional (work, worship, shopping, and civic group) ties.

26. Coined by social theorists especially worried about the effects of individualism on American society (Bellah et al. 1985), the term "lifestyle enclave" seems intended to evoke the most pernicious of consequences from individual choices. The term "new voluntarism," as used in Roof and McKinney 1987, is much more neutral. Much of this literature, however, adopts the "shopping" metaphor to describe the process of choice and as a consequence denigrates the resulting choices. See, for example, Marler and Roozen 1993.

27. Hammond 1992 is a careful study of the relationship between ideas about individual autonomy and actual parish involvement (measured as membership, attendance, salience, and identification). More educated, mobile people do indeed place more value on autonomy and are thereby less involved in local parish life. This finding lends credence to the arguments that individu-

alism erodes commitment. It certainly forces a redefinition of the nature of commitment. It is also important to note, however, that much of Hammond's effort to measure decline in religion is in fact a measurement of the decline of nineteenth-century evangelical orthodoxy and practice.

28. Warner 1994.

29. Wuthnow 1988.

30. Warner 1988.

31. Wuthnow 1994.

32. Among those who have written about this intertwining are T. Wilson (1993) and Evans and Boyte (1986).

33. The classic theoretical statement on this issue is Mead 1934. A more recent, very helpful exposition of the interdependence of self and society is found in Shotter 1984.

34. A classic statement on this issue is Simmel 1971 [1908]. See also Coser 1991.

35. Wuthnow 1994c, 322, 330.

36. I am indebted to Mary Jo Neitz for this critique of Wuthnow's use of "domestication" to describe the religious practices of small groups. In her 1995 presentation to a session of the American Sociological Association, focused on Wuthnow's book, she noted that such everyday concerns have always been the domain of women's religious practice and that they are equally prevalent in a variety of non-Protestant and non-Western traditions.

37. Philip Selznick (1992) makes the familiar primary/secondary distinction in this way. He points to the coexistence of both types of attachments in modern society but retains the basic dichotomy, failing to recognize the place of social arrangements that in themselves combine both styles of attachment.

38. These are issues emphasized by Peter Berger (especially 1969). In recent conversation (and in Berger 1992), he has struggled with the reality of strong modern commitments. In spite of the absence of certitude and of ascribed communities, people like himself choose to have faith.

39. On these issues, see Warner 1993.

40. Berger 1992, 88–89.

41. The cultural power of religious organizations is the subject of Demerath and Williams 1992. For an elaboration on the concept, see Ammerman 1993a.

42. Warner 1994, 63.

43. Niebuhr 1929, 25.

44. Bender 1978.

45. One way to understand nineteenth-century U.S. history is through the lens of conflicts between the nation-state and rival tribalisms—among others, the confederates in the South and the Mormons in Utah, both drawn against their will into a nation wishing to dominate the whole North American continent. See Stryker 1992.

46. Habermas 1984.

47. Fraser 1990.

48. James Luther Adams (1986) points to the degree to which nineteenth-century missionary societies served the same function, especially for women.

49. Douglas 1977.

50. See chapter 1 of Whitley 1969 for a review of classic community studies that make this assumption.

51. Scott 1992 and Epstein 1981.

52. Carnes 1989.

53. Janoski and Wilson 1995.

54. See Selznick (1992, 193–201) for a discussion of the need for both particularity and universalism in moral judgment.

55. Warner 1988.

56. Among those who emphasize the role of cross-cutting loyalties and the interconnection of networks are Claude Fischer (1982), J. Miller McPherson (1983), and Thomas Bender (1978).

57. Hunter 1994.

58. Swidler 1986.

59. For more detail, see Ammerman 1994b.

60. The full report is forthcoming. Preliminary findings are reported in Olson and Carroll 1992.

61. Carroll and Marler 1995.

62. Reported in Mock 1992.

63. Becker 1995.

64. Wuthnow 1993.

65. Brueggemann 1989, 26.

66. Stephen Warner (1994, 72–73) speaks of such congregations as "protected enclaves in a hostile world."

67. Stephen Warner (1993, 1072–1073) makes the argument that denominations and other national organizations often give legitimacy and opportunity to groups that might be silenced in more homogeneous local assemblies.

68. Milofsky and Hunter 1995.

69. Demerath and Williams 1992 contains fascinating accounts of the way such formal and informal networks operate in Springfield, Massachusetts.

70. Orr et al. 1994, 19.

71. Salamon 1987.

72. This analysis shows that "turning over" social service delivery to state, local, and nonprofit entities stands to do grave harm to the system already in place. It would disrupt the stream of funds on which nonprofits depend and cease setting democratic standards that would ensure that all constituencies receive care. While local nonprofits might gain a measure of autonomy from government-imposed paperwork, they would likely have to add significant fund-raising functions to maintain their delivery of services.

73. While a good bit has been written about denominations, we know much less about emergent generalist coalitions (both those sponsored by megachurches like Willow Creek or Calvary Chapel and those existing independently like the Cooperative Baptist Fellowship) or about the "parachurch" organizations like Habitat for Humanity that draw together coalitions around specific causes or ministries. On Calvary Chapel, see Balmer and Todd 1994. On emergent denominational forms, see Ammerman 1993b.

74. Thanks to both Jay Demerath and Rhys Williams for persisting in asking this question and thereby pushing me to think about these issues.

75. Christopher G. Ellison and Linda K. George, "Religious Involvement, Social Ties, and Social Support in a Southeastern Community" (*Journal for the Scientific Study of Religion* 3 [1994]: 46–61).

76. Warner 1994.

77. This is not to ignore the fact that subaltern counterpublics can silence their own dissenters as easily as they themselves are silenced by the larger society.

78. Lincoln 1982.

79. Brady et al. 1995.

80. Martin 1990, 286–287.

81. Verba et al. 1995, especially chaps. 11–12.

82. Miyakawa 1964.

83. Wood and Bloch 1995.

84. Putnam 1995, 70.

85. Orr et al. 1994, 16.

86. Wuthnow 1994a, 242–243. This mobilization of religious people into voluntary efforts in behalf of the larger community may not be universally the case, however. John Wilson and Thomas Janoski (1995) show that active conservative Protestants are actually less likely to be involved in secular volunteering. Their energy seems to go into their own congregations, rather than into the community at large.

87. Hodgkinson and Weitzman 1993, 19–20.

88. Wuthnow 1994a, 236.

89. Wuthnow 1991, 197.

90. Ammerman and Roof 1995.

91. Brown and Hall forthcoming.

92. Ammerman forthcoming.

93. Berger 1969, 95–96.

94. Ibid., 99.

95. Turner 1977.

96. Durkheim 1915.

97. See, for example, Wood 1994; 1991. For Susan Harding (1992), ritual *is* social action, accomplishing the transformation in its very performance.

98. Fields 1985; Comaroff 1985.

99. Milofsky 1995, 1.

100. Warner 1993; Max Weber, *The Protestant Ethic and the Spirit of Capitalism* (Boston: Beacon, 1905 [1958]).

101. This is at the heart of the concerns of Wuthnow 1994b.

102. Levine 1992, 15–16.

Selected Bibliography

Adams, James Luther. 1986. "The Voluntary Principle in the Forming of American Religion." Pp. 171–200 in *Voluntary Associations: Socio-Cultural Analyses and Theological Interpretation*, ed. J. Ronald Engel. Chicago: Exploration.

Ahlbrandt, Robert S. Jr. 1984. *Neighborhoods, People, and Community*. New York: Plenum.

Alexander, Bobby C. 1991. "Correcting Misinterpretations of Turner's Theory: An African American Pentecostal Illustration." *Journal for the Scientific Study of Religion* 30:26–44.

Althauser, Robert P. 1990. "Paradox in Popular Religion: The Limits of Instrumental Faith." *Social Forces* 69:585–602.

Altman, Irwin, and Abraham Wandersman, eds. 1987. *Neighborhood and Community Environments*. New York: Plenum.

Ammerman, Nancy T. 1987. *Bible Believers: Fundamentalists in the Modern World*. New Brunswick, N.J.: Rutgers University Press.

———. 1990. *Baptist Battles: Social Change and Religious Conflict in the Southern Baptist Convention*. New Brunswick, N.J.: Rutgers University Press.

———. 1993a. "Review of *A Bridging of Faiths* by N. J. Demerath and Rhys H. Williams." *Society* 31 (1): 91–93.

———. 1993b. "SBC Moderates and the Making of a Post-Modern Denomination." *Christian Century* 110:896–899.

———. 1994a. "Accounting for Christian Fundamentalisms: Social Dynamics and Rhetorical Strategies." Pp. 149–170 in *Accounting for Fundamentalisms*, ed. by Martin E. Marty and R. Scott Appleby. Chicago: University of Chicago Press.

———. 1994b. "Telling Congregational Stories." *Review of Religious Research* 36:289–301.

———. Forthcoming. "Golden Rule Christianity: Lived Religion in the American Mainstream." In *Practicing the Religious: Lived Religion in America*, ed. David Hall.

Ammerman, Nancy T., and Wade Clark Roof, eds. 1995. *Work, Family, and Religion*. New York: Routledge.

Ashbrook, James B. 1966. "The Relationship of Church Members to Church Organization." *Journal for the Scientific Study of Religion* 5:397–419.

Balmer, Randall. 1989. *Mine Eyes Have Seen the Glory*. New York: Oxford University Press.

Balmer, Randall, and Jesse T. Todd, Jr. 1994. "Calvary Chapel, Costa Mesa, California." Pp. 663–698 in *Portraits of Twelve Religious Communities*. Vol. 1 of *American Congregations*, ed. James P. Wind and James W. Lewis. Chicago: University of Chicago Press.

Barron, David N., Elizabeth West, and Michael T. Hannan. 1994. "A Time to Grow and a Time to Die: Growth and Mortality of Credit Unions in New York City, 1914–1990." *American Journal of Sociology* 100:381–421.

Bartunek, Jean M. 1984. "Changing Interpretive Schemes and Organizational Restructuring: The Example of a Religious Order." *Administrative Science Quarterly* 29:355–372.

Baum, Gregory, and Andrew Greeley, eds. 1974. *The Church as Institution*. New York: Herder and Herder.

Baum, Joel, and Steven Mezias. 1992. "Localized Competition and Organizational Failure in the Manhattan Hotel Industry." *Administrative Science Quarterly* 37:580–604.

Baum, Joel, and Jitendra V. Singh. 1994. "Organizational Niches and the Dynamics of Organizational Mortality." *American Journal of Sociology* 100:346–380.

Baumgartner, Mary Pat. 1988. *The Moral Order of a Suburb*. New York: Oxford University Press.

Becker, Penny. 1993. "Religion, Culture, and Organizational Process in One Sample of Congregations." Paper presented to the Chicago Area Group for the Study of Religious Communities, April.

———. 1995. "'How We Do Things Here': Culture and Conflict in Local Congregations." Ph.D. diss., University of Chicago.

Becker, Penny, Stephen J. Ellingson, Richard W. Flory, Wendy Griswold, Fred Kniss, and Timothy Nelson. 1993. "Straining at the Tie That Binds: Congregational Conflict in the 1980s." *Review of Religious Research* 34:193–209.

Beckford, James. 1973. *Religious Organization*. The Hague: Mouton.

Bellah, Robert N., Richard Madsen, William M. Sullivan, Ann Swidler, and Steven M. Tipton. 1985. *Habits of the Heart*. Berkeley and Los Angeles: University of California Press.

Bender, Thomas. 1978. *Community and Social Change in America*. New Brunswick, N.J.: Rutgers University Press.

Bennett, Larry. 1990. *Fragments of Cities: The New American Downtowns and Neighborhoods*. Columbus: Ohio State University Press.

Benson, J. Kenneth, and Edward Hassinger. 1972. "Organization Set and Resources as Determinants of Formalization in Religious Organizations." *Review of Religious Research* 14:30–36.

Benson, J. Kenneth, and James H. Dorsett. 1971. "Toward a Theory of Religious Organizations." *Journal for the Scientific Study of Religion* 10:138–151.

Berger, Peter L. 1961. *The Noise of Solemn Assemblies*. Garden City, N.Y.: Doubleday.

————. 1969. *The Sacred Canopy*. Garden City, N.Y.: Doubleday.

————. 1992. *A Far Glory: The Quest for Faith in an Age of Credulity*. New York: Free Press.

Berger, Peter L., and Richard John Neuhaus. 1977. *To Empower People*. Washington, D.C.: American Enterprise Institute.

Berger, Peter L., and Thomas Luckmann. 1967. *The Social Construction of Reality*. Garden City, N.Y.: Doubleday.

Blackwell, James E. 1991. *The Black Community: Diversity and Unity*. New York: HarperCollins.

Bluestone, Barry, and Bennett Harrison. 1982. *The Deindustrialization of America: Plant Closings, Community Abandonment, and the Dismantling of Basic Industry*. New York: Basic.

Bolden, Dean A. 1985. "Organizational Characteristics of Ecumenically Active Denominations." *Sociological Analysis* 46:261–274.

Bolman, Lee G., and Terrence E. Deal. 1991. *Reframing Organizations: Artistry, Choice, and Leadership*. San Francisco: Jossey-Bass.

Bourdieu, Pierre. 1979. *Outline of a Theory of Practice*. New York: Cambridge University Press.

————. 1990. *The Logic of Practice*. Stanford, Calif.: Stanford University Press.

————. 1991. *Language and Symbolic Power*. Cambridge: Harvard University Press.

Brady, Henry E., Sidney Verba, and Kay Lehman Schlozman. 1995. "Beyond SES: A Resource Model of Political Participation." *American Political Science Review* 89:271–294.

Brannon, Robert C. L. 1971. "Organizational Vulnerability in Modern Religious Organizations." *Journal for the Scientific Study of Religion* 10:27–32.

Brewer, Earl D. C., Theodore H. Runyon, Jr., Barbara B. Pittard, and Harold McSwain. 1967. *Protestant Parish: A Case Study of Rural and Urban Parish Patterns*. Atlanta: Communicative Arts.

Brown, Anne S., and David D. Hall. Forthcoming. "Family Strategies and Religious Practices in Early New England: An Essay in the History of Lived Religion." In *Practicing the Religious: Lived Religion in America*, ed. by David D. Hall.

Brown, Karen McCarthy. 1991. *Mama Lola: A Vodou Priestess in Brooklyn*. Berkeley and Los Angeles: University of California Press.

Browning, Don S. 1988. "Pastoral Care and the Study of the Congregation." Pp. 103–118 in *Beyond Clericalism: The Congregation as a Focus for Theological Education*, ed. Joseph C. Hough, Jr., and Barbara G. Wheeler. Atlanta: Scholars.

Brueggemann, Walter. 1989. "The Legitimacy of a Sectarian Hermeneutic: 2 Kings 18–19." Pp. 3–34 in *Education for Citizenship and Discipleship*, ed. Mary C. Boys. New York: Pilgrim.

Budros, Art. 1993. "An Analysis of Organizational Birth Types: Organizational Start-up and Entry in the Nineteenth-Century Life Insurance Industry." *Social Forces* 72:199–221.

Burman, Stephen. 1995. *The Black Progress Question: Explaining the African American Predicament*. Thousand Oaks, Calif.: Sage.

Burns, Jeffrey M. 1994. "Que es Esto? The Transformation of St. Peter's Parish, San Francisco, 1913–1990." Pp. 396–463 in *American Congregations: Portraits of*

Twelve Religious Communities, ed. James P. Wind and James W. Lewis. Chicago: University of Chicago Press.

Butler, Jon. 1990. *Awash in a Sea of Faith*. Cambridge: Harvard University Press.

Calas, Marta B., and Linda Smircich. 1992. "Re-Writing Gender into Organizational Theorizing: Directions from Feminist Perspectives." Pp. 227–253 in *Rethinking Organization: New Directions in Organization Theory and Analysis*, ed. Michael Reed and Michael Hughes. London: Sage.

Calhoun, Craig, ed. 1991. *Religious Institutions*. Greenwich, Conn.: JAI.

Cameron, Kim, Robert I. Sutton, and David Whetten. 1988. "Issues in Organizational Decline." Pp. 3–19 in *Readings in Organizational Decline: Frameworks, Research, and Perspectives*, ed. Kim Cameron, Robert I. Sutton, and David Whetten. Cambridge, Mass.: Ballinger.

Cantrell, Randolph L., James F. Krile, and George A. Donohue. 1983. "Parish Autonomy: Measuring Denominational Differences." *Journal for the Scientific Study of Religion* 22:276–287.

Carlos, Serge. 1970. "Religious Participation and the Urban-Suburban Continuum." *American Journal of Sociology* 75:742–759.

Carnes, Mark C. 1989. *Secret Ritual and Manhood in Victorian America*. New Haven, Conn.: Yale University Press.

Carpenter, Joel A. 1984. "From Fundamentalism to the New Evangelical Coalition." Pp. 3–16 in *Evangelicalism in Modern America*, ed. George M. Marsden. Grand Rapids, Mich.: Eerdmans.

Carroll, Glenn R., and J. Richard Harrison. 1994. "On the Historical Efficiency of Competition between Organizational Populations." *American Journal of Sociology* 100:720–749.

Carroll, Jackson. 1991. *As One with Authority: Reflective Leadership in Ministry*. Louisville, Ky.: Westminster/John Knox.

Carroll, Jackson, and David A. Roozen. 1990. "Congregational Identities in the Presbyterian Church." *Review of Religious Research* 31:351–369.

Carroll, Jackson, and Penny Long Marler. 1995. "Culture Wars? Insights from Ethnographies of Two Protestant Seminaries." *Sociology of Religion* 56:1–20.

Carroll, Jackson, Carl S. Dudley, and William McKinney, eds. 1986. *Handbook for Congregational Studies*. Nashville: Abingdon.

———. Forthcoming. *The New Handbook for Congregational Studies*. Nashville: Abingdon.

Casanova, José. 1994. *Public Religions in the Modern World*. Chicago: University of Chicago Press.

Castelli, Jim, and Joseph Gremillion. 1987. *The Emerging Parish: The Notre Dame Study of Catholic Life since Vatican II*. San Francisco: Harper and Row.

Champion, A. G. 1989. *Counterurbanization: The Changing Pace and Nature of Population Deconcentration*. London: Edward Arnold.

Chaves, Mark. 1991. "Family Structure and Protestant Church Attendance: The Sociological Basis of Cohort and Age Effects." *Journal for the Scientific Study of Religion* 30:501–514.

Chaves, Mark, and David E. Cann. 1992. "Regulation, Pluralism, and Religious Market Structure: Explaining Religion's Vitality." *Rationality and Society* 4: 272–290.

Cheal, David. 1992. "Ritual: Communication in Action." *Sociological Analysis* 53:363–374.

Chopp, Rebecca S. 1989. *The Power to Speak: Feminism, Language, God.* New York: Crossroad.

Claritas, Inc. 1994. "Demographic Overview Report" (from *1990 U.S. Census of Population and Housing*). New York: Claritas, Inc.

Clark, Linda J. 1991. "Hymn-Singing: The Congregation Making Faith." Pp. 49–64 in *Carriers of Faith,* ed. Carl S. Dudley, Jackson W. Carroll, and James P. Wind. Louisville, Ky.: Westminster/John Knox.

Cohen, Michael D., James G. March, and Johan P. Olsen. 1972. "A Garbage Can Model of Organizational Choice." *Administrative Science Quarterly* 17:1–25.

Cohn, Steven F. 1993. "Ministerial Power and the Iron Law of Oligarchy: A Deviant Case Analysis." *Review of Religious Research* 35:155–173.

Coleman, James S. 1988. "Social Capital in the Creation of Human Capital." *American Journal of Sociology* 94 (Supplement): S95–S120.

Collins, Patricia Hill. 1985. "Learning from the Outsider Within: The Sociological Significance of Black Feminist Thought." *Social Problems* 33:514–532.

Comaroff, Jean. 1985. *Body of Power Spirit of Resistance.* Chicago: University of Chicago Press.

Cormode, D. Scott. 1995. "Neighborhood Religion: Membership and Community in Churches and Secular Voluntary Organizations in Chicago's West Town, 1870–1920." Louisville Institute Dissertation Fellows Seminar, Louisville, Ky. Typescript.

Coser, Rose Laub. 1991. *In Defense of Modernity: Role Complexity and Individual Autonomy.* Stanford, Calif.: Stanford University Press.

Cott, Nancy. 1977. *The Bonds of Womanhood: 'Woman's Sphere' in New England, 1780–1835.* New Haven, Conn.: Yale University Press.

D'Antonio, William V. 1995. "Small Faith Communities," Pp. 237–259 in *Work, Family, and Religion,* ed. Nancy Tatom Ammerman and Wade Clark Roof. New York: Routledge.

D'Antonio, William V., James Davidson, Dean Hoge, and Ruth Wallace. 1989. *American Catholic Laity.* Kansas City, Mo.: Sheed and Ward.

Davidman, Lynn. 1991. *Tradition in a Rootless World.* Berkeley and Los Angeles: University of California Press.

Davis, James H., and Robert L. Wilson. 1966. *The Church in the Racially Changing Community.* Nashville: Abingdon.

Day, Thomas. 1991. *Why Catholics Can't Sing: The Culture of Catholicism and the Triumph of Bad Taste.* New York: Crossroad.

Demerath, N. J., III, and Rhys H. Williams. 1992. *A Bridging of Faiths: Religion and Politics in a New England City.* Princeton, N.J.: Princeton University Press.

DiMaggio, Paul. 1992. "The Relevance of Organization Theory to the Study of Religion." Working Paper #174. New Haven, Conn.: Program on Non-Profit Organizations, Yale University.

DiMaggio, Paul, and Helmut K. Anheier. 1990. "The Sociology of Non-Profit Organizations and Sectors." *Annual Review of Sociology* 16:137–159.

DiMaggio, Paul, and Walter W. Powell. 1983. "The Iron Cage Revisited: Institutional Isomorphism and Collective Rationality in Organizational Fields." *American Sociological Review* 48:147–160.

Dolan, Jay P., ed. 1987. *The American Catholic Parish: A History from 1850 to the Present.* 2 vols. New York: Paulist.

Douglas, Ann. 1977. *The Feminization of American Culture.* New York: Knopf.

Douglass, H. Paul. 1927. *The Church in the Changing City.* New York: Doran.

Douglass, H. Paul, and Edmund S. de Brunner. 1935. *The Protestant Church as a Social Institution.* New York: Harper and Row.

Driggers, B. Carlisle. 1977. *The Church in the Changing Community: Crisis or Opportunity?* Atlanta: Home Mission Board, SBC.

Ducey, Michael. 1977. *Sunday Morning: Aspects of Urban Ritual.* New York: Free Press.

Dudley, Carl S. 1978. "Neighborhood Churches in Changing Communities." *New Conversations* 3 (1): 4–10.

———. 1993. "Pluralism as an Ism." *Christian Century* 110:1039–1041.

Dudley, Carl S., and Sally A. Johnson. 1993. *Energizing the Congregation: Images That Shape Your Church's Ministry.* Louisville, Ky.: Westminster/John Knox.

Durkheim, Emile. 1915. *The Elementary Forms of the Religious Life.* New York: Free Press.

Edmonston, Barry, and Jeffrey S. Passel. 1994. "Ethnic Demography: U.S. Immigration and Ethnic Variations." Pp. 1–30 in *Immigration and Ethnicity: The Integration of America's Newest Arrivals,* ed. Barry Edmonston and Jeffrey S. Passel. Washington, D.C.: Urban Institute Press.

Eiesland, Nancy. 1994. "Contending with a Giant: The Case of a Mega-Church in Exurbia." Paper presented at the Society for the Scientific Study of Religion, Albuquerque, November.

———. 1995. "A Particular Place." Ph.D. diss., Emory University.

———. Forthcoming. "Irreconcilable Differences: Conflict and Schism in a Small-Town/Suburban United Methodist Congregation." In *Mainstream Protestants and the Pentecostal and Charismatic Movements,* ed. Edith Blumhofer. Carbondale: University of Illinois Press.

———. Forthcoming. "Mapping Faith: Choice and Change in Local Religious Organizational Environments." In *Beyond Two Parties: A Survey and Analysis of American Protestantism, 1960–1995,* ed. William Trollinger and Douglas Jacobsen.

Emirbayer, Mostafa, and Jeff Goodwin. 1994. "Network Analysis, Culture, and the Problem of Agency." *American Journal of Sociology* 99:1411–1454.

Epstein, Barbara L. 1981. *The Politics of Domesticity: Women, Evangelism, and Temperance in Nineteenth-Century America.* Middletown, Conn.: Wesleyan University Press.

Erickson, Victoria Lee. 1993. *Where Silence Speaks: Feminism, Social Theory, and Religion.* Minneapolis: Fortress.

Etzioni, Amitai. 1961. *A Comparative Analysis of Complex Organizations.* New York: Free Press.

Evans, Sara M., and Harry C. Boyte. 1986. *Free Spaces: The Sources of Democratic Change in America.* New York: Harper and Row.

Farley, Reynolds, and William H. Frey. 1994. "Changes in the Segregation of Whites from Blacks during the 1980s: Small Steps toward a More Integrated Society." *American Sociological Review* 59:23–45.

Farnsley, Arthur Emery, II. 1994. *Southern Baptist Politics: Authority and Power in the Restructuring of an American Denomination.* University Park: Pennsylvania State University Press.

Feldman, Martha. 1989. *Order without Design: Information Processing and Policy Making.* Palo Alto, Calif.: Stanford University Press.

Feldman, Martha, and James March. 1981. "Information as Signal and Symbol." *Administrative Science Quarterly* 26:171–186.

Fichter, Joseph. 1951. *Southern Parish: Dynamics of a City Church.* Chicago: University of Chicago Press.

———. 1954. *Social Relations in the Urban Parish.* Chicago: University of Chicago Press.

Fields, Karen E. 1985. *Revival and Rebellion in Colonial Central Africa.* Princeton, N.J.: Princeton University Press.

Finke, Roger, and Rodney Stark. 1988. "Religious Economies and Sacred Canopies: Religious Mobilization in American Cities." *American Sociological Review* 53:41–49.

———. 1992. *The Churching of America.* New Brunswick, N.J.: Rutgers University Press.

Fischer, Claude S. 1975. "The Study of Urban Community and Personality." Pp. 67–89 in *Annual Review of Sociology,* ed. Alex Inkeles. Palo Alto, Calif.: Annual Reviews.

———. 1982. *To Dwell among Friends: Personal Networks in Town and City.* Chicago: University of Chicago Press.

———. 1991. "Ambivalent Communities: How Americans Understand Their Localities." Pp. 79–90 in *America at Century's End,* ed. Alan Wolfe. Berkeley and Los Angeles: University of California Press.

Fowler, James. 1991. *Weaving the New Creation.* San Francisco: Harper.

Fraser, Nancy. 1990. "Rethinking the Public Sphere: A Contribution to the Critique of Actually Existing Democracy." *Social Text* 25/26:56–80.

Freedman, Samuel G. 1993. *Upon This Rock: The Miracles of a Black Church.* New York: HarperCollins.

Freeman, John. 1982. "Organizational Life Cycle and Natural Selection Processes." Pp. 1–32 in *Research in Organizational Behavior,* ed. Barry Staw and L. L. Cummings. Greenwich, Conn.: JAI.

French, John R. P., Jr., and Bertram Raven. 1968. "The Bases of Social Power." Pp. 259–269 in *Group Dynamics,* ed. Dorwin Cartwright and Alvin Zander. 3d ed. New York: Harper and Row.

Frey, William H. 1989. "United States: Counterurbanization and Metropolis Depopulation." Pp. 34–61 in *Counterurbanization: The Changing Face and Nature of Population Deconcentration,* ed. A. G. Champion. London: Edward Arnold.

Gagliardi, Pasquale. 1990. "Artifacts as Pathways and Remains of Organizational Life." Pp. 3–38 in *Symbols and Artifacts.* New York: Aldine de Gruyter.

Galaskiewicz, Joseph. 1979. "The Structure of Community Organizational Networks." *Social Forces* 57:1346–1364.

Garreau, Joel. 1991. *Edge City: Life on the New Frontier.* New York: Doubleday.

Geertz, Clifford. 1973. "Religion as a Cultural System." Pp. 87–125 in *The Interpretation of Cultures.* New York: Basic.

Genette, Gerard. 1980. *Narrative Discourse: An Essay in Method.* Ithaca, N.Y.: Cornell University Press.

Gibbs, James O., and Phyllis A. Ewer. 1969. "The External Adaptation of Religious Organizations: Church Response to Social Issues." *Sociological Analysis* 30:223–234.

Gillespie, Joanna B. 1993. "Gender and Generations in Congregations." Pp. 167–221 in *Episcopal Women,* ed. Catherine Prelinger. New York: Oxford University Press.

Goodwin, Carole. 1979. *The Oak Park Strategy.* Chicago: University of Chicago Press.

Gorman, E. Michael. 1992. "The Pursuit of the Wish: An Anthropological Perspective on Gay Male Subculture in Los Angeles." Pp. 87–106 in *Gay Culture in America: Essays From the Field,* ed. Gilbert Herdt. Boston: Beacon.

Gottdiener, Mark. 1994. *The New Urban Sociology.* New York: McGraw-Hill.

Greeley, Andrew M. 1988. "Evidence That a Maternal Image of God Correlates with Liberal Politics." *Sociology and Social Research* 72:150–154.

Grierson, Denham. 1984. *Transforming a People of God.* Melbourne: Joint Board of Christian Education of Australia and New Zealand.

Griffin, Larry J. 1993. "Narrative, Event-Structure Analysis, and Causal Interpretation in Historical Sociology." *American Journal of Sociology* 98:1094–1133.

Guest, Avery M., and Barrett A. Lee. 1987. "Metropolitan Residential Environments and Church Organizational Activities." *Sociological Analysis* 47:335–354.

Gustafson, James M. 1961. *Treasure in Earthen Vessels.* Chicago: University of Chicago Press.

Habermas, Jurgen. 1984. *The Theory of Communicative Action.* Boston: Beacon.

Hadaway, C. Kirk. 1981. "The Demographic Environment and Church Membership Change." *Journal for the Scientific Study of Religion* 20:77–89.

———. 1982. "Church Growth (and Decline) in a Southern City." *Review of Religious Research* 23:372–390.

———. 1990. "Denominational Defection: Recent Research on Religious Disaffiliation in America." In *The Mainstream Protestant "Decline": The Presbyterian Pattern,* ed. Milton J. Coalter, John M. Mulder, and Louis B. Weeks. Louisville, Ky.: Westminster/John Knox.

Hadaway, C. Kirk, and Penny Long Marler. 1993. "All in the Family: Religious Mobility in America." *Review of Religious Research* 35:97–116.

Hadaway, C. Kirk, Penny Long Marler, and Mark Chaves. 1993. "What the Polls Don't Show: A Closer Look at U.S. Church Attendance." *American Sociological Review* 58:741–752.

Hall, David. 1990. *Worlds of Wonder, Days of Judgment: Popular Religious Belief in Early New England.* Cambridge: Harvard University Press.

Hall, Peter Dobkin. 1994. "Religion and the Origin of Voluntary Associations in the United States." Working Paper #213. New Haven, Conn.: Program on Non-Profit Organizations, Yale University.

———. 1995. "The Evolution of Small Religious Nonprofits: An Historical Overview." Paper prepared for the Lilly Endowment Working Conference on Small Religious Nonprofits, Chicago, October.

Hamberg, Eva M., and Thorleif Petterson. 1994. "The Religious Market: Denominational Competition and Religious Participation in Contemporary Sweden." *Journal for the Scientific Study of Religion* 33:205–216.

Hammond, Phillip E. 1992. *Religion and Personal Autonomy: The Third Disestablishment in America.* Columbia: University of South Carolina Press.

Hammond, Phillip E., Lewis Salinas, and Douglas Sloane. 1978. "Types of Clergy Authority: Their Measurement, Location, and Effects." *Journal for the Scientific Study of Religion* 17:241–253.

Hannan, Michael, and Glenn R. Carroll. 1992. *Dynamics of Organizational Populations: Density, Competition, and Legitimation.* New York: Oxford University Press.

Hannan, Michael, and John Freeman. 1977. "The Population Ecology of Organizations." *American Journal of Sociology* 82:929–964.

———. 1984. "Structural Inertia and Organizational Change." *American Sociological Review* 49:149–165.

———. 1986. "Where Do Organizational Forms Come From?" *Sociological Forum* 1 (1): 50–72.

———. 1989. *Organizational Ecology.* Cambridge: Harvard University Press.

Harding, Susan. 1992. "The Gospel of Giving: The Narrative Construction of a Sacrificial Economy," ed. Robert Wuthnow. London: Routledge.

———. 1994. "The Politics of Apocalyptic Language in the Moral Majority Movement." In *Accounting for Fundamentalisms,* ed. Martin E. Marty and R. Scott Appleby. Chicago: University of Chicago Press.

Harrison, Michael I., and Glenn R. Carroll. 1991. "Keeping the Faith: A Model of Cultural Transmission in Formal Organizations." *Administrative Science Quarterly* 36:552–582.

Harrison, Michael I., and John K. Maniha. 1978. "Dynamics of Dissenting Movements within Established Organizations: Two Cases and a Theoretical Interpretation." *Journal for the Scientific Study of Religion* 17:207–224.

Harrison, Paul M. 1959. *Authority and Power in the Free Church Tradition.* Princeton, N.J.: Princeton University Press.

Hart, Stephen. 1992. *What Does the Lord Require? How American Christians Think about Economic Justice.* New York: Oxford University Press.

Hatch, Nathan G. 1989. *The Democratization of American Christianity.* New Haven, Conn.: Yale University Press.

Hauerwas, Stanley. 1981. *A Community of Character: Toward a Constructive Christian Social Ethic.* Notre Dame, Ind.: Notre Dame University Press.

Hawley, Amos H. 1950. *Human Ecology: A Theory of Community Structure.* New York: Ronald.

Heilman, Samuel. 1973. *Synagogue Life.* Chicago: University of Chicago Press.

Herberg, Will. 1960. *Protestant-Catholic-Jew.* Rev. ed. Garden City, N.Y.: Doubleday.

Herman, Nancy J. 1984. "Conflict in the Church: A Social Network Analysis of an Anglican Congregation." *Journal for the Scientific Study of Religion* 23:60–74.

411

Herrell, Richard K. 1992. "The Symbolic Strategies of Chicago's Gay and Lesbian Pride Day Parade." Pp. 225–252 in *Gay Culture in America: Essays from the Field*, ed. Gilbert Herdt. Boston: Beacon.

Hinings, Robin C., and Bruce D. Foster. 1973. "The Organization Structure of Churches: A Preliminary Model." *Sociology* 7:93–106.

Hodgkinson, Virginia A., and Murray S. Weitzman. 1993. *From Belief to Commitment: The Community Service Activities and Finances of Religious Congregations in the United States*. Washington, D.C.: Independent Sector.

Hodgkinson, Virginia A., Murray S. Weitzman, and Arthur D. Kirsch. 1988. *From Belief to Commitment: The Activities and Finances of Religious Congregations in the United States*. Washington, D.C.: Independent Sector.

———. 1990. "From Commitment to Action: How Religious Involvement Affects Giving and Volunteering." Pp. 93–114 in *Faith and Philanthropy in America: Exploring the Role of Religion in America's Voluntary Sector*, ed. Robert Wuthnow and Virginia A. Hodgkinson. San Francisco: Jossey-Bass.

Hoge, Dean R. 1994. "Patterns of Financial Contributions to Churches." *Review of Religious Research* 36:101–244.

Hoge, Dean R., Benton Johnson, and Donald A. Luidens. 1994. *Vanishing Boundaries: The Religion of Mainline Protestant Baby Boomers*. Louisville, Ky.: Westminster/John Knox.

Hoge, Dean R., and David A. Roozen, eds. 1979. *Understanding Church Growth and Decline*. New York: Pilgrim.

Holifield, E. Brooks. 1988. "The Historian and the Congregation." Pp. 89–101 in *Beyond Clericalism: The Congregation as a Focus for Theological Education*, ed. Joseph C. Hough, Jr., and Barbara G. Wheeler. Atlanta: Scholars.

———. 1994. "Toward a History of American Congregations." Pp. 23–53 in *American Congregations: New Perspectives in the Study of Congregations*, ed. James P. Wind and James W. Lewis. Chicago: University of Chicago Press.

Holton, Robert J., and Bryan S. Turner. 1986. "Against Nostalgia: Talcott Parsons and a Sociology for the Modern World." Pp. 207–234 in *Talcott Parsons on Economy and Society*, ed. Robert J. Holton and Bryan S. Turner. London: Routledge and Kegan Paul.

Hopewell, James F. 1987. *Congregation: Stories and Structures*. Philadelphia: Fortress.

Hornsby-Smith, Michael P. 1989. *The Changing Parish: A Study of Parishes, Priests, and Parishioners after Vatican II*. New York: Routledge.

Hough, Joseph C., Jr., and Barbara G. Wheeler, eds. 1988. *Beyond Clericalism: The Congregation as a Focus for Theological Education*. Atlanta: Scholars.

Hougland, James G., and James R. Wood. 1979. "Determinants of Organizational Control in Local Churches." *Journal for the Scientific Study of Religion* 18:132–145.

———. 1982. "Participation in Local Churches: An Exploration of Its Impact on Satisfaction, Growth, and Social Action." *Journal for the Scientific Study of Religion* 21:338–353.

Hudnut-Beumler, James. 1994. *Looking for God in the Suburbs*. New Brunswick, N.J.: Rutgers University Press.

Hunter, Albert. 1987. "The Symbolic Ecology of Suburbia." Pp. 191–221 in *Neighborhood and Community Environments*, ed. Irwin Altman and Abraham Wandersman. New York: Plenum.

Hunter, James Davison. 1983. *American Evangelicalism: Conservative Religion and the Quandary of Modernity*. New Brunswick, N.J.: Rutgers University Press.

———. 1991. *Culture Wars: The Struggle to Define America*. New York: Basic.

———. 1994. *Before the Shooting Begins*. New York: Free Press.

Iannaccone, Laurence R. 1988. "A Formal Model of Church and Sect." *American Journal of Sociology* 94 (Supplement): S241–268.

———. 1990. "Religious Practice: A Human Capital Approach." *Journal for the Scientific Study of Religion* 29:297–314.

———. 1994. "Why Strict Churches Are Strong." *American Journal of Sociology* 99: 1180–1211.

Ingram, Larry C. 1980. "Notes on Pastoral Power in the Congregational Tradition." *Journal for the Scientific Study of Religion* 19:40–48.

Janoski, Thomas, and John Wilson. 1995. "Pathways to Voluntarism: Family Socialization and Status Transmission Models." *Social Forces* 74:271–292.

Johnson, Douglas W., Paul R. Picard, and Bernard Quinn. 1974. *Churches and Church Membership in the United States, 1971*. Washington, D.C.: Glenmary Research Center.

Johnson, Sally A. 1992a. "The Influence of Community Context on How a Project Develops." *Church and Community Brief Paper*. Chicago: Center for Church and Community Ministries.

———. 1992b. "Partnership for Community Ministry." *Church and Community Brief Paper*. Chicago: Center for Church and Community Ministries.

Jones, Ezra Earl, and Robert L. Wilson. 1974. *What's Ahead for Old First Church?* New York: Harper and Row.

Kanter, Rosabeth Moss. 1972. *Commitment and Community*. Cambridge: Harvard University Press.

Kanter, Rosabeth Moss, Barry A. Stein, and Todd D. Jick. 1992. *The Challenge of Organizational Change: How Companies Experience It and Leaders Guide It*. New York: Free Press.

Kelley, Dean M. 1977. *Why Conservative Churches Are Growing*. 2d ed. San Francisco: Harper and Row.

Kincheloe, Samuel C. 1989. *The Church in the City*. Ed. Yoshio Fukuyama. Chicago: Exploration.

Kloetzli, Walter. 1961. *The City Church: Death or Renewal*. Philadelphia: Muhlenberg.

Knight, Walker L. 1969. *Struggle for Integrity*. Waco, Tex.: Word.

Knoke, David. 1981. "Commitment and Detachment in Voluntary Associations." *American Sociological Review* 46:141–158.

Knoke, David, and James R. Wood. 1981. *Organized for Action: Commitment in Voluntary Associations*. New Brunswick, N.J.: Rutgers University Press.

Kunda, Gideon. 1992. *Engineering Culture*. Philadelphia: Temple University Press.

Lamont, Michele, and Marcel Fournier, eds. 1992. *Cultivating Differences: Symbolic Boundaries and the Making of Inequality*. Chicago: University of Chicago Press.

Land, Kenneth C., Glenn Deane, and Judith R. Blau. 1991. "Religious Pluralism and Church Membership: A Spatial Diffusion Model." *American Sociological Review* 56:237–249.

Laumann, Edward. 1969. "The Social Structure of Religious and Ethnoreligious Groups in a Metropolitan Community." *American Sociological Review* 34:182–196.

Laumann, Edward, Joseph Galaskiewicz, and Peter Marsden. 1978. "Community Structure as Interorganizational Linkages." *Annual Review of Sociology* 4:455–484.

Leavitt, Barbara, and Clifford Nass. 1989. "The Lid on the Garbage Can." *Administrative Science Quarterly* 34:190–207.

Lee, Richard Wayne. 1992. "Unitarian Universalists: Organizational Dilemmas of the Cult of the Individual." Ph.D. diss., Emory University.

Lenski, Gerhard. 1963. *The Religious Factor.* New York: Doubleday.

Levine, Daniel H. 1992. *Popular Voices in Latin American Catholicism.* Princeton, N.J.: Princeton University Press.

Lewis, James W. 1994. "Going Downtown: Historical Resources for Urban Ministry." *Word and World* 14:402–408.

Lincoln, C. Eric, and Lawrence H. Mamiya. 1990. *The Black Church in the African American Experience.* Durham, N.C.: Duke University Press.

Lincoln, James R. 1982. "Intra- and Inter-Organizational Networks." *Research in the Sociology of Organizations* 1:1–38.

Lindbeck, George. 1984. *The Nature of Doctrine.* Philadelphia: Westminster.

Lottes, Ilsa L., and Peter J. Kuriloff. 1994. "The Impact of College Experience on Political and Social Attitudes." *Sex Roles* 31:31–54.

Luckmann, Thomas. 1967. *The Invisible Religion.* New York: Macmillan.

Lynch, Frederick R. 1992. "Nonghetto Gays: An Ethnography of Suburban Homosexuals." Pp. 165–201 in *Gay Culture in America: Essays from the Field,* ed. Gilbert Herdt. Boston: Beacon.

McCann, Joseph F. 1993. *Church and Organization: A Sociological and Theological Enquiry.* Scranton, Pa.: University of Scranton Press.

McKinney, William. 1979. "Performance of United Church of Christ Congregations in Massachusetts and in Pennsylvania." Pp. 224–247 in *Understanding Church Growth and Decline,* ed. Dean Hoge and David Roozen. New York: Pilgrim.

McKinney, William, and Dean R. Hoge. 1983. "Community and Congregational Factors in the Growth and Decline of Protestant Churches." *Journal for the Scientific Study of Religion* 22:51–66.

McLeod, Hugh. 1978. "Religion in the City." *Urban History Yearbook* 5.

McMullen, Mike. 1994. "Religious Polities as Institutions." *Social Forces* 73(2): 709–728.

McPherson, J. Miller. 1983. "An Ecology of Affiliation." *American Sociological Review* 48:519–532.

———. 1990. "Evolution in Communities of Voluntary Organizations." Pp. 224–225 in *Organizational Evolution: New Directions,* ed. Jitendra V. Singh. Beverly Hills, Calif.: Sage.

McPherson, J. Miller, and Lynn Smith-Lovin. 1987. "Homophily in Voluntary Organizations: Status Distance and the Composition of Face-to-Face Groups." *American Sociological Review* 52:370–379.

Manning, Peter K. 1992. *Organizational Communication.* New York: Aldine de Gruyter.

March, James. 1978. "Bounded Rationality, Ambiguity, and the Engineering of Choice." *Bell Journal of Economics* 9:587–608.

Marciniak, Edward, and William Droel. 1995. "The Future of Catholic Churches in the Inner City." *Chicago Studies* 34:172–186.

Marler, Penny Long. 1995. "Lost in the Fifties." Pp. 23–60 in *Work, Family, and Religion,* ed. Nancy Tatom Ammerman and Wade Clark Roof. New York: Routledge.

Marler, Penny Long, and C. Kirk Hadaway. 1993. "Toward a Typology of Protestant 'Marginal Members.'" *Review of Religious Research* 35:34–54.

Marler, Penny Long, and David A. Roozen. 1993. "From Church Tradition to Consumer Choice: The Gallup Surveys of the Unchurched American." Pp. 253–277 in *Church and Denominational Growth,* ed. David A. Roozen and C. Kirk Hadaway. Nashville: Abingdon.

Martin, David. 1990. *Tongues of Fire: The Explosion of Protestantism in Latin America.* Oxford: Basil Blackwell.

Mead, George Herbert. 1934. *Mind, Self, and Society.* Chicago: University of Chicago Press.

Mechanic, David. 1962. "Sources of Power in Lower Participants in Complex Organizations." *Administrative Science Quarterly* 7:349–364.

Melvin, Patricia Mooney. 1985. "Changing Contexts: Neighborhood Definitions and Urban Organization." *American Quarterly* 37:357–368.

Metz, Donald L. 1967. *New Congregations: Security and Mission in Conflict.* Philadelphia: Westminster.

Miller, Zane L. 1981. "The Role and Concept of Neighborhood in American Cities." Pp. 3–32 in *Community Organization for Urban Social Change,* ed. R. Fisher and P. Romanofsky. Westport, Conn.: Greenwood.

Milner, Murray, Jr. 1994. "Status and Sacredness: Worship and Salvation as Forms of Status Transformation." *Journal for the Scientific Study of Religion* 33:99–109.

Milofsky, Carl. 1987. "Neighborhood-Based Organizations: A Market Analogy." Pp. 277–295 in *The Nonprofit Sector: A Research Handbook,* ed. Walter W. Powell. New Haven, Conn.: Yale University Press.

———. 1995. "Reinforcing Social Capital in Small Towns: A Role for Religious Nonprofits." Paper prepared for the Lilly Endowment Working Conference on Small Religious Nonprofits, Chicago, October.

Milofsky, Carl, and Albert Hunter. 1995. "Where Nonprofits Come From: A Theory of Organizational Emergence." Paper presented at the Southern Sociological Society, Atlanta, April.

Minkoff, Debra C. 1994. "From Service Provision to Institutional Advocacy: The Shifting Legitimacy of Organizational Forms." *Social Forces* 72:943–969.

Miyakawa, T. Scott. 1964. *Protestants and Pioneers: Individualism and Conformity on the American Frontier.* Chicago: University of Chicago Press.

Moberg, David O. 1962. *The Church as a Social Institution.* Englewood Cliffs, N.J.: Prentice-Hall.

415

Mock, Alan. 1992. "Congregational Religious Styles and Orientations to Society: Exploring Our Linear Assumptions." *Review of Religious Research* 34:20–33.

———. 1992. "Theological Perspectives and Involvement in Community Ministries: Exploding a Myth." *Church and Community Brief Paper*, ed. John Koppitch. Chicago: Center for Church and Community Ministries.

Morgan, Gareth. 1986. *Images of Organization*. Beverly Hills, Calif.: Sage.

Muller, Thomas, and Thomas J. Espenshade. 1985. *The Fourth Wave: California's Newest Immigrants*. Washington, D.C.: Urban Institute.

Neitz, Mary Jo. 1987. *Charisma and Community*. New Brunswick, N.J.: Transaction.

———. 1989. "Sociology and Feminist Scholarship." *American Sociologist* 20:3–13.

Nelson, Geoffrey K. 1971. "Communal and Associational Churches." *Review of Religious Research* 12:102–110.

Newman, William M. 1975. "Religion in Suburban America." Pp. 265–278 in *The Changing Face of the Suburbs*, ed. Barry Schwartz. Chicago: University of Chicago Press.

Niebuhr, H. Richard. 1929. *The Social Sources of Denominationalism*. New York: World.

Noyce, Gaylord. 1975. *Survival and Mission for the City Church*. Philadelphia: Westminster.

Olson, Daniel V. A. 1987. "Networks of Religious Belonging in Five Baptist Congregations." Ph.D. diss., University of Chicago.

———. 1989. "Church Friendships: Boon or Barrier to Church Growth?" *Journal for the Scientific Study of Religion* 28:432–447.

———. 1993. "Fellowship Ties and the Transmission of Religious Identity." Pp. 32–53 in *Beyond Establishment: Protestant Identity in a Post-Protestant Age*, ed. Jackson W. Carroll and Wade Clark Roof. Louisville, Ky.: Westminster/ John Knox.

———. 1993. "Making Disciples in a Liberal Protestant Church." Research report. Typescript.

Olson, Daniel V. A., and Jackson W. Carroll. 1992. "Religiously Based Politics: Religious Elites and the Public." *Social Forces* 70:765–786.

Orr, John B., Donald E. Miller, Wade Clark Roof, and J. Gordon Melton. 1994. *Politics of the Spirit: Religion and Multiethnicity in Los Angeles*. Los Angeles: University of Southern California.

Orsi, Robert. 1985. *The Madonna of 115th Street: Faith and Community in Italian Harlem, 1880–1950*. New Haven, Conn.: Yale University Press.

Parsons, Talcott. "Religion and Modern Industrial Society." Pp. 273–298 in *Religion, Culture, and Society*, ed. Louis Schneider. New York: Wiley, 1964.

———. 1951. *The Social System*. New York: Free Press.

Perrucci, Carolyn C., Robert Perrucci, Dean B. Targ, and Harry R. Targ. 1988. *Plant Closings: International Context and Social Costs*. New York: Aldine de Gruyter.

Pfeffer, Jeffrey. 1992. *Managing with Power: Politics and Influence in Organizations*. Boston: Harvard Business School Press.

Pfeffer, Jeffrey, and Gerald Salancik. 1979. *The External Control of Organizations*. New York: Harper and Row.

Pinto, Leonard J., and Kenneth E. Crow. 1982. "The Effects of Size on Other Structural Attributes of Congregations within the Same Denomination." *Journal for the Scientific Study of Religion* 21:304–316.

Pondy, L. R. 1983. "The Role of Metaphors and Myths in Organization and in the Facilitation of Change." Pp. 157–166 in *Organizational Symbolism*, ed. L. R. Pondy. Greenwich, Conn.: JAI.

Pope, Liston. 1942. *Millhands and Preachers*. New Haven, Conn.: Yale University Press.

Powell, Walter W. 1990. "Neither Market nor Hierarchy: Network Forms of Organizations." Pp. 295–336 in *Research in Organizational Behavior*, ed. Barry M. Stah and Larry L. Cummings. Greenwich, Conn.: JAI.

Powell, Walter W., and Paul J. DiMaggio, eds. 1991. *The New Institutionalism in Organizational Analysis*. Chicago: University of Chicago Press.

Prelinger, Catherine M., ed. 1992. *Episcopal Women: Gender, Spirituality, and Commitment in an American Mainline Denomination*. New York: Oxford University Press.

Prell, Riv-Ellen. 1989. *Prayer and Community: The Havurah in American Judaism*. Detroit: Wayne State University Press.

Putnam, Robert D. 1995. "Bowling Alone: America's Declining Social Capital." *Journal of Democracy* 6 (1): 65–78.

Ray, Melissa. 1991. *Blest Be the Ties That Bind: Interpretive Appropriation of External Mandates in an Organizational Culture*. Ph.D. diss., University of Wisconsin, Madison.

———. 1994. "Partial Alienation as Organizational Parent-Member Accommodation: An Urban, Midwestern Catholic Parish." *Sociology of Religion* 55:53–64.

Reynolds, Charles H. 1988. *Community in America: The Challenge of "Habits of the Heart."* Berkeley and Los Angeles: University of California Press.

Riesman, David. 1950. *The Lonely Crowd*. New Haven, Conn.: Yale University Press.

Rivlin, Leanne G. 1987. "Neighborhood, Personal Identity, and Group Affiliations." Pp. 1–34 in *Neighborhood and Community Environments*, ed. Irwin Altman and Abraham Wandersman. New York: Plenum.

Roberts, Keith A. 1993. "Ritual and the Transmission of a Cultural Tradition: An Ethnographic Perspective." Pp. 74–98 in *Beyond Establishment: Protestant Identity in a Post-Protestant Age*, ed. Jackson W. Carroll and Wade Clark Roof. Louisville, Ky.: Westminster/John Knox.

Roof, Wade Clark. 1978. *Community and Commitment*. New York: Elsevier.

———. 1993a. *A Generation of Seekers*. San Francisco: Harper.

———. 1993b. "Religion and Narrative." *Review of Religious Research* 34:297–310.

Roof, Wade Clark, and William McKinney. 1987. *American Mainline Religion*. New Brunswick, N.J.: Rutgers University Press.

Roof, Wade Clark, Dean R. Hoge, John E. Dyble, and C. Kirk Hadaway. 1979. "Factors Producing Growth or Decline in United Presbyterian Congregations." Pp. 198–223 in *Understanding Church Growth and Decline*, ed. Dean R. Hoge and David A. Roozen. New York: Pilgrim.

Roozen, David A., and C. Kirk Hadaway, eds. 1993. *Church and Denominational Growth*. Nashville: Abingdon.

Roozen, David A., William McKinney, and Jackson W. Carroll. 1984. *Varieties of Religious Presence*. New York: Pilgrim.

Rothauge, Arlin J. N.d. *Sizing Up a Congregation for New Member Ministry*. New York: Congregational Development Services, Episcopal Church Center.

Salamon, Lester M. 1987. "Partners in Public Service: The Scope and Theory of Government-Nonprofit Relations." Pp. 99–117 in *The Nonprofit Sector: A Research Handbook*, ed. Walter W. Powell. New Haven, Conn.: Yale University Press.

———. 1994. "The Rise of the Nonprofit Sector." *Foreign Affairs* 73:109–122.

Sanderson, Ross. 1932. *The Strategy of City Church Planning*. New York: Institute for Social and Religious Research.

Schneider, Mark, and Thomas Phelan. 1993. "Black Suburbanization in the 1980s." *Demography* 30:269–279.

Schreiter, Robert J. 1985. *Constructing Local Theologies*. Maryknoll, N.Y.: Orbis.

Scott, Ann Firor. 1992. *Natural Allies*. Urbana and Chicago: University of Illinois Press.

Scott, Tracy. Forthcoming. "What's God Got to Do with It? Protestantism, Gender, and the Meaning of Work in the United States." Ph.D. diss., Princeton University.

Selznick, Philip. 1992. *The Moral Commonwealth: Social Theory and the Promise of Community*. Berkeley and Los Angeles: University of California Press.

Shotter, John. 1984. *Social Accountability and Selfhood*. New York: Basil Blackwell.

Simmel, Georg. 1971 [1908]. "Group Expansion and the Development of Individuality." Pp. 251–293 in *Georg Simmel on Individuality and Social Forms*, ed. Donald N. Levine. Chicago: University of Chicago Press.

Singh, Jitendra V., ed. 1990. *Organizational Evolution: New Directions*. Newbury Park, Calif.: Sage.

Singh, Jitendra V., and Charles J. Lumsden. 1990. "Theory and Research in Organizational Ecology." *Annual Review of Sociology* 16:161–193.

Singh, Jitendra V., David J. Tucker, and Agnes G. Meinhard. 1991. "Institutional Change and Ecological Dynamics." Pp. 390–422 in *The New Institutionalism in Organizational Analysis*, ed. Walter W. Powell and Paul J. DiMaggio. Chicago: University of Chicago Press.

Smircich, Linda. 1985. "Is the Concept of Culture a Paradigm for Understanding Organizations and Ourselves?" Pp. 55–72 in *Organizational Culture*, ed. Peter J. Frost, Larry F. Moore, Meryl Reis Louis, Craig C. Lundberg, and Martin Joanne. Beverly Hills, Calif.: Sage.

Smith, Donald P. 1990. "Closing the Back Door: Toward the Retention of Church Members." Pp. 86–101 in *The Mainstream Protestant "Decline": The Presbyterian Pattern*, ed. Milton J. Coalter, John M. Mulder, and Louis B. Weeks. Louisville, Ky.: Westminster/John Knox.

Smith, Dorothy. 1979. "A Sociology for Women." Pp. 135–187 in *The Prism of Sex: Essays in the Sociology of Knowledge*, ed. J. Sherman and E. Beck. Madison: University of Wisconsin Press.

Spradley, James P. 1980. *Participant Observation.* New York: Holt, Rinehart and Winston.

Stackhouse, Max L. 1990. "Religion and the Social Space for Voluntary Institutions." Pp. 22–37 in *Faith and Philanthropy in America: Exploring the Role of Religion in America's Voluntary Sector,* ed. Robert Wuthnow and Virginia A. Hodgkinson. San Francisco: Jossey-Bass.

Stinchcombe, Arthur L. 1965. "Social Structure and Organizations." Pp. 142–193 in *Handbook of Organizations,* ed. J. G. March. Chicago: Rand McNally.

Stone, Jon. 1990. "The New Voluntarism and Presbyterian Affiliation." Pp. 122–149 in *The Mainstream Protestant "Decline": The Presbyterian Pattern,* ed. Milton J. Coalter, John M. Mulder, and Louis B. Weeks. Louisville: Westminster/John Knox.

Stonebraker, Robert J. 1993. "Optimal Church Size: The Bigger the Better?" *Journal for the Scientific Study of Religion* 32:231–241.

Stout, Harry S., and D. Scott Cormode. 1995. "Institutions and the Story of American Religion: A Sketch of a Synthesis." Yale University. Typescript.

Stryker, Susan. 1992. "Making Mormonism: A Critical and Historical Analysis of Cultural Formation." Ph.D. diss., University of California, Berkeley.

Sullins, D. Paul. 1993. "Switching Close to Home: Volatility or Coherence in Protestant Affiliation Patterns?" *Social Forces* 72:399–419.

Sweetser, Thomas. 1983. *Successful Parishes: How They Meet the Challenge of Change.* San Francisco: Harper and Row.

Swidler, Ann. 1986. "Culture in Action: Symbols and Strategies." *American Sociological Review* 51:273–286.

Thung, Mady. 1976. *The Precarious Organisation: Sociological Explorations of the Church's Mission and Structure.* The Hague: Mouton.

Tipton, Steven M. 1982. *Getting Saved from the Sixties.* Berkeley and Los Angeles: University of California Press.

Tocqueville, Alexis de. 1969 [1835]. *Democracy in America.* Garden City, N.Y.: Doubleday.

Troeltsch, Ernst. 1931. *The Social Teachings of the Christian Churches.* New York: Macmillan.

Turner, Victor. 1977. *The Ritual Process.* Ithaca, N.Y.: Cornell University Press.

Tushman, M. L., and E. Romanelli. 1985. "Organizational Evolution: A Metamorphosis Model of Convergence and Reorientation." *Research in Organizational Behavior* 7:171–222.

U.S. Bureau of the Census. 1972. *U.S. Census, General Characteristics of the Population.* Washington, D.C.: U.S. Department of Commerce.

———. 1982. *U.S. Census, General Characteristics of Persons.* Washington, D.C.: U.S. Department of Commerce.

———. 1991. *Census of Population and Housing, STF1.* Washington, D.C.: U.S. Department of Commerce.

Verba, Sidney, Kay Lehman Schlozman, and Henry E. Brady. 1995. *Voice and Equality: Civic Voluntarism in American Politics.* Cambridge: Harvard University Press.

Vidich, Arthur J., and Joseph Bensman. 1958. *Small Town in Mass Society: Class Power and Religion in a Rural Community.* Princeton, N.J.: Princeton University Press.

419

Wald, Kenneth D., Dennis E. Owen, and Samuel S. Hill. 1988. "Churches as Political Communities." *American Political Science Review* 82:531–548.

Walrath, Douglas A. 1979a. *Leading Churches through Change*. Nashville: Abingdon.

———. 1979b. "Social Change and Local Churches: 1951–75." Pp. 248–269 in *Understanding Church Growth and Decline*, ed. Dean R. Hoge and David A. Roozen. New York: Pilgrim.

Warner, R. Stephen. 1985. "Dualistic and Monistic Religiosity." Pp. 199–220 in *Religious Movements: Genesis, Exodus, and Numbers*, ed. Rodney Stark. New York: Paragon.

———. 1988. *New Wine in Old Wineskins*. Berkeley and Los Angeles: University of California Press.

———. 1991. "Starting Over: Reflections on American Religion." *Christian Century* 108:811–813.

———. 1993. "Work in Progress toward a New Paradigm for the Sociological Study of Religion in the United States." *American Journal of Sociology* 98:1044–1093.

———. 1994. "The Place of the Congregation in the Contemporary American Religious Configuration." Pp. 54–99 in *New Perspectives in the Study of Congregations*. Vol. 2 of *American Congregations*, ed. James P. Wind and James W. Lewis. Chicago: University of Chicago Press.

———. 1995. "The Metropolitan Community Churches and the Gay Agenda: The Power of Pentecostalism and Essentialism." Pp. 81–108 in *Sex, Lies, and Sanctity: Religion and Deviance in Contemporary North America*, ed. by Mary Jo Neitz and Marion S. Goldman. Greenwich, Conn.: JAI.

Warner, W. Lloyd. 1963. *Yankee City*. New Haven, Conn.: Yale University Press.

Watt, David Harrington. 1991. "United States: Cultural Challenges to the Voluntary Sector." Pp. 243–280 in *Between State and Market*, ed. Robert Wuthnow. Princeton, N.J.: Princeton University Press.

Webber, George W. 1964. *The Congregation in Mission: Emerging Structures for the Church in an Urban Society*. Nashville: Abingdon.

Weber, Max. 1946. "The Protestant Sects and the Spirit of Capitalism." Pp. 302–322 in *From Max Weber*, ed. H. H. Gerth and C. Wright Mills. New York: Oxford University Press.

———. 1947. *The Theory of Social and Economic Organization*. New York: Free Press.

Welch, Michael, ed. 1989. "Methodological Issues in Congregational Studies." *Review of Religious Research* 31 (special issue): 113–174.

Wellman, Leighton B. 1979. "Networks, Neighborhoods, and Communities." *Urban Affairs Quarterly* 14:363–390.

Westerhoff, John H., and Gwen Kennedy Neville. 1974. *Generation to Generation: Conversations in Religious Education and Culture*. Philadelphia: Pilgrim.

Wheeler, Barbara G. 1990. "Uncharted Territory: Congregational Identity and Mainline Protestantism." In *The Presbyterian Predicament: Six Perspectives*, ed. Milton J. Coalter, John M. Mulder, and Louis B. Weeks. Louisville: Westminster/John Knox.

Whetten, David A. 1987. "Organizational Growth and Decline Processes." *Annual Review of Sociology* 13:335–358.

———. 1988. "Sources, Responses, and Effects of Organizational Decline." Pp. 151–174 in *Readings in Organizational Decline: Frameworks, Research, and Perspectives*, ed. Kim Cameron, Robert I. Sutton, and David Whetten. Cambridge, Mass.: Ballinger.

White, Dana F. 1982. "The Black Sides of Atlanta: A Geography of Expansion and Containment, 1970–1980." *Atlanta Historical Journal* 26:199–225.

Whitley, Oliver Read. 1969. *The Church: Mirror or Window? Images of the Church in American Society*. St. Louis: Bethany.

Whyte, William H. Jr. 1957. *The Organization Man*. New York: Doubleday.

Wilken, Paul H. 1971. "Size of Organizations and Member Participation in Church Congregations." *Administrative Science Quarterly* 16:173–179.

Williams, Melvin D. 1974. *Community in a Black Pentecostal Church*. Pittsburgh: University of Pittsburgh Press.

Williams, Rhys H. 1992. "Social Movement Theory and the Sociology of Religion: 'Cultural Resources' in Strategy and Organization." Working Paper #180. New Haven, Conn.: Program on Non-Profit Organizations, Yale University.

Wilson, Gerald, Joann Keyton, G. David Johnson, Cheryl Geiger, and Johanna C. Clark. 1993. "Church Growth through Member Identification and Commitment: A Congregational Case Study." *Review of Religious Research* 34:259–272.

Wilson, John, and Thomas Janoski. 1995. "The Contribution of Religion to Volunteer Work." *Sociology of Religion* 56:137–152.

Wilson, Robert L. 1977. "Resources of People, Money, and Facilities for the Small Congregation." Pp. 125–138 in *Small Churches Are Beautiful*, ed. Jackson W. Carroll. New York: Harper and Row.

Wilson, Robert L., and James H. Davis. 1966. *The Church in the Racially Changing Community*. New York: Abingdon.

Wilson, Thomas C. 1991. "Urbanism, Migration, and Tolerance: A Reassessment." *American Sociological Review* 56:117–123.

———. 1993. "Urbanism and Kinship Bonds: A Test of Four Generalizations." *Social Forces* 71:703–712.

Wilson, William Julius. 1987. *The Truly Disadvantaged: The Inner City, the Underclass, and Public Policy*. Chicago: University of Chicago Press.

Wind, James P. 1990. *Places of Worship*. Nashville: American Association for State and Local History.

Wind, James P., and James W. Lewis, eds. 1994. *American Congregations*. 2 vols. Chicago: University of Chicago Press.

Winter, Gibson. 1961. *The Suburban Captivity of the Churches*. Garden City, N.Y.: Doubleday.

———. 1967. "Religious Organizations." Pp. 408–491 in *The Emergent American Society*, ed. W. L. Warner. New Haven, Conn.: Yale University Press.

Wirth, Louis. 1938. "Urbanism as a Way of Life." *American Journal of Sociology* 44:1–24.

Witten, Marsha. 1992. "The Restriction of Meaning in Religious Discourse: Centripetal Devices in a Fundamentalist Christian Sermon." Pp. 19–38 in *Vocabularies of Public Life*, ed. Robert Wuthnow. London: Routledge.

Wood, James R. 1970. "Authority and Controversial Policy: The Church and Civil Rights." *American Sociological Review* 35:1057–1069.

———. 1981. *Leadership in Voluntary Organizations*. New Brunswick, N.J.: Rutgers University Press.

Wood, James R., and Jon P. Bloch. 1995. "The Role of Church Assemblies in Building a Civil Society: The Case of the United Methodist General Conference's Debate on Homosexuality." *Sociology of Religion* 56:121–136.

Wood, Richard L. 1994. "Faith in Action: Religious Resources for Political Success in Three Congregations." *Sociology of Religion* 55:397–417.

Wuthnow, Robert. 1987. *Meaning and Moral Order*. Berkeley and Los Angeles: University of California Press.

———. 1988. *The Restructuring of American Religion*. Princeton, N.J.: Princeton University Press.

———. 1991. *Acts of Compassion: Caring for Others and Helping Ourselves*. Princeton, N.J.: Princeton University Press.

———. 1993. "Seeking the Center: American Religion and the 21st Century." Paper presented at the Cathedral Heritage Conference, Louisville, Ky., October.

———. 1994a. *God and Mammon in America*. New York: Free Press.

———. 1994b. *Producing the Sacred*. Urbana: University of Illinois Press.

———. 1994c. *Sharing the Journey*. New York: Free Press.

Wuthnow, Robert, Virginia Hodgkinson, and Associates, eds. 1990. *Faith and Philanthropy in America*. San Francisco: Jossey-Bass.

Yanow, Dvora. 1992. "Supermarkets and Culture Clash: The Epistemological Role of Metaphors in Administrative Practice." *American Review of Public Administration* 22:89–109.

———. 1993. "Reading Policy Meanings in Organization-Scapes." *Journal of Architectural and Planning Research* 10:308–327.

Contributors

Nancy Tatom Ammerman is Professor of Sociology of Religion at the Center for Social and Religious Research at Hartford Seminary. She joined the Hartford faculty in 1995, after eleven years at Emory University. She is the author of *Bible Believers: Fundamentalists in the Modern World* and *Baptist Battles: Social Change and Religious Conflict in the Southern Baptist Convention,* both from Rutgers University Press. *Baptist Battles* was the winner of the annual book award from the Society for the Scientific Study of Religion.

Tammy Adams was, in 1992, a Master of Divinity student at Candler School of Theology. She presently works at the American Academy of Religion as their office manager and computer specialist. She is responsible for producing all of the print materials for the executive office and programs of the AAR. In her spare time she is writing a book entitled "More Than Getting By: An Everyday Theology for the Rest of Us."

Penny Edgell Becker did this research as a doctoral student in sociology at the University of Chicago. She is currently an assistant professor in the Sociology Department at Cornell University. Her dissertation is entitled "How We Do Things Here: Culture and Conflict in Local Congregations."

Brenda Brasher completed her work in Religion/Social Ethics at the University of Southern California in 1995. Her dissertation is entitled "Godly Women: Female Fundamentalists in a Postmodern Age." She is currently assistant professor of religion at Thiel College, where her most recent research focuses on the intersection of religion, technological socialization, and popular culture.

Thomas Clark was, in 1992, a doctoral student in religion at the University of Southern California, intending to write a dissertation in theology. In 1994, he was diagnosed with cancer, and in early 1995 he lost his battle with the disease.

Joan Cunningham worked on this project as a student in Indiana University, Purdue University at Indianapolis (IUPUI) Public History Master's Program. She is currently a research archivist at the Indiana State Archives.

Nancy Eiesland was a doctoral candidate in the Department of Sociology of Religion at Emory University when she did this research. She is currently assistant professor of sociology of religion at Emory University. Her dissertation, entitled "A Particular Place: Exubanization and Religious Change in a Sunbelt City," is forthcoming from Rutgers University Press.

Barbara Elwell was a doctoral student in ethics and society at Emory University. She is currently marketing and production coordinator for the American Academy of Religion and the Society of Biblical Literature in Atlanta, Georgia.

Arthur E. Farnsley II, associate director of this research project, is a senior research associate at Indiana University's POLIS Center, where he coordinates several initiatives within the Project on Religion and Urban Culture. A graduate of Wabash College, Yale Divinity School, and the Religion and Society Program at Emory University, he is author of the book *Southern Baptist Politics* (Pennsylvania State Press, 1994).

Michelle Hale was a graduate student in the Public History Program at Indiana University, Indianapolis, in 1992, where she is currently a research associate at the POLIS Center.

Diana L. Jones received her M.A. in sociology from Emory University in 1992. She is currently working as a recreation director at Haygood Memorial United Methodist Church in Atlanta, Georgia. She is also an adjunct professor of sociology at Oglethrope University and research consultant with the Georgia Indigent Defense Council.

Virginia Laffey was, in 1992, a doctoral student at Boston University. She is currently working on her dissertation entitled "'The Invisible Regiment': The Waiting Wives, Mothers, and Girlfriends of American Soldiers in Vietnam."

Stacey Nicholas was a master's student at Indiana University–Purdue University at Indianapolis in 1992. Currently, she is co-publisher and general manager of the *Colchester Chronicle*, a weekly newspaper. She is a part-time lecturer at Spoon River College in Macomb, Illinois.

Marcia Robinson is a doctoral student in historical theology at Emory University in Atlanta, Georgia. Her dissertation is on beauty and selfhood in Søren Kierkegaard's religious thought. In the fall of 1996, she will become assistant professor of church history at Eden Theological Seminary in St. Louis, Missouri.

Mary Beth Sievens is a doctoral student in American history at Boston University. She is currently working on her dissertation, "Stray Wives: Marital Expectations and Conflict in Vermont, 1790–1830."

List of Contributors

Daphne C. Wiggins was, in 1992, a doctoral student in the Graduate Institute of Liberal Arts at Emory University. She began an appointment as assistant professor of religion at Texas Christian University in August 1996. Her dissertation is entitled "An Exploratory Study of the Socio-Cultural Determinant of Church Attendants among African American Women."

Connie Zeigler was a graduate student in history at Indiana University, Indianapolis, in 1992. She currently is a freelance author for antiques and historical publications and owns an antiques business.

Index

Index

Index

Index